S0-AYT-217

PETER CALVERT was born in Co. Antrim
and took degrees at the Universities of
Cambridge and Michigan. He joined the
University of Southampton in 1964 as
Lecturer in Politics and since 1971 has been
Senior Lecturer. He has also held posts
as Teaching Fellow at the University of
Michigan (1960–61); Visiting Lecturer at
the University of California, Santa
Barbara (1966); and Research Fellow,
Charles Warren Center for Studies in
American History, Harvard University
(1969–70).

Dr Calvert is the author of *The Mexican
Revolution 1910-1914: the Diplomacy of
Anglo-American Conflict*; *Latin America:
International Conflict and International Peace*;
Revolution; and *A Study of Revolution*. He has
also contributed to the *Annual Register,
International Affairs, Political Studies,* and the
Journal of Latin American Studies.

NATIONS OF THE MODERN WORLD

ARGENTINA	H. S. Ferns
	Professor of Political Science,
	University of Birmingham

AUSTRALIA   O. H. K. Spate
Director, Research School of Pacific Studies,
Australian National University, Canberra

AUSTRIA   Karl R. Stadler
Professor of Modern and Contemporary History,
University of Linz

BELGIUM   Vernon Mallinson
Professor of Comparative Education,
University of Reading

BURMA   F. S. V. Donnison, C.B.E.
Formerly Chief Secretary to the Government of Burma
Historian, Cabinet Office, Historical Section 1949–66

CHINA   Victor Purcell, C.M.G.
Late Lecturer in Far Eastern History, Cambridge

CYPRUS   H. D. Purcell
Professor of English,
University of Libya, Benghazi

DENMARK   W. Glyn Jones
Reader in Danish, University College London

MODERN EGYPT   Tom Little, M.B.E.
Former Managing Director and General Manager of
Regional News Services (Middle East), Ltd, London

ENGLAND   John Bowle
A Portrait   *Formerly Professor of Political Theory, Collège d'Europe,*
Bruges 1950–67

FINLAND   W. R. Mead
Professor of Geography, University College London

| EAST GERMANY | David Childs |
| | *Lecturer in Politics, University of Nottingham* |

| WEST GERMANY | Michael Balfour, C.B.E. |
| | *Professor of European History, University of East Anglia* |

MODERN GREECE — John Campbell
Fellow of St Antony's College, Oxford

Philip Sherrard
*Lecturer in the History of the Orthodox Church,
King's College, London*

HUNGARY — Paul Ignotus
*Formerly Hungarian Press Counsellor, London, 1947–49, and
Member, Presidential Board, Hungarian Writers' Association*

MODERN INDIA — Sir Percival Griffiths, K.B.E., C.I.E., I.C.S. (RET.)
President India, Pakistan and Burma Association

MODERN IRAN — Peter Avery
*Lecturer in Persian and Fellow of King's College,
Cambridge*

ISRAEL RESURGENT — Norman Bentwich, O.B.E.
*Late Professor of International Relations,
Hebrew University of Jerusalem*

ITALY — Muriel Grindrod, O.B.E.
Formerly Editor of International Affairs *and*
The World Today
Assistant Editor The Annual Register

KENYA — A. Marshall MacPhee
*Formerly Managing Editor with
the* East African Standard *Group*

LIBYA — John Wright
Formerly of the Sunday Ghibli, *Tripoli*

MALAYSIA — J. M. Gullick
Formerly of the Malayan Civil Service

MEXICO — Peter Calvert
*Senior Lecturer in Politics,
University of Southampton*

NEW ZEALAND	James W. Rowe *Professor of Economics, Massey University, New Zealand* Margaret A. Rowe *Tutor in English at Victoria University, Wellington*
NIGERIA	Sir Rex Niven, C.M.G., M.C. *Administrative Service of Nigeria, 1921–54 Member, President and Speaker of Northern House of Assembly, 1947–59*
NORWAY	Ronald G. Popperwell *Fellow of Clare Hall, and Lecturer in Norwegian, Cambridge*
PAKISTAN	Ian Stephens, C.I.E. *Formerly Editor of The Statesman, Calcutta and Delhi, 1942–51 Fellow, King's College, Cambridge, 1952–58*
PERU	Sir Robert Marett, K.C.M.G., O.B.E. *H.M. Ambassador in Lima, 1963–67*
POLAND	Václav L. Beneš *Professor of Political Science, Indiana University* Norman J. G. Pounds *Professor of History and Geography, Indiana University*
PORTUGAL	J. B. Trend *Late Fellow, Christ's College, and Emeritus Professor of Spanish, Cambridge*
SOUTH AFRICA	John Cope *Formerly Editor-in-Chief of The Forum and South Africa Correspondent of The Guardian*
THE SOVIET UNION	Elisabeth Koutaissoff *Professor of Russian, Victoria University, Wellington*
SPAIN	George Hills *Formerly Correspondent and Spanish Programme Organizer, British Broadcasting Corporation*
SUDAN REPUBLIC	K. D. D. Henderson, C.M.G. *Formerly of the Sudan Political Service and Governor of Darfur Province, 1949–53*

SWEDEN   Irene Scobbie
              Senior Lecturer in Swedish,
              University of Aberdeen

SYRIA   Tabitha Petran

TURKEY   Geoffrey Lewis
              Senior Lecturer in Islamic Studies, Oxford

YUGOSLAVIA   Stevan K. Pavlowitch
              Lecturer in Balkan History, University of
              Southampton

NATIONS OF THE MODERN WORLD

MEXICO

F
1231.5
.C273
1973b

MEXICO

By

PETER CALVERT

LONDON
ERNEST BENN LIMITED

GOSHEN COLLEGE LIBRARY
GOSHEN, INDIANA

First published 1973 by Ernest Benn Limited
25 New Street Square, Fleet Street, London, EC4A 3JA

Distributed in Canada by
The General Publishing Company Limited, Toronto

© *Peter Calvert 1973*

Printed in Great Britain

SBN 0 510-37905-2

Preface

WRITING A BOOK on Mexico for an English-speaking readership presents two main problems. The history of the country is seldom familiar, which rules out an entirely topical presentation, and a purely chronological approach is not only dull but necessarily unsuccessful. Some topics simply do not fit easily into a narrative framework.

Furthermore, few sources for the history of Mexico are easily available outside specialist libraries. This limits the reader's opportunity to whet his wits on the material presented to him.

To meet both problems, I have departed somewhat from the usual pattern of the 'serious' printed book. Novelists have for a long time explored various arrangements which try to free the reader from the traditional chapter-by-chapter sequence, though costs limit the practicability of varying typeface, juxtaposing columns, and similar devices. I have made use of one such pattern in the construction of *Mexico*: a simple interlocking sequence of short sections, with continuity between types of section as well as between consecutive sections.

The sections themselves are of four kinds:

1. A basic historical *narrative* of the Mexican Revolution (as the Mexicans themselves conceive of it), as a unity between past and present;

2. Sections dealing with *topics* related to, or deriving from, aspects of the narrative;

3. *Biographical* treatments of prominent Mexicans of the recent period, not necessarily in chronological order;

4. Brief, impressionistic, collections of *quotations*, loosely linked to the time sequence in subject, inserted at irregular intervals, and chosen for their clash of ideas.

The pattern makes no special demands on the reader. The book is meant to be read simply from beginning to end like any other book. What I have tried to do is to show something of the richness, complexity, and charm of Mexico; whether or not this has been achieved, I leave to the reader to judge.

A bibliographical study has been incorporated as an extended

9

topical section at the end of the book. An earlier version of this appeared separately as 'The Mexican Revolution; theory or fact?' in the first issue of the *Journal of Latin American Studies*, and I am grateful to the Editors of that journal for permission to reproduce it here.

Southampton   P.A.R.C.
July 1972

Contents

List of Illustrations

Maps

Acknowledgements

ACKNOWLEDGEMENT for kind permission to reproduce illustrations is made to the following, to whom the copyright of the illustrations belongs:

Camera Press Limited: 15, 17, 18, 19, 20, 23
Señor Don Agustín Casasola Zapata, Mexico City: 4, 12, 16
Mexican Tourist Department, Mexico City: 21, 22, 25, 26, 27
The Other Cinema, London (from the film *Mexico: the Frozen Revolution*): 5, 9, 11
Paul Popper Limited: 1, 2, 6, 8, 10, 13, 14, 24
Radio Times Hulton Picture Library: 3, 7

List of Abbreviations

BUO	Bloque de Unidad Obrera
CGOCM	Confederación General de Obreros y Campesinos de México
CGT	Confederación General de Trabajadores
CNC	Confederación Nacional Campesina
CNOP	Confederación Nacional de Organizaciones Populares
CROC	Confederación Revolucionaria de Obreros y Campesinos
CROM	Confederación Regional de Obreros Mexicanos
CRPI	Confederación Revolucionaria de Partidos Independientes
CTAL	Confederación de Trabajadores de América Latina
CTM	Confederación de Trabajadores Mexicanos
FdePPM	Federación de Partidos Populares Mexicanos
OAS	Organization of American States
PA	Partido Antireeleccionista
PAN	Partido de Acción Nacional
PARM	Partido Auténtico de la Revolución Mexicana
PCM	Partido Communista Mexicana
PCN	Partido Cooperatista Nacional
PDM	Partido Democrático Mexicano
PL	Partido Laborista
PLC	Partido Liberal Constitucionalista
PLM	Partido Laborista Mexicano
PNR	Partido Nacional Revolucionario
PNRep	Partido Nacional Republicano
PP	Partido Popular
PPS	Partido Popular Socialista
PRI	Partido Revolucionario Institucional
PRM	Partido de la Revolución Mexicana
PRUN	Partido Revolucionario de Unificación Nacional
PSF	Partido Socialista Fronterizo
SLP	San Luis Potosí
UGOCM	Unión General de Obreros y Campesinos de México
UNAM	Universidad Nacional Autónoma de México

Prologue: The Past

MEXICO. A country whose grandeur of scenery shows directly the immense power of the geological forces that formed it. The southernmost of the three great states that today make up the North American continent, in shape it resembles on the map one of those ornate cornucopias used in fanciful classical decorations. Certainly Mexico as a country is a state in the classical mould, but there the resemblance ends. Mexico is a country chronically short of arable land, the basic resource without which no full human life is possible.

Current belief is that the present-day isthmus of Panama and Central America is a fairly recent geological formation, probably caused by the collision of the continent of North America with its fellow-continent to the south. If so, then Mexico's geographical individuality is caused by this fundamental collision. The mountains of the Sierra Madre which run from north to south and divide the country throughout its length are formed along the line of instability that runs from Alaska to Cape Horn. Not only is Mexico a country of beautiful extinct or dormant volcanoes, it is also a country of active volcanoes and frequent earthquakes. It is hardly surprising therefore that many Mexicans are fatalistic about natural catastrophes; it would be more surprising if they were not.

In 1942 a farmer ploughing in the field felt the ground tremble under his feet and ran for shelter. When he looked round, he saw a volcano appear where he had been, and three weeks later it was a cone more than a thousand feet high, in full eruption. Today Paracutín is extinguished, but still regarded as active, and certainly no one can take it for granted, as they do the peaks of Popocatepetl and Orizaba near Mexico City. In this region geology has formed a high table land with a relatively temperate climate, and it is this central region (the 'Core') where the majority of the Mexican population lives today.

This region lies just south of the Tropic of Cancer, so it is not surprising that vertical differences are much more important than horizontal ones in giving Mexico different climates. Seasons, too, are not of great significance. Apart from the *tierra templada* of the plateau and the *tierra fría* of the peaks, there are two other types of climate which can be distinguished. Along the shore of the Gulf of Mexico and in the Isthmus of Tehuantepec to the south there is the *tierra caliente* – hot, steamy jungle, until recently almost impassable, both as a physical barrier and because of the diseases present in the swamp. And to the north, where the Sierra Madre divides into two parallel ranges, there is desert. Not the desert of sand dunes and date palms that come to the mind of those who know deserts only from Hollywood, but a desert of rock and dust, broken only sparsely by wiry scrub and spectacular branching cactuses. Here distance itself is a barrier to communication, for the scale of settlement is stretched out in striking contrast to the pocketed landscape of mountain and valley familiar elsewhere.

When and how man first arrived on this formidable stage is still uncertain. We are not even absolutely certain whether he entered, so to speak, from left or right. There is very little doubt, however, that it was in fact the former; that is to say, from Asia across what is now the Behring Straits, probably by a land bridge existing during the last Interglacial Period and so down the west coast of North America. Whether or not men also arrived later and therefore by sea, and possibly by other routes, is a much more open question. It is certain that about 10000 B.C. men were already living in the area of the Southern Core region; that the climate in the region was then somewhat cooler than it is now; and that the inhabitants were nomadic and hunters of small game such as antelope and jack rabbits.

About 6500–5000 B.C. the climate began to get warmer and the game withdrew north. The resulting shortage of animal food was met by the systematic collection of vegetable foods: squash, peppers, avocados, and even cotton seeds, and then by the systematic planting of crops. After 5000 B.C. a new crop was added to the diet – a wild grass, which was to prove the most productive food crop in the world and (with squash and beans) forms the essential nutritive basis for New World civilization. About 3500 B.C. permanent settlements of huts began to appear, and ultimately between 2300 and 1500 B.C. the discovery of fired pottery opened up new possibilities of food storage. In the more favourable conditions of the Isthmus, with the resources of sea food, it only required the clearance of patches of soil in the forest uplands to enable these techniques to produce the abundant crops needed to support an urban population. And it is now known that such a culture did appear, with a suddenness that until recently would not have been believed.

By 1100 B.C. the area archaeologists know as Mesoamerica was thickly populated by people living in settled villages. What these people called themselves, we do not know; today they are known as the 'Olmecs'.[1] They forced themselves on modern scholarship by the size and complexity of their great ceremonial centre at La Venta in the State of Tabasco. Here at this early date they built a vast clay mound on which they erected temples, pits, and platforms. To it they brought offerings of the most precious substance known to them: jade, richly worked and carved. We believe that the mound and others like it subsequently constructed elsewhere were, for the inhabitants of the Gulf region, models of the volcanoes which they had worshipped in the regions to the north. Certainly some association with fire seems indicated by the discovery of many polished stone mirrors, laboriously ground in a parabolic curve, which could have been used to focus the rays of the tropical sun on tinder.

In later years the inhabitants of Mexico possessed only a dim recollection of this period, when their civilization was centred on the area now known as San Lorenzo Tenochtitlan. They recollected only that this was the first stage in a series of migrations. The reasons for these migrations are still hotly debated, but the general consensus is that the main cause was the exhaustion of the soil by the primitive form of 'slash and burn' cultivation. Some form of insurrection may also have taken place – the monuments at San Lorenzo seem to have been deliberately demolished and subsequently abandoned. The inhabitants moved away from the Gulf, south into the highlands of Chiapas and Guatemala, and east into the Yucatán peninsula, where, between the fourth and tenth centuries A.D., there flourished the Classic Age of the Maya civilization.[2]

In the Olmec period the Mesoamericans had already devised the complex calendar which had such a great significance to the Mayas. Based on a vigesimal notation, it achieved an even more exact measure of the length of the year than that which formed the basis for the Gregorian calendar we use today. This degree of accuracy, achieved without the use of telescopes, was probably attained by the building of specialized observatories such as that which today is known as the Caracol at Chichen Itzá. Even more interesting was the purpose to which it was put. The entire life of the Mayas was to a unique extent regulated by the calendar their ancestors had devised. They believed that the world had in the past undergone a series of catastrophes, from which on each occasion men had only barely escaped. Every fifty-two years a similar catastrophe might happen again. Accordingly at a jubilee period great ceremonies were held to avert the end of the age, including the enlargement of the stepped pyramids of limestone into which by now the primitive mounds had been translated.

It is to the related civilization of the Zapotec of Monte Albán in Oaxaca, however, that the Mayas owed the priceless benefit of a fully flexible system of writing. This enabled them to record not only their calendrical calculations (which we can read), but also anything else they wished (which, regrettably, we still cannot read properly). Sadly, they seem to have used this priceless invention, like most other civilizations, primarily for writing down dynastic lists, famous battles, and lists of tribute. For the Maya political system of the Classic Age appears to have been a collection of warring states, formed from time to time into larger confederations by the military ascendancy of individual cities and their dynasties. Yet it was a vigorous culture, distinguished by its great temple complexes in which a brilliant architecture triumphed over problems of roofing with the corbelled vault and of constructing satisfactory doors and windows with only wood for lintels. Not only were the buildings themselves beautiful, but they were covered with delicate reliefs and ornamented inside with elegant mural paintings, some of which, fortunately, have survived.

About A.D. 900, this civilization was disrupted, whether by invasion or by internal stresses is not certain. The disruption coincided with the appearance of elements from a new culture, which, from its centre having been located at Tula, in the modern State of Hidalgo, was known as the Toltec. It appears that about the beginning of the Christian era, the Mesoamerican civilization had finally reached the area which today is known as the Valley of Mexico, where over the next six hundred years it followed a separate course of development, and where the vast temple complex centred on what are today the ruins of Teotihuacan, just north of modern Mexico City, was built. Teotihuacan itself was violently destroyed about A.D. 650; but after a period of disturbances a new dynasty came to power in Tula and brought about reunification.

The family resemblances between these civilizations are very much more striking than their differences. The Mayas worshipped a god which they called Kukulcan ('Feathered Serpent'); the king of the Toltecs who turned his attention to the conquest of the Mayas of the Yucatán peninsula had the same designation. The Toltecs, however, brought a greater emphasis on human sacrifice to the Maya religion than seems previously to have been the case, and the recurrent wars became much more serious. The Mayas are said to have resisted the Toltec incursions for a time by the so-called 'Triple Alliance' of the states of Uxmal, Chichen Itzá, and Mayapan, but in time the first two succumbed and only Mayapan was left unconquered by A.D. 1500.

By then, however, the Toltec hegemony in the Core of Mexico had been displaced by a warrior-culture of an even more ferocious type, though one still manifesting the marks of its common origin. This was the culture of the Aztecs, who called themselves the Mexica.[3] It developed around the island settlement of Tenochtitlan on Lake Texcoco in the Valley of Mexico, and through alliance and conquest secured a brittle hegemony over the whole Core region before about 1500. The motive force of the endless wars of the Aztecs was the need to obtain captives for human sacrifice, which they practised on an unparalleled scale. At a major public festival they might sacrifice ten thousand victims. The warrior class and the priests stood therefore at the head of a rigidly stratified society, geared to the needs of successful warfare. Those who failed in battle were executed; those who failed in other ways were enslaved; and the dread of the Aztecs among their allies became such that by 1519 they were on the verge of open revolt against Aztec domination.

It was at this juncture that Hernán Cortés and his small band of followers arrived at Vera Cruz. Clad in armour and mounted on horseback they certainly represented a new dimension in warfare, hitherto quite unknown in Mesoamerica. It was not their tiny numbers, however, but what they stood for, that enabled them to conquer. Everyone, from Moctezuma II, last but one emperor of the Aztecs, downwards, saw these pale-faced, bearded strangers as the reincarnation of their principal deity, Quetzalcoatl – the Aztec version of Kukulcan, the Feathered Serpent. And after the Spaniards had declared themselves politically by taking the to them entirely religious step of opposing the barbarous religion of the Aztec state, they found themselves surrounded by allies from other tribes. It was the tragedy of the rulers of these states that in backing the Spaniards to destroy the Aztecs, they backed a conquering power that, unlike all previous conquering powers known to them, would not leave them in the possession of power itself.

For the majority of Mexicans the establishment of Spanish rule, essentially completed during the four years from 1519 to 1523, was merely the imposition of a new hierarchy on top of the one they already had. For their rulers and priests it was their reduction to the status of their former subjects. But for all of them, despite the plagues that resulted from unfamiliar European diseases such as consumption and measles, and the disastrous population collapse that followed, it was a relief from endless war and the terrors of human sacrifice. The disadvantages of the bargain were in many ways only to appear in retrospect. We can now pass, therefore, directly to the end of the Spanish colonial system, leaving its details for consideration in the appropriate place.

[1] Michael D. Coe, *America's First Civilization; Discovering the Olmec* (Washington, D.C., The American Heritage Publishing Co., 1968).
[2] See *inter alia* Michael D. Coe, *Mexico* (London, Thames & Hudson, 1962) and *The Maya* (Harmondsworth, Penguin Books, 1971); Sylvanus G. Morley, *The Ancient Maya* (Stanford, Stanford University Press, 1946).
[3] See George C. Vaillant, *The Aztecs of Mexico* (Harmondsworth, Penguin Books, 1968).

The Revolution I: Independence

THE PROBLEM OF MEXICAN INDEPENDENCE was that it was in origin an accidental by-product of events in Europe. Mexico, as New Spain, was the governing centre of the Spanish Indies. When in 1808 the forces of Napoleon first deposed King Charles IV of Spain, and then tried to place Napoleon's brother Joseph on the throne instead of the rightful heir, there was nowhere in the empire where the change was received with more horror than in the city of Mexico. But only among the *peninsulares* – the Spaniards born in Spain who, down to that time, had held a near-total monopoly of political power. They realized at once what the absence of legal authority might mean for them personally and joined together to proclaim their own viceroy.

The *criollos* – the persons of Spanish blood born in the Indies who were badly affected by the silver crisis brought on by the war – failed to act, purely because they had no previous experience in deciding what to do. They agreed only on one thing: they hated the *gachupines*.[1] A group of them tried to plan an abortive *coup* at Valladolid, Michoacán, in December 1809. They were surprised, and most of them were arrested by the authorities, but some escaped. One was a parish priest whose lands had been confiscated for debt,[2] Miguel Hidalgo y Costilla, from the town of Nuestra Señora de los Dolores in Guanajuato. He was chosen by the others as their leader, both because of his personality and because he was a priest, and they wanted (but did not get) the support of the Church. The other was a captain of dragoons, Ignacio José Allende Unzaga. Both were *criollos*.

Allende went to the town of Querétaro – of particular significance in Mexican history – and formed under the cover of a social club a conspiracy of his fellow-*criollos* among the army. Once again the plot was discovered, and orders given for the arrest of the ringleaders. This time, however, Allende was warned by the wife of the *corregidor* of Querétaro, Señora Josefa Ortiz de Domínguez, and he in turn warned Hidalgo. They resolved to raise all the popular support they could. At first light on the morning of 16 September 1810 the village of Dolores was awakened by the tolling of the church bell for Mass, and, when its inhabitants gathered before the church, their priest

24

summoned them to 'defend their religion and their homes'. It is a measure of the gulf between *criollo* and *gachupín* that he called upon his *mestizo* and Indian audience to do so by fighting to 'recover from the hated Spaniards the lands stolen from our forefathers three centuries ago'.

To the cry of 'Mueran los gachupines' ('Death to the Spaniards') some eighty male inhabitants of Dolores then followed their priest to the nearby town of Atotonilco, where they found the image of the Virgin of Guadalupe. The dark-skinned Virgin of Guadalupe was by papal command regarded as the patroness of the Indies, as its mystical origin was the first miraculous act to be recognized as such in the New World. With the image of the Virgin at its head the *criollo* revolt became one that was truly national. Among other acts of Hidalgo's short-lived provisional government in the area his forces held were the abolition of slavery and of levies on the Indians. The countryside was soon aflame with insurrection, and at the beginning of November Hidalgo stood at the head of a huge army on the outskirts of the capital. Only a tenth of his numbers stood between him and the dramatic capture of the seat of Spanish power. Unfortunately, against the advice of Allende, he judged, incorrectly, that he did not have the strength to proceed; his retreat led first to the separation and then to the destruction of his army, and in March 1811 he was captured with his remaining followers near Nuevo Laredo. Unfrocked by an ecclesiastical court, he was executed by firing squad on the morning of 30 July and his head exhibited in Guanajuato.

The measure of Hidalgo's achievement was not that he failed, but that he came so near to succeeding. His death therefore did not mean the end of the movement he had begun. Its leadership passed to one of his principal followers, but a man who, though also a priest, came from a humble background and possessed the military genius which Hidalgo had lacked: José María Morelos y Pavón. Morelos had been fortunate: he had been detailed to leave the main force and to capture the port of Acapulco for the insurgents. When the news of the execution of his leaders reached him, he expanded his forces and his territory until he effectively commanded a great arc running round the Pacific and Gulf coasts and encircling the capital. In meeting this threat the viceregal government lacked the sureness which had characterized its handling of the first revolt. The proclamation of the Spanish Constitution of 1812 in Mexico gave an official stamp to the doctrine that sovereignty rested not in the Crown but in the nation, and its liberal views on the freedom of the press ended the restrictions on those who argued that nation, for Mexicans, meant Mexico.

On 14 September 1813 Morelos convened a congress at Chilpancingo, today the capital of the State of Guerrero. Here, some 230 miles south of Mexico City, on 6 November was adopted a 'Solemn Act of the Declaration of Independence of North America [América Septentrional]'. Tragically, the ending of the war in Spain itself and the establishment on the Spanish throne of the reactionary and embittered Ferdinand VII meant a new viceroy in Mexico City in 1814: Félix Calleja, the general whose daring at the Bridge of Calderón had been responsible for the destruction of Hidalgo's army. Soon he was receiving fresh reinforcements from Spain and was able to take the strategic initiative. By the time the congress reconvened, the insurrectionary government was already under serious military pressure and had to move periodically to avoid capture; so it met at Apatzingan. There on 22 October 1814 it ratified the first constitution of the country which was now called 'Mexican America [América Mexicana]', a liberal, republican, and nationalist document which stands as a monument to the most clearsighted of the leaders of Mexican independence.

Morelos himself, leading the forces he had commanded so successfully, was finally captured near Tehuacán, and like Hidalgo, tried, unfrocked by an ecclesiastical court, and then shot (22 December 1815). Though the army of the congress survived him for several months, it too rapidly wasted away under the conciliatory policy of the new viceroy, Juan Ruiz de Apodaca. A filibustering expedition raised in the United States and England, led by Francisco Javier Mina, landed on the Gulf Coast in 1817 and penetrated as far as Guanajuato. It was destroyed and its leader executed. There remained only tiny guerrilla bands, too small, it seemed, to menace the restored power of the Spanish Crown and the conservative landowners. Two of the leaders of these bands, Miguel Ramos Félix Adaucto Fernández, who symbolized his faith in the republican cause by taking the name of Guadalupe Victoria, and Vicente Ramón Guerrero Saldana, were to play much bigger roles in the future of their country.

In 1820 the reactionary policy of Ferdinand finally brought about a Liberal revolution in Spain itself. The Constitution of 1812 was again proclaimed, and the conservative *gachupines* and *criollos* found their regained privileges once again in danger. The only hope for their own survival seemed to be in making Mexico an independent but conservative state. The principal royalist general, Agustín de Iturbide, who had played the principal role in the defeat of Morelos, now seized his chance. Leading an army south from the capital on the pretext of attacking Guerrero, instead he met the guerrilla leader at the town of Iguala and there came to an agreement with him. The fruit was the Plan of Iguala (24 February 1821), the document under which Mexican independence was finally attained.

In one sense the Plan was exactly what Iturbide wanted; in another it was the only possible formula under which the disparate ambitions of the liberal and conservative *criollos* could be reconciled. Its basic principle of independence linked all parties; the fact that it spoke vaguely of Mexico as 'this kingdom' was not in itself offensive to any. But it did provide for a monarchical government under either Ferdinand VII or another European prince, or if neither were possible, that the viceroy name a government to be backed by the conjoint army of the Three Guarantees. And the Three Guarantees were absolute independence, racial equality, and the maintenance of the Catholic religion.

The Liberals accepted the independence the Plan offered by supporting the army to which it gave birth. The viceroy, Apodaca, was deposed; his successor, Juan O'Donojú, arrived from Spain, summed up the situation, and accepted the inevitable. On 27 September 1821 the Army of the Three Guarantees occupied Mexico City and a regency was proclaimed under Iturbide. Though the Spanish government subsequently refused to accept the agreement, it was too late, and Mexico was launched on her career as an independent state and, as she had been both before and during Spanish rule, as a monarchy.

But where was the monarch to fill the vacant throne? If Ferdinand did (as it seems) toy with the idea of accepting it, and migrating to the New World as the Braganças had done to Brazil, in the end he decided against it. This was not necessarily a proof of commonsense. It was the throne of Spain herself he was trying to keep, and the French were prepared to help him keep it by military force. If Spain were secure, the force might be found to recover Mexico, where at the mouth of the harbour of Vera Cruz a Spanish garrison still held the sinister island fortress of San Juan de Ulua. As Iturbide had no doubt foreseen, when their hoped-for monarch did not come, the monarchist supporters of the Bourbons gave up their dream and accepted political reality. But as he did not foresee, the majority of those present at the Constituent Assembly which met in February 1822 decided to support the republic of the Liberals rather than a monarchy with Iturbide as monarch. Seeing his chances on the wane, on 18–19 May Iturbide carried out a *coup d'état* and forced the hostile Congress to elect him emperor under the title of Agustín I (*sic*).[3]

Just ten months later – on 19 March 1823 – the emperor abdicated. Having first purged and then dissolved Congress, he had tried the desperate expedient of nominating a hand-picked assembly and writing yet another stillborn constitution, before bankruptcy forced him once again to summon the representatives of what was now, by his making, unmistakably the Mexican nation. They behaved generously to him by voting him an annual pension on his abdication; he behaved ungenerously to them by conspiring to return with European aid. When he did so, in July 1824, he was promptly arrested and executed. It was now the turn of the republicans.

Law

The problem facing the interim governing junta was more serious than merely restoring order after a simple change of government. For just over three hundred years New Spain had been a conquered dependent territory. Within that territory all the threads of government had been in the hands of Spain, and all had led back to the Council of the Indies at Seville.

Maintenance of orderly rule over such a vast area had been achieved in two ways. First, a tremendous effort had been made to remove the need for independent thought by the codification of the entire law relating to the Indies. The *Recopilación de las leyes de las Indias*, originally formulated shortly after the Conquest, was reprinted several times, but not substantially altered. Secondly, all administrators and their administrations were checked both by councils representing the various interests in the area concerned, and by periodic roving inquests charged with hearing complaints about their use of power.

Mexico also inherited three things. Firstly, as the former seat of the viceroyalty she inherited claims over a vast territorial area stretching from the Captaincy-General of Guatemala in the south to San Francisco in Upper California in the north. The loss of Louisiana to Napoleon and of Florida to the United States in the last years of Spanish rule were a warning that Mexican rule in the outlying territories would have to be made good if it were to be heeded. Secondly, she inherited a strongly centralist system of government. Towns, under their medieval charters and *fueros* (privileges), were the only subordinate unit of government that had any tradition of self-government. But much of the value of that tradition had been lost for many years past, since the right to seats on town councils had become something available only by inheritance or purchase. Moreover, even within towns, all citizens were not equal before the law. The Church, the army, and the learned professions of medicine and law enjoyed *fueros* applicable to their members, freeing them from the jurisdiction of the ordinary courts and giving them important safeguards against, for example, proceedings for debt. Outside the towns the great nobles had even more extensive privileges and on their vast estates there was no one to check their opportunity to abuse their powers.

And thirdly, since such a rigid system would otherwise have been unworkable, Mexico inherited a tradition of observing the letter rather than the spirit of the law, and of observing it rather than obeying it. These three disadvantages brought disaster to Mexico for her first thirty years of independence. The one thing that survived that disaster was the republic.

It was significant, for example, that the governing junta made no attempt to put into effect the republican constitution they already had. The strength of regional feeling had been one of the greatest assets of the guerrilla leaders in their struggle against the Spanish, and in the struggle against Iturbide there had been added to the names of Guadalupe Victoria and his colleagues as regional military heroes that of a young officer in Vera Cruz, Antonio López de Santa Anna. Though Guatemala itself had at first voted to join Mexico, it had now changed its mind; Chiapas might follow suit, and the unity of Mexico was tenuous. The solution propounded by the dominant faction in the Constituent Assembly of 1823–24 was a federal union such as that under which Mexico's northern neighbour, the United States, had been able to attain a dramatic unity. This plan was adopted in the Constitution of 1824.

Under this constitution Mexico, or 'the United Mexican States', became a federal republic of nineteen self-governing states. The executive power was entrusted to a President, the first holder of that office (1824–28) being Guadalupe Victoria. The Congress of the Union was to consist of two representatives from each state; the states themselves being created *de novo* out of the old Spanish provinces. Several of the provinces were renamed, with Indian rather than Spanish names; others created with the names of heroes such as Hidalgo and Morelos. But they remained obstinately provinces rather than states.

The Federalists, the dominant faction, who were ultimately to become known in the 1840s as Liberals, were opposed by the so-called Centralists, subsequently to become the Conservatives. The struggle between them was carried on under various names – not usually complimentary ones. It was the tragedy of Mexico, like all newly independent nations, that her leaders saw their old links of comradeship in war gradually disappear. It was Mexico's special tragedy that her leaders had so few links in the first place. The principal reason for this (among many others) was that in the struggle for independence the power had passed directly from Spain, not to the *criollos*, who had believed in the Spanish manner that they were necessarily destined to inherit it, but to men of the 'new race' that was purely Mexican – the *mestizos*. Iturbide himself was a *mestizo*; so too were both Victoria and his successors from the Federalists.

Victoria saw out his four-year term, though growing debility weakened his political touch near the end. While he still held office,

Nicolás Bravo, Republican hero of the War of Independence, led a Centralist force against the government, but was defeated at the hands of Vicente Guerrero. Guerrero naturally hoped to succeed Victoria, but Victoria's Secretary of War, Manuel Gómez Pedraza, had forestalled him and with army support he won the election of 1828. Guerrero appealed to arms and civil war broke out. To add further spice to the situation, the Spanish government tried to take advantage of Mexican divisions to reconquer their lost colony, but by the time their expeditionary force arrived, Guerrero had prevailed and become President (1829–30). Weakened by yellow fever from the marshes around Tampico, they were easily defeated by a force under Antonio López de Santa Anna, who emerged as a Liberal and national hero.[4]

At this juncture the Centralists, with *criollo* support, revolted against the policy of the *puros* ('extremists'), as the Guerrero wing of the Federalists were known. They were temporarily successful, but their ruthless attempts to exterminate the Liberals under the dictatorship of Anastasio Bustamante (1830–32) brought their own nemesis. Guerrero was dead – treacherously murdered after being invited to a meeting on board ship in 1831 – and the Federalists were able to reunite for long enough to restore Gómez Pedraza to serve the last few days of the term to which he had been elected four years previously.

The striking thing about these four years of Mexican politics is the way in which legalism destroyed the rule of law. Guerrero could not accept that he might not have been elected. He had contested the 1828 election; therefore he must be the 'legal' President. The Centralists could not accept that it was legal for a Federalist to hold office. It was irrelevant that the Federalist government was as centralist in practice as any Mexican government before or since. But they made no pretence of legality in seizing power in 1830, and they had no warrant whatsoever for their repressive measures against the Federalists. Moreover, worse was to come.

With the striking blend of shrewdness and inconsequence which was to become all too familiar to Mexicans in the next two decades, Santa Anna simply failed to turn up to be sworn in as President and his Vice-President, Valentín Gómez Farias, became acting chief executive. His short-lived Liberal administration was a striking attempt to tackle the major ills of the republic: to cut back the size of the army, improve primary education, limit the powers of the Church, and, above all, to make the government's power effective, especially in the north. It was a disastrous failure, in that it united all his enemies. From his hacienda Santa Anna watched until his time was ripe, then returned to the capital to assume power for the first of the eleven times he was to do so in the name of saving Mexico, between 1833 and 1853. But Santa Anna had no remedy for the evils of division except his own absolute rule. Hence, though his successive tenures of power, and the efforts of the Liberals to prevent them, resulted in a crop of more or less conservative constitutions, they resulted in no important social advance. And as the administrative machinery inherited from the Spanish slowly ran down, it was not repaired. The secession of Texas, the French invasion of 1838, and the disastrous war of 1845–48 with the United States only made manifest a weakness that was in one way or another apparent to almost everyone.

Despite the important contribution to the débâcle made by Santa Anna himself, conservatism was so bankrupt that Santa Anna actually returned to power in 1853 in quasi-monarchical guise. He did not dare to reach more closely to the throne of Iturbide than to adopt the style of 'Most Serene Highness' and live with the splendour of a prince on the proceeds of the sale of the Mesilla Valley (the Gadsden strip) to the United States. It was two whole years before the revulsion of all classes at this combination of proved recipes for disaster moved them to eject him. Mexico confronted the need for a virtual constitutional revolution: the period known in Mexican history as 'the Reform'.

Voices: Independence Period

'My children, this day comes to us as a new dispensation. Are you ready to receive it? Will you be free? Will you make the effort to recover from the hated Spaniards the lands stolen from our forefathers three centuries ago? Today we must act! The Spaniards are bad enough themselves, but now they have sold our country to the French. Will you become Napoleon's slaves? Or will you, as patriots, defend your religion and your homes?

'We will defend them! Long live Our Lady of Guadalupe! Death to the bad government! Death to the gachupines!'

[1] A derisive term for Spaniards.
[2] D. A. Brading, *Miners and Merchants in Bourbon Mexico, 1763–1810* (Cambridge, Cambridge University Press, 1971), epilogue.
[3] See William Spence Robertson, *Iturbide of Mexico* (Durham, N.C., Duke University Press, 1952).
[4] See Wilfrid Hardy Calcott, *Santa Anna* (Norman, University of Oklahoma Press, 1936), also the same author's *Church and State in Mexico 1822–1857*.

The Revolution II: The Reform

On 7 August 1855 Santa Anna embarked at Vera Cruz on the *Iturbide* for his final exile. He was to return to Mexico as a broken and poverty-stricken old man, and to die peacefully in the national capital in 1876. Perhaps it was a portent of a more generous age to come, but for the moment it was still far away. The new President, and the moving spirit behind the Liberal manifesto, the Plan of Ayutla, was Juan A. Álvarez, then, at sixty-five, the last of the significant veterans of the army of independence raised by Morelos. His last achievement, after assuming power, was to reunite the Liberal Party in a broad-based administration, and to give it the first impulse on the way to radical reform by backing the *Ley Juárez*, named after the Indian lawyer from Oaxaca who was his Minister of Justice and Ecclesiastical Affairs.[1]

The *Ley Juárez* was something more than the Liberal riposte to twenty years of military and clerical support for Santa Anna. By abolishing outright the old *fueros* of these two groups, it fulfilled the aim of the heroes of independence of establishing the basis for a new society in which the distinctions made by the Spaniards between class and class no longer existed. In fact, of course, these distinctions reflected equally the privileged position of the same two classes under the Aztecs. Having established the Reform, Álvarez then retired and handed over the Presidency to Ignacio Comonfort, his principal lieutenant in the struggle against Santa Anna. Without further delay the *Ley Juárez* was followed up by the *Ley Lerdo*, the product of Comonfort's Secretary of Finance, Miguel Lerdo de Tejada. The *Ley Lerdo* removed the great landholdings of the Church from ecclesiastical ownership. It did not prescribe for them to be put under state control and in due course they mostly passed into the hands of the private corporations. But the Church did not get them back.

Having dealt with the Church, the Liberals turned their attention to the state.[2] The Plan of Ayutla, conceived in the aftermath of the great territorial losses of Mexico to her northern neighbour, had stressed the need for stability. The Constitution of 1857, however, bore more of the marks of the American constitution than any of its predecessors. Like it, it was a compromise between the moderates, who wanted to restore the Constitution of 1824, and the *puros*, who wanted to enshrine the complete separation of Church and state in a new form. It was a new constitution, but it was moderate in tone: a political fact which did not prevent it from being singled out for the almost unique denunciation of Pius IX. Article 5 prohibited the state from prescribing a man's religious belief; Article 13 confirmed the *Ley Juárez*'s provisions on the abolition of the *fueros*, and Article 28 went beyond the *Ley Lerdo* in prohibiting the Church from owning any property other than buildings specifically devoted to religious purposes.

With papal encouragement, the archbishop of Mexico denounced the constitution and declared that Catholics could not accept it. Comonfort, who had become increasingly hesitant, tried to avert an open collision; then, when he found it inevitable, decided to outflank it. Being elected the first President under the new constitution, he assumed dictatorial powers and suspended it only ten days later – leading, in effect, a revolt against his own government. At this signal the Conservatives, under General Félix Zuloaga, pronounced for the Church. Comonfort yielded his troops to the Conservatives and fled into exile. But the Liberals of 1857 were determined to win. They rallied behind Comonfort's Vice-President, Benito Juárez, and proclaimed him President. In early 1858 it seemed improbable that he could do much, but it turned out that they could hardly have made a better choice.

Benito Juárez

Benito Juarez[3] is one of those figures who have come to be regarded as having a symbolic significance beyond his own time and his own country. His career was marked at one and the same time by heroism, by tragedy, and by success. As with other great historical figures, the myth has become solidified to the point at which it obscures the facts. He has become a figure of legend, and the legends are inconsistent in a way that the human being was not. It is doubtful in fact whether Mexicans today regard him – to use the too-obvious comparison – as the Americans view Abraham Lincoln, his contemporary. Even in his lifetime he was a much more remote figure, and though he was in a very real sense a man of the people, he was not a popular man. As a result it is his achievements, rather than his humanity, that are remembered, and this makes him much more impersonal.

He was born in 1806 in San Pablo Guelatao, high in the mountains of Oaxaca, of Indian parents in a wholly Indian hamlet, and his parents died when he was four. He was brought up as a herdsman for one of his uncles. At the age of twelve he escaped from virtual serfdom by running away to the town of Oaxaca, where he was fortunate enough to find a Franciscan priest who taught him to read and write, and, pleased with his pupil's success, enrolled him for theological training.

Like all young Oaxacans, Juárez was inspired by his native state's greatest son, Vicente Guerrero, also of Indian extraction and a hero of the war against Spain. For him to become a dedicated Liberal was almost automatic. Though he remained a devout Catholic, he decided that he had a vocation in the secular and not the religious sphere, and the success of the republic and the impetus it gave to secular education enabled him to study at the new Institute in Oaxaca. In due course he became a lawyer and a magistrate. Already he had served briefly on the state legislature. However, he devoted himself to his legal duties, and it was not until 1847, when the governor of the state went off to lead a military force against the invading Americans, that Oaxaca's leading civilian citizen became governor.

Subsequently elected to the governorship in his own right, he gave the state a stable administration almost unique in the troubled months following the war and gave up his post at the conclusion of his term in 1852. The return of Santa Anna in 1853, however, was followed by his immediate arrest and deportation. From Havana he made his way to join his Liberal friends in New Orleans and played a major role in planning the revolt against Santa Anna that culminated in the Plan of Ayutla. During this time he worked as private secretary to Álvarez and was given the portfolio of Justice and Ecclesiastical Affairs in his short administration with the express purpose of curtailing the power of the Church of which he continued to be a member. In Comonfort's government he was advanced to the key post of Secretary of *Gobernación* (Interior), and in the first elections under the Constitution of 1857 was chosen as President of the Supreme Court and consequently as Vice-President under a constitution which made no other provision for the succession. Then Comonfort's *volte-face* left him as the only possible leader of the Liberals. Yet he had virtually no forces at his command and was, moreover, wholly a civilian, with no military training nor desire for military training. Soon his government was forced to leave Querétaro, where the rump Congress had chosen him as President, and fall back on Vera Cruz. There at least he retained sea links with the outside world and could get in much-needed supplies. The only problem was that there was a chronic shortage of money, not only to buy arms, but to maintain any of the processes of government.

In their extremity the reservations of the moderate Liberals against attacking the property of the Church, to whom they owed their current misfortunes, rapidly evaporated. In July 1859 the Liberal government passed the Law for the Nationalization of the Properties of the Secular and Regular Clergy. At one stroke it affected the separation of Church and state and the curbing of the Church. But only in the small area still left under the control of the Liberal government, and, what was more serious, that area by this time was too small for the return on the nationalization of the church property it held to be sufficient to fuel the war effort.

Meanwhile, on the Conservative side the Presidency had been transferred from Zuloaga, whom the clerical party distrusted, to the twenty-seven-year-old general who was commanding the Conservative armies with such success. The young Miguel Miramón was a *criollo*, with a personal antipathy for 'the Indian Juárez'. Within days he had prepared what he hoped would be the final blow against the Liberals by sending three ships to cut off Vera Cruz from the sea. At this point the Liberals were unexpectedly saved by the intervention of the United States, whose government, though itself on the brink of civil war, was concerned about the Conservative alliance with Spain and the implications it held for the renewal of European intervention on the American continent. A small American flotilla under Admiral J. R. Jarvis challenged Miramón's fleet, disabled it, and then escorted it to New Orleans where its commanders were charged with piracy. The United States then recognized the government of Juárez. His Minister of Foreign Relations, Melchor Ocampo, was virtually forced in return to sign a treaty – the McLane-Ocampo Treaty – ceding the territory of Lower California, passage rights across Mexican territory, and the perpetual right of intervention to protect United States interests. Fortunately it was rejected not only by Juárez's Congress, but also by the Republican majority in the United States Senate. Yet it was the nearest the Liberals had yet come to handing away Mexican sovereignty, as their Conservative opponents had so freely done in the past.

And they were to do it again. 1859 closed with the Conservatives still unable to win decisively, while the Liberals had cast down a further challenge to the Church by establishing a civil ceremony of marriage – potentially a serious blow to church revenues. Miramón had borrowed from a Swiss banker named Jecker 619,000 pesos to build a new fleet. The fleet failed, but Jecker received in exchange bonds with the impossible face value of fifteen million pesos. Conservative hopes of further loans had been annihilated before the loans themselves had been raised. Worse, European investors had been given a pretext for intervention. The failure at sea, however, was only a prelude to failure on land. The turning-point came at the battle of Silao on 9 August 1860 and on 1 January 1861 Liberal forces finally reoccupied the national capital. The Three Years War was over and the Liberal laws against the Church were now a fact. Ten days later

Juárez himself entered the city, a civilian in civilian clothes, in a plain black carriage, almost unnoticed. On 15 June 1861 he began his rule as elected President of Mexico.

As such he inherited not only the Liberal but also the Conservative debts of three years of civil war; a ravenous army, and a horde of place-seekers determined to recoup their losses at the hands of the Conservatives; numerous Conservative guerrillas operating in the states to the west of the capital where their support was strongest; an unstable Congressional majority in which Jacobin deputies scorned the painful attempts of the President to restore order and bayed for blood; the prospect of the intervention by a Spanish force already fitting out in Havana to recover Spain's lost territory; and the temporary loss of effective support from the Republican administration in the United States which, since Fort Sumter, had been entirely occupied with its own seceding Southern states. Only the last could be put right at once, through the creation of an amicable relationship with the United States minister urgently seeking tacit Mexican support, but it seemed a useless gesture in 1861 and in any case alienated further strength at a critical time.

For the first task of the shaky government was to deal with the financial situation, and there was no alternative to the conclusion that it was hopeless. Even without the Conservative debts it would have been bad enough. On 17 June 1861 Congress formally ratified the suspension of payment of the national debts for a space of two years, and at once the governments of Britain and France broke off diplomatic relations. Together with the government of Spain, the two governments proceeded to act together to demand the resumption of payments, their action culminating at the beginning of 1862 in the arrival of ships at the port of Vera Cruz, and its joint occupation. On reaching a satisfactory agreement the British and Spanish forces thereupon withdrew.

But not the French. The enthusiasm of the *parvenu* Napoleon III in pressing for payment for the bonds of the Swiss Jecker which were mostly held in London had hitherto seemed rather mysterious. Now that French forces had actually landed in Mexico it became plain that the joint expedition, in which Napoleon had been the moving spirit, was simply a cover for the pursuit of *la gloire*. Dazzled by the stories of the traditional wealth of the Spanish treasure fleets, the emperor intended to create a French protectorate in the New World, confident that the United States to the north would never again be able to interfere, and that the Conservatives in Mexico would help him.

Once their allies had left, therefore, the French forces set off for the capital, issuing increasingly insolent proclamations as they went. At Puebla, on 5 May 1862, they were repulsed by forces under the command of General Ignacio Zaragoza. In this action the young Porfirio Díaz, newly promoted general for gallantry against the Conservatives, added fresh laurels to his reputation. Small though the forces involved were, the Mexicans were inferior in numbers, and the achievement was considerable. The battle of the *Cinco de Mayo* forced a radical reassessment of the situation in France. Meanwhile, the French retired to Orizaba to await reinforcements from France under a new and abler commander, General Forey, and in the meantime General Zaragoza died of typhoid fever. His successor, General Ortega, though less able, held out in Puebla for two months against the French reinforcements before being forced to surrender. On 31 May the government of the republic had to abandon Mexico City, which was in due course occupied by French forces.

The Mexican Conservatives were now to receive a different sort of shock from those to which they had become accustomed. General Forey, speaking from the strength of military success, made it clear that they were not to set up their own government, as they had hoped. Instead Mexico's Notables – carefully selected for the purpose – convened in Mexico City and invited Archduke Maximilian of Habsburg, brother of the Emperor Francis Joseph, to accept the throne of Mexico. Unfortunately for him, he accepted, though only after asking for assurances that he had been popularly chosen, which caused the French authorities inordinate trouble in arranging 'elections'.

For the republic still survived. Throughout 1864 and 1865 guerrilla bands still fought on throughout the country. No less important, their government stayed in being, though Juárez had to retreat first to Saltillo, then to Monterrey, then to Chihuahua, and finally to the last possible point, El Paso del Norte, on the northern frontier with Texas. News reached him even there of some successes and many defeats; the most serious news, the campaign of General Bazaine in Oaxaca which led to the capture of Porfirio Díaz, being relieved somewhat by the later news of Díaz's daring escape from imprisonment in Vera Cruz. Finally the American Civil War came to an end, and the United States, which had continued to recognize Juárez when all the European powers recognized the empire, made threatening gestures and allowed arms to cross the frontier to the Republicans.

Maximilian, who had arrived in Mexico in May 1864, was distinguished-looking, honourable, and well-meaning.[4] Faced with the demands of the Church, from the Vatican downwards, for the restoration of church lands, he did not know which way to turn. Like all its predecessors, his government spent much money but was in fact bankrupt. In his liberal inclinations he was wiser than his ministers, and it was with the best intentions that he virtually endorsed the Laws of the Reform. What he could not do, as a foreigner, was to attract sufficient military support; thus, driven back into the arms of the Conservatives, he was persuaded in 1865 to sign a decree ordering that anyone caught in arms against the empire be shot out of hand. Finally, his very existence annoyed his principal backer, Napoleon III, by reminding him of the damage the Mexican adventure was doing to the French budget. Eager to rid himself of the burden, Napoleon needed no persuasion from the United States (which offered it anyway) to withdraw French forces from Mexico, and in the event the outbreak of the Seven Weeks War in Europe brought forward the timetable. The last French troops left Mexico City in February 1867 under the command of General Bazaine. Honourably, Maximilian himself decided to remain. Betrayed by one of his Conservative followers, he eventually fell into the hands of General Escobedo at Querétaro after trying to arrange safe-conducts for his followers at the price of his own life, and there, at the place where he surrendered, he was shot on 19 June 1867.

Mexico City surrendered to the Republican general, Porfirio Díaz, and Juárez returned once again as the leader of a triumphant government, this time with appropriate ceremony. To Congress he justified the execution of Maximilian on the grounds that it was proper: severity to leaders enabled mercy to be granted to their followers. This was the policy that the government continued to pursue, though its application caused considerable dissension. The country continued in a very turbulent state, and if the Treasury was still empty, at least there was no one now to dispute how it was to be filled – no one outside Mexico, for Juárez had already met with opposition among his own ranks when he had had to prolong his own Presidential mandate in 1865, and though there were few to dispute his right to re-election in 1867 (when elections could again be held), there were many who looked to a change in 1871.

Slowly the economy began to recover. Foreigners were not welcome, though they could deal with the Mexican government on Mexican terms. Some were prepared to do so: Juárez soon had the satisfaction of seeing Spain become a liberal monarchy under the rule of General Prim and ultimately France herself a republic. Both joined the United States in recognizing Mexico. Consequently trade did pick up, though endemic banditry was discouraging to major expansion. The power of the Church seemed for a moment at least to be scotched, but the Congress and press were restless with a government that had lived so long with emergency legislation that it had forgotten the slowness of democracy. Sebastián Lerdo de Tejada, brother of Miguel and now Chief Justice and *de facto* Vice-President, hoped to become constitutional President in 1871, but he was impatient with fools and not popular. In this position, after he had suffered a stroke and his

devoted wife had died after a long illness, Juárez took the difficult
decision to run for a further term.

He won, though not at all by an absolute majority. Lerdo came
third; it was Porfirio Díaz who came second. At this point Díaz made
a fateful mistake. Ever since the end of the war, military conspiracies
among the greatly inflated army had been fairly common. Díaz had
stayed aloof; some of his supporters had been among the revolutionaries, but officially his line was to criticize the government for not
taking stronger action to suppress revolt. Now he himself 'pronounced'
against the re-election from his hacienda of La Noria, claiming that the
election had been rigged. Juárez was granted extraordinary powers,
and the revolt broken by the accident that General Félix Díaz, governor of Oaxaca and Porfirio's brother, fell into the hands of a peasant
band who shot him forthwith. With the country still in turmoil,
Juárez himself had a heart attack and died on the evening of 18 July
1872.

Voices: The Reform

'I die in a just cause. I forgive all, and pray that all may forgive me.
May my blood flow for the good of this land. Long live Mexico'.[5]

'The Clergy is my main reliance, & there are powerful persons
appealing to its interests to lend me its aid & influence. The new
Government is wholly dependent upon the Church for support, all the
Coasts and Customs Houses being in the hands of the "Coalition". The
Church has already loaned its credit to the Government to the amount
of a Million and a half of Dollars. It will be very difficult to negotiate
these securities, and, at most, not more than fifty per cent can be
realized upon them; because Capitalists fear to risk the stability of the
Government, and know that, if the *Puros* come in, the Church property
will be declared National. The Church is thus between two fires; in
danger, first, of being ruined at a blow from the *Puros*, and equally
sure of being ruined by its friends, the present Government. There is
no escape but in filling the Treasury from abroad'.[6]

'The people and the government shall respect the rights of all.
Between individuals as between nations, respect for the rights of others
is peace'.[7]

'The execution at Querétaro was necessitated by the gravest
motives of justice, combined with the imperious necessity of securing
peace in the future and putting an end to the internal convulsions and
all the calamities inflicted by the war on our society. The application
of the law to those in the first rank among those most guilty has permitted the use of great clemency towards all the others'.[8]

[1] Wilfrid Hardy Calcott, *Liberalism in Mexico, 1857–1929* (Stanford, Stanford
University Press, 1931).

[2] Walter V. Scholes, *Mexican Politics during the Juárez Regime 1855–1872* (Columbia, Mo., University of Missouri Studies, 1957).

[3] The principal biography of Juárez in English is Charles Allen Smart, *Viva Juárez* (London, Eyre and Spottiswoode, 1964).

[4] Biographies are plentiful. H. Montgomery Hyde, *Mexican Empire* (London, Macmillan, 1946) is still interesting.

[5] Emperor Maximilian, in Bertita Harding, *Phantom Crown; the Story of Maximilian and Carlota of Mexico* (London, Harrap, 1935), 205.

[6] John Forsyth, US Minister to Mexico, 1858, in Scholes, op. cit., 31.

[7] Juárez, manifesto, 1867, in *Discursos y manifiestos de Benito Juárez*, ed. Ángel Pola (Mexico, Á. Pola, 1905), 290.

[8] Juárez, address to Congress, 8 December 1867, in Smart, op. cit., 381.

The Revolution III: Porfiriato

THE SUDDEN DEATH OF JUÁREZ came as such a surprise that the legal succession was not disputed. The aspirations of Porfirio Díaz had suffered a temporary setback after his unsuccessful revolt in 1871, and the pretext of *continuismo* was annulled by Juárez's death.

Sebastián Lerdo de Tejada proved a capable President.[1] He was no Juárez – but then no man could have hoped to fill that exacting and heroic role, and he sensibly did not try. No one had any doubts that in the end Díaz would try again, and it is a measure of Lerdo's success and the influence of the ideas of constitutionalism propagated, though not practised, by Juárez, that the revolt came at the end of his term, when the question of succession was once again about to be solved by re-election. The Plan of Tuxtepec, issued by Díaz to signal his revolt early in 1876, embodied the specific goal of no re-election together with demands for the strict observance of the Laws of the Reform and the Constitution of 1857. Accordingly, after the brief campaign had led to Lerdo's resignation, Díaz installed a Provisional President and held elections before assuming power himself early in 1877.

During his first term (1877–80) Díaz ruled very much as a party leader and as a constitutionalist. However, although he was studious to avoid offending any one section of opinion, he had no hesitation in taking severe action against the endemic guerrilla warfare which was a relic of the French intervention. His methods were uncomplicated, and, as far as they went, effective. Reporting an abortive conspiracy in Vera Cruz, which had involved the crew of a ship, Governor Mier y Terán used the newly installed telegraph to ask for instructions. Díaz replied that he should first catch the ship, then shoot the officers and a tenth of the crew. The hysterical governor interpreted this to mean that he could shoot whom he pleased, in an episode that has become a legend in Mexican history.[2] There were no further revolts in Vera Cruz while Díaz ruled, but Díaz himself never went there again until 1911.

When the elections of 1880 came round, Díaz introduced a new variant to Mexican politics by securing the return of his childhood friend and *compadre* Manuel González. González, an imposing figure with an impressive forked beard, looked every inch a President. As a general he had a good war record, and as an individual he rewarded his friends and was on good terms with others. Inevitably he gained political support in his own right. But he was pledged to return the Presidency to Díaz in 1884, and, having amended the constitution to make that possible, he duly did so, but not before the partisans of Díaz had spread stories that González was hopelessly corrupt and quite unfitted to rule.

Certainly it was under González that the economic development of modern Mexico really began, with the advent of railway construction and the introduction of foreign capital on a large scale. In 1883 diplomatic relations were restored with Great Britain, and in 1884, by the completion of the Central Railway, Mexico was connected to the United States. The influx of wealth which accompanied these developments benefited those in office at the time and enabled Díaz to form a new alliance between the central government and the regional *caciques* (bosses) who held the state governorships.

González kept his bargain, but after Díaz returned to the Presidency in 1884 he showed that the anxieties of the preceding four years had left their mark on him. Perhaps he no longer trusted anyone but himself, or perhaps he became convinced of his own indispensability. It is hard to say. In any case, the hero of the Plan of Tuxtepec had Congress amend the constitution in 1887 to permit his immediate re-election for a further term, and before that was up, a further amendment had abolished all restrictions on re-election. In 1888, 1892, 1896, and 1900, therefore, he was returned to the Presidency by the customary overwhelming majorities, though never without at least nominal opposition, and in 1896 with quite a lot of openly expressed discontent.

The Díaz motto was 'Little politics, much administration'. The *Porfiriato* was a very personal government, but it had much in common with other Latin American dictatorships that proved less durable.

To begin with, Díaz relied for his assistants and subordinates on his old colleagues of the War of Intervention. It was they who filled the ministries and occupied the state governorships. As they grew older with him, into their fifties, their sixties, their seventies . . . the system became rigid. It could not be changed, for it allowed no opportunity for change. Its enemies called it the 'full car' (*carro completo*). Waiting to get on, if not sufficiently assiduous to hold minor positions, were a whole generation of Mexican intellectuals, many of whom recognized – with greater or lesser enthusiasm – that the price of the new stability was that the car stayed in one place.

In its early years the system benefited most from the exhaustion born of the War of Intervention. Few then were disposed to question the pleasures of quietism. It was so long since anything resembling quiet in any sense had been known in Mexico. By the time that doubts began to appear, important changes had taken place. As one of the first acts of his government, Díaz had organized a vast force of rural police, the *Guardia Rural*. They wore smart grey uniforms with a broad red stripe down the seams of the trousers, and picturesque floppy hats, and they were heavily armed as a military force. Like many similar forces they were remotely related to Napoleon's gendarmerie, designed, like their model, to meet any threat to public security up to and including all-out war. They were not noted for asking questions, and people who made themselves objectionable or merely inconvenient to them were reported 'shot trying to escape'.

The *rurales* supported the régime in two ways. Most obviously, they disposed of opponents or potential opponents. They created besides a very strong sense of the omnipresence of the government which hitherto had been notably lacking. It was said that a woman could walk on foot unmolested from one end of Mexico to the other. It is just possible that that was true. It is even more likely that the prevalence of summary 'justice' untouched by legal process merely resulted in very low crime statistics. Either way, the government gained kudos.

Secured in the physical sense, the *Porfiriato* then executed two more complex and delicate political manœuvres which brought it untold extra strength. On the one hand, by 1888 the enforcement of the Laws of the Reform against the Church was tapered off and the Church, appropriately grateful, became the principal organized supporting group of the régime. Most of the great revolutionaries of the future were, therefore, given good clerical educations. Simultaneously, the old Liberal Party, of which Díaz had become the nominal head, was allowed to fall into decay. To replace it, there began to emerge a new faction, which though not in fact a party, performed some of the functions of a political party in a one-party state, in that it decided important policies, put forward candidates, and linked together the principal financial and commercial interests of the state. These men came to be known, at first derisively, later with more circumspection, as the *científicos*, or scientists.

The *científicos* were those members of the government who believed that through the philosophy of Auguste Comte they could attain – indeed, had attained – a knowledge of social processes so accurate that revolution would become impossible. These processes would be regulated by a combination of coercive sanctions and inducements, or, as the epigrammatic motto had it, 'bread or the stick' (*pan o palo*). It would be a self-sustaining process. Once stability had been achieved, a programme of capital development could be undertaken based on the foreign capital it attracted. Economic development, meaning financial stability, would then maintain internal adherence while retaining the foreign capital indefinitely. Dictatorship and technological progress were therefore seen as connected and interdependent.

To us, the most striking thing about the system was that it did indeed work, to some extent. As we have already seen, the capital did come in, and Mexico did progress economically. Too many of the benefits, however, stuck in the top ranks of the government for the process to work for more than a small fraction, and the rest suffered considerably more than before.

Financial stability in international trade meant adherence to the gold standard. For the world's largest silver-producing nation this meant sharp deflation, emphasizing the gap between rich and poor.

Colonization of the northern deserts swallowed up a great deal of money and annoyed a great many people without attracting any substantial addition to the labour force. The bulk of the population continued to be squeezed into the Core.

Laws designed to promote private ownership of mines and other resources were enacted to encourage investment. In the scramble for these resources, and in the pressure for land, unchecked for the favourites of the régime by any fear of the corrupt and inefficient legal system, individuals, hamlets, and even villages were deprived of their land, which rapidly passed into the hands of a few wealthy supporters of the régime, the political and economic bosses of their own regions.

Those who dissented (or whose resources were coveted) were deliberately reduced to peonage, and thousands died on the *henequén* (sisal) plantations of Yucatán, harvesting the sharp spiny leaves for a pittance which kept them in permanent bondage to the company store.

As so often during the nineteenth century, science seemed to have very strange results in Mexico. In 1910 the roads of Mexico were essentially as the Spaniards had left them. But already in the other great cities of the world the new horseless carriages were gliding over Mexican asphalt as a matter of course. The American magnate who owned the wells had been unable for a long time to find enough oil and he had to sell the asphalt to recover his costs.

The United States

It was the hallmark of the *Porfiriato* that it shifted the entire orientation of Mexico. From facing eastward across the sea to Europe, by 1910 she was joined to the United States to the north. This development was resisted strongly by all Mexicans, and even by the government, but it occurred anyway.

It is impossible to understand the story of Mexico in the twentieth century without trying to understand her relations with the United States.[3] They are not easy to assess. Few have attempted to do so who are neither Mexicans nor *norteamericanos*, and their accounts are inclined all too often to approximate to traditional stereotypes. For tourist purposes, some of these stereotypes are extremely profitable to maintain, which makes their true assessment very much more difficult.

In 1810 the United States was very much smaller than Mexico – in fact, the Kingdom of New Spain was then the largest single political unit in the world. Yet in a sense American incursions had already begun. When Napoleon sold the Louisiana territory to the United States in 1803, it had only just ceased to be Spanish territory – the Plaza de Armas in New Orleans is witness to this day to the fact that Spanish rule there lasted much longer than French. The Mexican War of Independence was still in progress when the United States went to war with Spain in 1818 and captured the territory of Florida. However, once Mexican independence had been secured and the republic proclaimed, the government of President Monroe welcomed it to the company of the free nations of the world and accredited a minister to its government. To the rest of the world the name of this minister – Joel Poinsett – is known today only by the name of the beautiful Mexican flower he popularized.[4] The Mexicans, however, regard him as a bungling meddler who, by introducing the York Rite of Masonry into their country gave the pretext for the division in the republican party which brought so much misery upon them. Probably they credit him with too much influence; the divisions were there anyway.

A second stage in Mexican-American relations opened with the establishment of the Centralist republic in 1833. For the previous twelve years settlers, led by Stephen Austin, had been moving, with the agreement of the Mexican government, into that part of the State of Coahuila which was known as Texas.[5] They were welcomed as colonists in what Austin himself described as a 'howling wilderness'. But they were not universally welcomed, because they wanted to bring slavery with them. The Mexicans enforced abolitionism in the territory, and the Texans, anxious to obtain statehood for themselves, were refused it not only by the Federalists but also by the Centralists who had no qualms about repealing the decree against slavery. After this events moved speedily to a break. The Centralist government sent a force to Texas under the command of General Martín Perfecto De Cos. It was stopped by a force of Texans who defeated it in a pitched battle at San Antonio on 4 December 1835. Determined to avenge the defeat, Santa Anna himself led reinforcements to San Antonio, where he found only 150 defenders in the old Franciscan mission of the Alamo and massacred them to a man. The news reached the leaders of the newly proclaimed Republic of Texas that their state had received its first martyrs and that the Mexican President himself was continuing

GOSHEN COLLEGE LIBRARY
GOSHEN, INDIANA

his advance on the San Jacinto River. On 21 April 1836, while the Mexican forces were asleep, the remainder of the Texan forces, only 800-strong, fell on the heavily superior Mexican force and took it completely by surprise. Santa Anna fled from the battlefield in his nightgown and slippers. Soon captured, he was not allowed to return to Mexico until he had signed the Treaty of Velasco, recognizing Texan independence.

The United States too recognized Texan independence. There were many in the South who wanted to annex Texas forthwith, as the Texans desired, but Northern opposition to slavery and its extension prevented any further move at that time. In fact the United States did not even have to lend anything more than moral support to Texas, since that state proved perfectly capable of maintaining its independence without it. What turned the situation into real tragedy was the election in 1844 to the Presidency of the United States of James Knox Polk, a tough-minded Ulster Scot who was determined on the territorial expansion of the United States, and who, unique among American Presidents, was prepared to sacrifice even a second term of office for a successful Presidency as he saw it.

Polk knew that he could not persuade the Senate to ratify a treaty for the annexation of Texas by the necessary two-thirds majority. Instead Congress was persuaded to authorize the action by a Joint Resolution which required only a simple majority. It was a dubious expedient, but it worked, backed by the preposterous argument that if it were not done, Texas would fall into the hands of Great Britain.

Polk was no less anxious to get hold of the territory of Upper California, the possession of which was indispensable to any dream of the United States as a vast country stretching from coast to coast. He next sent a commissioner, John Slidell, to Mexico City, authorized to purchase Upper California together with the territory now known as Arizona and New Mexico. As minister to Mexico, Slidell was also commissioned to make United States gains good by settling the boundary with Texas on the Río Bravo, the river the Americans call the Rio Grande. Since the Mexicans did not recognize Santa Anna's recognition of the secession of Texas, quite naturally no designated boundary had been agreed, but traditionally the frontier of Texas had lain rather further north, at the Río Nueces. The expulsion of Slidell from Mexico was the necessary move for any Mexican government to make when news of his mission leaked out, but it was just the pretext that Polk needed for war. He ordered General Zachary Taylor to establish a military presence on the Río Bravo and on 25 April 1846 a clash between his forces and those of the Mexicans inaugurated the War of 1847, known in the United States as the Mexican War.

Faced with an actual state of war, the American Congress gave Polk the declaration of war he needed, and American troops advanced on Monterrey. Simultaneously forces under John Charles Frémont occupied the thinly populated settlement of Upper California. In Mexico a Liberal revolt toppled the government and unity was sought behind the only available military leader, Santa Anna, who had added to his laurels in 1838 by routing a French debt-collecting force (the 'Pastry War') at Vera Cruz and losing a leg in the action. While the political changes were still taking place, however, American forces had already landed at Vera Cruz under General Winfield Scott, and had begun the long ascent to the capital. At the battle of Cerro Gordo Scott's troops routed the Mexican forces under Santa Anna. Santa Anna, however, retreated with his rearguard to Puebla. There he actually succeeded in persuading Scott, who had to halt for reinforcements, to bribe him with $U.S.10,000, and used it to raise another army for the last-ditch stand in the Valley of Mexico.

Only in this extremity did the Liberals and Conservatives stop killing one another and form a united front against the invaders. Both they and Santa Anna had hitherto underestimated the courage and tenacity of the small American force, toiling uphill in their thick uniforms in the hot sun much as had the soldiers of Cortés before them. As they marched they sang 'Green Grow the Rashes O' – hence *gringo*, the Mexican term of derision for a North American. Both ruses and guerrilla warfare failed to delay them more than three weeks, and they fought their way into Mexico City on 14 September 1847 only two days before the annual celebration of the *Grito de Dolores*. The military cadets who defended the Castle of Chapultepec for their part fought until there were only six left alive, and they wrapped themselves in the Mexican flag and jumped to their death off the battlements rather than surrender. Today a monument to the boy soldiers (the 'Niños Heroes') marks the place where they made this last sacrifice.

Santa Anna had already been deposed by a Congress which saw no alternative to a negotiated peace. That peace, the Treaty of Guadalupe Hidalgo (1848), was one of the most severe ever signed by any nation. By it Mexico lost half the national territory to the northern republic, in compensation for a cash payment of only 15 million U.S. dollars. Yet only five years later Santa Anna, as we have seen, sold a further strip of territory on the border on the last occasion that he was recalled to power. Only then did the period of territorial aggrandisement of the United States come to an end, owing to the growing strains over slavery which the acquisition of Texas had done much to accelerate. In this sense Polk's actions may be said to have brought their own terrible nemesis.

With the election of Abraham Lincoln in 1860 relations between Mexico and the United States moved into a happier period. This was not immediately apparent since, after all, the United States did not even recognize the government that appeared to be in control of Mexico from 1862 to 1867. Her support of the Liberals and of Juárez, however, was to be the precursor of a long period of mutual suspicion coupled with increased respect on both sides. Then after 1880, a fourth period began in which American capital began to move into Mexico – the first country to feel the power of the growing industrial nation of the modern world during the time that it was emerging into great-power status. The influx of capital was essential to the economic success of the *Porfiriato*. By the turn of the century its effects were so widespread that Mexico's leaders began to have their doubts about the advisability of cultivating it further. Before they had had time to make any more than the most hesitant moves to change their policy, however, they were to be swept away, and the establishment of a new relationship with the northern republic was to be a major preoccupation of all twentieth-century Mexican governments.

Porfirio Díaz

Nowhere in Mexico today will you find a statue of Porfirio Díaz; no street bears his name; and few Mexicans speak of him except as the name of an age. For that is just what he was. It is as if, for example, one spoke of the 'Victorian Age' without referring to the ruler who gave her name to it. To this day Díaz's record of twenty-seven years' continuous office (1884–1911) is unequalled in the Latin American republics, and only Trujillo in the Dominican Republic has equalled his total period of personal rule. The rule of Díaz is one of the most important formative influences on the making of modern Mexico and its general characteristics cannot be ignored, but still less can the character and achievements of the man at the centre of it all.

Díaz was always a man who was admired rather than liked. Juárez observed of him, critically, that he was a man who wept while killing, and it is the suspicion of hypocrisy which made him most un-attractive to his critics. He was undoubtedly highly emotional; he was equally undoubtedly very insensitive to the pain and suffering of others. Beals takes up the obvious reference to his name (*Porfirio* = por-phyry) and describes him as a man of stone, like the jade figurines of his native Oaxaca, and so in a sense he was.[6] Perhaps he had to be. He was an Indian boy who lost his father at the age of three, and from his earliest youth had to work to support his mother, Petrona Mori de Díaz, and his younger brother, Félix. He was a bright boy, however, and after the customary religious education he began the study of law. Then when he was sixteen, in 1846, came news of the American intervention and, like many others, he volunteered but was never mobilized for action.

His entry into politics, then, came with the Plan of Ayutla and the Liberal triumph, out of which he received the lowly job of being sub-prefect of Ixtlán. It was the first step in his political career. But it was the military, and not the civilian, ladder that he was destined to climb, for, significantly, his first steps in the army were taken during the Three Years War, fighting against his own countrymen. At the end of that time, at the age of thirty-one, he was promoted to brigadier-general. For a few weeks he held the virtual sinecure of a Federal deputyship, a reminder that he had ambition and might be expected to go higher. The War of the French Intervention turned him from a promising young officer into a national hero.

After his first distinction in the battle of the *Cinco de Mayo*, Díaz was among the forces guarding Puebla against the invaders. Like other high officers he was taken prisoner at the inevitable surrender, but unlike them, his daring escape over the rooftops of Vera Cruz enabled him to return to action and gain further laurels. His first success came with his capture of Taxco, after which he was sent south to liberate his home State of Oaxaca. Again he had the misfortune to fall into enemy hands, and again a daring escape, from the Convent of Saint Cather-ine, Oaxaca, enabled him to resume the fight. In the appalling condi-tions of 1864 he maintained the nucleus of a guerrilla army in the hills, harassing the French forces at every opportunity. By 1865 he was the one high commander actually in the field who could serve as the rallying-point for the Republican forces.

Then in September 1865 the tide turned. A long series of victories ultimately brought Díaz to the gates of the capital on 21 June 1867, and the following month he was able to turn a working government in possession of its city over to Juárez at his long-delayed triumphal entry. His work done, he stated his intention of retiring into civil life, and though he retained his military post as a divisional commander, he retired to Tehuacán, in the State of Puebla, from where he watched the political scene without comment. Clearly he hoped to be drafted to the Presidency. The election of Juárez cut short his immediate hopes, however, and early in 1868 he obtained leave of absence and settled down in Oaxaca on the hacienda of La Noria given to him by its grateful legislature. Still only thirty-eight, he could afford to wait for the elections in 1871.

There can be no doubt that Díaz must have seen the decision of the ageing Juárez to run for a third term as a personal affront to himself; his own campaign was well organized, and the large number of votes credited to him reflect a real popularity which Juárez at least never ignored. Had he not made the serious mistake of backing the futile revolt of La Noria, which failed even to capture the state capital, his ascent to power would have been much less painful. As things turned out, it was to take another four years and the permanent disruption of the Liberals to achieve the end-product he desired. Even then it was a close thing.

The revolt of Tuxtepec in 1876 was based on a double strategy. Díaz's friends were to raise Oaxaca and proclaim their support for him, while he himself went, by way of New Orleans, to the north in order to recruit support there. He was moderately successful, but in the primitive state of Mexican communications of the day the plan was doomed to failure. Eventually he abandoned the attempt and made his way back by sea to Vera Cruz, whence in considerable risk of being captured and shot, he made his way across the country to Oaxaca, revived the flagging energies of the revolt, and struck as soon as he dared at the seat of power. He was greatly aided by the attitude of President Lerdo's Vice-President, the President of the Supreme Court, José María Iglesias. By refusing to recognize Lerdo's re-election he brought about a deep split in the government ranks which worked entirely in favour of Díaz. With the capture of Puebla, his road to power was at last open.

Having entered the capital (24 November 1876) and established his military presence, Díaz proceeded with the utmost legality. Congress was persuaded to implement the constitutional provision of no re-election. Díaz turned the Presidency over to a colleague, General Méndez, for the duration of the elections. Since he was the sole candidate, his victory was a foregone conclusion. And as we have seen already, his first period of office was entirely constitutional, if centralist in a sense which would have been more appropriate to one of the defunct Conservatives than to a nominal Liberal. It was only after his return to power in 1884 that the era of continuous re-election and of *personalismo* as a system of government became an accomplished fact. Again, apart from the corruption of power, we can only guess at the reasons. First among them, perhaps, was the loss of his brother after the revolt of La Noria. (Only after that time did he lose the ability to trust people.) Partly, again, we must not forget that until Díaz had done it, no one knew just what a long period of continuous personal rule might lead to. It is certainly significant that the only Latin American dictators to rule in the same style for anything like so long were Dr Francia in Paraguay (1816–40) and Manuel Estrada Cabrera in Guatemala (1898–1920). Of these the last came to power when Díaz still ruled and modelled himself on him, yet seemed in some ways to learn from his experience.

Many great achievements were claimed by the Díaz régime, and some, as we have seen, were substantial. Its major failure, it can easily be argued, was overconfidence. But it is important to discern what kind of overconfidence, for it was political rather than economic. Surrounded with the incense of adulation (some of the most sickly from foreigners), its centre and *raison d'être* came to believe in the legend of his own beneficence. So when in 1908 he came to give an interview to an American journalist, James Creelman, about his life's work and intentions Díaz was wholly sincere when he envisaged himself as a paternal ruler whose task it had been to pave the way for democracy in his native country. Díaz was not content with being a merely national figure; he must be a world figure, and in 1900 the invitation to Mexico to join the conference at The Hague must have seemed to him to confirm the reception of Mexico into the league of civilized nations.

The evil days of the past were over, he told Creelman. Then it had been necessary to be hard. A man might kill if the interests of the nation demanded it. How many soldiers, it might not be asked, would not have said the same? But democracy was the thing of the future, and anyone who wished could stand for election. This was not wholly untrue: Díaz had always permitted one official opposition candidate at his elections after 1884, the thankless task having been discharged for some years by a lawyer from the capital named Don Nicolás Zuñiga de Miranda. This man Díaz considered to be a madman, and naturally so, for who could wish to bring back the evil of the old days?

It was a serious misjudgement when Díaz mistook the youthful enthusiast from Coahuila, Francisco Madero, for another of the same type. With military pretenders to the succession, like General Reyes, he knew how to deal: he merely left them to the rivalries of his entourage and kept his control on the states, the place where the votes were counted and the elections 'made'. But the idea of maintaining control of the states with a number of constantly changing officeholders – as the anti-re-electionists wanted – was then inconceivable. The machincry for selecting them simply did not exist. For if it had, it would have been incompatible with the continued supremacy of Díaz himself. The prohibition of re-election, which Madero and his Anti-re-electionist Party proclaimed, was the crucial challenge to the key political factor in the whole system. Madero was right. It was on the re-election of Díaz that all else depended, and without it the economic and social changes which so many others had come to see as necessary could not have been secured.

It was this failure of comprehension, understandable in a man of eighty, that allowed Díaz to let Madero become an official candidate against him in 1910. At the last minute he realized that he had made a mistake. The orders went out, and the candidature was quashed. But by then it was too late. Coahuila had been a disappointment to him in 1876; in 1910 it was a disaster.

[1] Frank A. Knapp, Jr, *The Life of Sebastian Lerdo de Tejada, 1823–1889* (Austin, University of Texas Press, 1931).

[2] Daniel Cosío Villegas, *Historia moderna de México: El Porfiriato, vida política interior, Primera Parte* (Mexico, Editorial Hermes, 1970), 322–44, covers the incident exhaustively, showing that although the notorious telegram 'Aprendidos infragranti, matalos en caliente' never existed, the orders that were given were equally barbarous.

[3] The definitive study is Howard F. Cline, *The United States and Mexico* (revised edition, Cambridge, Mass., Harvard University Press, 1967).

[4] *Euphorbia pulcherrima*, 'deciduous shrub, 2 to 10 ft. h., branched. *l.* ovate-elliptical to lanceolate, entire, toothed or lobed. fl. yellow, bracts vermilion'. The Royal Horticultural Society, *Dictionary of Gardening*, II.

[5] As in 'México' the 'x' represents an aspirate nowadays rendered in Castilian usage by 'j'.

[6] Carleton Beals, *Porfirio Díaz, Dictator of Mexico* (Philadelphia, J. B. Lippincott, 1932); cf. Todd Downing, *The Mexican Earth* (New York, Doubleday Doran, 1930), 207.

The Revolution IV: Outbreak

ON 16 SEPTEMBER 1910 Mexico celebrated the centenary of the *Grito de Dolores*. The ceremony when, at midnight, President Díaz stepped out on to the balcony of the National Palace and rang the bell that Father Hidalgo had rung so long before, was but the climax to a whole month of festivities. Collectively they were designed to show Mexico's emergence to an equal place among the nations of the world, the achievement of Díaz as the ruler who had held power longer than any other in Latin American history.

As the representatives of the nations of the world were slowly dispersing, the Chamber of Deputies was considering a petition for the nullification of the elections in which Díaz had just been returned to power for an eighth term. They rejected it. Their action was the signal that all legal remedies had been exhausted by the Anti-re-electionists. After successfully escaping to the United States Madero reluctantly agreed on armed insurrection. As the first step he issued a manifesto, the Plan of San Luis Potosí, in which he proclaimed himself Provisional President. His reluctance stemmed from his own personal nature and his desire for peace, but in any case he and his forces lacked both arms and money. Nevertheless, under the impetus of his optimistic brother Gustavo, letters were sent out to centres of support in Mexico, and eventually it was planned to launch a nationwide insurrection on 20 November.[1]

Needless to say, such a widespread and diffuse conspiracy could not be kept from the ears of the Porfirian police. A purchase of arms was noted, and inquiries made. On 16 November the government struck first, rounding up hundreds of suspects and transferring them to the capital for interrogation. At 7 o'clock in the morning of 18 November, a detachment of police arrived at the house of a shoemaker named Aquiles Serdan, in the centre of the city of Puebla. Serdan, his brother, and sister were indeed the principal organizers for the anti-re-electionist plot in the city, and had been warned. They fired on the police detachment, who called in the *rurales* to reduce the opposition. There were initially only eleven men and three women in the house, reinforced after the initial battle by five men and a boy; yet the twenty defenders resisted the overwhelming weight of government forces

53

for almost 24 hours and killed 158 men before being wiped out.[2]

The deaths of Serdan and his family and followers gave the Revolution its first martyrs. As yet, however, there was no certainty that the Revolution would follow. Madero himself had no army; the organization of the nationwide uprising had been broken; and in any case the essential element of surprise had been lost. In the general despondency, which led Madero's family to urge him to flee to Europe, it was some time before the continuing existence of revolutionary bands in the deserts of Durango, Chihuahua, and Coahuila was noted at all. Madero crossed the frontier to put himself at the head of his troops, but was unable to find them, and had to return to El Paso, Texas, where the agents of the *Porfiriato* were searching eagerly for evidence to get the United States government to have him arrested. It was for this reason that he once again crossed into Mexican territory at the beginning of February 1911. This time, fortunately, he was able to make contact, and joined the force led by a young ex-farmer named Pascual Orozco in Chihuahua.

This was, in fact, the most active centre of revolutionary mobilization. In no way was the guerrilla band a match for the government forces. Fortunately, however, the government was confused by the reports of 'bandits' which seemed to be springing up on all sides. Moreover, its sophisticated army depended very largely upon rail transport and so found it difficult to concentrate in support of the local counter-guerrilla activity. The most spectacular manifestation of revolution, and the one which achieved the most publicity abroad, was actually by far the least important in strategic terms. This was the outbreak in the peninsula of Baja California, closely connected with anarchist groups in Los Angeles and led by the brothers Flores Magón with the goal of setting up a socialist republic.[3] Out-of-work film actors and similar publicity hunters crossed the frontier to take part, found little or nothing there, and returned with glowing tales of their own heroism. Elsewhere, except in the north, though there were many who had heard stories of revolutionaries in action, they were always somewhere else.

Francisco I. Madero

Francisco Indalecio Madero was an improbable figure to be leading a revolution against Latin America's greatest *caudillo* of all time.[4] Born in 1873, he was the eldest son of Francisco Madero, a rich businessman of Parras, Coahuila. His grandfather, Evaristo Madero, the patriarch of an enormous family, had served as governor of the State of Coahuila under Manuel González. After Díaz had returned to power, the family had, more or less voluntarily, withdrawn from politics. But with the ascent of the *científicos* they had more than made up for their retirement in influence, since the family were on extremely close terms with Limantour, the Secretary of *Hacienda* (Finance), their acknowledged leader. By the end of the century, the family were immensely wealthy from banking, copper mining, stock-holding, and their considerable estates. Yet in their native State of Coahuila political power rested with others who enjoyed the favour of Díaz himself.

The young Francisco grew up on the family estate, accustomed to an outdoor life and fully at home in the saddle. Early in his life the family began to express concern at his small stature, which put him at a considerable disadvantage in childhood games. Otherwise he led the normal life of a son of a rich family, was sent to a Jesuit school at the age of twelve, and at fourteen by way of New York to France, where he was given a detailed business education.

It was the degree of equality with which he, as a young Latin American visitor, was received in Paris that first awoke in Madero his admiration for democracy as a way of life. He was, it seems, in any case looking for a new faith. At any rate, it was at this time, after his experience of a Jesuit school, that he dropped his baptismal name of Ignacio and replaced it with the less 'committed' Indalecio which he used in adult life. In Paris he encountered the new and modern religion of Spiritualism and was converted to it. It provided certainties not often offered to political leaders, and in one particular prophecy, a prediction that he would one day occupy the Presidential chair of his native country.

At the end of five years he hastened back to Mexico to see his family. After a few months spent perfecting his English at the University of California at Berkeley, he returned finally to take up the management of one of the family plantations, as he had been trained to do. He took from the first an intense interest in the people who worked on the plantation, in their history and problems, and this contributed in no small part to his success as an agriculturist. Not only did he ensure that adequate and better-quality housing was built, but he took a particular interest in the provision of adequate medical facilities, being himself a follower of the homoeopathic school. In this capacity he did much diagnosis and attempted cures himself, recording details and gaining confidence as he went on. His mother's escape from typhoid in 1901 was believed to be due to his attention.

Madero's developing social conscience was strengthened by his religious beliefs. The impulse to act upon them was to some extent inherent in his own energy, though after his marriage to the daughter of a neighbouring landowner in 1903 he might easily have settled down to plantation life uninterrupted by thought of politics had circumstances been different. As it was, no landowner attempting to grow cotton in the north of Mexico, who understood the economics of the crop and was involved in the larger question of irrigation, could afford to keep his eyes solely on his own territory. It was through his interest in this question that he first began to deal with the central government direct, and it was this contact, brief as it was, that established the essential difference between Madero and other possible contenders for power. He was not afraid of the government.

Díaz was seventy in 1900, and already those who had grown up under the shadow of the *Porfiriato* were manœuvring to be in the right position to take over power. Leading among the contenders was General Bernardo Reyes, the governor of the State of Nuevo León, who had made his reputation by punitive expeditions against the Indian tribes who still lingered in the north-west. Reyes was a bluff, imposing soldierly figure, but his nerve was not equal to his pretensions to power. Early in 1903 he was challenged on his own territory in the key northern industrial city of Monterrey by peaceful demonstrations in favour of an opposition candidate. His troops fired upon the crowd, killing a number of people, a stupid and unnecessary act which caused widespread disgust.

The reason for Reyes's nervousness was plain enough. In 1904 there was to be a Presidential election. If the seventy-four-year-old Díaz were to stand, he would be elected for his seventh term; so much was sure. What was not so clear was that he would survive that term. Accordingly by general agreement the constitution was once again altered. The Presidential term was extended from four to six years, and the post of Vice-President, abolished in the Constitution of 1857, was reinstated. The Vice-Presidency was the prize at stake, and Reyes was determined to get it. He organized a network of Reyista clubs throughout Mexico to push his candidature and went about making speeches.

Díaz was quite happy as long as his would-be heirs fought against one another, and the more so as he knew Reyes was very unpopular with the *científicos*. In the end he exercised his privilege to choose his own Vice-Presidential candidate, and in Ramón Corral chose a candidate who was equally unpopular with both factions, and, indeed, so unpopular generally that there was no likelihood that anyone would wish to edge Díaz out in his favour.

The activities of Reyes were, however, a very visible reminder that the forms of democracy in Mexico had not been suppressed. It was, apparently, still open to anyone to launch a political campaign, provided he did not challenge the authority of the President himself. Madero did not propose to do that. In the best traditions of democratic politics, once he had organized a Democratic Club (in the name of Benito Juárez) at San Pedro, Coahuila, his first target was the municipal elections of 1904, from which base he hoped to launch a contest for the governorship of the state. Naturally he was not allowed to win, and on the occasion of the gubernatorial elections, orders for his arrest were given which were only countermanded at the last moment from Mexico City. Despite this he did not lose hope for the democratic process. He turned back to the basic groundwork of founding a nationwide chain of clubs. This activity, so long as it did not involve actual electoral contests, was not actually prohibited, and in the new climate of shifting political alignments the work went well if laboriously. In these years Madero lent money to the Flores Magón brothers to continue to publish their magazine *Regeneración* in the United States, but he was not impressed by the failure of their very inadequate efforts to procure armed revolt.

Then came the Creelman interview which was published in English in *Pearson's Magazine*. As an important part of its work in promoting economic development, the régime had always tried to offer a good face to the outside world, subsidizing the production of favourable literary works, often quite embarrassingly eulogistic.[5] On this occasion Díaz had merely expressed the usual platitudes about his desire to see the principles of democracy in Mexico firmly rooted in the future. Looking back on his life's work, he considered that this had now been achieved. Accordingly, he said, at the end of his term he did not intend to stand again for re-election.

The word, though intended primarily for external consumption, speedily got back to Mexico, where it passed from mouth to mouth, and within days had got into print. There followed a keen debate about what it meant, but since few expected Díaz to live until 1910 (not, perhaps, even Díaz himself), the debate soon turned to the more significant question of what should be done about it.

Madero's own contribution to the debate was a book – *La sucesión presidencial en 1910*. It was written for the occasion, very much as a political manifesto. Though not lacking in classical references, it therefore lacked many of the verbose contortions that were then the fashionable literary method of signalling profundity. Its simple and unadorned style and its matter-of-fact content led to considerable disparagement from the self-styled intellectuals of the day; even indeed to a suggestion of its style being too 'Anglo-Saxon' to be taken seriously. Such criticism misses the point entirely. What Madero wished to do was to establish the view that the principal fault of Mexico lay in her political structure; that there was little basically wrong with the charter of 1857 as a system of government; and that what was wrong with the system was the way it had been treated by Díaz, great as his achievements had been. Two things were needed to make the system work: effective suffrage (i.e., no governmental interference with the electoral process) and no re-election. One thing was needed to achieve them: an effective, nationwide democratic party.

The success of the book was shown by its rapid passage through three editions, each change showing signs of its political relevance. The formation of a rival Democratic Party before the book's publication led to the name of Madero's organization being changed to the unwieldy but effective Anti-re-electionist Party. Moreover, at the beginning Madero had still been thinking of himself as a possible alternative Vice-President. The events of 1909 and the success of the tour he made of the country convinced him that he had the following to aim directly at the Presidency. Initially he saw Díaz as a good ruler at the head of a bad system. His closer experience of the system demonstrated that the system was the conscious creation of, and was consciously maintained by, the old dictator. Even at the beginning of 1910 he was still a long way from outright revolution, correctly recognizing that there was no difference between revolution and a *coup d'état* such as had brought Díaz himself to power save in the number of people who would be killed. His humanitarian spirit abhorred such a solution.

Early in 1909 Díaz went back on his predictions and allowed himself to be 'pushed' by his supporters into running for re-election. Reyes, the only alternative 'strong man', had tried for power too early. Díaz with the aid of the *científicos* forced him to submit to the renomination of Corral. Corral had continued as Vice-President to be as unconditionally loyal to Díaz as he had been when he had served as Secretary of *Gobernación* (Interior), the key post in the internal security of the government and the one responsible for the conduct of elections.

Reyes, therefore, was destroyed and humiliated. He was no longer a serious political force. However, while Díaz had been concentrating on him, Madero had been able to gain sufficient sympathy among the normally cautious local officials to be able to speak directly to the people. In a daring stroke, the national convention of the Anti-re-electionist Party was held in Mexico City itself, and, though many did not dare to come or were detained, once there, the convention did take place, and nominated Madero for President and Dr Francisco Vázquez Gómez for Vice-President. At this point the government began to take an interest in the Anti-re-electionists, and their second tour was much interrupted. Boldly, Madero wrote directly to Díaz and secured an interview with him. The old dictator, who had nothing but contempt for this young and insignificant man who dared to challenge his supremacy, said little. His cryptic words were 'that the people should choose between them who should hold the power'.

When Madero attempted to resume his campaign he found the harassment had not diminished. He made a further appeal to Díaz, who said in reply that he could not interfere with the sovereignty of the states, and that, though further disturbances were unlikely, Madero would find his surest safeguard against them in the law. In a sense, he did, but only in a sense, for on the night of 6 June 1910 he was arrested at Monterrey and thrown into prison. The wholly false charge was one of shielding another man from arrest. Only after the election was he released on bail, and while free, he escaped to the United States.

Transport

It was the revolution in transport that was both the making and the undoing of the Díaz régime. Mexico had been very slow to get railways for two reasons. The natural terrain, as the soldiers of Cortés had found so long ago, was incredibly mountainous and broken. Outside the Core region of the Valley of Mexico roads were poor and broken by flood and landslip. A generation of wars after independence had led to such neglect that the task of restoration alone seemed almost hopeless. Moreover, the turmoil made investors very reluctant to support the provision of any alternative. The first short stretch of railway in Mexico was opened in 1864 because of French confidence in the stability of the empire, and not for any better reason. But this railway, the Mexican Railway Company, did not link Mexico City to the port of Vera Cruz until 1873.

It was not an easy line to build, and it was not an easy line to travel on. Its ascent of 5,500 feet in the first 95 miles and then 2,500 feet in 12 miles to the edge of the central table-land presented enough problems in itself, but the broken nature of the countryside made matters worse. After crossing the Infiernillo viaduct, 6 miles north of Nogales, the curves were so sharp and close together that the duplex double-boiler Fairlie engines would frequently find themselves on three curves at once. Accidents were frequent, one, at Alta Luz in 1915, costing the lives of 300 people. The greatest elevation of the line was even then not attained, for the table-land is broken by high peaks, and the line reaches a maximum of 8,323 feet in two places before descending into the Valley of Mexico to the relatively low altitude of 7,348 feet.

By contrast, the building of the Mexican Central Railway, running north from Mexico City to reach the frontier at Ciudad Juárez 1,224 miles away was a straightforward business. The company was incorporated in Massachusetts in 1880 and building began almost at once. The line was opened as it went, to Tula in 1881, and to Querétaro the following year; it was finished on 8 March 1884. Despite sharp curves and some bridges on the southern part, especially between Tula and Querétaro, its construction was attended by no special technical difficulties. Leaving the Valley of Mexico the line made use of the Tajo de Nochistongo, the vast excavation dug between 1607 and 1789 to drain the waters of the Valley of Mexico.

The difficulties of the Mexican Railway Company led to the formation in London in 1888 of a rival company, the Interoceanic Railway, which planned to amalgamate existing narrow-gauge lines into a single system linking Vera Cruz with Mexico City and thence with Acapulco on the Pacific Coast. In fact it never got further than Puente de Ixtla in the south-westerly direction, but its line to Vera Cruz offered easier grades and a safer ride. A similar process of amalgamation created the line from Laredo to Mexico City by way of Monterrey and Saltillo. By 1903 this route had been reconstructed in standard gauge and because of its directness offered particular advantages to the visitor from the United States. At the same period the first line was driven into the difficult mountain country south of Mexico City to link the capital with Oaxaca. Although the total distance from Puebla to Oaxaca was only 228 miles, the line required extensive construction of tunnels and bridges to cross the intervening mountain ranges. The winding track ran through gorges at high level to avoid flooding, but in at least one place it was necessary to divert a river, and throughout the wear and tear on the rolling stock was such that it became a major consideration in operation.

By the turn of the century, therefore, the capital of Mexico was linked to all parts of the country by rail in some degree, with one principal exception. No connection existed between the independent railway system of Yucatán and that of the rest of the country, though south of Vera Cruz, in the Isthmus, there existed a connecting line which could serve as a link. The purpose of this link was to connect with the Tehuantepec National Railway, a line finished in 1895 to link the two sides of the Isthmus and to enable Mexico to benefit from the international trade that was expected to use it. Unfortunately, after some forty-five years of construction, the 188 miles of track proved almost unusable, and the government had to take the drastic step of having it completely reconstructed. The task of reconstruction, undertaken by the British firm of S. Pearson & Son, was completed in 1907, but unfortunately for the line's success, not until work was already well under way on the Panama Canal that was to render it obsolete. In 1913, however, the TNR was linked by the so-called Pan American Railway to the Guatemalan frontier at Suchiate.

It was always the conscious policy of the Díaz régime to build railways to unify Mexico strategically and to open up country hitherto remote from inspection. The lines were designed to tap all important centres of population and all sites which might be economically productive. If the process was still far from complete, this was in great part a result of the deficient technology of the day, or, frankly, the unsuitability of railways as a means of linking valley settlements in a very mountainous country. A great network of small branch lines, usually narrow gauge, and tramways, particularly in the Core region, reinforced the unifying effect of the principal lines. Nowhere was the impact of the railways more marked than in the desert north.[6]

Basically, the railways shifted, within a couple of decades, the political centre of the country from the south, where it had been since the rise of Juárez, to the northern states with frontiers on the United States. It was in the north that the leading supporters of Díaz could be rewarded with vast estates of land hitherto inaccessible, but now potentially valuable. So-called 'unused lands' (*terrenos baldios*) could be 'denounced' and taken over by anyone who had the political influence and the financial resources to make use of the legal code. Moreover, he could after 1884 also enjoy the incalculable benefits of the private ownership of mineral resources under the Mining Law of that year. There were snags, in particular the resistance of the Yaqui of Sonora to being deprived of their lands. Such disturbances were ruthlessly suppressed.

There was, however, another side to the northern problem. Though much of the land was now accessible as never before, it was still extremely unproductive. Efforts to build Mexico into a big power by colonization foundered on two obstacles: the resistance of the big landowners themselves, and the lack of capital to provide the irrigation and other facilities which the colonist required.[7] If the state was not going to provide these – and no one had yet thought of this solution – then they would have to be provided by private capital. And the nearest source for such capital was in the United States.

When Díaz came to power, the United States was just beginning the long-drawn-out pacification of Arizona and New Mexico. The Indians of those parts took no account of the white man's boundaries, and Geronimo himself took refuge in the mountains of Sonora, before allowing himself to be talked into returning to the United States to lead his people into captivity in Florida. As the pacification continued and the railways spread, the railroad promoters in New York naturally turned their attention to the economic advantages that might flow from linking their systems with the Pacific ports of Mexico. Thus several companies were projected to link the northern states with the United States, their natural economic hinterland, rather than with Mexico City. Two of the most important were the Kansas City, Mexico, and Orient line through Chihuahua to Topolobampo, and the Piedras Negras to Tepehuanes Railway, tapping the coalfields of Coahuila, which was intended to be completed to Mazatlán. But the biggest was the Southern Pacific line from Nogales, just south of Tucson, linking California and Arizona to Guaymas, Mazatlán, and Tepic.

Finally, the railways made the Revolution of 1910 possible, and determined the course that it took. At the beginning of the decade of fighting they were the sole, modern, efficient means of transport.

Percy N. Furber, one of the pioneers of oil in Mexico, took one of the first motor-cars to that country as late as 1909, and the only road it could run on even then was the Paseo de la Reforma.[8] The destruction of the railways during the Revolution, however, was so great that the development of Mexican transport was virtually halted until the age of the aeroplane.

Voices: Porfirians

'Nature does not go forward by leaps, and between the absolute power of General Díaz and the absolute reign of the Law, there is found a great distance, which cannot be traversed in the days which remain of the life of the Hero of Peace.

'If we return to anarchy, we immediately run the risk of losing our nationality. While we two destroy each other, foreign interests which amount to hundreds of millions, would call to their aid foreign powers, who would end up by conquering us and imposing on us a Caesar who would govern us as we deserved'.[9]

'It was better that a little blood should be shed that much blood should be saved. The blood that was shed was bad blood; the blood that was saved was good blood'.[10]

'The Yaqui trouble is a military question pure and simple, while the so-called debt servitude practised among the Mayas on the henequen plantations is a feature, not of slavery, but of peonage, the result of patriarchal conditions and habits many centuries old. ... They [the Yaqui] insisted upon having their own government, carried on by their chiefs, under their whimsical, unwritten laws, without respect for anything else'.[11]

'It can be seen, then, how complex has been the work of General Díaz, and how complex has had to be his responsibility. He is a unique man, who in a single nation, has had to govern and has governed wisely, many different peoples, living at different periods of evolution, from the prehistoric to the modern. We believe sincerely that on few occasions has the human intelligence embraced what his has embraced'.[12]

'26 June [1910] Day of the elections (???...) Naturally, I did not vote, in spite of the fact that legally I am considered a citizen in full enjoyment of my rights and obligations, either in the city of Mexico or here in San Ángel. What is the point? Let authorities and politicians play their comedy, as long as I in these pages judge it freely and criticize it frankly, however much one might have been convinced that in any place there take place completely free elections; would that it might be better; as well to stick with the judgement of a statesman of the stature of General Díaz, worthy sampler of men and admirable statesman, unimpeachable patriot and honest as well as anybody, as the brutal judgement of the mass or the mercenary and muddy one of political leaders and little bosses. The first is preferable and the best if one is dealing with a people such as ours, hardly at the spelling-book of their civic education'.[13]

'That's why I say there was justice in those times. It is true that we were almost enslaved, but *don* Porfirio was *don* Porfirio and his was a true government. There were not so many little governments then, no Agrarian Department or Forestry Department, or so many courts to fatten themselves. There was only *don* Porfirio and although he favoured the rich, laws were obeyed and the poor got justice. Now, if you have money there is justice; without money there is none!'[14]

'Each day I regret more and more what is happening and the impossibility on my part of helping in any manner to prevent the evils which are derived from the situation created for the country in general and especially for your family, by the foolish acts of your grandson, who, as you will say, by taking the part of redeemer, has sacrificed everybody. I understand perfectly how delicate and annoying is the situation in which you find yourself in respect to the government and also in respect to the men of order and good judgement. It must, however, be understood that this straining of relations is the fatal consequence of the disturbance of public order, responsibility for which does not assuredly rest on the government, and of certain acts which would not have been interpreted in a manner unfavourable to you and your family if from the beginning, and even now, all the members of the family had adopted a resolute and energetic attitude which would have allayed even the suspicion of sympathy, if not with the cause, at least with the persons who have initiated and upheld sedition'.[15]

' "I might have reestablished order, – it would not have been the first time" (here he paused for an instant, doubtless reviewing in memory the blood of battles and the bending of lawbreakers' wills) "but it could only have been done by a fratricidal war which would have destroyed the industries and commerce of the country and exposed it to international complications" '.[16]

[1] Stanley Robert Ross, *Francisco I. Madero, Apostle of Mexican Democracy* (New York, Columbia University Press, 1955); Charles Curtis Cumberland, *Mexican Revolution: Genesis under Madero* (Austin, University of Texas Press, 1952), 119–24.

[2] Ross, op. cit., 122.

[3] See Lowell L. Blaisdell, *The Desert Revolution, Baja California, 1911* (Madison, Wis., The University of Wisconsin Press, 1962).

[4] Ross, op. cit., is the definitive biography.

[5] e.g. David Hannay, *Diaz* (London, Constable, 1911).

[6] See F. W. Powell, *The Railroads of Mexico* (Boston, The Stratford Co., 1921); David M. Pletcher, 'The Building of the Mexican Railway', *Hispanic American Historical Review*, XXX (1950), 26.

[7] Moisés González Navarro, *La colonización en México, 1877–1910* (Mexico, 1960).

[8] Percy N. Furber, *I took chances. From windjammers to jets* (Leicester, Edgar Backus, 1954), 140.

[9] L. Lara y Pardo, *La sucesión presidencial* (1903), 12; quoted Callcott, *Liberalism in Mexico*, 156.

[10] Díaz speaking to James Creelman, *Pearson's Magazine*, XIX (March 1908), 241.

[11] James Creelman, *Díaz, Master of Mexico* (New York & London, D. Appleton & Co., 1911), 405–6.

[12] Andrés Molina Enríquez, *Los grandes problemas nacionales* (Mexico, Imprenta de A. Carranza e Hijos, 1909), 77.

[13] Federico Gamboa, *Mi diario: mucho de mi vida y algo de la de otros* (Mexico, 1938), V, Segunda Serie, II, 170–1.

[14] Oscar Lewis, *Pedro Martinez; a Mexican Peasant and his family* (London, Panther, 1969), 129.

[15] Limantour–Evaristo Madero, from Paris, 27 January 1911, in Edward I. Bell, *The Political Shame of Mexico* (New York, McBride Nast & Company, 1914), 38.

[16] Díaz speaking to Mrs O'Shaughnessy in Rome, Easter morning 1913, in Edith L. C. O'Shaughnessy, *Intimate Pages of Mexican History* (New York, George H. Doran, 1920), 17.

The Revolution V: Mobilization

IT WAS THE GOVERNMENT of the United States that was to prove the *deus ex machina* in the developing revolution of Francisco Madero. More specifically it was President Taft, an unlikely agent for the task – a man of peace, a man of law, and possibly the most efficient administrator the United States has ever had in her top administrative office. One of the first acts of his administration had been to confirm its good relations with Díaz. Taft met him at the frontier in Ciudad Juárez, Chihuahua, and El Paso, Texas, on 16 October 1909. By so doing, Taft became the first President of the United States to leave her territory during his term of office.

In 1911, however, Taft had to reckon with the mid-term elections, and a state of developing insurgency in his own party preoccupied him. He had little time to spare for Mexican affairs, and was in any case curiously impatient with Díaz for not being able to manage his own insurgents. So when his ambassador, Henry Lane Wilson, returned to Washington to tell him of the woes of Mexico as he saw them, he was anxious to act quickly. On the other hand, his military advisers were pressing him strongly to make use of the new military and naval strength of the United States which had been built up in the time of his predecessor, President Roosevelt. The result was a hasty decision that had precisely the opposite effect to what was intended.

On 8 March 1911 President Taft ordered the mobilization of 20,000 men in the area of Texas adjoining the Mexican border. The intention was to demonstrate the power of the United States government to intervene in Mexico to protect the lives and property of its nationals if need be. As he said himself in his instructions to General Wood, commanding the forces:

It seems my duty as Commander in Chief to place troops in sufficient numbers where if Congress shall direct that they enter Mexico to save American lives and property, an effective movement may be promptly made. Meantime, the movement of the troops to Texas and elsewhere near the boundary, accompanied with the sincere assurances of the utmost goodwill towards the present Mexican Government and with larger and more frequent patrols along the border to prevent insurrectionary expeditions from American soil will hold up the hands of the existing government and will have a healthy moral effect to prevent attacks upon Americans and their property in any subsequent general internecine strife. . . .[1]

In Mexico the action served to raise general alarm, and specifically cast doubt on the ability of the government to suppress the insurrection. So far, in fact, the revolutionaries had done little even in the north to disturb the peace. Some sabotage on the railways, a few raids on mines to obtain arms and explosives, that was about the extent of their impact. The imposition of martial law which followed the American mobilization was not accompanied by any significant intensification of effort. Indeed it was at this point that Limantour, who had hitherto taken advantage of his absence in Paris for talks on the refunding of the National Debt, returned to take charge of government policy and was gratefully given what proved to be a thankless task.

Limantour had made the most of his passage through New York to talk not only to members of the United States government, but also to members of the Madero family and the chief revolutionary agent, Francisco Vázquez Gómez. It seems clear that he had decided to save the Díaz régime, if necessary by jettisoning the President himself. Corral was known to be mortally ill; next in line of succession Limantour now placed Francisco de la Barra, the Mexican ambassador to Washington, who was given the portfolio of External Relations. De la Barra was an amiable and diplomatic personality of not very strong Catholic political affiliations and he was acceptable as a figurehead to moderate opinion. Limantour's strategy was straightforward: to get Díaz to outbid the revolutionaries by offering them a programme of reforms, then to disperse them with force while they were disunited. But the President's offer of reform was regarded with universal suspicion, and even in the Congress that had sat for so many years obedient to Díaz's wishes, the loudest cheers greeted the news of the acceptance of the principle of 'no re-election'.

Within a month, therefore, the government opened formal negotiations with the revolutionaries. From this point on the government proceeded to collapse of its own inertia, with scarcely a shot fired on either side. On 14 April 1911 the revolutionaries captured the border town of Agua Prieta, giving them the opportunity legally to import arms through the customs house there. Madero's forces then surrounded the key stronghold of Ciudad Juárez, with the same intention. The government spun out the negotiations, hoping to divide the revolutionary ranks, and they did so, but not in quite the way intended. It was the radicals who, after briefly and unsuccessfully trying to arrest Madero himself, gained the upper hand with the troops and initiated the attack on the city which led to its capture. The loss of this major and symbolically named strongpoint led to general agreement in the capital that Díaz must resign.

Even at the time one shrewd newspaperman noted that Limantour's perverse behaviour resembled 'the accomplishment of a definite undertaking'. As he commented: 'Every measure which seemed to me essential was neglected, almost every possible folly was committed, and complete disaster was achieved in sixty-six days'.[2]

José Yves Limantour

It is impossible to understand Limantour[3] without trying to understand the *científicos*. Basically, they were the product of the search for reassurance in lay thinking, which was in turn the product of the secularization of education brought about by the Reform. As Mexico continued to be strongly influenced by French ideas, it was the positivism of Auguste Comte that was adopted as the official ideology of the Porfirian régime. The *científicos* were simply the most authoritative exponents of it. To them positivism offered a definite creed for the maintenance of social stability, which was both 'scientific' and authoritarian.

At first, however, the *científicos* were only a group of young men recently arrived on the political scene, who came into the public eye with the emergence of Limantour as Secretary of *Hacienda*. The success of Limantour in establishing the finances of the country gave them great strength, and office after office fell to a growing circle of friends and protégés of his. Many of these were not *científicos* in the original strict sense of members of the small group, but they were the men who were popularly known as the *científicos*. Not until 1910 was their control of the machinery of government in the name of progress and prosperity completed, when the aged Ignacio Mariscal died and was succeeded by Enrique C. Creel as Secretary of External Relations. Their emergence as a quasi-party can be dated to the year 1892, when their alliance with the Díaz machine gave them a political standing as a group.[4]

Lastly *científico* gained a pejorative meaning. Most of the quasi-party were rich. If not, they became so. Through them, the stream of wealth from investment and production behind tariff walls, as well as contracts of all kinds, was directed by various boards of directors of which they were members. Some of them, such as Pablo Macedo, were lawyers; others, such as Emilio Pimentel of Oaxaca, Olegario Molina of Yucatán, Enrique Creel of Chihuahua, Guillermo de Landa y Escandón of the Federal District, and Ramón Corral himself, were governors of states; yet others, such as Joaquín Casasus, were involved in banking; but all figured on numerous boards of directors. It is not surprising that they were accused of corruption. It would not be surprising if in fact they were corrupt. It *is* surprising to find that there is virtually no evidence, even circumstantial, to show that any of them really were corrupt, as far as their personal dealings went. On the other hand, the intimate connection between business and government had an undesirably corrupting effect, especially in the states, while the Federal judiciary was venal to a degree. So the *científicos* became a by-word for all that the reformers found detestable in the Díaz régime. Carleton Beals expresses that view very well.

> The Científicos talked science and positivism; their real program was scientific stealing. Close advisers to the various ministries, they drew up new laws, revised old codes: the Commerce Law, the Banking Law; the Railway code; the Monetary Law – all with a positivist criterion, which meant that the old Roman-Spanish-Aztec legal bases were substituted by Roman-Napoleonic-Anglo Saxon tendencies, more adopted [*sic*] to laissez-faire doctrines of capitalistic development and private property tenure.

This he claims, and rightly, was a legal revolution, and it was designed primarily to facilitate foreign investment. 'These laws', as he puts it, 'which overthrew basic legal structure were meant to facilitate land-grabbing, mine-grabbing, oil-grabbing, and a new conquest of Mexico by Europe – this time by northern Europe and the United States'.[5]

Under this view, of course, the fact that the financial operations of the state were conducted through the so-called 'Scherer-Limantour Paris banking house' and the French National Bank, which had *científico* directors, is scandalous enough. Beals, however, claims that the commission that members of the *científico* group took in their respective capacities was in intention corrupt, and was accompanied by large-scale financial irregularities. This view is difficult to uphold. When so much could be made legally and above board there would seem no need for the principals to resort to illegality.

The argument rages most fiercely around the figure of Limantour himself. José Yves Limantour was born on 19 March 1855.[6] His father, J. Y. Limantour, was a French *émigré* who is notable in the history of California for having secured grants on large tracts of land, including what is today most of San Francisco, from the Mexican government in 1843. After the accession of California to the United States he pressed for his claims to be recognized, but they were disallowed in 1858, after, it is said, the mysterious disappearance of two Mexican witnesses (in his favour) on their way north. Despite this, his son inherited a sizeable fortune. Bell wrote of him: 'He was rich already; he was not to be bought', and asserts that his government 'as revealed to foreign gentlemen in heavy transactions covering many years, was characterized by remarkable integrity'.[7]

Beals opens his portrait of Limantour in very different style:

> Limantour was an illegitimate son of a French adventuress, Adela Marquet, taken to wife by Julio Limantour, a man run out of San Francisco by the Vigilantes. Julio became a trafficker in arms with the Reform movement and was rewarded with Church properties in Mexico City from Bolivar Street to the plaza, presently to become the main business section, making him fabulously wealthy.[8]

But even he gives no instances of Limantour's personal participation in corrupt practices.

Limantour, again, received this tribute from Mrs Edith O' Shaughnessy, wife of the First Secretary at the American embassy who at the time, however, had only been a month in Mexico:

> There is a clean-cutness about him and his Gallic origin is written all over him in an unmistakable elegance. He is considered by friend and foe alike to be absolutely incorruptible, and the only thing I have ever heard whispered *against* him is that he is *rich*. However, the Romans that made the roads doubtless got rich, but they made the roads, which is what mattered to the Romans.[9]

It does, however, point the way to an assessment based on achievements, and in the sphere of finance Limantour's achievements were undoubtedly great. He achieved as a matter of course a balanced budget, something only once before achieved, under the much-vilified Manuel González. In 1904 he placed Mexico on the gold standard. In 1907 he carried out the vast merger that constituted the National Railways under direct government control, and so averted the threat of American railroad monopoly. Finally in 1909–11 he succeeded in refunding the National Debt on a 4 per cent basis, unparalleled in any Latin American country for decades to come, by which the Treasury saved a vast sum in interest.

It is highly improbable that a man of less than the maximum standard of probity could have got the confidence necessary to secure any of these achievements. It is equally unlikely that they could have been achieved without the aid of a unique network of associates, conducting the bulk of their negotiations in absolute secrecy. Secrecy breeds suspicion of motives, and Limantour's impeccability in the financial world seems to be clear.

He did have his weak point, however – his vanity. Under the dictator, financial success might at any time be put to the hazard by a political error; as early as 1892 his position was endangered by a *canard* that he wished to run for the Presidency. In 1910 he was still liable at any moment to become involved in the struggles which Díaz provoked continuously to keep possible successors at bay. There can be little doubt that Limantour regarded himself as fully fitted for the exercise of the supreme power; nor that he bitterly resented the methods of his rivals who alleged that he was disqualified because not of Mexican birth.

Yet Limantour believed that it was he, rather than Díaz, who upheld the fabric of the *Pax Porfiriana*. This belief was heightened, it is clear, from the growing dependence of Díaz upon him, as the President and almost his entire Cabinet passed the age of seventy-five! In the Cabinet of old men, Limantour was the only one who was middle-aged, until at the death of Mariscal he was joined by Creel. His dangerous separation from the facts of Mexican life was demonstrated in his decision to remain in Paris throughout the Centenary celebrations and even through the early weeks of the Revolution.

Money

The *científico* programme of economic development of Mexico presupposed the willingness of foreign investors to provide the necessary capital. Clearly, stable government, guaranteeing the payment of regular interest, was the prime necessity for Mexico's structure of credit, and its lapse the most serious hazard to long-term growth. On one major occasion at least (1896), representatives of foreign concerns in Mexico organized a major demonstration on behalf of the Díaz régime. In those days, no one seems to have found this at all peculiar.

In 1910 the Mexican economy, in the words of Sanford A. Mosk, was properly described as a 'colonial economy': an economy characterized by the high proportion of exports to national income, and dependence on the flow of foreign investment. Always erratic, this last might in time of crisis cease completely. Fluctuations in conditions in the industrial nations, therefore, had a dual effect in time of depressions, as in the years after 1907: first, of cutting off investment; secondly of reducing the demand for exports, thus precluding effective government counter-measures through control of imports.

These fluctuations in the 'modern sector' of the Mexican economy in turn influenced the much larger 'subsistence sector' by returning workers to it. 'This shift', Mosk has said,

which is both regional and occupational, explains why unemployment never reaches large proportions in a Latin American country.

Instead of suffering absolute unemployment in time of depression, workers transfer themselves to much less productive occupations.[10]

What measure of control did the government of the *Porfiriato* have over the economy? To begin with, taxation was rudimentary. The two principal sources were import duties and stamp revenue, the former being by far the most important. Government spending was heavily weighted towards the maintenance of the standing army and the *rurales*; public building was limited to the capital and carried out principally for the sake of prestige, building within the twenty-seven states being the province of the local governments. Virtually all expenditure, it should be noted in passing, was on behalf of the executive branch and virtually no constitutional strain was required to channel all the wealth of the state into any channel which might be selected.[11]

The banking system was unique, 'based upon a plurality of banks of issue, with a simple institution at the centre without numerous branches, but maintaining a large metallic reserve and supporting the local banks by rediscount'. As one writer put it in 1913: 'The system thus combines some of the features of the central banking system, which is all but universal in Europe, with the system of isolated independent banks of issue which prevails in the United States'.[12]

A major strain on the system was provided by one of Limantour's major achievements—the adoption of the gold standard. This was deemed necessary to establish a permanent rate of exchange against the currencies of investing countries, for the fall of the price of silver in the 1880s and 1890s had meant that investors lost heavily on the exchange on their otherwise handsome profits from Mexican enterprises. In 1902 a Commission, consisting of Enrique C. Creel, Luis Camacho, and Eduardo Meade, advised in favour of it. In practice, however, McCaleb held that the decision was 'probably a tremendous blunder'.[13] The gains of stopping the continuous export of silver to the extent of some $100 million (Mexican) per annum were almost certainly outweighed by the cost of the balancing operation. This had to be financed in 1904 by a loan from Speyers of $6 million (Mexican) in $4\frac{1}{2}$ per cent Treasury notes and again in 1904–05 of $40 million in $4\frac{1}{2}$ per cent bonds floated at 89, and occupied the time of the Treasury to an alarming extent. Until 1909 borrowing had to be maintained to offset shrinkage. Moreover, the internal effects were drastic, the mass of the people finding themselves markedly worse off in terms of purchasing power and liquid currency. 'It was better', remarks McCaleb, 'to have a peso with a fluctuating purchasing power than to have no peso at all'.[14]

Sadly enough, this widening of the gap between rich and poor was a prime characteristic of the Díaz régime as well as of *científico* economic development. It took several forms.

Land held since pre-Spanish times in common ownership by village communities (*ejidos*) was thrown open to exploitation by big plantation-owners (*hacendados*) or foreign corporations by a law permitting them to 'denounce' and enclose it. It is estimated that some 134,547,885 acres, or *one-quarter* of the area of Mexico, passed into the hands of the *hacendados* in this way. In 1910 there were not more than 834 of these, all owning more than 21,945 acres apiece.

Secondly, the régime itself pursued a deliberate policy of reducing unruly elements in particular and the poor in general to a state of peonage. From the *ejidos* alone came 3,103,402 *peones de campo*, bound by a form of wage slavery to till the lands they had formerly owned. In Yucatán criminals, beggars, and the merely poor, together with imported contract labour, were swallowed up by the thousands in the toil of the *henequén* plantations—among the planters was Olegario Molina himself, for long governor of the state. The exposure of the appalling conditions by John Kenneth Turner in *Barbarous Mexico*[15] did much to turn public sentiment in the United States, and later in Britain, against the Díaz régime. Previously they had, as Madero had seen the Mexican nation itself, been 'lulled to sleep by the noise of steam whistles, dazzled by the multiple and admirable applications of electricity, completely occupied with its economic development, trusting in the word of its Leader'.[16] Yet, as Madero pointed out, for Mexicans the alternative was the *ley fuga*, the custom by which inconvenient prisoners were 'shot trying to escape'.

The idea of rights in common was a very deep one in the Mexican rural mind, where the arid nature of the country makes the existence of a strict code of water rights a necessity. The Aztecs had such a code; the Spaniards maintained it. A similar tradition existed in the rights of the subsoil. The Spanish code ruled that only the surface of the land belonged to its owner; the subsoil was the province of the Crown, as indeed it had previously been of the Aztec state. The Mining Law of 1884—unconstitutionally according to some—adopted instead the Anglo-Saxon concept of landownership as something that extends downwards to the centre of the earth. By enabling the exploitation of mineral deposits through the simple process of buying the surface rights—as opposed to obtaining a concession from the government—the régime thus greatly stimulated investment in mining and allied industry. It also, however, established numerous colonies of noticeably wealthy foreigners in the poorest and most infertile parts of the country. Above all, perhaps, it stimulated resentment towards those foreigners because they were able to exploit the wealth which the original owners of the land could not.

Lastly, the régime devoted much time and effort to securing colonization, both by Mexicans and by foreigners, of the *terrenos baldíos* (untilled lands) in the north. These colonists were intended to extend agricultural production, and, it was hoped, by the example of their success to leaven, as it were, the sour lump of primitive Mexican agriculture. Most of these colonies failed. Mexico, unlike Brazil or Argentina, did not attract significant numbers of European settlers in the late nineteenth century, only a few Mormon colonies in Durango having any real achievement to show for much hard work. Furthermore, the Mexican *peones* did not welcome the settlers; coveted the lands the exploration and settlement companies had delimited; and on occasion even attempted to take them over by force, since they saw the settlers as the vanguard of an army that would eventually deprive them of everything. There was reason, on the face of it, for this alarm. Texas had been lost in such a way. But the numbers involved were so small that only in the sparsely populated and remote Territory of Quintana Roo, adjacent to British Honduras on the Yucatán peninsula, did foreigners attain 25 per cent of the population.

It was from the ranks of these peasants that the majority of the soldiers of the Revolution were recruited. This fact explains how it was economically possible to finance a decade of war, to say nothing of endemic violence for many years afterwards. The peasant soldier lived as he had always lived – off the land. He was accompanied as he went by his wife, legal or illegal, and the crowd of *soldaderas* that accompanied the troops, riding where necessary on the roofs of the trains, were an inseparable part of the fighting machine.

Their officers financed themselves by taking what they wanted. Few people dared to argue with them, and fewer still were successful. Madero's own revolution against Díaz required some formal financing to maintain its diplomatic representation abroad; this period passed; there seem always to have been sufficient exiles, of all political hues, to represent any government or opposition that happened to need their services.

---

[1] Peter Calvert, *The Mexican Revolution, 1910–1914: the Diplomacy of Anglo-American Conflict* (Cambridge, Cambridge University Press, 1968), 55.

[2] Bell, op. cit., 100.

[3] There has been no biography of Limantour since Carlos Díaz Dufoo, *Liman-tour* (Mexico, 1922). His memoirs were published in Mexico in 1954.

[4] Mexico, Fondo de Cultura Económica, *México: cincuenta años de Revolución, III: La política* (Mexico, 1961), 500.

[5] Beals, op. cit., 328.

[6] Bell, op. cit., 3–4.

[7] ibid., 83–5.

[8] Beals, op. cit., 317.

[9] Edith Louise Coues O'Shaughnessy, *Diplomatic Days* (New York & London, Harper & Brothers, 1917), 35–6.

[10] Sanford A. Mosk, *Industrial Revolution in Mexico* (Berkeley, University of California Press, 1950), 13.

[11] cf. James W. Wilkie, *The Mexican Revolution: Federal Expenditure and Social Change since 1910* (Berkeley & Los Angeles, University of California Press, 1967), 276 ff.

[12] México, Secretaría de Hacienda, *The Mexican Year Book: a Financial and Commercial Handbook, compiled from Official and other Returns* (London, McCorquodale & Co., 1913), 40.

[13] Walter Flavius McCaleb, *The Public Finances of Mexico* (New York & London, Harper Brothers, 1921), 177.

[14] ibid., 182.

[15] London, Cassell, 1911.

[16] Francisco Indalecio Madero, *La sucesión Presidencial en 1910* (Mexico, Librería de la Viuda de Ch. Bouret, 1911, tercera edición: copia de la segunda), 155, also 147.

The Revolution VI: Collapse of Díaz

FOLLOWING THE CAPTURE of Ciudad Juárez on 8 May 1911 Federal resistance collapsed entirely. Government forces even abandoned the key railway town of Torreón, and in the interval between their departure and the arrival of the startled revolutionaries, the laundry-women of the town took advantage of the opportunity to massacre the Chinese settlers who of late had been taking their business.

Only Díaz seemed unaware that all was lost. Not only was he an old man and deaf, but he had been suffering from toothache, and a badly extracted tooth gave rise to sepsis of the jaw. As he lay confined to bed in his own home, the sympathizers with the revolutionaries emerged into the streets of the capital itself. The news of the agreement between the government and the revolutionaries at Ciudad Juárez gave rise to general rejoicing. But still the news that Díaz had resigned did not come. The crowds in the streets grew thicker, their temper rose. On 25 May serious rioting broke out in the vicinity of the National Palace and Zócalo, fanned by the visible signs of the soldiers sent in to repress it. Fortunately for all concerned, it was cut short by one of those torrential rainstorms which make all outdoor activity impossible. In the early hours of the following morning, Díaz finally consented to resign and signed the instrument of resignation in the presence only of his wife, María del Carmen Romero Rubio de Díaz.

The British chargé reported that

> preparations were made with the utmost secrecy for the departure of President Díaz, one or two Englishmen being invited to assist and giving all the aid that was possible, and he left the City by the Interoceanic Railway at 4 o'clock on the morning of the 26th, arriving at his destination at 4 p.m., after a brush with the revolutionaries or bandits at a place called Tepeyahualco. He is reported to have lead [sic] the troops who were escorting him, himself. The assailants were easily beaten off. He is staying, pending the departure of his steamer, in the house of an Englishman belonging to the firm of Messrs Pearson and Son.[1]

Evidently the departure was neither so secret nor so early that the usual gigantic crowd did not have time to gather and cheer the stout gentleman in top hat and frock coat as he boarded the train–a scene recorded for posterity by the primitive hand-cranked cinematograph, which accompanied him on his journey, ultimately to take a farewell shot on board the *Ypiranga* itself. It was Díaz's original intention to go to Spain, where ex-Vice-President Corral was already living, but once he had arrived there, he made his way to Paris, the city that had influenced directly or indirectly so much of his career. There he died, of old age, in 1915.

Hispanidad

Class differences in Mexico, and indeed in most of the other countries of Latin America, have traditionally long been synonymous with racial differences. The Spanish Conquest represented the imposition of a caucasoid ruling class on an essentially Indian population. Spanish settlers, however, were always comparatively few and the first *conquistadores* established the precedent of marrying Indian women, who in due course gave birth to the first *mestizos*.

It is often believed that *mestizaje* is incompatible with racial prejudice. Unfortunately this is not so. In the Mexican case it merely added a new dimension to it. At first, indeed, scholars debated, as scholars will, the weighty problems of the Conquest, such as whether the Indians were in fact the children of Adam and whether or not they had souls.[2] But the Church answered this question decisively in the affirmative. The Indians were human beings. Church and Crown constituted themselves the protectors of the Indians against the rapacity of the *conquistador* who was solely out for money. But this protection began to open up the crucial gulf that we have already remarked existed between the *peninsular* and the *criollo*.

Furthermore, the admission that the Indians had souls opened up the awkward question of whether by that fact, and still more by the fact of their baptism and reception into the universal Church, they were not freed from the stigma of inferiority and hence from the obligation to work for their conquerors. In medieval times baptism would have been deemed to have had this effect. Yet for the universal reason that always lies behind prejudice–the fear that if distinctions of colour are not maintained then those distinguished against may become economic rivals, or even superiors–colonial society maintained a very rigid concept of racial classification.

Like the sixteen quarterings of the *Almanach de Gotha*, the colonial *criollo* maintained the knowledge of his ancestry to the fourth generation, and refused to admit to his circle those for whose antecedents he could not vouch. Corresponding to this, no less than sixteen distinctions of racial origin were maintained in everyday speech; thirty-two for more specialized purposes. For example, *mestizo* (properly speaking) originally referred only to the offspring of a Spaniard and an Indian woman. Such distinctions survived unofficially into the time of the republic, as social distinctions tend to outlive the societies in which they had meaning.

Independence, however, was inextricably mixed up with the self-assertion of the Indian. The refuge against this fatal possibility, in *criollo* eyes, was politics. Three times the *criollos* attempted to assert their hegemony in an independent Mexico–under Iturbide, under Santa Anna, and finally under Maximilian. Given the fact of the *Porfiriato*, they were eventually left with no alternative to accepting what they had, the rule of a pure-bred Zapotec Indian. It says much for the habit of generations of subservience that even Díaz, that tough yet strangely credulous man, seemed to accept the myth of *criollo* superiority. Surrounding himself with *criollo* ministers, ambassadors, and guards, and accepting the homage of Europeans and even *gringos*, he came, as has already been shown, to permit the *científicos* to formalize the system.

And yet, in a sense, he was merely following the nineteenth-century ideal of progress from which even Juárez was not immune. It was left to Madero to become the first modern Mexican politician to accept his country as a nation essentially Indian and *mestizo*. In *La sucesión presidencial en 1910* he names first the Indians as the victims of what he saw as viceregal despotism. He mentions first the wars against Tomóchic, the Yaqui, and the Mayas when he discusses the harm done by despotism in his own time.

How did this happen? Madero freely admitted: 'I belong, by birth, to the privileged class; my family is one of the most numerous and influential in this state. . . .'[3] Yet they could not, even had they wished, assert *criollismo*, for, according to their neighbours, they were by origin Jewish. It has since proved impossible to show whether this assertion was correct or not. It was probably derived from the family's visible success in making money–but given the (to us) extraordinary prejudices of the time, the fact of the assertion was enough to make their acceptance in high society impossible. Ironically enough, once young Francisco became a revolutionary, this alone seemed to some of his enemies to prove the case!

In Latin America as a whole racial distinction therefore involves social, economic, and cultural denominators. It operates at various levels. Thus, culture is a more important denominator than skin colouring. An Indian who adopts Hispanic culture by speaking Spanish and wearing European dress 'passes' as a *mestizo*. But the cultural denominator depends on economic condition: wealth, freedom to pursue a non-menial occupation, leisured life in an urban environment, higher education in one of the learned professions, and, in present-day Mexico, conspicuous expenditure and imitating the way of life of the middle-class citizen of the United States–these are the marks of cultural *criollo* status. Manual, and more especially menial, work is associated with Indian and, where applicable, negro blood. 'Indian' accordingly was (and is) the townsman's casually contemptuous way of designating someone from the country.

Most of these denominators stem from the fact of Spanish conquest, though the Quetzalcoatl myth, with its belief in the return of a white-skinned and bearded god to lead his people, must powerfully have aided their initial acceptance. Colonial rule was rule not from Madrid, but from Seville; rule not by Spain as a whole, but by Castile. And Castile was the land of the *reconquista*, the terrible seven-century-long struggle against the Moors that was ended only in the year of Columbus's first voyage.

Castile was a hard country and poor. The Castilian nobleman valued his descent the more since his possessions were few. The most honourable path to success in life lay in skill with the sword; defence of material possessions and of the values of the Church went hand in hand. In constant conflict with what he saw as the infidel, the Castilian's maintenance of the purity of 'the race' was an obsession; if it were not so, the long struggle might cease to have any meaning. Such attitudes die hard. With the added dimension of Indianism, Hispanic culture shows itself in modern Mexico in a whole range of small ways that add up to the modern equivalent of a very ancient social system.

Thus the modern middle-class Mexican practises an elaborate courtesy and an agreeable ceremony in meeting and taking leave even of his friends. For strangers he will have an elaborate visiting card engraved with his status-conferring titles. In the street he will proceed in a leisurely pattern, unhurriedly from place to place, or sit for as long as possible at a pavement café. Social life takes place in the street or restaurant and not in the home, where the womenfolk are immured for safety, though today Mexican upper-class women are among the most emancipated in Latin America. He will in no circumstances if he can avoid it be seen carrying a parcel, even a small one, though a newspaper or book or even a slim briefcase in good-quality leather may be appropriate; like the North American he stands for long periods having his shoes cleaned by an Indian boy to whom he negligently gives a vast, apparently silver, coin before moving off.

Hispanic culture, however, goes much deeper than this. The possession of the Spanish language gives the Mexican who uses it access to a vast literature, both in the original and in translation. It is a literature that has traditionally been limited to a rather small clientele, and both books and newspapers have small circulations in numbers of copies bought. But they are read widely. A Latin American novelist or poet will be read by the intellectual élite from the Río Bravo to Cape Horn; he will be a national figure of pride, to whom much is forgiven that would not be to lesser men, and an international figure welcomed wherever he goes. So a poet can lead the liberation of Cuba, a novelist become President of Venezuela, or a university professor President of Guatemala. But artistry in some sense is expected of any politician of any pretensions: a sense of style. As the new technology and the new professions have expanded in Mexico, all these cultural traits have been transferred to them, at least in some degree.

Francisco Bulnes

'Pancho' Bulnes was the most formidable intellectual defender of the Díaz régime. His many friends admired his ability to find out what was really going on. His many enemies had to admit wryly that he had a knack of asking awkward questions.

If Limantour was the Grand Vizier of the *Porfiriato*, Bulnes was its court jester. Protected by humour, he could attack even its foundations. Though he did so, he also played a major role in justifying in philosophical terms the equation of dictatorship with material progress. Born in Mexico City in 1847, he was trained as an engineer, and in Latin America that qualification is worn proudly, as a title for life. He might have aspired to be nothing more (or nothing less) than a professor in the National School of Engineering. But his formidable physical presence and talent for polemic opened the way on to the larger stage of national politics.

Engineers were rare enough in Mexico in the age of the Restored Republic. Engineers who were witty and articulate, and passionately interested in national improvement, were too valuable to be overlooked by any government. Bulnes combined the theoretical and the practical in a curious combination; he was a meteorologist who also taught classes in political economy. It was an age when meteorology retained connections–later to become attenuated–with astronomy. Mexico still kept local time, was still poorly mapped, but badly needed more information about hurricane prediction and more knowledge about earthquakes. The essential prerequisite to better understanding was accurate measurement, and for Bulnes the link between his major interests lay through mathematics.

In 1874 there occurred a transit of Venus across the sun's disc. This is a very rare event–a further transit occurred in 1882, but the next will not occur until 8 June 2004. For astronomers it seemed to offer then the best possible occasion for determining exactly how far the Earth is from the Sun, and this calculation in turn is basic to a wide range of others. On this occasion, therefore, the Mexican government sent an expedition to Japan to carry out the simultaneous observations required. Bulnes was appointed recorder to the expedition. On his return he published an account of his travels under the title of *Eleven thousand leagues across the Northern Hemisphere.*[4]

His name now established as an author, the young Bulnes moved naturally into that circle of trained positivist thinkers who were ultimately to rise to power with Limantour. Though, as we have seen, it is hard to define who were and who were not *científicos*, Bulnes was certainly among the dozen most prominent members of the circle, though, unlike most of the others, he was little involved in financial manipulations on his own account. His talent lay with the pen. He turned his attention first to the emergence of the Mexican nation, critically examining the War of Independence and its heroes.

It was not hard for the young Bulnes to find much to criticize. More important was the use to which he was to put his working knowledge of history. For him it was a two-way process: applying his knowledge of positivism to Mexican life; and educating others in the meaning of the doctrine itself. It can be traced most clearly in the ultimate exposition of *científico* belief, the massive three-volume study edited by Justo Sierra, *Mexico y su evolución social* (1903). Bulnes here expounded the thesis that the cause of Mexico's revolutions in the past had invariably been the financial difficulties of governments. In retrospect the problem with this judgement was not that it was incorrect, but that it excluded the possibility that if the governments had survived their financial difficulties, they might not necessarily have perished of other causes.

In the critical year of 1904, he followed up with his most important work, *El verdadero Juárez*. Cynics felt that its sole purpose had been to elevate Díaz by denigrating his great predecessor and one-time teacher. Certainly the book could not have appeared without the President's tacit approval. In fact, so highly was the name of Juárez still regarded that the book aroused a storm of protest, and initiated a debate that has continued to this day. What Bulnes was able to demonstrate so easily was that the personal rule of Díaz was built on the foundations Juárez had laid; that it was Juárez who had used emergency decrees even to prolong his own term of office, who had introduced re-election to the Mexican political system, who had not hesitated (in 1867) even to bypass the formal system of amending the sacrosanct Constitution of 1857–which was more than Díaz had ever done, mainly because he did not have to.

Bulnes, who was then at the height of his powers, entered into the controversy with gusto, eventually writing a whole book to refute his attackers. Díaz never discouraged controversy where it did not directly attack him or his government, and this formidable polemicist thrived on it. When the Revolution came, it was all too easy for him, in the columns of *El Universal*, to make fun of its absurdities, its stupidity, and its dishonesties. 'A revolution is the violent healthy reaction of an organism against the infection that has invaded it', he wrote afterwards.

A revolution is what the crowd know as a simple indigestion or a fatal fever. It is plain that the intensity of the reaction must correspond to the intensity of poisoning. In the fever, nausea, diarrhoea, copious sweats, are not the sickness, but symptoms of the healthy means by which the organism cures itself by self-disinfection.[5]

And the cause of the infection? Well, the author of *El verdadero Juárez* was also the author of *El verdadero Díaz*, first published in Mexico in 1920, five years after the old man's death. It was a stinging indictment of Díaz himself, rather than of those who surrounded him, though they were not overlooked. Before this Bulnes had made his own contribution to the debate on the reform of Mexico in *Los grandes problemas de México*, and though deservedly overshadowed by its forerunner, a key text for the early revolutionaries, Andrés Molina Enríquez's *Los grandes problemas nacionales* (1909), still showed a grasp of Mexican realities which was far above most of his contemporaries. He also published in 1916 a bright little attack on President Wilson's policy towards Mexico which was the best of a rather poor lot.

The collision between Mexico and the United States involved a crucial area of Bulnes's thinking, and one in which he made his own individual contribution. It involved the central question of race.

In every age there have been foolish people who have believed that the temporary ascendancy of one or other national horde was a proof of its innate superiority. There have also always been a few highly intelligent people who have pointed out the importance of eugenics in determining which élite group attained this temporary ascendancy and why; and why it fell, but that is another story. The problem remained of explaining why customs, and particularly political customs, varied from one part of the world to another. Was, for example, despotism something particularly distinctive to Eastern cultures? Was Latin America particularly given to political violence? If so (and those who make these statements can seldom produce any statistics which have any meaning) why?

The great eighteenth-century French political scientist Montesquieu was one of the most 'scientific' of political thinkers, and deservedly influential. It is to him that we owe the first statement of the influence of climate on politics. Bulnes, educated in the French tradition, would have known of it. 'People are . . . more vigorous in cold climates', Montesquieu had written.

Here the action of the heart and the reaction of the extremities of the fibres are better performed, the temperature of the humors is greater, the blood moves more freely towards the heart, and reciprocally the heart has more power. This superiority of strength must produce various effects; for instance, a greater boldness, that is, more courage; a greater sense of superiority, that is, less desire for revenge; a greater opinion of security, that is, more frankness, less suspicion, policy, and cunning.[6]

Elsewhere, Montesquieu spoke of another geographical determinant of political life: the abundance and fertility of the soil. 'The cause of there being such a number of savage nations in America', he wrote,

is the fertility of the earth, which spontaneously produces many fruits capable of affording them nourishment. If the women cultivate a spot of land round their cottages, the maize grows up presently; and hunting and fishing put the men in a state of complete abundance. Besides, black cattle, as cows, buffaloes, etc., thrive there better than carnivorous beasts.

In Europe, if the land were left uncultivated, 'it would scarcely produce anything besides forests of oaks and other barren trees'.[7]

It is quite understandable that a Mexican should be interested in the effects of climate on politics. The major variations in temperature and vegetation caused by either vertical or horizontal movement within the country are its most striking feature. The history of Mexico in the nineteenth century, as we have seen, had been one of regional *caudillos*. And cutting across this was the division between *criollo* and Indian, and their offspring, who were neither one nor the other, the *mestizos*.

By accident or by design Bulnes produced a formula for climatic effects which was not only plausible, but acceptable to a *criollo* régime ruled by an Indian dictator. It was, perhaps, understandable that a meteorologist should have been able to do this, since he did not, like Montesquieu, think of weather primarily as something that affects human beings. Crops are much more important. There are three main food plants in the world, each, as we should say now, paramount in a complex of plants giving a balanced diet: wheat, maize, and rice. Bulnes therefore divided the peoples of the world into wheat-eaters, maize-eaters, and eaters of rice. He then asserted that wheat-eaters were bound to dominate maize-eaters, and maize-eaters those who ate rice. Thus he offered not only an explanation, but also a remedy.

Bulnes's theory, though very popular in its day, probably did not contribute much to the outbreak of European restaurants in Mexico

City. It did contribute a good deal to *científico* self-confidence. Most of all, however, it left a legacy to the twentieth century in the form of a question. What was the Mexican, and what was to be his place in the world?

[1] Thomas B. Hohler–Sir Edward Grey, 27 May 1911, no. 110. Foreign Office Papers 1911, 371/1148 file 1573/23268, cf. Calvert, op. cit., 72.

[2] See Lewis Hanke, *The Spanish Struggle for Justice in the Conquest of America* (Philadelphia, University of Pennsylvania Press, 1949).

[3] Madero, op. cit., 26.

[4] *Sobre el Hemisferio Norte once mil leguas. Impresiones de viaje* . . . (Mexico, 1874).

[5] *El verdadero Díaz y la revolución* (Mexico, Editorial Hispano Mexicano, 1920), 5.

[6] *The Spirit of the Laws*, trs. Thomas Nugent, intro. Franz Neumann (New York & London, Hafner, 1966), 221.

[7] ibid., 275.

The Revolution VII: The Interinato

FRANCISCO DE LA BARRA WAS SWORN IN as President on 26 May 1911, only a few hours after his predecessor had made his early-morning escape from the capital. Large crowds in the streets welcomed him with applause, though there can have been few among them who knew anything much about him.

In appearance he was dignified and benign, with silver hair and a rubicund, distinctively *criollo* appearance. He had the polish of the experienced diplomatist, and had already shown as foreign minister that he had a mind of his own and was prepared to use it. He was, like Madero himself, entirely a civilian. It was generally agreed that he was both honourable and honest, but there was considerable doubt as to whether he would be firm and decisive enough to suppress the brigandage that seems inseparable from the success of a revolutionary movement. Fears on this score, however, proved to be rather premature, since the two weeks after the inauguration passed largely without incident.

Meanwhile Francisco I. Madero, after two weeks of joyous progress from his base at Ciudad Juárez through the northern states, had finally made his triumphal entry into the capital. He was heralded by a violent earthquake in the early hours of the morning of 7 June which cracked buildings and broke the water-mains. The vast crowds awaiting the arrival of the man they had come to regard as almost a living saint were at first inclined to see the incident as an ill omen; in the course of the morning the more optimistic interpretation prevailed that the very earth trembled before him. When he actually arrived, stepping imperturbably over the fissures in the station platform, and rode through the streets to his headquarters the ovation dwarfed anything ever seen in the capital before. The day passed entirely without incident. At Madero's own request no soldiers were seen in the streets, and order was maintained entirely by unarmed members of Madero's party organized by Gabriel Robles Domínguez.

The presence of Madero undoubtedly acted to stabilize the situation at first. But as the crowds continued to gather outside his house, where daily he saw petitioners and spoke to his supporters, the difficulty of his position became more apparent. He was, however influ-

ential, only a private individual. And from the beginning he met with
difficulties in working with a government to whose appointment he
had agreed, but which was motivated by a very different philosophy
from his.

Compromise and caution were inherent in the nature of the *interinato*, as they must be in any government whose sole aim as a government is to transmit power to another. Promises and optimism were
inherent in the Maderista Party, as they must be in any small group of
men who set out to overthrow a seemingly great, powerful, and ever-
lasting government—and find it collapses before they have got to grips
with it. Again, the success of the movement had brought with it many
problems. Many had jumped on the bandwaggon at the last moment,
and their real beliefs and devotion to the leader of the movement were
seriously in doubt. General Reyes was the most spectacular of the
opportunists. Others were perforce men of ability who had no qualms
about changing sides. Of such, Manuel Calero was probably the most
outstanding. And the personal reliance of Madero on members of his
own family to fill high positions necessarily gave rise to criticism—a
criticism, however, not levelled at de la Barra, whose needy nephews
were not forgotten.

Madero's supporters were, therefore, a mixed bag. His name was
the key to everything, and they were ready to pledge it for him to any
project that caught their fancy. The problem was that Madero was
not in a position to 'deliver'. Bell said that 'from the day Madero
entered Mexico City, de la Barra was president in name only'.[1] Unhappily this was far from true. The President did not use his powers to
prevent open political discussion and freedom of the press. Nor did he
restrain—at first—the activities of the Maderista ministers designated
by the treaty. But Madero could not act himself, and his offices
at 99, Paseo de la Reforma could only receive and transmit complaints.

The inevitable results were not long delayed, and of course they
were pushed on by the gossip of Madero's opponents. In the Cabinet
the 'old guard' intrigued against the Maderistas, trying to persuade
the President that his dignity was threatened. In the country at large
there was hostility between the regular army and the irregular revolutionary forces—and this was much more serious. Madero himself, as a
constitutionalist, held that with the treaty the moment for armed
revolt had passed. His supporters should now disband and return to
their homes. Many of them, represented by the Secretary of *Gobernación*, felt with reason that if they did so, the gains of the Revolution
would speedily be lost. On the other hand, the Porfirian army had not
been defeated, and the interim government contained a majority that
preferred to rely for public order on its relatively disciplined troops.

The army was still there if they chose to try to make use of it to disarm the revolutionaries.

The Secretary of *Gobernación*, Emilio Vázquez, was responsible for the disbandment of the revolutionaries. Following Madero's wishes, he began by paying them off handsomely, thus discharging the obligations his leader undoubtedly felt towards them. There was, however, one problem. The payment encouraged men once disbanded to take up arms again, to be disbanded a second or even a third time, and others simply chose to forgo payment. Still, enough did not. Soon the lavish way in which Vázquez handled the funds of the Treasury, refusing to be accountable for them and subsequently bullying his co-signatory, the Secretary of War and Marine, into putting his name on piles of blank forms, aroused first concern, then alarm, and finally fury among the more conservative members of the Cabinet. It was hardly likely that they would have approved of him anyway, since it was his task to build political support and arrange state elections, and this he did with great zest.

The crisis first broke at the end of June over the position of Emiliano Zapata, already regarded as the leader of the agrarian revolt in Morelos. He had been one of many who had received commissions in the revolutionary forces from Madero. He was eager to be recognized, and Madero did recognize him as leader of the revolutionary forces in the state. After a public outcry from the alarmed residents of the capital, the appointment was withdrawn. But the irregular forces remained in being, and the incident was sufficient to bring de la Barra over to the conservative side. Threatening to resign, he forced Madero to agree to a repressive policy.

In the end the President, aided by his own personal inclinations, decided to exert his authority. To begin with, he wanted to appoint a competent Minister of War. The situation was ironic, since the Ministry of War was the one post under the treaty he had been allowed to fill with his own nominee. Even though the designated replacement, General José González Salas, was a Maderista, the proposal met with considerable opposition in Congress from the Maderista deputies. They feared–in the event correctly–that the change heralded an attempt to pursue a military policy which would hit at their potential support. Their suspicions were confirmed when a Porfirista, General Villaseñor, was appointed as the new chief of *rurales*.

With the strong encouragement of the President, Madero had meanwhile left the capital and taken up residence at Tehuacán, a small watering place in the State of Puebla some 240 miles to the south-east of Mexico City. In his absence, there had begun that series of scurrilous personal attacks on him from the conservative press which was so to harass him later, and the conservatives were rapidly regaining confidence. What they lacked, though, was a standard-bearer. The ineffable Reyes decided in the changed climate of opinion to proclaim himself a candidate for the Presidency. His judgement was as ever at fault. Outside a narrow circle in the capital Madero was still very powerful. And his radical supporters were getting rather impatient.

Madero himself, who always found it hard to think unkindly of others, steered a conciliatory course. He saw Villaseñor, and after talking with him, agreed to his appointment. But he said nothing about Emilio Vázquez. In the end, de la Barra realized that if he wanted his resignation, he would have to ask for it, and did so.

The President's perseverance was finally rewarded on 2 August when he received Vázquez's letter of resignation. It was militant, stating clearly that he was resigning only on the orders of the President. A band of his followers were so stirred up by it that they armed themselves and marched up to the castle of Chapultepec. Exhausted by the long tramp, they were received by the President, who told them plainly that their words and actions served more than anything to confirm him in his request. After this, Madero sent a telegram to the press in approval of de la Barra's action, censuring the policy of the fallen Secretary.

The new Secretary, Alberto García Granados, was, however, not a Maderista, as had been expected, but a devout Catholic of particularly reactionary sympathies and an irritating and offensive manner into the bargain. It was an unfortunate choice, and one which strengthened the growing suspicion that de la Barra was working in secret against Madero. Madero himself made matters much worse by saying publicly that Vázquez was a latecomer to the Revolution, which was far from being fair. When the new Secretary of *Gobernación* opened his period of office by ordering the arrest of 102 of Vázquez's supporters for the 'crime' of signing an abusive memorial to the President, the fat was in the fire. The result was a split in the anti-re-electionist movement, which was welcomed as much by Madero as by the Vazquistas.

The Vazquistas, rather confusingly, were the ones who retained the anti-re-electionist label. Under the direction of Madero's brother, Gustavo, a cheerful and gregarious organizer who, from the accident in youth that had cost him the sight of one eye, was known familiarly as 'Ojo Parado', the Maderista support had been reorganized as the Progressive Constitutional Party. The reorganization had enabled the brothers to shed both dead wood and inconvenient enthusiasts, one of the first casualties being Vázquez's brother, Francisco, who had been candidate for Vice-President with Madero in 1910.

On the government side, there had been a pronounced increase in the size of the regular army, to some 28,000 men. Of the former revolutionary army, 5,000 had gone home, and 6,000 had been drafted as *rurales*. This left a force of some 6,000 – still a considerable number. The best-known, and most feared, group among these was the irregular bands associated with the name of Zapata in Morelos. So near were these to the city that some of them crossed the line into the Federal District, and the smallest act of banditry in Morelos was headline news in the capital, where the jittery nerves of the conservatives were daily played on by reports – mostly imaginary – of terrible incidents in all parts of the country. It is reasonable to say that the greater part of these represented little more than the normal rate of crime to be expected in a country where central authority had recently undergone something of an eclipse. But it was natural that the first target of new government policy should have been Morelos, and forces were despatched there without delay, under the command of the Federal General Victoriano Huerta.

Hearing of the attack, Madero decided to intervene. No secret had been made of the intentions of the force, which was to destroy the agrarian revolt by destroying Zapata and if necessary all his followers. Madero had an obligation to do something about it. He notified the President that he was going to Morelos to mediate. The conservative majority in the Cabinet rejected the suggestion, but de la Barra could hardly refuse it and retain his authority. Madero passed through the Federal lines to Cuautla and met Zapata. On 18 August he reported to the President that a settlement had been reached.

Far more dramatic was his accusation that General Huerta was an agent of General Reyes, working to reimpose the tyranny of the past. Zapata, on the other hand, he praised as 'that most valiant and most upright soldier of the revolution'.[2] The sensation was immense. The government was forced to halt its forces, and in the ensuing state of inaction Madero returned to the capital; thereafter, however, the troops went ahead unimpeded while Madero turned his attention to what had now become the pressing question of the elections. He had lost even more sympathy with the old guard and was in danger of losing still more among his own supporters.

The Progressive Constitutional Party met in convention in the first days of September: what the American chargé described as the 'first untrammelled political convention' ever held in Mexico.[3] Madero was nominated unanimously for the Presidency. The Vice-Presidential nomination went at the second ballot to the hitherto unknown José María Pino Suárez of Yucatán, after the first ballot had given him a lead of 615 to 600 over Francisco Vázquez Gómez, who was to allege all his life that Pino Suárez had been 'imposed'. In fact Madero was almost certainly only following North American practice, the choice being dictated by nothing more sinister than a desire to 'balance the ticket'.

The period was marked by a general restoration of order, and the election campaign was, in the circumstances, surprisingly calm. It was quickly apparent that Madero would win. Reyes attracted little support, and even the American ambassador, Henry Lane Wilson, was so disgusted with his performance that he described him as 'an opera-bouffe soldier and patriot' who had 'become a by-word and a jest in the arena of politics'.[4] In the end he had to take the ultimate resort of Mexican politicians, and left the country ostentatiously, in the hope that someone might think he was being unfairly treated. By a strange coincidence Emilio Vázquez left Mexico the same day for the same destination.

The elections, which were held on 1 October, were undoubtedly the fairest elections ever held in Mexico down to that time. There was certainly a good deal of trickery, false returns, and ballot stuffing. Many of the voters had very little idea of what was going on, but since they had no recent experience of contested elections, this was not surprising. The important thing was the absence of overt intimidation and of political control except on a local level. It is hard to be more precise, as in the indirect voting system then used no accurate official returns of the voting of the very small electorate were compiled. There can, however, be no doubt that those who voted were overwhelmingly in favour of Madero, and that the sentiments of those who were not able to vote would have increased rather than decreased his majority.

In the last few days of the *interinato* there were still some who hoped that Congress, still the Congress that had been elected in 1910, would refuse to certify the elections. Considerable pressure was already being brought to bear against Madero, as it had been throughout the campaign, and now that the elections were over, de la Barra no longer had much interest in preserving his stance of impartiality, since the Presidential lightning was clearly not going to strike him. He resolved to resign as soon as possible, and not to wait until the official inauguration date of 1 December. First, however, the conservative members of the Cabinet forced the resignation of Francisco Vázquez Gómez, and conservative opinion in the Chamber of Deputies forced the resignation of the Secretary of War and Marine, General González Salas, for failing to defeat Zapata. Simultaneously, his fall brought the resignation of García Granados. There was no escaping the fact that the tide of opinion was with Madero and that the majority still hoped for much from the new order.

The Congress had always been habituated to obey. In its extremity it remained true to form. The official returns of the Presidential election were certified by 153 votes to 15 on 2 November. Two days later the deputies applauded vigorously a farewell statement by de la Barra, and on 6 November, with equal enthusiasm, they welcomed the new President when he came before them to take the oath of office.

Emiliano Zapata

Outside Mexico, few people could say who they thought was the greatest of all Mexicans. It would be invidious to do so, anyway, since the concept of 'greatness' as human beings habitually use it is not quite as complimentary as they think it is. There can be no doubt, however, that there is one Mexican of whom far more people have heard than any other. That Mexican is Emiliano Zapata.

Zapata today is a myth, not a man. His personality, like that of all myths, is almost indiscernible under the shiny layers of hero-worship and vilification. Even the facts about his life are hard to discover, and some are even harder to believe. Strangely enough, the fictional presentation, which in this case Hollywood tried so hard to avoid, is in fact the view of Zapata that most people find most comfortable.

Emiliano Zapata was born at Anenencuilco in the State of Morelos on 8 August, most probably of the year 1879.[5] Besides Emiliano, an elder brother Eufemio (?1873–1917) and two sisters lived to maturity. Their parents, Gabriel and Cleofas, were simple countryfolk who had some land and livestock, and lived in a proper adobe-and-stone house. Emiliano himself never had to work as a day labourer on the hacienda that hemmed his native village in. He farmed his land and some more that he rented, and he dealt in livestock, horses, and mules. So he could afford a good horse for himself, and the smart cowboy clothes which good horsemen affected.

As a boy he had, of course, little time or opportunity for schooling. He got his introduction to politics the hard way, as one of a group of young men who sought to carry on the traditions of the village against the encroachment of the *hacendados*. After the death of his parents, he was involved in 1906 in a movement to defend land titles in the vicinity of Cuautla, and had to hide from the *Porfiriato* police for several months. When he returned to the village, dissensions among the planters had led to an unheard-of opportunity, a split in the ruling élite about who was to succeed as governor of the state. The opposition to the sugar-planters' nominee, a society dandy of no particular ability, was strong and came from Francisco Leyva himself, who before Díaz's time had been responsible for the creation of the state in the first place. The opposition crystallized on behalf of his son, and when it led to riots in Cuautla, the police had to step in and fix the elections openly. It was a great lesson to a young man that the régime was not immutable.

Sugar made Morelos different from all the other states. It was fantastically profitable, but the need for complex and expensive machinery forced large-scale production and gave the planters an insatiable appetite for lands. There was also the danger of exhausting the fertile volcanic soil. The problem was that in giving right to individual land titles, the Reform had unwittingly opened the way for these apparently progressive landowners to increase their holdings in full accord with prevailing notions of progress. They could denounce and take over the lands of adjoining villages; they could also, in any case, pay lawyers and judges indefinitely until they secured the decisions they wanted, and it could bankrupt a village simply to try to fight them. As the *Porfiriato* went on, it became easier and easier to stamp out resistance. Troublemakers were all too often simply arrested and, if not shot 'trying to escape', deported to the penal settlements of Yucatán or Quintana Roo. Alternatively one might be impressed into the army.

Emiliano was impressed into the army. It happened in February 1910, and he was released at the instance of Díaz's son-in-law, Ignacio de la Torre y Mier, a month later. The reason has not been explained, but probably was to do with Zapata's expertise in horse-flesh, which would have been known to one of Morelos's biggest landowners. At any rate, he then went to work for de la Torre in his stables in Mexico City. Disliking the atmosphere of creeping and corruption, he left and returned home, apparently without hindrance. He found his village in a critical state. It was a crisis that had been brewing for many years and the villagers had taken every step they could to meet it.

In September 1909, in order to defend their lands, they had chosen, with the approval of the village elders, young men to lead the village in their struggle—who could fight with guns if necessary. Emiliano Zapata was elected their leader. He was just thirty. He was, however, the nephew of the previous chief elder and a relative of José Zapata, who had helped Díaz to power. His immediate task was to defend his village against the long-feared further encroachment of the local proprietor; his strength, however, lay not just in his local connections and the trust of his fellow-villagers, but in the network of contacts he had built up in the Villa de Ayala municipality and the Cuautla district generally. For it was there that the people had been goaded to desperation by the blatant attempts of the new governor to remove all restrictions on haciendas and their expansion, and an explosion was bound to come. Overconfidence had driven almost all the *hacendados* to go too far, and Madero's abortive summer campaign was the sign the Morelenses were awaiting that there were other forces for change outside their little state.

When he returned, Zapata had the answer. Backed by his companions, he went to the fields the hacienda had taken, asked the sharecroppers to leave, and took them over again. When the local *jefe político* came to enquire, his small escort was outnumbered ten to one. No longer certain of his backing, he went away again.

Thus, when Madero called for revolt, there was already a small revolt in Morelos, and the possibility of much more. However, as it happened, the leader designated by Madero for that region was one of those arrested in the mid-November police sweep that preceded the rising at Puebla. The revolt in Morelos therefore started off as a decentralized affair under a number of regional chiefs. Zapata was only one of these, but he stood out among the others, and he received unintentional distinction by being chosen as the first the frightened *científicos* tried to negotiate with. One thing he and his companions had in common was that they did not propose to be dictated to by anyone else. They had had enough of that. They would recognize the authority of Madero as their leader, but not that of anyone who did not speak directly for him. In this they were prudent.

In the adjoining State of Guerrero, however, the brothers Ambrosio and Francisco Figueroa were attempting something much more ambitious. They wanted to be recognized as regional chieftains of the south, and therefore they wanted control of Morelos. Zapata acted to forestall all other parties. In alliance with other regional chiefs, he engineered the capture of Yautepec, Jonacatapec, and ultimately, in full siege, of Cuautla itself. At the Treaty of Ciudad Juárez he was, therefore, the strongest leader in Morelos. Nevertheless the Figueroas, with the aid of the planters who were anxious to end the fighting somehow, took Jojutla and within days Cuernavaca, the state capital. Once there they aided the planters to name the interim governor, and things were back where they had been before the fighting began, at least on paper.

Zapata went to Mexico City, where he was one of the first to confer with Madero after his triumphant entry into the capital in June 1911. Madero must have regarded the sombre Zapata with some misgiving. The proximity of his operations to the capital had already caused him to be labelled as a bandit, and there was no knowing how far a bandit might go. Zapata soon reinforced this impression. Observing that Madero was wearing a very fine gold watch, he asked him whether, if he took advantage of the fact that he was armed and he were to take it, and they later met again, Madero would have the right to ask for it back. Madero agreed that he would. Zapata pointed out that that was the position with regard to his soldiers' lands. They wanted them back –and they wanted them back at once.

Madero wanted disarmament first, however, so that the era of constitutional rule could begin as soon as possible. He was confident that he was going to achieve the Presidency, and he honestly intended to carry out his promises. But he did not appreciate the need for haste that others felt and did not understand that a very large number of people were attempting to sabotage what plans for reform he had. The Treaty of Ciudad Juárez had left them all in a very strong position, with only the President of the Republic to act as arbiter. And though de la Barra's intentions were good, he was not strong enough to carry them out consistently.

Zapata accepted Madero's good faith. The little revolutionary leader accepted his invitation to come to Morelos, though it seems that he believed the ruined buildings of Cuautla after the siege were evidence of pillaging and riots sanctioned by Zapata. Yet by demanding he trust him, Madero put Zapata in the position of having to agree to disband his men. This was therefore done, to all appearances completely and for good. Having carried this out, Zapata was understandably disconcerted to find that Madero, who, it will be remembered, held no official position in the government, did not 'deliver' the official appointment as chief of police which was the minimum he expected in return. But after a further interview with Madero he accepted the position, which left him only a personal escort of fifty men, and retired to private life.

It was now up to the planters. However, much to their distress, the situation did not improve. There was no police authority in the state and unofficial bands of near-bandits still roamed it, even though they were not supposed to exist. The fact that they had no connection with Zapata was a distinction most of the well-to-do did not appreciate and in any case would hardly have been keen to publicize. Zapata himself was being talked of for governor, while they had no candidate of any ability to propose in the new democratic age.

Meanwhile Zapata was alert. His former chief-of-staff, Abraham Martínez, had been given a commission by Emilio Vázquez as head of the revolutionary forces in Puebla. Hearing of a threat to assassinate Madero when he visited the city, Martínez arrested several people. But they included a Federal deputy, and Martínez was in turn arrested by the Federal commander, who attacked the revolutionary headquarters, killing more than fifty people. Before he had the opportunity to hear that Madero had blamed the revolutionaries for the incident, Zapata had already mobilized his forces in support of Madero and told him he stood ready to march. This time they stayed in arms, despite the protests of the new Secretary of *Gobernación*, the right-wing Alberto García Granados, himself a *hacendado* from Puebla.

Zapata had decided to marry and settle down formally in his native village. No doubt he would have done so, but he was too busy or too suspicious to go to visit Madero in Tehuacán, and he did not know of the determination of de la Barra to back the new tough policy to stamp out bandits and rebels. By keeping his men illegally in arms he had unwittingly given his enemies in the government the excuse they needed for suppressing him forthwith without inconvenient questions. He was still at his wedding feast when news arrived that the 32nd Infantry Battalion, under the Federal general Victoriano Huerta, had entered the state.[6]

With great energy Huerta proceeded to invade and occupy the state in the same way that he had been accustomed to carry out punitive campaigns in Sonora and Yucatán. First, he needed reinforcements, but, more importantly, he needed to be able to do as he liked. On 12 August, therefore, the President suspended the state government and enabled Huerta to impose martial law. Before he could move, however, Madero arrived to mediate. Faced with the evidence of governmental hostility, Zapata raised his terms for disarmament. He required a custodial force to be maintained in being and political changes to remove the governor and facilitate revolutionary legislation on land tenure. But he did offer to disarm, and so Madero left Cuernavaca to go to meet him. While he was travelling in the belief that Federal operations had been suspended, Huerta ordered behind his back a Federal attack on Yautepec. Though he stated that this was only a 'manœuvre' and not an attack, Madero protested vigorously. There can be no doubt that when he declared that Zapata was 'that most valiant and most upright soldier of the revolution', he meant what he said; nor that when he accused Huerta of conspiring with General Reyes to impose a new tyranny, he did so from information universally known in the state, namely that Huerta's right-hand man was a known agent of Reyes. Moreover, he rightly told de la Barra that the presence of Huerta and Blanquet was the principal reason for trouble, that they were known to be looking for it, and that if Morelos was to return to peace, they should be withdrawn at once.

Incredibly, when Madero had brought the chiefs of the state, with the aid of Zapata, to the actual disarmament of their forces, troop movements were resumed. Disturbances by unattached bands of outlaws were grist to the mill of government propagandists who blamed Zapata for all the troubles of Morelos. By the end of August the settlement had completely collapsed, and the state was being occupied, not just from the north by the Federals, but also from the south by the Figueroas, who hanged inconvenient opponents as they advanced. Meanwhile Madero, denied access to the President, had left for Yucatán.

Zapata was lucky to escape with his life. He remained in Cuautla to the last, protesting that he had not sought a fight and remained loyal to the Revolution. Then he escaped to Chinameca, where he was trapped and encircled by the Figueroas' men. Fortunately they were too impatient, and the shooting as they tried to storm the front gate warned him to flee. Heading south, he crossed into Puebla on a donkey, and was fortunate enough to meet up with Juan Andreu Almazán, with whose forces he took to the mountains. It was from Puebla that on 26 September he issued his first manifesto to a national audience, the nucleus of the agrarian Plan of Ayala.

Meanwhile Huerta's pacification, correct enough in a military sense, was daily creating recruits for the man who had now emerged as the agrarian leader, riding round his flank to reappear in Morelos as the elections were held. The resurgence of the Zapatistas as a fully-fledged revolt discredited Huerta himself, and forced his replacement, along with those of his superiors who had commissioned him. Whether or not Madero would have survived to be inaugurated later, de la Barra's decision to hand over power at the beginning of November, the earliest possible opportunity, was certainly conditioned by this failure. Madero himself had once again stated that his earlier promises at Cuautla would be honoured once he took office. Zapata returned to Villa de Ayala to await him.

Madero no doubt had the preoccupations of a national leader. Morelos was undeniably important to any régime precisely because of its proximity to Mexico City, where the metropolitan papers were daily screaming about fresh outrages said to have been committed by 'the Attila of the South'. But on 6 November Madero became President of a country stretching from Baja California to Chiapas. Only two days later his emissary, Gabriel Robles Domínguez, arrived in Cuautla to negotiate. Robles Domínguez had no difficulty in reaching terms for a settlement acceptable to Zapata, but when he came to return to Mexico City, he discovered that one important factor had been overlooked. While the negotiations had been in progress, General Casso López, commander of the Federal forces and Huerta's former subordinate, had surrounded them and refused to allow anyone to leave.

Nevertheless, Robles Domínguez got through the Federal lines and, returning to the capital, secured an audience with Madero at Chapultepec. Madero gave him a letter demanding immediate submission, and assuring Zapata that if his men were disarmed he had nothing to fear. But when he returned to Cuautla, Casso López refused to let him through, though he did permit him to send on Madero's letter accompanied by a note of explanation. In the circumstances, any explanation could hardly seem convincing. Hardly had Zapata finished reading the letters when the Federal artillery began to fire. With characteristic ineptness, the Federals allowed Zapata to escape through their lines, and once more he took refuge in Puebla.

To this day it has not been explained whether Casso López was acting on instructions from higher authority, or whether he was merely acting on his own initiative. An engineer by training, and a career military officer of long standing, he was just the sort of officer who could be expected in default of instructions to continue operations already under way. Like Huerta, he was a veteran of the most significant punitive campaign of the *Porfiriato*, that against the forces of Canuto Neri in Guerrero (1895). In any case, given that it was Sunday, it is improbable that Madero could easily have secured countermanding orders through the complex military bureaucracy. Whatever the cause of the muddle, Zapata read it as a cold-blooded attempt at betrayal. It was the crucial incident that sundered him from the Maderista movement, and his next step was to proclaim, not just his independence from it, but his undying hostility to Madero himself, whom he described as 'the most fickle, vacillating man' he had ever known.

The Plan of Ayala, the campaign statement of the Zapatistas, was issued in late November from a little village in the mountains of Puebla. It was written by Otilio Montano on Zapata's own orders, typed out by a parish priest, and published in the metropolitan daily *Diario del Hogar* on 15 December with the prior approval of Madero himself.

It sought first to proclaim the Morelenses as truly national revolutionaries, seeking to carry through the plan of the original Revolution which, they claimed, had been betrayed by Madero himself, out of boundless ambition and the desire to make himself a tyrant. They therefore adopted as their own the Plan of San Luis Potosí. To supply the want of a leader of truly national standing, they called upon the services of Madero's former chief general, Pascual Orozco. If he did not choose to serve, leadership would devolve on Zapata himself. The one addition to the original Plan was the section calling for immediate expropriation of lands seized by the *científicos*, landlords, or bosses. In his provision that any of these who opposed the Plan might have their own lands nationalized and used to indemnify the widows and orphans of the revolutionary forces, the Zapatista author followed explicitly the precedent pioneered by the Reform in application to the nationalization of church lands.

The Zapatistas plainly believed that the Madero régime was a house of cards that would collapse at the first puff. They did not know, or care, that outside Mexico City Madero's personal popularity was still immense; that by choosing (they said 'imposing') Pino Suárez he had ensured stability in the south; and that the very rigidity of the Federal army which had almost cost them their lives was for a long time to defend him, and most effectively, in the north. The rebellion did succeed in dislodging the Figueroas from Morelos, but this in turn enabled Madero to secure the support of the moderates, who feared worse. Control of the state was regained by elected officers, and Madero appointed a new Federal commander in the state.

The appointment, of General Juvencio Robles, was very nearly disastrous for the moderates, but it was far more serious for the Zapatistas. Robles put into effect a punitive policy which rivalled the worst that the Díaz régime had managed. Zapata's relatives were arrested as hostages. Suspects, particularly those holding official positions, were summarily shot. Whole villages were burnt to the ground and their populations 'resettled' in a parody of counter-insurgent warfare in Cuba, South Africa, and the Philippines. His viciousness swelled the ranks of the rebels, but the Federal superiority in arms denied them the chance to capture and hold towns. The fact was that Morelos was too isolated and too far from a port to have access to adequate supplies of ammunition, and in the end Zapata was reduced to threats to invade the capital which caused a great panic there, but which he was quite powerless to effect. In mid-1912 'constitutional rule' was at last restored to Morelos.

The immediate effect of this, as far as the rebels were concerned, was the welcome recall of Robles and the appointment of Felipe Ángeles as his successor. Under Ángeles's conciliatory policy, the rebels began to return to their villages, as the constitutional legislature of the state made a real effort to attack the problem of agrarian grievances. The next lot of legislators, mistaking a respite for a permanent settlement, were less wise. They were slow to enact what had by now become a bare minimum, and they were essentially townspeople who mistook peace in Cuernavaca for peace in the countryside. Perhaps by now savagery had bitten too deep, and it was impossible for some of the chiefs to believe that they would ever now be allowed to return to civilian life until the battle they had begun had been fought to a finish. It was certainly some of his principal lieutenants who persuaded Zapata to take up arms again towards the end of the year.

Now a hardened guerrilla fighter, and no longer just an amateur strategist of brilliance, Zapata had accumulated a staff and now set himself to accumulate money. It was easily done. Up to this time his levies had fallen on towns and villages, and, however loyal they were, there were always some who were alienated. Now he directed his attention instead to the plantations. They would pay protection money, or suffer having their canefields burnt to the ground. The planters complained bitterly to the government. But many of them paid up.

When the news came of Madero's fall, Zapata was in a difficult

position. During the last crisis the removal of Federal forces had permitted his followers to move back into hitherto occupied towns and
villages. Madero, whom he had come to hate, had fallen, but his
successor, General Huerta, was no improvement. Still, there were
some in Morelos who had forgotten his campaign, particularly since
it had been overshadowed in their memories by that of Robles. And
aided by judicious inducements from Mexico City, and the news that
their erstwhile hero Pascual Orozco had made his peace with the new
government, many defected from the agrarian forces. It was left to
Huerta to save the situation for Zapata. This he did first by announcing the appointment of Robles as military commander in Morelos;
then by supporting him in imposing himself as governor of the state
after arresting all the legislators he could find.

With Huerta's backing, Robles then proceeded to surpass himself.
What was now afoot was the mass deportation of thousands of citizens
of Morelos. All country people were to be treated as Zapatistas. When
they were removed, Huerta promised the planters, new labourers
would be sent in to work the fields. Mrs King in Cuernavaca was one
of the few who had the temerity to tell Robles what she thought of this
latest barbarism. 'Why, I am trying to clean up your beautiful
Morelos for you', he replied. 'What a nice place it will be once we get
rid of the Morelenses! If they resist me, I shall hang them like earrings
to the trees'.[7]

Those who were not hanged were impressed into the army or used
as pioneers in the Federal campaigns in the north. Fortunately for
them, however, after the initial shock few were caught. Federal
forces moved so slowly and ponderously that all they could usually do
was to burn the villages after the villagers had left. When they returned to the smoking ruins, there were always more recruits for the
Zapatistas. In Puente de Ixtla, even the women took to arms, and
formed their own battalion, which was regarded with respect by their
menfolk.

At the end of May 1913 Zapata had regained control over his
forces and issued an amendment to the Plan of Ayala. Huerta was
formally pronounced 'worse than Madero'–something of an under-
statement; Orozco was proclaimed 'a social zero'. Zapata himself for
the first time assumed the headship of the agrarian cause in his own
name.

Robles was heading for trouble. He had repeated every mistake of
1911. Zapata's mother-in-law had again been arrested and consigned
to a military prison in Mexico City. The zealous burning of nests of
Zapatistas had not spared even important municipalities. Yet the
Zapatistas were raiding into Mexico City itself. Now Robles staged
an enormous set-piece battle to capture what he proclaimed as the

rebel 'headquarters' with its archives, rifles, etc. Robles was promoted to divisional general. But he was then removed from his command. The strain had been too much for the system and the six thousand troops were needed for real battles in the north. All that was left was a garrison strong enough to keep Zapata at bay.

The situation was dramatically altered by events in October. Within days of Huerta's dissolution of Congress Zapata arranged an urgent conference, as a result of which a vital decision was taken. Huerta was on the point of collapse. It was time to abandon the traditional independence of the south and to seek a coalition with the north. Above all, what the south needed was fresh supplies of arms and ammunition, for Zapata was now building a revolutionary force that extended outside Morelos into Guerrero, Puebla, and the Federal District itself. It took six months to prepare, for no arms could yet come through the Federal lines; but the capture of the famous state capital of Guerrero, Chilpancingo, at the end of March 1914 finally put Zapata on the national map.

At this promising point, however, Zapata was doomed to failure. He had counted on the victory at Chilpancingo to supply him with the material he needed for an assault on Mexico itself. But though he had done well, he had not done that well. And though he had achieved the breakthrough to the outside world that he desired by securing the access to Acapulco that enabled him to bypass both the Federals and the north, it was a difficult route by muleback and it did not enable him to bring in ammunition in any quantity. Last but not least, there was nothing movable left in Morelos to sell and he had no money to buy arms.

Such was Zapata's situation when Huerta fell, and his great opportunity decisively to alter the course of national policy came. He did not take it. There was no conclusive march of the pyjama-clad hordes of Morelos into the trembling city. Why not remains something of a mystery. He had offered trust to the revolutionaries of the north, but they had never yet in any positive sense reciprocated it. Even when news came that Obregón was negotiating for the surrender of the city, Zapata did not move, and by then it was almost too late. The camp-fires of his followers were still visible on the hills to the south as Constitutionalist soldiers took over the posts of the defeated Federal army. And, significantly, those Federal posts included those that had long watched south, towards Morelos.

Provincialism

The provincialism of the early days of the Mexican Revolution is an important and characteristic stage in the evolution of a modern state. Its principal significance in this case was that the divisions it implied halted the initial impetus for wholesale reform, and by diverting part of the revolutionaries' energies into competition and dispute among themselves, made the ultimate settlement far more broadly based than would otherwise have been the case.

We have already seen several times how the strength of a local region, such as Oaxaca, or Guerrero, or Morelos, could be such as to resist utterly the power of the central government to command more than its temporary allegiance. Quite understandably, the reason for this is very little understood outside Mexico. The apparent simplicity of the Spanish Conquest of 'the Aztecs', and the fact that the colonial period lasted so long, suggested, especially to the French, that the conquest of Mexico was an easy proposition. What they forgot was that Mexico in 1519 was not one country. She was even more divided than Spain herself; and the centralism imposed by the Crown of Castile was always illusory.

The Spanish found the Aztecs in Tenochtitlan holding down with difficulty a loose federation of states united only under the military conquest of one dynasty, backed by ferocious sanctions for disobedience. So hated was the Aztec rule that the Spaniards had no difficulty in being welcomed as allies, rather as the British were later to become part of the power game of eighteenth-century India, or even (at a different level) the North American settlers the backers of one Indian nation against another. The name of Doña Marina, known as Malinche, the Indian princess who acted as interpreter to Cortés, has been attached in the twentieth century to a form of treasonable behaviour against the Mexican nation (*malinchismo*), but this is wholly retrospective and is an historical judgement of no relevance to sixteenth-century conditions. The Zapotecs of Oaxaca, who were later most bitterly to resist both the Spaniards and subsequently the French, were among the most important allies of Cortés himself.

But regionalism in Mexico went very much deeper than that. To this day there are more than three hundred languages spoken in Mexico; each of them the distinguishing characteristic of a tribe or nation of pre-Conquest times. The language of the ancient Mayas was in 1960 still the sole tongue of 81,013 people. Náhuatl, the language of the Aztec Empire, was the sole tongue of 297,285 and is a living language, though one considerably altered by time. The Yaqui of Sonora survived into the time of Díaz as an independent entity, and were reduced in a series of punitive campaigns under General Bernardo Reyes that were as vast and as tragic as the Arizona campaigns of the 1870s and 1880s. Language too, as numerous anthropological studies show, is not the only badge of difference: dress, customs, ritual, all mark off the *patria chica* of the Indian.

As the ancient Mexicans lived their lives in villages or hamlets

interlinked to ceremonial centres, and came together in rituals com-
memorating divine actions, so to this day the villagers of Mexico carry
their saints in annual processions. Possession of saints and their relics
is of the utmost significance in rivalry between villages; within
villages it is the cause around which a strong hierarchical organization
maintains encapsulated the social structure of a separate entity. This
social structure was and is important, since the concept of individual
ownership of land was unknown before the Conquest, and communal
ownership implied communal organization. Large estates were carved
out by the *conquistadores*, like that of Cortés himself, where one can
stand at the former hacienda building, now a modern hotel, and see in
every direction as far as the horizon land that was under his control.
Usually, however, they incorporated the villages rather than broke
them down. The peasants merely gave their forced labour to Spanish
rather than Indian overlords.

The Liberals of the Reform believed that the introduction of
individual landownership would promote democracy, and enable all
citizens to protect their own. In practice, even before the *Porfiriato*
became so fossilized as to insulate the *hacendados* from the complaints of
those they victimized, it had just the reverse effect. Introduction of
documents of land title in individual names meant that villages simply
would not seek titles. No such inhibitions restrained the *hacendado*, who
could take over lands adjoining his own simply by 'denouncing' them,
and then relying on his 'pull' with courts or government to add them to
his own holdings.

When this occurred, the Indians who lived on the land passed into
his power too. They knew of no alternative; they had been bound to
the land since before the Conquest.

By 1910, therefore, there were three different sorts of land problem.
Firstly, there were lands still under communal Indian ownership, but
these usually survived only because they were too poor, too mountainous, or too remote to be worth seizing. Secondly, there were many
Indian villages that retained an identity, but had been swallowed up
in great haciendas, to which their inhabitants had to give compulsory
service. Lastly, there were villages that had been completely destroyed
and their inhabitants reduced to virtual servitude; they had no separate identity and were wholly dependent on the hacienda economy, for
better or for worse.

The hacienda itself was run like a paternalistic substate. The
authority of the *hacendado* himself was virtually absolute. Where he was
sufficiently powerful, he was in a position to assert his authority as
cacique (boss) of the state in which his lands lay. Every political leader
of independent Mexico before Díaz had had to come to terms with
these regional *caciques*; the more so since, with a curious echo of the

Constitution of the United States, the individual states could maintain their own armed forces and usually did so. In any case, under Díaz the alliance between the *cacique* and the President included the understanding that the *rurales* would act in the *cacique*'s interest if necessary.

Madero's Revolution overthrew this system by overthrowing the men who then operated it. But it could not destroy the regional identities on which it was based, and which always made the Mexican states something more than departments of a centralized government.

The principal reason why not, was that until a very late stage in Spanish colonial rule, the viceroyalty had retained essentially those territorial divisions found by the first Spaniards to arrive in the area. Kingdoms, *gobernaciones*, *alcaldías mayores*, and *corregimientos* varied as wildly in size as they did in title, and the network of overlapping jurisdictions, though confusing in the extreme, provided too convenient an excuse for litigation and procrastination to be swept aside. Don José de Gálvez, between 1761 and 1774, was the first to recommend that the confusion be swept away and replaced in the Bourbon manner with a number of *intendencias*, each based on an important regional city, such as Mexico, Puebla, Vera Cruz, Oaxaca, Valladolid, Guadalajara, etc. The reform itself was not implemented until 1789. Even then it only affected the southern part of the country, including Yucatán, which in those days was easily accessible only by boat.

The sparsely inhabited north was placed under a different authority, the so-called *Comandancia de Provincias Internas*, in 1776. The objectives were twofold: to provide for the control of invading Plains Indians from the north and to guard against the possibility of either British or Russian colonization of Upper California. (The British had already claimed California in the time of Drake, long before the Spaniards got there; Russian exploration of the same coast was the immediate cause of President Monroe's warning of 1823.) The *Comandancia* was later roughly subdivided into western and eastern provinces, the northern frontier being guarded at the time of independence by thirteen *presidios* or military districts permanently garrisoned.[8]

Iturbide was the first ruler of an independent Mexican government to formalize its internal subdivisions. Following colonial precedent and the proposals of the earlier revolutionaries, his government divided Mexico equally into provinces, twenty-one in all, to which was subsequently added a twenty-second, that of Centroamerica (Central America), the former Captaincy-General of Guatemala. When the First Empire fell, its principal relic was the accession of Chiapas from Central America, together with the disputed district of Soconusco, which was subsequently added to it.

The division of Nueva Vizcaya into Durango and Chihuahua, the separation of Sonora from Sinaloa, Tabasco from Yucatán, and the

Isthmus from its neighbours, gave the twenty-five provinces which formed the republic. However, the choice of a federal form of government was accompanied by the establishment of some provinces as states and the placing of the rest in the subordinate character of Federal territories. With Sonora and Sinaloa re-amalgamated, the result was that the Constitution of 1824 enumerated nineteen states and four territories, the four being Alta California (modern California and Nevada), Baja California, Colima, and Santa Fé de Nuevo México (modern Arizona and New Mexico with part of Colorado).

It would be tedious to enumerate the divisions and alterations of boundaries during the struggle between federalism and centralism. Of the major losses of territory to the United States we have already spoken. The real curiosity as far as internal government was concerned was that they did not result in the disappearance of the concept of the territory: new territories were lopped off former states from time to time as the government of the day thought fit. Colima, the only one of the original territories to survive the War of 1847, became a state in 1857. The new territories were usually very sparsely populated areas, and those surviving to this day, Baja California del Sur and Quintana Roo in the Yucatán Peninsula, are also very remote. In strategic terms it could be potentially risky to leave them to their own devices.

Today's northern states are very small compared with the huge territories that once lay to the north of them. But they are still very large compared with the states of the Core and south. It was in the immediate area of the capital that state formation proceeded most rapidly in the nineteenth century, the State of the Valley of Mexico suffering most. First came the creation of the Federal District as the seat of the national government. The District was created by the 1824 Constitution and has continued to be ruled by the central government of the day. Under the Federal constitutions of 1857 and 1917 it is administered by a governor appointed by the President of the day, who is invariably a particularly trusted follower. The city of Mexico has today spilt over the bounds of the District into the State of Mexico and its maximum increase is continuing to take place there, with a corresponding strain on planning and amenities.

The creation of the Federal District, however, did not end the process of subdivision. The State of Mexico lost the region of Tlaxcala in 1847, the State of Guerrero in 1849, and the States of Hidalgo and Morelos in 1869. Nor was Mexico the only state to suffer in this way. Thus Aguascalientes was carved out of Zacatecas, Tepic (now Nayarit) from Jalisco, and so forth. A special case arose in part from the rebellion of Yucatán, which attempted to secede in 1841, giving rise to a long war (the *Guerra de Castas*, or Caste War; 1841–49). This in turn stimulated separatism in Campeche, which separated itself from

Yucatán in a *coup d'état* on 6 August 1857. Continuing distrust of Yucatecan motives was undoubtedly a factor in leading the government of Díaz to carve off it the Territory of Quintana Roo in 1902. In fact, only one state, Michoacán, today occupies even roughly the same area as its colonial predecessor, the *intendencia* of Valladolid. Its shape too has been altered at various times since independence.

How did all this come about? Firstly, as can be seen, because of the domination of the central government and its desire to assert its supremacy. Secondly, because some kinds of regional feeling were so strong that they seemed to be a threat to central rule. And lastly, because of the changes in patterns of provincial leadership. The new states of the nineteenth century were created by and for regional *caudillos*, who obtained independence for them as the price of their political support for the central government. This process can be seen most clearly in the case of the formation of the State of Guerrero, which, though created largely out of the State of Mexico, also included part of Puebla and a tiny part of Michoacán. This was the territory of the regional *caudillo* Juan A. Álvarez, the same who was later to become the first President of the Reform. Subsequently the presence of strong leadership maintained the original boundaries, as in the case of the State of Morelos, which began its independent career as a military district under the Second Empire and achieved statehood under the leadership of General Leyva, or more recently, in the case of Baja California, where the ascendancy of Abelardo L. Rodríguez was an important factor in maintaining its independence of Sonora.

The entire process involves the same nationalisms, and the same sort of boundary disputes, that characterized the separation of the independent countries of South, or still more Central, America. Two factors have acted to bring it to an end. The upheavals of the Revolution resulted in widespread movements of people and of ideas which acted as a fresh set of unifying factors. When these came to an end, the improvement of communications and the greater commitment of central government to social betterment acted in the same way. Today, however, there has begun to emerge a consciousness of a new sort of differentiation between the Mexican states—an economic one. The Core region and the Gulf, together with Baja California (because of its proximity to the United States), are getting richer much faster than the rest.[9] It remains to be seen what remedies will be found for this, or for its consequences, which include, most importantly, the return of political power to the Valley of Mexico.

Voices: The Early Revolutionaries

'This has demonstrated, that for a man in power, and above all when he has ascended to it by means of a revolution, it is relatively

easy to keep it if he persists in it and observes a moderate policy, since
the more the people become civilized, the more they flee from revolutions, and prefer to support a relatively bad government to suffering
the disastrous consequences of a revolution. This is certain for people
in their normal state; on the other hand, when they are victims of
political convulsions or have just sustained great wars, stable government is rare, since after those shakings there are left behind many
germs of revolution, many leaders (*caudillos*) who reward [them-
selves]; in a word, the disastrous plague of militarism; while on the
other hand there are few interests as a foundation in support of the
constituted government'.[10]

'Madero, seen at close range, is small, dark, with nose somewhat
flattened, expressive, rather prominent eyes in shallow sockets, and
forehead of the impractical shape. But all is redeemed by expression
playing like lightning over the shallow, featureless face and his pleasant, ready smile. ... There is something about him of youth, of
hopefulness and personal goodness; but I couldn't help wondering, as
I looked at him during the dinner, if he was going to begin the national
feast by slicing up the family cake'.[11]

'... in appearance and manner he was [Madero] the reverse of
impressive'.[12]

'It is wonderful how circumstances have brought such a man as he
appears to be to his present heights, and I have great difficulty in
believing that he will last'.[13]

'Hardly a day passed that I did not spend hours with de la Barra,
arguing, cajoling, persuading but always taking care to treat him with
the utmost deference and speaking as if the Government was a highly
civilized one, to which extraordinary events chanced to be happening.
The results were excellent and compared very favourably with those
effected by my American and Spanish colleagues whose subjects were
being despoiled and even killed right and left'.[14]

' "I do not want to kill my people to make them good", he declared
in a shrill voice. ... "I could have controlled them", he went on. "I
am preparing to open lands to them. I am arranging employment at
good wages for all Maderista soldiers and many other men, on public
works. Does your government suppose that I have given no thought to
conditions here, or that extensive plans such as mine can be carried
out by magic in a day? I ask of no man or government anything but a
reasonable chance. Why is this unfriendly effort made to force me to
violate my pledges against the shedding of blood? What influence is at
work secretly to accomplish this injustice? Surely the United States
has nothing to gain by making me a tyrant and a madman!" '[15]

'Gustavo Madero was completely cynical (all the wise were) about his brother's promises of free land, finding them also stupid and dangerous. He told me . . . "The people won't get the land, they never do anywhere. It's not only in Mexico as foreigners seem to believe. And as a cry for developing social unrest, it can't be beaten", he added, somewhat treacherously to the Maderista creed'.[16]

'The Maderos, who were staring at Limantour as if he were a god, did not say a word in reply; but I, appearing to be the person directly spoken to, answered without leaving my seat:

"I do not believe that there will be an American intervention, but if there is, you will be responsible".

"Why do you say that?" replied Limantour.

"You know – I said – that the occasion of the revolution was the imposition of Señor Corral as Vice President of the Republic; and the man who imposed the candidature on Díaz was you".

"And how do you know that?" asked Limantour.

"Because General Díaz told me so, on the 24th June last year, at Chapultepec, at six o'clock in the evening".

Before such an emphatic affirmation from me, without raising myself or abandoning my chair, Limantour, raising his hands to his head and sitting down violently, said:

"The sin is mine" '.[17]

[1] Bell, op. cit., 109.

[2] Calvert, op. cit., 93.

[3] ibid., 94–5.

[4] Henry Lane Wilson–Philander C. Knox, 22 September 1911, Confidential. State Department Files 812.00/2384.

[5] John Womack, Jr, *Zapata and the Mexican Revolution* (New York, Knopf, 1969) supersedes all earlier biographies. See also Baltasar Dromundo, *Emiliano Zapata* (Mexico, Imprenta Mundial, 1934) and *Vida de Emiliano Zapata* (Mexico, 1961); Mario A. Mena, P., *Zapata* (Mexico, Editorial Jus, 1969).

[6] Huerta had been stationed there briefly at Cuernavaca in the last days of the Díaz régime. He had made no move to go to the aid of Cuautla.

[7] Rosa E. King, *Tempest over Mexico, a Personal Chronicle* (London, Methuen, 1936), 93.

[8] There were two more *presidios* in Yucatán. For further details see Edmundo O'Gorman, *Historia de las divisiones territoriales de México* (Mexico, Secretaría de Educación Pública, 1948).

[9] Vicente Verni, *El rescate de la provincia mexicana* (Mexico, Costa-Amic, 1964).

[10] Madero, op. cit., 135.

[11] O'Shaughnessy, *Diplomatic Days*, 74.

[12] Bell, op. cit., 112.

[13] T. B. Hohler–James Bryce, 16 June 1911. Bryce Papers USA 31 folio 253. Bodleian Library, Oxford.

[14] Sir Thomas Beaumont Hohler, *Diplomatic Petrel* (London, John Murray, 1942), 174.

[15] President Madero to Edward I. Bell, 13 February 1912, reported in Bell, op. cit., 155.

[16] O'Shaughnessy, *Intimate Pages of Mexican History*, 158.

[17] Francisco Vázquez Gómez, *Memorias políticas (1909–1913)* (Mexico, Imprenta Mundial, 1933), 96–7.

The Revolution VIII: Madero

EVEN BEFORE MADERO was sworn in, men were already talking of plots against his government, and one at least–General Reyes–was already, from a safe refuge at San Antonio, Texas, preparing to take up arms against him. Reyes's revolt, only a month after the new government had taken office, came as no surprise to anyone. But its failure was monumental. The general crossed the border with a mere handful of followers, failed to gain any response from the people, and, after wandering aimlessly for some days, was captured by a small troop of soldiers near Linares in his own State of Nuevo León.

Madero's Cabinet was one of moderates, and he defied the opinion of Congress from the start by recommending the name of General González Salas as Secretary of War and Marine, though the deputies had forced his resignation from that position only days before.

The Presidential Message at the opening of Congress outlined a programme of reform that would clearly take much time to put in hand. Zapata and his followers were not willing to wait–in fact, they did not even wait to find out what Madero did intend to do, for their programme, the celebrated Plan of Ayala, which incorporated a bitter attack on Madero himself, was published before the end of November. It says much for the freedom of speech permitted by the new government that it was openly circulated in the city itself. It was therefore clear from the beginning that whatever else the new President would have to face, the hostility of Morelos was certain, and hence, from the conservative side, pressure for the final suppression of the Zapatistas by force.

Early in 1912 the threat of counter-revolution began to appear in an indefinite form in the north. It centred on the State of Chihuahua, which had for so long been under the tight control of the Terrazas family. The Maderista governor, elected before Madero came to power, was a rock of offence to those who felt they had been supplanted. Abraham González came from relatively humble origins, was uncultivated and brusque, and had a sincere detestation of the great landowners which he was at no pains to hide. Furthermore, he was an important figure in the revolutionary movement, with a talent for organization, and trusted by the new President. This led to him being chosen as Madero's Secretary of *Gobernación*.

It was a doubly unfortunate choice. On the one hand, it removed this strong personality from his position in the state from which he could watch for any revolutionary attempt, and take measures to check it. On the other, it meant, under the constitution, that he was replaced by an acting governor, Felipe Gutiérrez, who in that capacity had only limited powers, many of his actions being subject to confirmation by the Federal government. This state of affairs was unhappily reminiscent of the days in which Enrique C. Creel had been Secretary of Foreign Relations, or ambassador, and the state had in his absence had a series of acting governors directly accountable to Díaz, who had permitted the Terrazas family to do very much as they chose.

In February Pascual Orozco was sent to Chihuahua. He set about building up a considerable force, calling periodically for reinforcements and additional equipment for them. Towards the end of the month he submitted his resignation, and, as soon as it had taken effect, went into open revolt, seizing control of the state government overnight. He had been one of the most prominent generals of the Revolution, and it is clear that Madero trusted in his loyalty until the facts could no longer be doubted.[1]

The crisis was sudden and immediate. General González Salas himself laid down the Secretaryship of War and Marine to become the Federal commander in the field; advanced rapidly northward by rail and met the rebel forces at the battle of Escalón on 26 March; and met with a repulse. He committed suicide in the train bearing him from the battlefield, for reasons that will never be entirely clear, but apparently because he believed he had lost his entire artillery train to the rebels – a belief which was mistaken.

The result was panic in Mexico City, and a general loss of confidence in the power of the government to maintain itself. Madero felt it necessary to declare that in no circumstances would he resign his office. It is clear that there were many, among the diplomatic corps as elsewhere, who in this new crisis returned automatically to consider the device which had been used at the fall of Díaz: compromise and an interim Presidency. In due course the return of de la Barra from France, against the expressed wishes of the Maderista Party, lent support to this. The situation was saved for the government by military success.

Victoriano Huerta

The general who was appointed as successor to González Salas had not previously been especially conspicuous. He had, however, enjoyed a good if undistinguished military record. Victoriano Huerta was born at Colatlán, in the State of Jalisco, on 23 December 1854.[2] His parents were poor peasants, of Indian stock. About the year 1871, when he was sixteen, he came to the attention of General Donato Cuerva, who introduced him to President Juárez and secured his entry as a cadet to the Chapultepec Military College, where he proved to be outstanding in topography and astronomy. He was still there when the battle of Tecoac (16 November 1876) gave the Presidency to Díaz.

Under the new régime, therefore, his duties seem to have been routine for some twenty years, though during this time he was employed on the Geographical Survey Commission and commended for the accuracy of his work. Then in 1895 he was given the task, which he successfully accomplished, of quelling the revolt of Canuto Neri against the imposition of an unpopular governor in the State of Guerrero. After a further spell on garrison duties, in 1901 he was called upon to suppress a further rising in the same state, led by Rafael del Castillo Calderón, which he did with a harshness that earned official approval; and then to suppress the revolt of the Mayas in the State of Yucatán. He succeeded in pacifying the peninsula by October 1902. For this he received promotion to the rank of major-general, and cemented a firm political alliance with General Reyes, with whose fortunes he continued to be identified until Reyes's ignominious collapse in 1909. He had, however, contracted a serious eye complaint which did not yield to treatment and from 1907 to 1910 he was absent on leave from the army as engineer at Monterrey.

We have already seen how, after the fall of Díaz, the provisional government employed Huerta in the campaign against Zapata in Morelos, and how he was chosen to escort the ex-President to Vera Cruz. We have also seen how before coming to the Presidency Madero had chosen him as his principal target in his criticism of the handling of Zapata. Huerta offered his resignation to the government as a result of this affair, but reconsidered his decision after correspondence and a meeting with Madero. At a banquet at the new President's inaugural he publicly reproved him for his former distrust of the army. Less than five months later he was in supreme command of the government forces for the first time.

For his campaign Huerta spent a considerable time in preparation, and clearly aimed to amass an overwhelming military superiority before commencing operations. Then within the space of a month, at the three battles of Conejos (12 May), Rellano (22/23 May), and Bachimba (3 July 1912), he inflicted progressively heavier defeats on the Orozquista forces, until after Bachimba they broke up in disarray and fled to the mountains of Sonora, ceasing thereby to be any serious threat to the government. Huerta, however, came under considerable criticism, both for failing to follow up the earlier battles adequately, and for failing to stop the escape of Orozco himself. He defended himself on the grounds that he was deficient in cavalry equipment, and in view of the fact that he had to operate within the confines of what was still substantially the ponderous military machine of the *Porfiriato* the criticism need not be taken too seriously. A more serious criticism—that he had failed to account for the expenditure of some million and a half pesos—and the fact that his promotion to divisional general was somewhat tardy, became new causes of irritation in his relations with the civilian authorities. Madero was unhappily involved in both controversies. However, a report in September that Huerta was involved in a conspiracy against the government, instinctively believed by the United States State Department, was refuted by the American consul Marion Letcher.

Conditions, it appears, were at their quietest point since 1910, when on 16 October there came news of a new *coup*. Soldiers in Vera Cruz, led by General Félix Díaz (nephew of Porfirio), had 'pronounced' against the government. The name of Díaz stirred strong emotions in many supporters of the old régime, and it is recorded that in army circles in the capital the greeting 'félices días' (happy days) enjoyed a sudden popularity. Rumour excelled itself: it was reported that Díaz held the entire port; that the fleet had mutinied and imprisoned their officers; that a rebellion had begun in the north of the State of Veracruz in support of Díaz; and that the army would refuse to move against him. All these rumours proved to be false. Díaz held only the barracks—which were outside the city—and the customs house and armoury—which were commanded by the guns of the *General Guerrero*, in port, and still loyal to the Federal authorities. His positions were inadequately defended, and he failed to make any advance, resorting instead to negotiations with the consular corps in the city for recognition by the United States and other countries. Within five days his prestige had evaporated. General Beltrán arrived from the capital with a small force, gave notice of his intention to attack, and ended the revolt with the capture of Díaz after less than four hours' desultory fighting.

The indignation of the old guard was exceedingly great. Beltrán was vilified by the press, accused of having resorted to 'treachery', and of having misused the white flag to secure an easy approach to the rebel positions. Madero was denounced for his refusal to intercede for the life of Díaz, who had been found guilty by court martial, and defended his refusal on the ground that militarism must not be encouraged; on appeal the courts commuted the sentence on a technicality to one of imprisonment, and Díaz was incarcerated in the fortress-prison of San Juan de Ulua (whose closure Madero had once promised would be among the first acts of his administration).

Peace–but for the perennial Zapatistas–was once more restored. But for the rumours of a further counter-revolutionary attempt, and the increasing virulence of press attacks on the government, the three months of November and December 1912, and January 1913, passed with a striking lack of incident. Interest centred, for the first time in many years of Mexican history, on the parliamentary struggles of senators and deputies in the outstandingly able XXVI Legislature. The long-drawn-out series of military actions had seriously depleted the Treasury, to the point at which the raising of a major loan to consolidate the country's debt appeared to be the only solution. This loan was carefully–even brilliantly–negotiated by the Secretary of *Hacienda*, but many elements in Congress combined to delay its acceptance. It had still not been approved when on the morning of 9 February 1913 a military *coup* in the capital, led by General Reyes and the newly released Félix Díaz, placed counter-revolutionary forces in control of the most important strongpoint in the city, and the bombardment that ensued occupied the remaining ten days of the administration's existence.

Militarism

It is a fascinating and so far unsolved problem why and at what point in a government's life it loses so much credibility that a military takeover becomes possible. In the case of the Madero government there were four principal groups whose alienation played a significant role in the final collapse. There were the 'old guard', the army itself, the officers of the Cabinet and the legislature, and the press.

To begin with the 'old guard'. Ambassador Wilson, in a revealing comment, considered at first that they would support Madero, even if they would do so without enthusiasm, because he had been 'honestly elected'. The ambassador, as we have seen, changed his mind about the honesty of the elections. Whether the 'old guard' did the same, or whether the ambassador had just been indulging in wishful thinking, the 'old guard' in fact did everything they could to make things difficult for the new government. At the most petty level, Mexican 'Society' boycotted Señora Sara Pérez de Madero's receptions at Chapultepec. Even the British minister was taken in by this to the point of believing that it represented a real lack of support in the country. At a more serious one, the network of rumour that they controlled incessantly transmitted hints of scandals in high places, newspapers reported such rumours as facts, banks refused credit to Maderistas–the list could be much longer. It is sufficient to note that the 'old guard', the upper classes, were nowhere more effective in their resistance than where they impinged on the circle of the embassy and the legations. Even the most responsible of representatives would have found it difficult to sift facts from rumours, and in the hothouse atmosphere of the capital suspicions and fears sprang up like poisonous orchids.

The government's relations with the army began well.[3] The generals were loyal to the government in power as long as their interests were not infringed, and if they had little enthusiasm for the civilians, they gave them a fair chance. They made no move to aid Reyes, but then he had had more chances than most to gather rivals and enemies. Orozco they did not help, but he was an ex-revolutionary and farmboy, and not one of themselves. When Félix Díaz rose in Vera Cruz it seemed to many inevitable the generals would give him their support. However, General Beltrán, having brought up his forces, gave ceremonial notice of his intention to take the city—and duly did so.

Beltrán's success was received with a storm of abuse intensified by the fact that Madero refused to grant Félix Díaz his life. It was saved on a technicality by the Supreme Court, but this infringement of the tradition that high officers enjoyed a virtual right of revolt was not forgiven. Even Porfirio Díaz had not broken the rule—he had anticipated the revolts before they occurred. For Beltrán there was a worse charge. He was accused of having violated the white flag, by allowing his men to advance under it. This, it may be said, was certainly not just: Félix Díaz, who had already shown fatal misjudgement in failing to consolidate and extend the territory he had gained on the first day of his revolt, putting his faith instead on negotiations for recognition by foreign powers conducted through a sympathetic consular corps, clearly believed that Beltrán's forces, after the customary ceremonial opposition, would join him. Equally clearly, some of them intended to do so, and displayed white flags at their entry. Their commander and his senior officers, however, had decided otherwise, and they rallied their troops with efficiency and determination. The paradox of the situation was that it was these senior officers who represented the old Porfirian army; it was the lower ranks who had been largely recruited from the former revolutionaries.

It must be remembered that the loyalty of the Mexican army was to the army first, and to any government a bad second. It is traditional to believe that in Britain and America the custom is otherwise, and so the Mexican brand of loyalty is stigmatized as disloyalty. There is, it is true, a distinction in degree between the Anglo-Saxon and the Latin views of the place of the soldier in the state, and the degree of obedience to be expected from him to his civilian masters. The difference in kind is harder to locate with certainty. Britain, for example, was at this time in the course of events leading up to the Curragh mutiny, and Churchill and Fisher led a navy largely divorced from cabinet control; and where Fisher and Sir Henry Wilson upheld a distinctive military or naval view, they had merely been anticipated by their Mexican counterparts a century before.

As Alfred Vagts has shown, there are two different types of militarism: the militarism of the military, a form of caste pride, and the militarism of civilians. It is the latter type, which he describes as 'self immolation on the altar of violence', which is the more far-reaching.[4] The pretensions of the military to constitutional guardianship of the state only gain significance in proportion to their uncritical acceptance by the civilian majority.

In the present instance, the origins of military pride are not hard to locate. To the glory won–however belatedly–against the French, Díaz had added the consciousness of power born of treating the military as a nascent aristocracy. Generals had attained almost feudal status. Only the habit of obedience to Díaz himself enabled him to maintain the system with so little expenditure of actual coercion. Even then, at his fall, most soldiers seem to have transferred their allegiance, without question, to his successors. Like their civilian counterparts, they had not been brought up to ask questions.

In time, those who were drawn from the Díaz circle weakened before the continual barrage of disparagement of the new President. It was they who made the first overt moves to reintroduce the military style. Their failure left the way open to others who did not share their class background, but did aspire to it. The *carro completo* had blocked these aspirations; the new régime permitted them, but it offered two possible routes for fulfilling them: the peaceful, which it preached, and the violent, which it had practised. It was this division, though not one specific to Mexico, which opened the way for the wave of violence to come.

Divisions within the Cabinet are not specifically Mexican phenomena either, and of the considerable number of divisions in the Madero Cabinet, not all were significant. The division between members of the Madero clan and the others was the most damaging; that between the extreme progressives, such as Abraham González, and the moderate conservatives, such as Ernesto Madero, the most persistent; and that between those who had achieved their ambition and those who wished to go yet higher the most spectacular. For a Cabinet that was so persistently denounced as lacking in administrative experience it was, on the whole, remarkably effective.

The most serious problems developed with the Secretaryship of Foreign Affairs, which carried with it the premiership of the Cabinet. As Calero has shown in his memoirs, even he could see no good reason why he should have been the first man chosen to fill this position under the new administration.[5] His ambition, however, was excited by his consciousness of his closeness to the Presidential succession, and a feud soon developed between Calero and Pino Suárez, who wished to take an active role in government and was finally brought in as Minister of Public Instruction. Calero, as Secretary, was very close to Ambassador Henry Lane Wilson, with whom he used regularly to dine, and they had a remarkable agreement to call on each other on request, a departure from normal diplomatic practice which could not but feed the ego of the ambassador, who received a sharp reprimand from the State Department when he let fall in a dispatch that he had 'summoned' the Minister of Foreign Affairs to the embassy. The presence of Calero in the Cabinet was clearly one of the main reasons why at first it was considered to be pro-American. It therefore became a question of whether Calero would resign or be dismissed first, and he chose to go as ambassador to the United States.

The knowledge of these and similar divisions circulated widely in the capital, and seriously weakened the government's control over its following in the key area essential to fulfilling its own promises.

Until after the mid-term elections of 1912 the government's relations with the legislature had remained fairly good, though in the last session the legislature achieved nothing. Gustavo Madero, as the leader of the *renovadores*, had chosen to manage this body himself. In consequence he was accused of corruption, of fixing the elections, even of setting up a strong-arm organization known as the *Porra* ('The Stick') which offered physical violence and worse to those individuals and newspapers who opposed the government.[6] It seems doubtful that such an organization existed, even in the somewhat loose standards of violence in the post-revolutionary era, for much money was spent by the ruling party on purchasing newspapers, and the most extreme pressure—far from democratic, it is true—known to have been exerted on a newspaper proprietor was a hint from the President that if he did not sell his journal, it would be suppressed.

Throughout the period the relations of the government with the press were, as has already been indicated, extremely bad, and the scurrilous and vulgar nature of some of the cheap news-sheets, and so-called 'comic' papers, such as *El Multicolor*, must have strained the patience of many. It is significant that the greatest offence to follow any action against a newspaper was caused by the confiscation of one issue of an American-owned journal which at the height of the peril from Orozco had announced a catastrophic—but wholly imaginary—defeat for the government forces. Gustavo Madero was forced to follow the old tradition of paying subsidies to newspapers to obtain even a reasonable semblance of impartiality. The *Mexican Herald*, which was among those subsidized, did not give the government even that.

These three factors—dissension in the executive, failure to produce speedy legislation, and the abuse of free speech—combined to produce a dangerous desire for authority and predictability at any price. The instrument was at hand. The only thing that stood between the army and power was the small remnant of the original revolutionary forces still in arms and the large force of *rurales* created from their former colleagues. But the urge to violence was already moving those revolutionaries who had fought for change and now seemed to see it slipping away from them. They were to be no less drawn to the military method, though in the service of a different cause. How things would turn out depended on the way in which the uneasy balance of power was disturbed, and by whom, but the militarization of Mexico in one way or another had become almost inevitable by February 1913.

[1] Pascual Orozco has been the subject of a detailed study by Michael Meyer, *Mexican Rebel, Pascual Orozco and the Mexican Revolution, 1910–1915* (Lincoln, University of Nebraska Press, 1967).

[2] William L. Sherman and Richard E. Greenleaf, *Victoriano Huerta, a Reappraisal* (Mexico, Centro de Estudios Mexicanos, 1960), has up to now been the only considerable biography but is frankly revisionist in purpose. The excellent *Huerta, a political portrait*, by Michael C. Meyer (Lincoln, University of Nebraska Press, 1972), appeared as this book went to press.

[3] See Edwin Lieuwen, *Mexican Militarism: The Political Rise and Fall of the Revolutionary Army, 1910–1940* (Albuquerque, University of New Mexico Press, 1968) for details.

[4] *A History of Militarism* (London, Hollis & Carter, 1959), Preface.

[5] Manuel Calero, *Un decenio de política mexicana* (New York, 1920), 71.

[6] cf. 'Pirra-purra' (pseudonym of Pedro Lamicq), *La parra, la perra y la porra* (Mexico, 1913).

The Revolution IX: The Tragic Ten Days

EARLY IN THE MORNING of 9 February 1913, troops from the garrison at Tacubaya and cadets of the Escuela Militar de Aspirantes arrived secretly in the capital by tramcar. Disembarking, they formed two columns.

The first headed for the military prison. The guards offered no resistance when they entered and released General Reyes, who had been warned in advance. They then hastened to the Penitentiary. The civilian governor saw at a glance that his men were heavily outnumbered, and surrendered at gunpoint Félix Díaz, who had been transferred there from San Juan de Ulua. The column then headed for the Zócalo and the National Palace.

For the other column, things had not gone so well. They had gone straight to the palace and taken it, incidentally seizing Gustavo Madero and the Minister of War. But Gustavo had been warned that an attempt was possible, and loyal troops were on hand to retake the building. When the first column arrived in the Zócalo and advanced on the building, believing that it was already in rebel hands, they were met by Federal troops under the command of General Villar. General Reyes advanced confidently on the palace, evidently believing that the tables would be turned in his favour, but was met instead by a burst of firing, in which he was killed instantly. In the crossfire that followed, hundreds, mostly civilians, were killed, but though the Federal commander was seriously wounded, the rebels had so clearly lost that Félix Díaz prudently withdrew.

Meanwhile President Madero, at Chapultepec, had received news of the engagement. With an entourage which included his uncle, Ernesto Madero, Secretary of Finance, and General Huerta, he made his way on horseback down the Paseo de la Reforma. At one point he had to take refuge in a photographer's shop while the last bullets of the Zócalo battle flew past. He has been reproached for his foolhardiness in risking his life so close to the fighting,[1] but it seems likely that he had his brother's danger in mind, and only secondarily, perhaps, the importance of being seen to be still in command of the situation. At the palace he took his most crucial, and ultimately fatal, decision. General Lauro Villar was incapacitated and recommended his

116

replacement, and on the advice of his Minister of War, Madero appointed General Huerta temporary commander in the field to eliminate the remaining rebels.

Meanwhile, however, the rebels had been able to rendezvous at the Caballito, and under the command of General Díaz, to make for the most important military target of the city. This was the arsenal or *Ciudadela*. It was not a strong fortress. During the long years of the Porfirian peace its walls had been breached by handsome windows, and its main hall was roofed in nothing stronger than glass. But it was the best available, and it contained a huge supply of arms and ammunition. Díaz took it with his battalion of cadets after a brisk exchange of rifle fire. His men then dug trenches to make their resistance to attack more effective. In the course of the city's expansion the Ciudadela no longer dominated it, and an active policy was impossible.

If the Ciudadela had been attacked at once by Federal troops there seems no reasonable doubt that it would have fallen within hours. But it was not attacked. Instead the government paused to consult, and Madero informed his Cabinet of his intention of going to Cuernavaca to get reinforcements from the one commander on whose loyalty he could entirely rely, General Felipe Ángeles. At 3 p.m. he left the city in an open car. The wildest reports were already circulating in the city and being propagated assiduously by the foreign press; this action seems to have given rise to the belief that Madero had fled and that Díaz was in command of the city. Before he left, the rebel General Ruiz and fifteen cadets were summarily executed, no one knows by whose orders.

Madero spent the night in Cuernavaca at the Hotel Bellavista, the property of an Englishwoman, Mrs Rosa King. On the evening of the next day, Sunday, he returned to the capital in the train bringing the reinforcements. In his absence no important steps had been taken against the rebels who had been able to establish outposts and position field-guns. The shops of the capital remained closed, and some prominent politicians took refuge in the American embassy and the legations.

Most important of all, a meeting took place between Félix Díaz, the rebel leader, and an agent of General Huerta, the new Federal commander, in the convivial surroundings of the El Globo café. It was agreed that the two principals would meet there the following day. News of such a meeting could hardly be suppressed, and Gustavo Madero informed the Cabinet of it. However, General Huerta so effusively protested his loyalty that Madero's suspicions were lulled. During the night the rebels established an outpost in the YMCA.

Just after 10 a.m. on 11 February a ferocious bombardment was opened by Federal forces on the Ciudadela. The rebels fired back, shells bursting among the residential suburbs to their rear and killing and wounding onlookers. Then for eight hours the shooting continued, while from all sides of the Ciudadela waves of Federal *rurales*, mostly loyal to Madero, were sent forward and were mown down in great heaps by the fixed machine-guns of the rebels. While the larger body of the loyal troops was thus being decimated, General Huerta met Félix Díaz in the house of Enrique Cepeda, known as the nephew, but actually the natural son, of the Federal commander. The fate of the government was sealed; the manner of its passing remained for Huerta to decide.

The grisly comedy was played out for eight whole days. A few well-placed shells could, of course, have ended the whole thing by demolishing Díaz and all his men. However, the batteries of General Ángeles were so placed that it was impossible for them to hit their target, while those of the other Federal commanders were observed by the German minister, Admiral von Hintze, to be firing nothing but shrapnel, which burst harmlessly against the walls of the Ciudadela. Led by Henry Lane Wilson, who was continually threatening, quite without authorization, the armed intervention of his government, the diplomatic corps tried to end the bombardment by the curious expedient of persuading the government to resign. Madero refused to do so, resolved, as he said, to die at his post. But he did agree to an armistice to allow civilians to reach safety or to emerge from their homes and get food. The rebels were not left out; no less than eighteen waggonloads of provisions evaded the scrutiny of the Federal forces, and they were able to improve their positions before the firing resumed again without warning.

There was by now a lot for Huerta to explain. On 17 February Gustavo Madero took him prisoner, but his brother ordered his release. Huerta had very nearly left it too late. The forces of General Ángeles had got dangerously near the Ciudadela, and though he had now been able to replace the palace guard with men of the 29th Battalion under General Blanquet, this made Blanquet himself dangerous. About 2 p.m. on 18 February Blanquet's troops, acting under his orders, arrested Gustavo Madero, the commander of the police, Felipe Ángeles, and finally the President and Vice-President, who were lodged with General Ángeles in the guardroom of the palace.

That night, Huerta and Díaz met with the American ambassador at the embassy and there came to a further agreement on the disposition of power. It was agreed that Huerta should become Provisional President, while Díaz would be allowed to be a candidate for the definitive Presidency at the next elections. The agreement, which was put on paper and signed, was known as the *Pacto de la Ciudadela*, but from the place and circumstances of its signing has always been known popularly as the *Pacto de la Embajada*.

At this point Madero was still President, although by proclamation Huerta had taken over the executive power. To legitimize his position, Huerta needed Madero's resignation. He had one strong argument: the custody of Madero's family. The supporters of Díaz were baying for blood. To appease them, Huerta handed over Gustavo Madero and Adolfo Basso, the superintendent of the National Palace. On the orders of General Mondragón, Gustavo was beaten, bayoneted, and eventually shot in the patio of the Ciudadela by a mob of drunken soldiery. After this there could only be the gravest concern for the possible fate of any other supporter of the Madero régime, above all for Madero himself.

In the morning an agent of Huerta's visited the captive President and Vice-President to demand their resignation. They eventually agreed to resign in exchange for a safe-conduct for members of their families, their own lives being guaranteed by the Chilean and Japanese ministers; their signed resignation was given to the Secretary of External Relations, Pedro Lascuráin. At this stage, Madero still did not know of the murder of Gustavo, and believed that if he could escape into exile, he might be able to lead a fresh revolution against his military successors.

It was nearly nine in the evening when Lascuráin appeared before the Chamber of Deputies with the letter of resignation. The deputies voted to accept it by 123 votes to 4 and 119 to 8 respectively. Lascuráin, constitutionally next in line, was proclaimed Provisional President of the Republic. He retired from the floor of the Chamber after taking the oath, and nominated General Huerta Secretary of the Interior (*Gobernación*), and, as such, his legal successor. He then resigned, after a Presidency of 56 minutes, which, even for Mexico, was something of a record.

So Huerta constitutionally became Provisional President of Mexico. When the news was brought to the prisoners in the palace, their spirits fell. They had pleaded with Lascuráin to ensure their departure before the resignations became effective, and he had failed to do so. Their usefulness was now at an end, and the train that was to have taken them and their families to Vera Cruz had not yet been made ready.

Some hesitation on the part of the government was understandable, as the governor of Veracruz had imprudently voiced his support for Madero. But there was general realization that the prisoners were in serious danger. Madero's wife went to see the American ambassador, who had had such influence on forming the new government, but he refused to intervene, stating gratuitously that he had not agreed with Madero. It was plain that he believed that the rule of Díaz was about to start again.

On the night of 21 February a meeting of the Cabinet decided that for safety the prisoners should be transferred to the Federal Penitentiary, which Félix Díaz had so recently vacated. The following day was the anniversary of George Washington's birth and the occasion for a reception at the American embassy, attended by the President, his Cabinet, and the diplomatic corps. At 11 p.m. a guard came to collect Madero and Pino Suárez from the National Palace. He had no orders about General Ángeles, to whom they gave an affectionate farewell. They were escorted into a large car. It was not a military vehicle, but a civilian car rented from a car-hire firm by Ignacio de la Torre y Mier, son-in-law of Porfirio Díaz and benefactor of Emiliano Zapata. The car then set off for the Penitentiary, but when it reached the main door it did not stop, but continued round to the back. The ex-President and his Vice-President were ordered to get out. As they did so, they were shot down by their escort.

The complicity of the government has never been proved. The commandant of the prison, Colonel Luis Ballesteros, had been appointed by Huerta, and was undoubtedly an accomplice. The commander of the escort, Major Francisco Cárdenas, who personally shot Madero, said that he received his orders from General Blanquet and General Mondragón, the Secretary of War. Not one member of the Cabinet, however, despite their protestations of innocence, went so far as to resign. Cárdenas himself was promoted. Later, when the Federal army was beaten by the Constitutionalists, he fled to Guatemala disguised as a mule-driver; faced with extradition after the change of government there in 1920, he committed suicide.

Before leaving the scene of the crime, where the bodies lay for some time, the escort riddled the cars with bullets to simulate an attack. The official story of the government was that such an attack, by supporters of Madero, had occurred and had been beaten off.

Madero was buried in the French cemetery the same evening, after which his family fled to Havana and his younger brothers, Emilio, Alfonso, and Raúl, made the long overland journey to safety in the United States. Before they got there, the situation had already begun to change once more.

Heroism

Significantly, however much his opponents disliked Madero, no one doubted his courage. No one accused him of anything other than arrogance or foolhardiness for staying in power to the last. Only one man, Manuel Calero, doubted his motives in agreeing to resign once he was arrested. Courage has at all times been the cardinal political virtue in Latin America.

To outside observers Madero displayed it in an unusual form. He had the strength of moral conviction; the courage of his beliefs. The history of Mexico suggests that this was indeed unusual. Mexico has few heroes in this sense, apart, perhaps, from Juárez himself. She has had many—perhaps too many—who have displayed plain physical bravery. Madero's strength was that he did this too; his weakness, perhaps, was that he was not afraid enough of the men around him.

Huerta, too, though eternally suspicious and defensive, was personally courageous. Mrs King described him thus when she saw him at Cuernavaca: 'He sat as though made of iron, without a motion of his body, his face without a smile, almost without expression, as careless of the bullets flying about him as though they were feathers'. Retrospectively, she went on:

> I marvelled at the incredible innocence of Mr. Madero, who seemed to think he could play fast and loose with men like this. He had made a foe of Zapata by just such an about-face, and now, to save Zapata, he had perhaps made a foe of the more formidable Huerta.[2]

Another feminine observer, wife of the First Secretary at the American embassy, saw Huerta as '*muy hombre*, a broad-shouldered, flat-faced, restless-eyed Indian with big glasses, rather impressive'.[3] In this she summed up perfectly (apart perhaps from the glasses) the archetypal appeal of the Mexican 'strong man'. In Latin America the phenomenon is called *machismo*, from *macho*, a he-mule, a male animal, and, by extension, a man of characteristically masculine attributes. How far it is characteristically Latin American—as Latin Americans like to believe—is another question. As a term it has a deceptively earthy simplicity, but earthy simplicities are precisely what human societies exist to get away from.

With his virile aggressiveness, military bearing, ability to withstand alike the ravages of bullets or of alcohol, and his publicly recognized illegitimate children, Huerta fits the stereotype very well. Pancho Villa, with his gusto, his outbursts of laughter or of rage, his warm-hearted generosity to his friends and ruthless pursuit of his enemies, fits it even better. Huerta's saturnine calm repelled many. This recalls better the extraordinary caricature of the Mexican perpetrated by D. H. Lawrence, full of slow, reptilian cunning washed only seldom by the dark tides of hot blood.[4] The fact is that warmth and impulsive generosity have in all ages been seen as the attributes of the leader. Where, as in Mexico, the claim to power is made effective through *coup* or counter-*coup*, then the military virtues will be valued accordingly as they give the ability to reward or punish. But even in time of war there are two possible paths to the top: the path of daring, that of the lion, and the path of the strategist, of the fox.

After the fall of Díaz there were very few in Mexico who sought a goal openly and fearlessly, or who found themselves trusted by all sides. With values in flux, it was hard to say who, if anyone, stood for the true values, and even harder to follow him, if, as was usual, he in turn had to follow another. No one should be surprised at the curious shifts and changes of alliances and loyalties that took place during these years. The Zapatistas proclaimed their adherence to principles rather than to a man, but the very fact that they retained their popular reputation, was proof of the extent to which they were associated with the personality of one man.

This is one of the most extraordinary aspects about Latin America: outsiders mutter disapproval of the 'personalism' that seems to be rampant in its societies. Certainly it is: as in the case of Mexico in 1913, adherence is to men and not to causes, and the most common form of *político* is the trimmer. But it was an American who described Lerdo de Tejada as the Mexican Lord Halifax. And anyone who can remember – or even read – the adulation heaped in our own time on the figure of a Kennedy, a Churchill, or a de Gaulle, should surely find the worship of Díaz more understandable? If Madero failed, it was because his followers had become too easily accustomed to his achieving the impossible.

Huerta, however, could not reconstruct the coalition of Díaz. Coming after him, he saw only the punitive measures of lesser men. To Díaz himself men had been bound by reciprocal ties of loyalty and obligation going back to the War of Intervention. Díaz, in short, was more than a dictator; he was also a hero.

It was to take a long time for the Revolution to be endowed with a similar mystique. Before that time came there were many false starts.

Felipe Ángeles

It is rare to find a truly heroic figure in an age of violence. The years from 1910 to 1920 in Mexico were years in which many men made their names. Often, however, it was at a heavy cost in moral standing, and most of them are in some sense equivocal. Felipe Ángeles is an exception.[5] Typically, later generations credited him with the very Spanish attribute of *hidalguía* – nobility, generosity, fine instincts. And he was in fact an Indian by birth, and in presence an *indio triste*, one who by his air of sadness seemed to mourn the Conquest.

Ángeles was born at Molango in the State of Hidalgo in 1869. He entered the Colegio Militar at the age of fourteen, and his ability was such that he graduated in the most technical of all military skills, that of artillery. In those days men still had a respect for this arm, which was a carry-over from the days of the artillerist Bonaparte who had made his way to a throne. In late nineteenth-century Europe, where Ángeles finished his studies in Paris, he was recognized as exceptional even by French standards. With such a record he became Director of the Colegio Militar, despite his relative youth and the fact that his publicly-proclaimed model of the ideal soldier was very far indeed above that which the *Porfiriato* actually produced.

Ángeles's association with the Revolution developed only after Madero became President. Madero charged him with one of the most difficult tasks imaginable: that of replacing Huerta and his successor Juvencio Robles as commander in Morelos. Ángeles had the difficult task of pursuing an essentially conciliatory policy with sufficient firmness to be taken seriously. Madero engaged more than his obedience as his superior officer, he also won his loyalty; but Ángeles was sufficiently clear-headed to see the perils that beset the President. Zapata, he believed, was wrong in maintaining his opposition to Madero, while Madero was doing his best to overcome the wiles and obstruction of the conservatives. Yet unlike other military commanders of the day he would tolerate no cruelty or injustice among his soldiers.

It was to Ángeles in Cuernavaca that Madero came for help at the beginning of the Tragic Ten Days. 'Seeing the two men together there in my drawing-room, the soldier and his frail-looking chief with the good face', Mrs Rosa King recalled many years later, 'it struck me that in the love Angeles had for Madero there was much of the protective feeling of a big boy for a little boy who is in for it'.[6]

Madero was under no illusions as to what lay in wait for him if he lost—he told his companions so in the military train which they boarded for the last part of the journey into Cuernavaca. One of those companions was later to take part in his arrest. Ángeles was also arrested at the same time, and so became, as we have seen, the last of his supporters to see the ex-President alive. After the murder of Madero and Pino Suárez he was released without explanation from his solitary custody in the guardroom of the National Palace. Prudently he did not stop to ask questions, but went into hiding in the capital.

'The treachery . . . that was what took the heart out of a man', he told Mrs King while he was still in hiding.

> It is one thing, Señora King, to face an enemy; but to look into the guns of–friends! . . . Imagine, if you can, *señora*, the moment when I opened fire on the Ciudadela and discovered that the focus of my cannon had been secretly destroyed! And poor Castillo and his men,–ordered by Huerta to the corner of Balderas and Morelos, where he knew they would be blown to pieces.

And, thinking of all the others who had been killed too, he said: 'God forgive us for what we have done to this city, all of us!'[7]

The new government appeared everywhere to be triumphant. Even Pascual Orozco, leader of the revolt against Madero, was reconciled to it, and if the movement headed by Zapata in Morelos took fresh strength, it remained confined to a very limited area. It seemed only a matter of time before the new military government destroyed it for ever. Ángeles had been offered a diplomatic commission, the traditional Latin American way of getting rid of awkward dignitaries without giving cause for offence. For Ángeles was, after all, a regular soldier, and a good one. However, his mind was made up when news reached him that on 26 March 1913 the governor of Coahuila, Venustiano Carranza, had proclaimed the Plan of Guadalupe, refusing to recognize Huerta and appointing himself First Chief of the Constitutionalist Army in charge of the executive power of the republic. This cumbersome terminology was necessitated by the fact that no one could properly be President without an election of some sort, and was in itself supposed to be a sign of his genuineness as a Constitutionalist.

The Constitutionalist revolt got off to a slow start. A serious political setback was the loss of the support of Abraham González, governor of the neighbouring State of Chihuahua. He had proclaimed himself in support of the revolt, but had then been seized by Federal troops and thrown under the wheels of the train that was carrying him to Mexico City. But the State of Sonora was already in revolt, and what was needed to weld a northern army together was a good general, precisely what Carranza did not possess.

When Ángeles arrived to join the Constitutionalists it was therefore natural that Carranza, who was a highly intelligent man, should welcome the opportunity to appoint him his Sub-secretary of War. His followers were very much less enthusiastic. Not only was there a huge gulf between their military attainments and those expected by one of the most able soldiers of the Federal army, but it was easy for those who were envious of him to spread rumours doubting his loyalty to the cause. Ángeles disliked this atmosphere of intrigue intensely, though it was, in fact, the way Carranza was always accustomed to work. His own isolation and refusal to be approached except through intermediaries made it almost inevitable. Furthermore, his chief general in the field, Pablo González, though very enthusiastic and absolutely reliable, had a knack for losing battles that no one else could have lost. By the end of 1913 Carranza was so far from having made progress that he had, in fact, been ejected from the State of Coahuila altogether and had to retreat across the Sierra Madre into Sonora.

The removal of political control in Chihuahua was filled, however, by the growth of an army around the picturesque figure of 'Pancho' Villa. A rough, virile, and emotional peasant, who had once nearly been shot for disobeying the orders of Victoriano Huerta, Villa had the ability to lead others and to inspire them with something of his own bravery. He was, besides, loyal; his tragedy was that he never had anyone to be loyal to. Carranza distrusted him, and he reciprocated the distrust.

In February 1914 Carranza found himself stuck in the north-west with no possibility of easily reaching the capital and getting close to the political centre of the country. Meanwhile Villa was winning battles in Chihuahua, and a third insurgent focus was developing in Zacatecas. He resolved to cross the mountains back to Chihuahua. On the way he received a message from Villa asking for the aid of Ángeles. Solving two of his problems at one stroke, he at once relieved Ángeles of his cabinet post and sent him off overland by way of the United States.

Villa's strategic problem was this: all major troop movements on both Federal and Constitutionalist sides had to take place by rail. The Federal government therefore had only to maintain strong garrisons at the principal rail junctions in order to be in effective control of the north, however much insurgency might actually be found there. To break this hold on the rail junctions, Villa needed to undertake a siege strategy, and for this he needed artillery. The guns themselves he had been able to capture from the Federals; handling them properly was another matter, and it was for this purpose that the Division of the North required the services of Mexico's leading artillerist. In the meantime Villa had been able to capture the port of Ciudad Juárez on the frontier, which gave him the opportunity to import arms and ammunition freely, and broke the Federal stranglehold in that respect.

Ángeles, it seems, found in Villa a commander who could reawaken his loyalty, and a leader who was sufficiently able to make full use of his military talents. Villa was impatient to recapture Torreón – the key railway junction in northern Mexico, which had been wrested from him by the Federals. Villa had already mastered the crucial combination of secrecy and rapid advance which was the key to his success. His troops moved quickly from Chihuahua to Yermo and there awaited his orders.

'At Yermo there is nothing but leagues and leagues of sandy desert sparsely covered with scrubby mesquite and dwarf cactus', wrote John Reed,

> stretching away on the west to jagged, tawny mountains, and on the east to a quivering skyline of plain. A battered water tank, with too little dirty alkali water, a demolished railway station shot to pieces

by Orozco's cannon two years before, and a switch track comprise the town. There is no water to speak of for forty miles. There is no grass for animals. For three months in the spring bitter, parching winds drive the yellow dust across it.[8]

Then came the Division of the North.

Along the single track in the middle of the desert lay ten enormous trains, pillars of fire by night and of black smoke by day, stretching back northward farther than the eye could reach. Around them, in the chaparral, camped nine thousand men without shelter, each man's horse tied to the mesquite beside him, where hung his one serape and red strips of drying meat. . . . Officers, orderlies, generals with their staffs, soldiers with halters hunting for their mounts, galloped and ran past in inextricable confusion.[9]

The clouds of smoke and dust were visible fifty miles to the south at the Federal outposts.

The vital arm in the battle to come would be the artillery.

'In a great circle ready for action, the artillery was parked, with caissons open and mules corralled in the center', Reed observed.

Colonel Servín, commander of the guns, sat perched high up on an immense bay horse, a ridiculous tiny figure, not more than five feet tall. He was waving his hand and shouting a greeting across to General Angeles, Carranza's Secretary of War—a tall, gaunt man, bareheaded, in a brown sweater, with a war map of Mexico hanging from his shoulder as he straddled a small burro.[10]

After four days Villa himself arrived. He had been to the wedding of a *compadre*, dancing all day and night at the festivities. Yet once he had arrived he took complete charge. With his characteristic sense of humour he used the telegraph to his own advantage; sending messages in the name of a Federal commander he had recently killed, in order to confuse and alarm the Federals. At Bermejillo he found the telegraph line to Torreón intact and got Ángeles to put through a call to the commander of the garrison, General Velasco, demanding his surrender. It was refused. The trains rolled on until they came to a halt eight miles north of the city where the tracks had been torn up.

There the terrible Villista cavalry left the trains and encircled the city of Gómez Palacio, key to the junction. The Federal commander held it in face of their frontal attack, and then fell back on Torreón itself. Despite terrible losses, the Villistas then pressed home their advantage. Five days of street fighting brought the Federals to the point of surrender; then the Federal commander used his artillery to lay down a diversion to the north and west, and took advantage of it and a fortunate dust storm to withdraw his forces to the east of Saltillo. The Villistas rode into Torreón on 2 April.

Villa's success made him the most powerful *caudillo* in Mexico overnight. He was, however, notionally subordinate to Carranza, and the First Chief, whose armies still resolutely failed to win battles on their own account, followed closely at his heels lest he might get to Mexico City without him. Despite his strategic blunders so far, however, Villa realized that he could not advance directly on Mexico City without first destroying Velasco's forces. In a fortnight of hot pursuit he succeeded in doing so, and was at last free to advance on the capital as soon as his men were rested and reprovisioned.

As Villa had risen, so Ángeles had become the closest adviser and confidant of Mexico's most powerful general. Yet at the height of his success there was one perplexity. Carranza refused to appoint Villa military governor of Chihuahua, though he was that and more in all but name. Instead he appointed one of his officers. And within a week Pablo González, for all his caution, had been unable to avoid occupying Monterrey, the second city of the republic, the major industrial centre of northern Mexico, and the key to the frontier State of Nuevo León. From there the Constitutionalist forces under Carranza could unite with the forces in Tamaulipas that were advancing on Tampico, the rich oil port. Carranza, in short, was at last becoming a military power in his own right. As such he would soon be in a position to demand whether Ángeles–and many others–would continue to follow Villa, or return to the allegiance of a First Chief who was determined to dispense with Villa's services.

1 Calero, op. cit., 112–13.
2 King, op. cit., 82, 87.
3 O'Shaughnessy, *Diplomatic Days*, 102 (attributed to 17 August 1911).
4 *The Plumed Serpent*, first published 1926 (London, Penguin Books, 1966), 79.
5 Ángeles was the subject of a short biography by Bernardino Mena Brito, *Felipe Ángeles, Federal* (Mexico, Ediciones Herrerías, 1936).
6 King, op. cit., 110–11.
7 ibid., 117–18.
8 John Reed, *Insurgent Mexico* (New York, Clarion, 1969), 155.
9 ibid.
10 ibid., 160.

The Revolution X: Huerta

ON PAPER, Huerta's government had much in its favour. The Cabinet included ex-President de la Barra as Secretary of External Relations and General Mondragón as Secretary of War and Marine, the post he had held under Díaz. The British minister described it, correctly, as 'distinctly good and strong'.[1] This government was backed by the army, which by now had lost the fat of the *Porfiriato* and was a formidable fighting force; it had also received the submission of almost all the state governors and was favourably regarded at the outset by diplomats and the major powers.

Only one fact stood in the way of its success: the murders of the ex-President and Vice-President. The other killings of the *Decena Trágica* might have been overlooked as being carried out *en caliente*—these could not. And they drew attention to the existence of an unsavoury element in the régime that also might have been overlooked. It was not that any of the things that happened were in themselves particularly unusual. It was simply that, though the government did not actually *need* respectability in order to survive, it desperately *wanted* it. And the want was to lead Huerta into such a tortuous maze of action and self-justification that in the end it collapsed under the strain.

Huerta's government wanted two things which were interdependent: recognition by the outside world and money. Recognition was necessary to enable the government to get loans from abroad; the idea of increasing taxation came to it only slowly and in a form that brought its own problems. The money was needed to service the national debt, which had been inherited from previous governments. However, none of these needs would have arisen had the government been able to live within its income, or had Huerta himself not wanted to stay in power.

His first task was to establish himself in power, and this meant restoring order. One state governor alone had had the temerity to speak openly against Huerta's seizure of power, Abraham González. He was arrested by a squad of Federal soldiers and escorted south to the capital. But he disappeared en route, as has already been related. After this the other governors came swiftly into line, with the sole exception of Venustiano Carranza of Coahuila, who, wiser than his colleague in Chihuahua, simply failed to answer any letters from Huerta until he had had time to gather his own forces.

His second problem was to appoint people loyal to himself in key positions. Here he made a disastrous mistake. His 'nephew', Enrique Cepeda, who had acted as his go-between in the *Decena Trágica*, was rewarded with the most crucial position of all, the governorship of the Federal District. Only a few days after his appointment, however, he went to the Penitentiary, ordered a political prisoner to be brought out, shot him with his own hand, and then ordered the body to be burned with petrol. When the news leaked out, as it rapidly did, Huerta protected him by having him certified as insane and removed into protective custody. Here, however, was a scandal that touched his own family, and one which made the official story of the murders of Madero and Pino Suárez look thinner than ever.

Thirdly, the government had to secure formal diplomatic recognition abroad. This task was in the hands of ex-President de la Barra. Rather rashly, he had promised to resign if it turned out that the government had had any connection with the murders. Though he did not at first do so, he retained sufficient goodwill from the period of his Presidency to take major steps towards general recognition. Britain, which was concerned only with whether or not the government was in effective control of the country, recognized the interim government on 31 March 1913, and was rapidly followed by the governments of other European and Latin American powers. It was, however, with the government of the United States that de la Barra was principally concerned.

The administration of President Taft, which went out of office on 4 March, had withheld recognition, despite the pleas of Ambassador Wilson, because it hoped to press a settlement of outstanding claims using recognition as a pretext. The administration of President Wilson, which succeeded it, involved a wholesale change of personnel in government and in particular at the State Department. It was therefore in no hurry to take up difficult problems, and for the time being simply allowed the Taft line to continue. Meanwhile arms continued to be exported from the United States both to the Mexican government and to the forces that were coming into being against it. In view of the very heavy United States investment in Mexico, and the pressures on her behalf for recognition, it seems quite possible that the United States might well have continued to deal with Huerta indefinitely.

However, Huerta was impatient. On 7 May the ambassador of the United States was summoned and told that Huerta considered his government's refusal to recognize him 'as unwise and susceptible of an unfriendly interpretation'. The ambassador was, of course, already pressing for recognition as hard as he knew how. Huerta's intervention merely alerted the United States government to the fact that he considered recognition important. And President Wilson instinctively wanted to exercise pressure on Huerta to promote the cause of democratic government in Latin America. Realizing at last that in the first three months of his Presidency he had not yet explained to the ambassador what he thought, he sent him on 15 June a telegram setting out his terms for the kind of bargain he had in mind. After explaining that his government felt there was a fundamental lack of confidence in Mexico in the good faith of those who had seized power, he stated:

> This Government awaits satisfactory proof of their plans and purposes. If the present provisional government of Mexico will give the Government of the United States satisfactory assurances that an early election will be held, free from coercion or restraint, that Huerta will observe his original promise and not be a candidate at that election, and that an absolute amnesty will follow, the Government of the United States will be glad to exercise its good offices to secure a genuine armistice and an acquiescence of all parties in the program.[2]

Huerta for his part did not want 'good offices'; he wanted recognition so that he could get a loan abroad. He had already agreed to arrange elections for 26 October, he had not promised not to be a candidate himself, and he could not promise on behalf of his successor that an amnesty would be granted. So he, like everyone else, remained in the dark as to what he was to get out of United States interference, as he saw it, in the domestic affairs of Mexico. However, at this point another factor entered the equation. President Wilson had sent a confidential agent to Mexico to provide him with a personal report on the situation. This agent, John Bayard Hale, a journalist who had written his campaign biography, now sent in a report demonstrating the ambassador's complicity in the events of the *Decena Trágica*. President Wilson now rejected decisively the arguments for recognition, recalled the ambassador, and dismissed him on his return to Washington. He did not wish to seem to condone a man who he believed had connived directly at the murder of ex-President Madero.

Meanwhile, in Mexico, two important political developments were taking place. With the backing of the American ambassador, Félix Díaz had come out of the *Pacto de la Ciudadela* with strong personal support in the Cabinet. The removal of de la Barra after his failure to get United States recognition began a series of cabinet changes, which in the course of time enabled Huerta to rid himself of all his Felicista ministers. This process was essentially complete by the end of July. However, at the same time Huerta was beginning to face another problem in managing Congress. Relations between the executive and the legislature had not greatly altered since the fall of Madero; the legislature, which contained a remarkable number of able and brilliant men, had contributed largely to the apparent failure of the Madero régime to solve Mexico's problems by their endless discussion and lack of resolution. Now, under Huerta, the legislators were still discussing, and Huerta lacked the political machine by the creation of which Gustavo Madero had attempted to exercise executive leadership. Intelligently, he met this problem by bringing the four outstanding deputies (the *Cuadrilatero*) within his government, but since he did not trust them, he did not get very good results.[3]

However, since the emergence of the focus of revolutionary activity in the north had become apparent, the legislators were emboldened. One senator, Belisario Domínguez from Chiapas, launched a public attack in speeches on 23 and 29 September on the re-emergence of the *ley fuga* and the growing militarization of the nation. He said courageously that the result of the speech might be his own death. Within days he was seized at night in his hotel and murdered. A deputy, Serapio Rendón, was murdered in similar circumstances. Their colleagues joined to resolve that if the executive could not protect the lives of legislators, they would be compelled to hold their sessions elsewhere. On 10 October, therefore, troops surrounded the Chamber of Deputies and arrested 110 members, after which, quite unconstitutionally, the Congress was declared dissolved and new elections called for the same day as the Presidential election, 26 October.

In fact, so far the revolt in the north had not had a very profound effect on the country as a whole. In the capital there was much more fear of the resurgence of Zapatista activity in Morelos, which was, after all, much nearer. The government was able to raise an internal loan with only moderate coercion, and negotiations were afoot for an external one. However, it is important to note that its financial problems were largely its own fault. The militarization which Senator Domínguez denounced was not in any sense a response to events in the north. It was the price Huerta was prepared to pay for continued military support, the expansion of the peacetime army to 80,000 effectives being announced in the President's message to Congress of 1 April. Though this represented a doubling in its size, the higher figure had already been exceeded by the beginning of September. The ranks were largely filled with the sweepings of the jails to begin with, and subsequently by conscription through press gangs operating at the bullfights or in the streets at night. But the army still cost a great deal of money, and peculation and theft were rampant at all levels of government.

Félix Díaz had now seen all his hopes of becoming President with Huerta's help crumble. Now he accepted the Special Embassy to Japan which Huerta offered him, though he actually went no further than Vera Cruz. The elections were duly held, but that was all. Huerta had not been able to find a man of straw, as Porfirio Díaz had in 1876, to hold the Presidency while he himself was a candidate, and so had been able to keep his promise. He was not a candidate. But the majority of votes, he later declared, were cast for him, and, since they were invalid, this meant that he continued to be Provisional President until fresh elections could be held.

After this, President Wilson of the United States was determined to do all he could to remove Huerta from office. He had already sent as his special envoy to the President John Lind, ex-governor of Minnesota, whose complete lack of tact or diplomacy succeeded in angering Huerta himself and, at the same time, helped him to rally support behind an anti-American stance. Lind settled down in Vera Cruz, where he was soon surrounded by Constitutionalist agents who fed him with much exaggeration about their successes in the north.[4] In fact the Constitutionalists, by capturing Torreón, had helped precipitate the dissolution of Congress, but they were not at this stage able to hold the city. Not realizing the true military position, first Lind and subsequently the United States government came to the conclusion that Huerta and his government were on the point of collapse. The only explanation of why he did not do so forthwith seemed to them that he was supported by the British government, who had recognized Huerta formally, and whose minister, Sir Lionel Carden, was openly urging support for him.

Washington moved as far as delivering Huerta a virtual ultimatum. This and other diplomatic pressures he counteracted in a novel way, by simply disappearing from view among the numerous cafés and bars of the city. His whereabouts were not particularly secret, and he sat out of doors quite openly, apparently unafraid of assassination himself. He also transacted government business in the large black car that swept him from place to place, and which, in an interesting contrast, never took the same route twice running. Ultimately Lind was reduced to threatening the one sanction overwhelmingly welcome to Huerta, his own departure, and duly carried it out.

Meanwhile the British government had been able to assure the government of the United States that they were not backing Huerta as such, though they were not prepared to interfere on their own account in Mexican affairs. Once satisfied of this, President Wilson took the next logical step, that of opening negotiations with the

Constitutionalists. It was a slow business, since so many factions were involved, and not until Villa's second, and final, capture of Torreón was it seen to be having much effect.

It was, therefore, not until February 1914 that the efforts of the northerners really began to erode the stability of the régime which by that time was under severe financial strain. The introduction of small-value notes in November stimulated a flight from silver; inflation, moreover, was compounded by the fact that the Constitutionalists issued their own money which effectively speaking had no backing but the bullet. The problem of the national debt was averted for a time by a loan floated in Paris, but the final expedient of calling a bank holiday on 22 December brought no relief and the ultimate default was only a matter of days. Default was, as ever, not as disastrous as it seemed beforehand. The government raised taxes, collected its customs dues in cash, and printed banknotes. President Woodrow Wilson, who had since December been engaged in what he called 'watchful waiting', decided that some more drastic form of interposition was needed than either diplomatic noises or financial starvation.

Venustiano Carranza

Ever since his death, the memory of Venustiano Carranza has been tended by a devoted band of followers. His house in Mexico City is a shrine, and his tomb, under the Monument to the Revolution, is a visible symbol of the importance of his contribution to the making of his country. Most writers agree that his personality was of crucial importance to the development of the Constitutionalist cause. What that contribution was is a more controversial question.[5]

The facts about his life are well known, but characteristically ambiguous. He was born on 29 December 1859 at Cuatro Ciniegas, Coahuila, the son of a well-to-do *hacendado*, and passed his early years in comfort, but without incident. His intention was to become a doctor, but his medical studies were brought to an end by the weakness of his eyesight, and at the age of twenty-eight he had to return to the family hacienda. Despite his nearsightedness, he was a tall and imposing figure, and in the year of his return to Coahuila was elected municipal president of his native town. He was re-elected to that post in 1894 and 1898, and despite his opposition to the imposition by Díaz of Governor Garza Galán–against whom he rose in revolt–he made his peace with the compromise candidate, and from then on rose swiftly up the career hierarchy of the *Porfiriato*. As an apparently loyal supporter of the régime he served in turn as state and Federal deputy, and then senator from Coahuila in the Federal legislature, until he became interim governor of Coahuila in 1908. As such he was a keen partisan of General Reyes.

With the rise of the anti-re-electionists, however, Carranza, at the age of fifty, became one of the earliest supporters of Madero's cause, and his political influence in Madero's native state undoubtedly facilitated the early course of the opposition. So important was his contribution that Madero named him to his shadow 'Cabinet' at Ciudad Juárez as Secretary of War and Marine, despite his entirely civilian status. As a result of the treaty, however, this post in the interim government went to another, and he returned to Coahuila as elected governor in his own right (1911).

Then came the tragic Ten Days and the accession of Huerta. We have already seen how Carranza, wiser than his fellow-governor of Chihuahua, sent no immediate reply to Huerta's telegram demanding adherence. His natural caution and hesitation, as it happened, made for the only course that he could have followed with any prospect of success. On 26 March it was Carranza, therefore, rather than anyone else, who issued the Plan of Guadalupe, and offered a standard to those looking for a rallying-point against the military government. How far the fortunate choice of name, which was that of Carranza's own hacienda, was deliberate is now impossible to say. But the vagueness of the Plan, and its deliberate adherence to the few principles established by Madero himself, were surely signs of personal commitment.

Within weeks the First Chief of the Constitutionalist armies had become the lonely figure whom John Reed saw, coming out of his hut to blink for a few minutes shortsightedly in the sun, before going back to the mass of papers that ever surrounded him. His material wants seemed to be few, his dedication to his self-imposed task considerable, but it was in those weeks and months that Carranza seems to have lost the ability to communicate with others. Perhaps it was the effect of responsibility without power – a strain which in those revolutionary years caused many people less secretive and more gregarious to behave oddly and unpredictably. Perhaps, on the other hand, it was the extraordinary sense of personal loyalty which Carranza was always able to evoke from a few. Jealously these few guarded their Chief from the outside world, reinforcing his wish that others communicate with him only through them.

As he became remote he became a figure of fun: 'Don Venus', the tall, untidy figure in the baggy uniform without badges of rank, looking, with his straggling white beard, a good decade or more older than he really was. Yet the distinguished-looking head concealed a brain of immense agility and perception, slow to act but politically trained, and backed by an inflexible will that could defeat the rages and the pleadings alike even of a Pancho Villa. Whatever its motivation (and there were many who said it was only personal ambition), it was effective because in the last analysis it was based on the maintenance of a simple and easily explainable minimum position. It was Carranza who chose the title of Constitutionalist for his forces: it was for Constitutionalism that they fought, and it was the Constitution of 1917 that eventually sealed their success.

Constitutions

The period from the collapse of the Huertista régime to the installation of the first President under the Constitution of 1917 – that is, the period from 13 August 1914 to 1 May 1917 – is known to modern Mexican historians as the Preconstitutional Era. This is, of course, a wholly retrospective judgement. After all, it came after the Constitution of 1857.

The retroactive validation of irregular methods of seizing power has been a commonplace in Latin American history. Retroactive validation is a technique with a respectable ancestry in Western political thought, going back in Christian times at least to St Thomas Aquinas, who gave it his blessing. In medieval times legitimacy – the right to rule – was conferred by the Church through ceremonies such as crowning, anointing, and investiture. In return the prospective or actual ruler was required to agree to a certain number of conditions, which sometimes he adhered to and sometimes he did not. In medieval Aragón the rights of subjects against their ruler were expressly recognized in the oath they swore, to obey only so long as the ruler should rule properly.

With the coming of secularism and the concept of power as being derived from the people, those establishing governments logically came to substitute a bargain with (or in the name of) the people for that previously made with the spiritual power. Such a document was the Social Contract of Locke or Rousseau made manifest. That of the United States was not the first of the genre, but it was the first to bear the title that later became universal, that of Constitution, which went back to medieval English legal practice.

In Latin America republican governments were established by the few, and consequently were not universally accepted. Their constitutions, therefore, came to be regarded as merely partisan documents, statements of intent that could be amended or substituted at will. It should not be thought that they were meaningless. They were very important documents. But they came to follow the transfers of power by registering changes of policy, rather than provide an agreed framework for government which might implement matters in a wide range of different ways. For this, Spanish legal rigidity, and the colonial habit of sticking to the letter of the law rather than the substance, bears much of the responsibility.

In the Spanish-speaking world the most significant base for constitutional rule was the Spanish Constitution of 1812. It was a very partisan document, the attempt of the *liberales* to fetter the king, and as such it became a model for the Liberal generation associated with the wars of liberation. It is not an easy document to summarize, not even, today, to find.[6] It contains 334 articles in ten divisions. Among its principal features are the following. The powers of government were divided between the king and the *Cortes* (the Spanish parliament); the latter being elected by universal suffrage with some important exceptions, but only indirectly. Deputies were eligible for re-election only after the interval of one *Cortes*, and could not accept offices from the king. The king had only a suspensive veto, which could be overridden. He had to take an oath to the constitution. The *Cortes* was given financial control, and to ensure its continued ability to function could neither be dissolved nor prorogued, but maintained a commission of seven members in being to keep an eye on the government when it was in recess.

The provinces were each governed by a *jefe político* appointed by the king and checked, in the French manner, by a provincial deputation. All towns of more than one thousand inhabitants were to form communes, and be governed by an *ayyuntiamiento* of magistrates, aldermen, and councillors under the presidency of the *corregidor*, the chief of police.

This constitution was of crucial importance in shaping the Mexican Constitution of 1824, a liberal document. It is interesting to notice that many of its features could be paralleled by the ancient *fueros* of the Spanish kingdoms, and that though in style it owed something to the French Constitution of 1791, it owed much more to actual military occupation of Spain by French forces. Similarly the Mexican Constitution of 1824 that was derived from it was developed in the light of Mexican experience with Iturbide, the concept of federalism derived from the United States being more a matter of terminology than actual influence.

The problem was that the restraints reasonable for a hereditary monarch after generations of absolute rule were irksome to elected Presidents chosen on what for those days was a fairly broad franchise. The conservative Constitution of 1836 was therefore at least partly a reasonable attempt to redress the balance and make government workable, as it was the expression of Santa Anna's impatience with a system that stopped him getting what he wanted. When the Liberals returned to effective power, they 'restored' the Constitution of 1824 (1846). But though, to emphasize its 'Centralist' character, the

Constitution of 1836 spoke of 'Departments' instead of 'States', the other differences were not great. And for long periods government was entirely 'provisional' and the constitution of the day had no effect.

It was Santa Anna's last period of rule that put an end to this state of affairs. Since it was entirely 'aconstitutional', the Plan of Ayutla in 1854 called for a Constitutional Convention in order to restore legal government. The convention duly met, and, with a moderate majority, appointed a drafting committee intended to scrutinize and revise the Constitution of 1824. In the changing political climate, however, the *puros* gained a majority in that committee, and opted to write an entirely new constitution. Their work eventually emerged on 5 February 1857. In fact the first government elected under that constitution lasted for only thirteen days, as we have seen, but the document itself survived foreign intervention and civil war, revolt and the Porfirian dictatorship, for over fifty years.

The most notable differences from the Constitution of 1824 referred to the Church. The 1824 document had proclaimed that 'the Mexican nation is and perpetually will be catholic, apostolic, Roman'. The 1857 charter, though issued 'in the name of God and with the authority of the Mexican people', was secular, and ultimately had added to it those parts of the Laws of the Reform restraining the powers of the Church. Although Díaz came to ignore some of those provisions, even he did not attempt to repeal them. The most important provision appeared in the constitution itself as Title 1, Article 27, which read in part:

> No corporation civil or ecclesiastical, whatever its character, denomination or object, will have the legal capacity to acquire property or to administer for itself real estate, with the sole exception of buildings intended immediately and directly for the service or object of the institution.[7]

This was, however, but one of the twenty-nine articles in Title 1 that sought to establish an essentially liberal state. Among their provisions were those for free education (Art. 3), freedom of occupation (Art. 4), religion (Art. 5), speech (Art. 6), and publication (Art. 7); the right of entry and exit from the republic (Art. 11); the abolition of imprisonment for civil debts (Art. 17); the right of habeas corpus (Art. 19); freedom from military oppression (Art. 26); and even the ultimate abolition of the death penalty, which was severely restricted (Art. 23). One of the few echoes of the United States Constitution was the reiteration of the right to possess and to bear arms 'for security and legitimate defense' (Art. 10).

The remainder of the document was, like its 1824 predecessor, quite brief. It established a Presidential system of government, but implied at least in part that ministers would be responsible to the Congress. The Congress itself was strengthened by sweeping away the old Senate and making it unicameral. Díaz was later to restore the Senate as a valuable vehicle for patronage. There was, as we have seen, no Vice-President, the President of the Supreme Court succeeding to the Presidency in the event of the demise of the chief executive. The President could not be of 'the ecclesiastical estate' and the oath which he was to take on entering office made no reference whatsoever to a Supreme Being. An important limitation of his power was a provision that he could not leave the area of the capital without the previous consent of the Congress or of its permanent commission – a restriction which Mexican Presidents, at least in normal times, seem always to have accepted as reasonable.

Amendment to the constitution required a vote of two-thirds of the Congress together with the approval of the legislatures of half the states. As has already been said, under Díaz the process of amendment was relatively straightforward, and in consequence the constitution was very extensively altered in a great many different respects. The most important of these amendments were those first introducing and then withdrawing the principle of no re-election, the creation of the Vice-Presidency, and the alteration of the law of succession. The abolition and restoration of the Senate had one curious consequence; that to this day the two Houses of the Mexican Congress meet in different, though neighbouring, buildings. Díaz had planned in the last years of his rule to incorporate both in a new Legislative Palace, but the Revolution broke out before anything had been constructed but the ironwork of the central portion bearing the dome.

Two forces combined to press for the creation of a new constitution after the death of Madero. Firstly, there was the consciousness that the old had failed in its essential purpose; that under Díaz dictatorship had always been 'constitutional'. Secondly, there was the desire to establish important new social rights – rights which were seen as being an integral part of a good social and political condition, and which were such important aspirations that they deserved no less than statement as part of the fundamental law. As we shall see, they were very much aspirations, and not fact. There was, accordingly, a good deal of 'faction constitutionalism' in their enunciation at this stage. But those who were impatient for their realization could take some small comfort from the fact that at least the Constitution of 1917 finally ended the controversy about the gains of 1857.

[1] Calvert, op. cit., 152.
[2] Calvert, op. cit., 181, 186.

3 Querido Moheno, *Mi actuación política despues de la Decena Trágica* (Mexico, Ediciones Botas, 1939), 25–41.

4 See also George Malcolm Stephenson's account of the negotiations in his *John Lind of Minnesota* (Minneapolis, University of Minnesota Press, 1935).

5 There is still no complete biography of Carranza. See Daniel Moreno, *Venustiano Carranza, Álvaro Obregón, Plutarco Elías Calles* (Mexico, Libro-Mex, 1960).

6 A good account is Karl Marx in New York *Daily Tribune* (24 November 1854), anthologized in K. Marx and F. Engels, *Revolution in Spain* (London, Lawrence & Wishart, 1939). For the texts of it and of early Mexican constitutions see Felipe Tena Ramírez, *Leyes Fundamentales de México, 1808–1967* (Mexico, Ed. Porrua, 3rd edn., 1967).

7 *Constitución federal de los Estados-Unidos Mexicanos* . . ., Mexico, 1857.

The Revolution XI: Tampico

ON 9 APRIL 1914 Mexico's second largest port, Tampico, was under siege from Constitutionalist forces. Owing to its low-lying situation it was extremely hard to defend from a land attack, and because of the presence of rich oil-wells, refineries, and storage tanks any battle in its vicinity was likely to be hazardous. United States, British, and German vessels were all stationed in the port to look after the interests of their nationals. Like their compatriots ashore, their officers had an exaggerated faith in the value of landing troops to do this.

The whaleboat that went ashore from the United States cruiser *Dolphin* on the morning of 9 April was, in fact, only going to pick up supplies of petrol. However, the regular supplies being exhausted, it went to land at a point some distance from the usual area, and, as it happened, very close to the Federal front line. In the circumstances it was not wholly surprising that, although the whaleboat was flying the United States flag at both ends and its sailors were in uniform, two of them were arrested at gunpoint by members of the state militia and marched a short distance through the deserted streets to the headquarters for questioning, before being released with profuse apologies. The ensign in charge of the boat reported the matter to his superior, and he in turn reported it to Rear Admiral Mayo, commanding the force. Mayo decided that the satisfaction offered was insufficient, and by so doing turned the trivial incident into a pretext for intervention.[1]

Mayo demanded that the Federal commander hoist an American flag at a convenient spot and salute it. On this he was quite inflexible. It did not occur to him that since his government did not recognize the government of Mexico, he was making rather a ludicrous request. It was, in fact, one which the Mexicans, with their punctilious attitude to such matters, were bound to refuse. Once the demand had been made, however, President Wilson seized upon the incident as an opportunity to deal a mortal blow to the government of the hated Huerta. The matter was taken up directly with Huerta through the American chargé d'affaires in Mexico City, Nelson O'Shaughnessy, and a major diplomatic incident had been created. It only remained for Wilson to order the Atlantic Fleet to Mexican waters to make an armed conflict almost inevitable.

When the salute was refused–giving the Huerta government the only real moment of popularity it ever enjoyed–the regular response of the United States fleet would be, in the custom of the day, to seize the port as a reprisal, or, perhaps, to bombard it. Bombardment of Tampico could have resulted in a fearful holocaust. It was in any case illegal in international law, since the port had no sea defences. And landing troops would have had to be done in small boats, and been costly in lives, even had it been effective. In fact the question was never put to the test. When he had received reinforcements and was preparing to land, Mayo, much to his astonishment, was ordered instead to steam south to Vera Cruz.

The reason why the landing was ordered at Vera Cruz was quite simple; the United States consul there had reported that the steamship *Ypiranga*–the same that had carried Díaz into exile–was due to dock on the 21st with a large cargo of arms and ammunition for the Federal forces. On 20 April Wilson asked approval from the United States Congress for his intervention; then, while the Senate still debated, in the early hours of the morning he ordered the American commander, Admiral Fletcher, to seize the customs house at once before the arms could be removed. Admiral Mayo, who had been withdrawn from Tampico to aid the intervention, was left outside Tampico harbour unable in any way to contribute or to aid the Americans in the city who had been relying on him for protection.

President Wilson seems to have had no realization that the landing at Vera Cruz might be opposed. He believed that the Mexicans were as anxious to get rid of Huerta as he was, and would instinctively grasp the rightness of his cause. Instinctively, since he had no way of enlightening them, and in any case did not even try to do so.

The Mexican Federal commander, General Maass, was in a difficult position. On paper, he had a substantial force. However, most of his men came from the local jail, and since the majority had been sent there in the first instance for deserting from the army, not too much confidence could be placed in their fighting abilities. On the other hand, like every other Federal official, the general knew of the notorious law of 1862 which prescribed death as the penalty for any collaboration, however well-intentioned, with a foreign invader. He determined to put up a token resistance and then retreat to await further orders. Orders from his superior officer, General Blanquet, arrived just too late to prevent bloodshed. Confident in their success in occupying the waterfront area, the party of marines advancing on the customs house were fired upon from cover. The shots inaugurated two days of street-fighting in which nineteen Americans and more than two hundred Mexicans died, and forty-seven Americans and more than three hundred Mexicans were wounded.

Eventually on the afternoon of the second day, with the aid of shell-fire from the naval guns in the harbour, armed resistance was crushed. More than six thousand Americans were landed to begin the vast task of tidying up, and, to their considerable embarrassment, they found themselves in complete charge of the city, none of the civil authorities being willing to aid them in any way.

The Huertistas called for a united front against the foreign invader. The Americans were, however, under the strictest orders not to advance outside the city–whatever the provocation. There was rioting in Mexico City and Monterrey; in the Pacific ports; and, most dangerously, in Tampico. At Tampico the American civilians were helpfully loaded aboard chartered ships; then, to their intense anger and grave financial loss, shipped back to the United States with virtually only what they stood up in. Those who returned to Mexico from Galveston had to do so at their own expense. So none of these local incidents gave rise to wider provocation. Rather more surprisingly, the considerable forces under General Maass received no orders to attack Vera Cruz.

The immediate effect of the American intervention was slight: it held up for a few days the Constitutionalist capture of Tampico. No doubt it held down for a time a number of troops that could have been sent north to strengthen the Federal lines. But despite Villa's victories, the Federal army was still strong, and Villa himself was diverted by Carranza to Saltillo, which he captured without resistance. Sure of himself, he now demanded of Carranza that the Carrancista generals co-ordinate their campaign with his. The Federal troops were in a bad way, retreating southward across the territory controlled by the Zacatecas revolutionaries under the Gutiérrez brothers. It was the time to harry them. Villa, however, could not do this without supplies and reinforcements, and at this point Carranza, determined to exert his authority over the northern movement, might take advantage of his position at the frontier to hold up supplies of arms and ammunition to Villa's army. For these he had to return to Torreón.

Carranza, however, had a much subtler move in store for him. In his capacity as his nominal superior, Carranza now demanded that Villa detach a brigade from his main force for the capture of Zacatecas. In his impulsive way, when he found that his arguments fell on deaf ears, Villa resigned. Carranza accepted his resignation with enthusiasm, but Villa's subordinate commanders, led by Ángeles, protested as a body. None was willing to take his place. Villa resumed his command and set off with his entire army for Zacatecas, which he stormed on 23 June, allowing the Federals once more to retreat southwards. Regarding this as an act of insubordination, and explaining it as such to his other commanders, Carranza now shut off supplies of coal and ammunition completely and immobilized Villa's forces.

All attempts by other commanders to mediate failed utterly. But it did not matter. Carranza had gained time for his plans. While this tragicomedy had been playing itself out in the northern strongholds, General Álvaro Obregón with the Sonoran Division of the north-west had been marching down the west coast of Mexico. Marching, because south of Tepic the railway had not yet been finished and it was necessary to manhandle supplies and guns over more than a hundred miles of craggy, mountainous country. Carranza was pinning all his hopes on the Sonoran general, whom he hoped and believed was entirely loyal to him personally. Then on 8 July the forces of Obregón marched into Guadalajara–second only to Mexico City in central Mexico–and, accordingly, within easy striking distance of the capital by rail.

Huerta, though he had gone through the motions of holding 'elections' the previous Sunday, saw that he had lost. On the following day he nominated President of the Supreme Court Francisco S. Carbajal Secretary of External Relations. On 15 July he submitted his resignation to the Chamber of Deputies, and fled to Puerto México in the Isthmus, where he embarked for exile on the German cruiser *Dresden*.

It will be recalled that the principal purpose in seizing the customs house at Vera Cruz was to deny Huerta the arms consignment due to arrive there on the German liner *Ypiranga*. The *Ypiranga* had duly arrived on the second day of the fighting, and the American naval authorities had boarded her and ordered her master not to discharge her cargo. This brought a stiff protest to the United States government from the German ambassador in Washington, as a result of which the ship was allowed to proceed, though not to discharge at Vera Cruz. She proceeded instead to the United States, and from there to Puerto México where she discharged the arms. The search had, however, cast an interesting light on the morality of arms supply, inasmuch as it emerged that the arms had originally come, not from Germany, but from the United States.

The United States government clearly believed that with Huerta gone, a general agreement of the warring parties could be obtained. To relieve themselves of the embarrassment of having landed in Vera Cruz they had agreed to the mediation of the governments of Argentina, Brazil, and Chile, and the 'ABC' powers' representatives were meeting at Niagara Falls, New York State, in the hope of bringing about a settlement. It was, despite this, much too late by this time for a negotiated settlement. The revolutionaries generally did not want a repetition of the *interinato*. Too much harm had been done in that time. They were determined to extirpate the old ruling order, even if (or especially if) like Carranza himself, they had been part of it. Besides, the Carbajal who was now acting President was the same man who had negotiated the Treaty of Ciudad Juárez on behalf of Díaz. He survived for almost a month, trying vainly to negotiate with anyone who looked like negotiating. No terms were offered but unconditional surrender.

There was still the hope that the revolutionaries would quarrel. This hope ended with the fall of Irapuato on the last day of July; Villa could not now advance on Mexico City because the forces of Obregón lay in the way. In the hope of saving lives Carbajal now tried to disband all Federal forces before the Constitutionalists arrived, but left a sufficient garrison in the capital to prevent it falling into the hands of the Zapatistas in Morelos. Finally he fled to Veracruz, leaving authority in the capital to Eduardo Iturbide, governor of the Federal District. On 13 August Iturbide signed the Treaty of Teoloyucan, by which the capital was to be handed over intact to General Obregón. On 15 August, a month after the flight of Huerta, Obregón's forces occupied the capital, Constitutionalist forces replacing the Federals at every point. The capital had been saved once again from the Zapatistas. But Carranza himself still had to reckon with them, and others like them—and with Villa too.

Adolfo Ruiz Cortines

On the day that the Americans landed, no one had much time for the ordinary residents of Vera Cruz. They were not wholly surprised: one very old lady remembered not only the arrival of the French in 1862 but also the previous visit of the Americans in 1847. When the shooting began, Doña María Ruiz, widow of Don Adolfo Ruiz Tejada, together with her sisters and her daughter María, took refuge in a warehouse belonging to the firm of Díaz Hermanos. It was Dr Díaz who took charge of the Mexican flag that had been flying over the Palacio Municipal.

Blockaded in the city, it was some time before Doña María could get word from her only son, who was serving with the Constitutionalists on the staff of Robles Domínguez. Adolfo Ruiz Cortines was a posthumous child, his father having died shortly before his birth in the city of Vera Cruz on 30 December 1890. His widowed mother had devoted every effort to bringing up her two children and to giving them the best education that was available. To begin with, this was the tuition given by the college under the care of their parish priest, Father Jerónimo Díaz. A Spaniard by birth, Father Díaz was remembered for his frankness and openness; a convivial person himself, he gave a liberal education. Ruiz Cortines (throughout his life he insisted on the use of his mother's name conjointly with his father's) then passed on to the Instituto Veracruzano.

Here he was exceptionally fortunate. In 1885 the governor of Veracruz, General Enríquez, had empowered a twenty-eight-year-old Swiss to draw up a comprehensive plan for education in the state. The life work of Enrique C. Rébsamen, together with that of Enrique Laubscher, a Bavarian disciple of Froebel who became the director of the Model School in Orizaba in 1883, had given Vera Cruz the best system of public education in the country. The young Ruiz Cortines[2] looked back on the four years of his baccalaureate, and on the teachers under whom he had had the good fortune to study, with such gratitude that in later life, when he was governor of Veracruz himself, he wrote a memoir on his old professor, Don Miguel Macias.

In fact he should have stayed for five years. But his family could not afford it, and it was time for him to get a job. In those days almost all the trade of Vera Cruz, and much of that of Mexico, was in Spanish hands. And Ruiz Cortines went to work for a large textile store owned by a Spaniard whose methodical and businesslike ways were enforced by the iron discipline customary in those days. Although his studies at the Institute had not been completed, he had shown great promise in accountancy and at the Casa Aragón his task was to learn the trade. The proprietor of the café next door recalled that he was one employee of the firm to whom he had never, as was his custom, had to lend money. 'You know he was always very meticulous', he explained.

Like any youth of his age he argued and disputed over coffee or wine; he also played baseball. Though very correct in his dress, he was not particularly sociable, nor did he enjoy dances. He preferred to observe and to discuss. And he was not impressed by the high society of the port, with its inflated provincial pretensions. He knew that his future with the Casa Aragón was a limited one, and like other young Mexicans of his age resolved to try his fortune in Mexico City, the true centre of culture and opportunity. He did better than he then knew, for the firm vanished in the turmoil of the Revolution, and in 1952 it had become a guest-house.

Ruiz Cortines left for Mexico City in December 1912, travelling to the chilly heights of the plateau by the spectacular route of the Mexican Railway. Before he left he had mingled with the crowd that had watched Díaz board the *Ypiranga* and Victoriano Huerta taking leave of him, and had read the accounts of the abortive revolt of Félix Díaz. He was not a stranger to politics. But at first in the capital he was very much on his own. With nothing to do in the evenings but to walk around the streets before returning to his lodgings, he absorbed at first hand that historical lesson. Then on 10 February along with thousands of others he read in *El Imparcial* of the uprising in the Zócalo, and of the appointment of the same Victoriano Huerta as chief of what were optimistically called the loyal forces. During the *Decena Trágica*, like many others, the young *veracruzano* left his lodgings when there was a break in the firing, in order to get food and if possible news. It was a dramatic education for the liberal youth to see at first hand the carnage and the destruction. He was filled with indignation at the betrayal which brought it to an end, but for those living in the capital in those days, with only scanty information about the very little that was going on in the north, it was hard to know how to carry indignation into action. What was different about Ruiz Cortines was that he actually did so.

The engineer Alfredo Robles Domínguez was already well known in the capital as one of Madero's earliest and most active supporters. It was he who, on horseback, heralded the arrival of his leader into the capital in 1911. A *morelense* who had taken part in the celebrated Leyvista election campaign of 1909, he had, under Madero, acted as one of his chief political organizers; his brother, Gabriel, was Madero's emissary to Zapata. On the fall of Madero, he had taken the bold decision to remain in the capital and had established contact with Carranza, who had appointed him as his agent there. Robles Domínguez badly needed able and active volunteers for the work of Constitutionalist propaganda.

Ruiz Cortines was one of these volunteers. It was dangerous work, for one of the chief targets of their efforts was the subversion of the Federal military forces. No one was under any illusions as to what they could expect at the hands of the Federals if they were caught. However, it was those who talked to the high officers in the smart cafés, like Alberto J. Pani, who were in the most danger. The young Ruiz Cortines dealt with lesser fry, and in his neat, inconspicuous dress he looked just what he had been until so recently, a young commercial clerk, like all of his type chronically short of money. Anything further removed from the popular image of the revolutionary could hardly be imagined.

His transformation into a civil servant occurred when Mexico City fell and Robles Domínguez was appointed governor of the Federal District by Carranza. It was an unenviable job. Carranza despised the capital as a nest of reactionaries. His followers (with some important exceptions) regarded it as a city to be sacked. The generals occupied the rich mansions on the Paseo de la Reforma; the junior officers and men broke into the stores and took anything for which they had a fancy. Huerta's police force had been kept in being to maintain order. It was now disbanded, and order began to collapse altogether. In all this turmoil, Robles Domínguez lacked the firmness that alone could have done anything to check the reign of the mob. Belatedly Carranza withdrew him and replaced him by General Heriberto Jara, and Ruiz Cortines remained as an aide to the new governor.

He had still been an active propagandist at the time of the American landing at Vera Cruz. His mother knew nothing of the danger he was in. Only after the fall of the capital to the Constitutionalist army had regular communication been renewed between the city and the port. However, Constitutionalist functionaries were not encouraged to visit the occupied city, where a great many supporters of the old régime had taken refuge in the vain hope that the Americans would not abandon them to the Constitutionalists. Nevertheless, Woodrow Wilson eventually found himself forced by domestic political considerations to order the troops to return home, and since Carranza as usual merely refused to answer repeated requests for guarantees of freedom from reprisals (especially in the shape of dual taxation), the forces were ultimately withdrawn on 23 December 1914 leaving the negotiations in the air. General Jara was ordered to occupy the city for the Constitutionalists, and the young Ruiz Cortines, now a captain in the Constitutionalist army, entered his native city just in time to see the last American ship leave the harbour.

He was not at home long, for, after Christmas, he was off again to join his old chief, Robles Domínguez, whom Carranza had named governor of Guerrero. He was attached to the headquarters of the Army of the South and promoted to first captain. However, the Constitutionalists were not to remain long in Guerrero; worsening relations between the factions led to their expulsion at the hands of the Zapatistas. He then moved north and continued his active service at the headquarters of General Jacinto B. Treviño, who was defending Constitutionalist positions in the State of Tamaulipas against the Villistas. There Ruiz Cortines was promoted to major and appointed paymaster-general. In these years, like so many other young Mexicans, he came in contact with people from all walks of life and all parts of the country. None of those who experienced this could ever again forget that their nation was much wider than the Valley of Mexico, and that political and social change had now moved out of the control of the lawyers in the capital into the hands of the soldiers in the field. When we come across him again, it will be at a critical moment in Mexican history, and it will not be in a city of any kind.

The City of Mexico

Of course the city of Mexico should never have been built where it was. The facts of its location, development, and expansion all fly in the face of commonsense. Yet they all have their particular reasons, and since it is where it is, the Mexicans have made the best of it.

And what a best it is. Today Mexico City is the third largest city in the world in terms of population, and one of the largest in terms of area. In 1970 eight million people lived in the metropolitan area, a concentration of population exceeded only in aggregate by New York and Tokyo. Its saving virtue is that it is not dense in proportion. Mexico City has expanded into the Valley of Mexico from which it takes its name, until a large proportion of it now lies outside the Federal District which is supposed to be its administrative unit. The governor of the Federal District, however, a personal appointee of the President, is certainly the world's most powerful civic executive, and that makes a considerable difference.

The city lies where it does, not because of economics, like so many other cities, but because of politics. Cortés as a deliberate act built his new capital on the site of Aztec Tenochtitlan, despite the fact that Tenochtitlan was built on artificial islands in the waters of Lake Texcoco, and joined to the land only by causeways and wooden bridges. He did so because he believed it was essential to show the Aztecs that the Conquest was a fact. Its principal symbolic act was the building of the huge cathedral, the first on the New World mainland, on the site of the great pyramid or *teocalli* of the Sun god. From the date of its building the vast stone edifice began to sink into the marshy ground of the lake bed, until today it is one storey lower than when it was built. And this has been the fate of every building built in the capital until modern times, to sink and to lean, until the frequent earthquakes impart cracks and twists of their own and the whole structure begins to look faintly improbable. Fortunately the splendid colonial Baroque retains its dignity even under these trying conditions, but the Palacio de Bellas Artes, for example, built in the last days of the *Porfiriato* in the style of the French Second Empire, has not worn so well, and the passer-by on foot finds the undulations of the pavements difficult for a constitution already under another kind of strain.

For Mexico City was not just built on a swamp–it was built on a swamp more than a mile above sea level. It is not long before the visitor notices the shortness of breath, particularly perhaps by waking up in the middle of the night. The inhabitants of the capital have long since suited themselves to it by adopting the stately pace and relaxed style of movement which makes it more tolerable. Only the children seem quite unaffected.

The colonial rulers of Mexico soon found the site of Mexico City a considerable nuisance from the point of view of expansion. The obvious solution was to drain some of the water out of the lake. Unfortunately this was a very difficult thing to do, as the ring of high mountains that surrounds the Valley of Mexico was almost unbroken, and to dig a tunnel through them with only manual labour and no adequate protection against landslip, explosion of gases, etc., was an incredibly rash project. Nevertheless one man, Enrico Martínez, believed it could be done, and in 1580 he made a proposal to that effect to the viceroy. After the usual interminable bureaucratic delays, the project was approved, and a later viceroy dug the first turf in 1607. The work continued literally for generations. In 1708, after a hundred years, the excavation, the Tajo de Nochistongo, was able to carry off some of the surplus water, but was still not deep enough to be really effective, and, despite the fact that work continued on it until 1789, flooding continued to be a major problem in the city after the heavy tropical downpours which occur regularly at certain seasons. Even to this day a sudden rainstorm in the mountains can bring flooding on the western side of the city almost without warning.

In the nineteenth century, with the drastic rise of the city's population, the inability to drain the valley became more serious. The consumption of water rose, so lowering the lakes and with them the level of the watertable. The swampy base began to contract more rapidly, accelerating the process of shrinkage and subsidence. Not only buildings and streets were affected, but also drains, while periodic flooding continued to bring havoc to the low-lying parts of the city. In 1895 Díaz invited the British firm of S. Pearson and Son to bring modern mechanical methods to bear on the problem. The Grand Canal, leading from the lake to two new tunnels through the mountainside near the Tajo de Nochistongo across the State of Mexico, was created with steam dredgers and for the first time the plans of Enrico Martínez were actually realized.

What was not appreciated, however, was the drastic effect that this would have on the stability of the city's foundations. Since 1900 the once enormous Lake Texcoco has been reduced to a small stretch of shallow ornamental water, while of the lake gardens so much admired by Cortés there remains only the so-called floating gardens of Xochimilco, where picturesque ornamental, flower-covered punts pass and repass slowly with their loads of Mexican families on weekend pleasure expeditions and American tourists photographing one another. The results have not been entirely happy, but they are nothing compared with the effect on the city centre. There the main drains now flow uphill and sewage has to be pumped. But where to? The Grand Canal itself has reversed its gradient over the first mile and a half. Ultimately the decision was taken to bypass the old system rather than to reconstruct it, and with the completion of the Western Interceptor to carry off the flood waters from the mountains, present-day Mexico City is once again able to cope in some degree with its drainage problems.[3]

What has made the problem so urgent has been the continued dramatic increase in the size of the city. Little remains now of the old city except the narrow streets around the Zócalo, or main square, and the few colonial buildings they contain are now sandwiched between huge department stores. Beyond the Alameda, or central park, with its kiosks, seats, and balloon-sellers, begins nineteenth-century Mexico, where the two great avenues of Insurgentes and the Paseo de la Reforma intersect. The Paseo de la Reforma, a gigantic boulevard intersected by other streets at *glorietas* (roundabouts), combines its Second Empire origins with the hotels and travel bureaux of the modern international world. Here is the Mexico City of the air traveller or businessman.

The city of the Mexicans is somewhere else again–in the old suburbs with their streets named after the capitals of Europe, in the large satellite towns of the outer ring, and in the shanty towns of the newest arrivals, the squatters and the urban workers. Though rehousing goes on at a frenetic pace (it is nothing to Mexico to cover a square mile with uniform blocks of workers' flats), the population pressure is still felt in every part of the city bar one–the fantastic homes of the rich built on the old lava flow known as the Pedregal. However, Mexico has solved the general Latin American problem of shanty towns on the approaches to the city in her own inimitable way: by offering piles of concrete blocks and cement to anyone who wants to build a proper home on otherwise waste land. A complication is that some otherwise evidently respectable members of the middle classes actually prefer to live in the shanty towns. As they do not officially exist, one cannot have an address, and if one does not have an address, one avoids taxes. But there is no escaping the fact that the outer suburbs of Mexico City are often dreary and frequently haphazard, like suburbs anywhere on the American continent. What redeems them is the evident vitality of the city as a whole, and its magnificent setting.

How such a magnificent whole evolved out of the disease- and pestilence-ridden city of the nineteenth century is largely a story of transport. The structure of the present city was laid in the 1880s and 1890s by the development of the tramway network–the creation of Fred Stark Pearson, a Canadian, who died in the sinking of the *Lusitania* in 1915. In the centre of the city the trams ran along the streets; outside the centre their tracks ran on their own rights of way, often flanked by the paths that in modern times were to become major avenues. The tramways were fast and cheap–the electric power for them came from the hydroelectric plant at Necaxa in the State of Puebla, on a headstream of the Tecolutla River. In 1916 there were in all 193 miles of electric tramways radiating from the capital to places as remote as Tizapán, Atzcapotzalco, and Xochimilco, and the limits established then have until very recently continued to shape the city of the present day.

Meanwhile the motor-car came on the scene. It was too late sub-stantially to alter the course of the Revolution, but it undoubtedly did much to promote the extraordinary development of the country after 1920. It had every advantage, for Mexican railways never really recovered from the destruction and over-use that accompanied the fighting. Though they remained substantially intact, they did not continue to expand, and it was only in the 1950s that major extensions were made to the network and Mérida, Yucatán, finally linked to the capital by rail. The motor-car, on the other hand, became the basic vehicle of the new post-revolutionary élite, the hard-drinking generals and their bodyguards, driving from the capital to their newly-acquired haciendas and back again. Victoriano Huerta conducted his state business in a motor-car; Pancho Villa was assassinated in one; but Cárdenas was to use his as a means of reaching parts of the country that had never seen their President before, and that was what counted.

Modern Mexico City would be inconceivable without it. The basic transport is the fleet of tiny taxis that ply everywhere, the most famous of which are the hordes that ply to and fro on the Paseo de la Reforma, taking individual passengers any distance on their route for only one peso (8 cents U.S.). The traffic moves with a freedom and self-expres-sion that is wholly Mexican.

In 1968 the continued challenge of the city's expansion to the capacity of its transport system was met by drastic reappraisal. The old tramcars which had carried so many generations of Mexicans so cheaply were finally scrapped. Instead the bus fleet was expanded and work begun on the Metro. The first line of the new underground railway, built in the French style with neat square cars with rubber tyres, ran initially from the airport past the Zócalo to Chapultepec. Two other lines were under construction at the time of its opening, forming a triangle around the old centre of the viceregal city.

The soft ground offered little resistance to the excavators, but the technical problems of drainage were considerable and there was some hesitation at the possible effects of earthquakes. An interesting by-product of the excavation was a mass of new evidence about ancient Tenochtitlan, now far underground. The main purpose was served when, for a low fare, Chapultepec, once the seat of the viceroys and of Presidents, but now a cultural and recreational centre for the people, was brought within reach of literally millions of people who travelled on the system in its first year of operation.

In the twentieth century three men stand out among those who have sought to beautify, develop, and improve the national capital. The first, now little remembered by present-day Mexicans, but none the less important, was José Y. Limantour himself, who as Secretary of *Hacienda* devoted particular attention to the city. It is to him, and to

Díaz's last governor of the Federal District, Guillermo de Landa y Escandón, that we owe the principal monuments of the period: the Independence Column, the monument to Juárez, the Palacio de Bellas Artes, which though an ugly building serves a praiseworthy purpose, and, more important, the consolidation of the new avenues with the old city.

Left unfinished at the Revolution was the vast steel structure designed to take the dome of the projected Legislative Palace, which stood for twenty years thereafter in the middle of the Plaza de la República, until Alberto J. Pani became Secretary of *Hacienda* for the second time. In his youth he had worked on the structure of the Palacio de Bellas Artes which, though complete outside, had yet to be completed inside. He set to work on this project and in July 1932 work was resumed. After the resignation of President Ortiz Rubio and his own reappointment, he learned that the remains of the Legislative Palace were to be sold for scrap. Immediately he pressed the President to allow him instead to turn them into a Monument to the Revolution, and this was done. At the foot of the monument were in due course reinterred with great ceremony the remains of Francisco I. Madero, Venustiano Carranza, and Álvaro Obregón, and on the death of Lázaro Cárdenas in 1970 he was buried there beside them.

Cárdenas himself, however, was not a lover of large cities, and he and his immediate successors devoted relatively little attention to this aspect of their work. The appointment in 1952 by President Ruiz Cortines of Ernesto P. Uruchurtu as governor of the Federal District was nevertheless taken as a sign that the government had now recognized the problems of its expansion were becoming acute. For sixteen years, until 1968, Uruchurtu remained in charge of the district, carrying out a mammoth programme of public works for the construction of housing, improved markets, urban renewal, the care and conservation of public works, and many other things besides. The construction of the Metro was the culmination of his work. It was the longest period since the Revolution in which a sustained and continued effort was made to cope with the problems of so large a city, and few other people have seen so many major projects through from inception to completion.

Voices: Constitutionalist Era

' "Yes", said the doctor, "there has been some little trouble. The General has not been able to walk for two months from rheumatism.... And sometimes, he is in great pain and comforts himself with *aguardiente*.... Tonight he tried to shoot his mother. He always tries to shoot his mother ... because he loves her very much". The doctor peeped at himself in the mirror, and twisted his mustache. "This *revolución*. Do not mistake. It is a fight of the poor against the rich. I was very poor before the *revolución* and now I am very rich" '.[4]

'We received instructions [from Carranza] to remain in the Chamber of Deputies, in our role of open opposition, and to join in any act that might weaken the authority of the usurper'.[5]

'I learned what I know about Mexico, which is not as much as I should desire, by hearing a large number of liars tell me all about it. At first I was very much confused because the narratives did not tally, and then one day when I had a lucid interval it occurred to me that it was because what I was told was not true'.[6]

'. . . in the natural order of things Obregón will be obliged to betray his chief'.[7]

'That afternoon at about five o'clock, Huerta arrived at the apartment where Madero was confined. He addressed Madero as "Mr President", but Madero interrupted, saying, "Oh, so I am still President". Huerta then began again: "Mr ex-President, I have already notified the Senate and the American Ambassador regarding what I have done, and they both approve my actions. Since I won the battle of Bachimba" – "Even then you were already a traitor", interposed Madero. This interruption caused Huerta to forget the speech he had been about to make, and after a few words, he took his leave. He shook hands with Mr Lascurain and Mr Hernandez, but on reaching Madero the latter refused to extend his hand. General Huerta then offered his hand to Mr Vazquez Tagle, who said: "I also refuse to shake hands with you, General". Huerta hesitated, then turned away saying "God be with you" '.[8]

'This amazing proceeding took place without a single word of warning, or declaration of war. But still more amazing, the Americans declared that it was not an act of war, and they were at peace with the Mexican Republic'.[9]

> 'In nineteen hundred and ten
> Madero was imprisoned
> In the National Palace
> The eighteenth of February
>
> 'Four days he was imprisoned
> In the Hall of the Intendancy
> Because he did not wish
> To renounce the Presidency
>
> 'Then Blanquet and Félix Díaz
> Martyred him there

They were the hangmen
Feeding on his hate

'They crushed . . .
Until he fainted
With play of cruelty
To make him resign'.[10]

'Huerta has a handsome, quiet-faced wife and eleven children.
These and a rented house (he has never lived at Chapultepec or at
the Palace) are, up to now, his only apparent worldly possessions. I
doubt whether he has the inclination or takes the time for an undue
amount of grafting. He is, from what I hear, very canny in the matter
of human equations, and seems full of vitality and a sort of tireless,
Indian perseverance. They say that the more he drinks, the clearer
his brain becomes.'

'[8 November 1913] N. finally ran Huerta down yesterday in the
El Globo café. He received the usual affectionate *abrazo*, and they had a
copita together, but Huerta never mentioned Lind any more than if he
were non-existent, and shied off at the remotest hint of "business".
Instead, he asked N., "How about the girls?" ("Y las muchachas?") a
phrase often used for opening or closing a conversation, in these
climes, much as we would ask about the weather. . . .'[11]

[1] This account follows Robert E. Quirk, *An Affair of Honor: Woodrow Wilson and
the Occupation of Vera Cruz* (New York, McGraw-Hill, 1964).
[2] The definitive source for his early years is Bernardo Ponce, *Adolfo Ruiz
Cortines, ensayo para una biografía política* (Mexico, Biografías Gandesa, 1952). This is
a 'campaign biography', but a good one of its genre.
[3] David J. Fox, 'Man-water relationships in metropolitan Mexico', *The Geographical Review*, LV, 4 (1965), 523.
[4] Reed, op. cit., 57.
[5] Félix Fulgencio Palavicini, *Mi vida revolucionaria* (Mexico, Ediciones Botas,
1937), 157.
[6] Statement attributed to Woodrow Wilson, 1919, by Carlos Pereyra, *México
Falsificado* (Mexico, Editorial Polis, 1949), I, 229.
[7] Francisco Bulnes, *The whole truth about Mexico. President Wilson's responsibility*
(New York, M. Bulnes Book Company, 1916), 352.
[8] Ramón Prida, *From Despotism to Anarchy* (El Paso, Texas, El Paso Printing
Company, 1914), 173.
[9] Hohler, op. cit., 191.
[10] Constitutionalist *corrida*, circa 1915, in Reed, op. cit., 65.
[11] O'Shaughnessy, *A Diplomat's Wife in Mexico* (New York, Harper & Brothers,
1916), 12, 41–2.

The Revolution XII: The Convention

THE STRUGGLE BETWEEN CARRANZA AND VILLA had already begun, as we have seen, before the defeat of Huerta. That between Carranza and Zapata was now to begin. The particular form it was to take, and the consequences for all three men, were determined by the actions of August 1914, while in Europe armies were similarly massing to change the face of the world.

By the Plan of Guadalupe, Carranza's original manifesto, he himself held only the irregular post of First Chief. On the occupation of Mexico City, the Plan assumed and all his supporters took for granted, he would then become Provisional President. With the constitutional order suffering only a slight check, the new government would then go on to remake Mexico in the Constitutional image. There were two problems about this. The first was that, if Carranza became Provisional President, he would be debarred by the principle of 'no re-election' from becoming President for a full term. This limitation he was as determined to evade as had been Huerta before him. And the second was that, for reasons that no one has ever been able to explain in creditable terms, Carranza did not just want to beat the Huertistas, he wanted to punish them. And this he could not do under a constitutional order in which his hands would be bound by legal guarantees, the right of *amparo*,[1] and the possibility of open political dissent. His first step after Mexico City had been occupied, therefore, was to suspend constitutional guarantees and to empower irregular tribunals to proceed against all who had fought against him on the precedent of Juárez's law of 1862.

Carranza's inflexibility made it impossible for him to see how the innocent suffered from his methods. The orgy of revenge and reprisal that took place in the capital did not disturb him. But it did disturb diplomatists who took it as evidence that Carranza had a very tenuous hold on the country he purported to govern. It may in part have been an inheritance from the *Porfiriato*, when to say a thing was equivalent to having done it. Carranza was a *caudillo* in the antique mould. But by this stage the young men who had done the fighting were beginning to assert themselves, and they were beginning to ask for action at once.

So although the First Chief acted according to precedent when he sent out a message to Zapata to come and meet him in the capital, times had changed since Madero had done the same thing and Zapata had gone as a matter of course. Treachery was rife. The Constitutionalists stood for the restoration of the legitimate government of Madero – popularly they were always known as *Maderistas*; never as Constitutionalists. But Zapata had been in rebellion against Madero himself, and he had little time for his self-proclaimed successor, whose Plan he considered 'more worthless' than what had gone before. The price of Zapata's adherence to any cause, and especially this one, was guaranteed agrarian reform. The Constitutionalists would have to accept the Plan of Ayala. Nothing less would do.

Carranza was invited to come to Morelos. He did not do so, probably, to do him full credit, for fear of his dignity rather than for fear of his life. He sent two emissaries instead. They found the Zapatistas inflexible. By this time it was already apparent that there was dissension in other quarters too. To assert his authority, and to ensure that as far as possible he could control any settlement that might take place, Carranza summoned a 'junta of chiefs' to meet in Mexico City on 1 October, and made no reply directly to Zapata. In short, he treated him, just as he had previously treated Villa, as a rebellious subordinate.

Matters were in the meantime passing out of his control. His leading general, Obregón, who had hitherto been entirely loyal, was now in the north talking to Villa about a settlement. He could not see why the First Chief should not now assume the Provisional Presidency, and agreed with Villa to settle all points of difference. To avoid being bound by this agreement, Carranza said that the matter could only be settled by the junta. Before it met, he made determined efforts to strengthen his position by securing recognition from the United States. However, no progress in that direction could be made without agreeing to President Wilson's request for guarantees before handing over Vera Cruz, though in principle the Americans were willing and even anxious to withdraw at once.

Meanwhile Obregón had again left the capital for the north in order to confer with Villa. He found that explosive personality in a difficult mood, obviously suspicious of his intentions. In the middle of their conference a telegram arrived announcing the outbreak of fighting between the forces of the Constitutionalist General Hill and the Villistas under Governor Mayortena of Sonora. Bad feeling between these two had been endemic for some time, and Obregón had leant over backwards to stop it coming to a clash. Now there was an angry scene between Villa and Obregón, whom he accused of breaking their earlier agreement. He demanded the immediate withdrawal of the Constitutionalist forces. Obregón refused. Villa threatened to have him shot. Villa's secretary helpfully summoned a squad of soldiers for the purpose. But Obregón refused to budge. A few minutes later, his anger evaporated, Villa was enveloping him in an *abrazo* and declaring his undying friendship for him. Subsequently the Constitutionalist general was treated to dinner and a ball held in his honour.

Villa too was now pinning his hopes on what was coming to be called the Convention of Revolutionary Chiefs. The change of name was significant. A Convention would be a sovereign body, empowered decisively to regulate affairs in the country. It was seen less as a constituent body than as a body competent to rule in its own right, in the fashion of the French Revolutionary Convention. In order to ensure a majority in it, Villa was angling for an alliance with the Zapatistas, who were, for similar reasons, willing to reciprocate. While Obregón was still with him in Chihuahua, he sent a telegram to Carranza demanding Zapatista representation.

At the same time that Carranza received this, he also heard from Sonora that Obregón had ordered Hill to withdraw his troops. Putting two and two together, he came to the conclusion that Obregón was now a prisoner in Villa's hands, and if this were so, a Villista attack on the capital was likely to follow. He therefore ordered the railway lines to be torn up. The news of this reached Villa after Obregón had already left for the capital, having, as he thought, reached a satisfactory agreement with Villa on the restoration of constitutional government, national assumption of the Villista debts, and assurances on the agrarian question. A former farmer himself, Obregón seems to have found all the demands, including the last, quite congenial. Villa and he had parted friends, to all appearances.

Then when Obregón's train was just north of Torreón, Villa ordered him to be brought back. He had now telegraphed Carranza to renounce any allegiance he might have to him, and once more harangued Obregón on Carranza's crimes, real and imaginary. Once again, Obregón's life was in danger, but Raúl Madero (brother of the late President), Felipe Ángeles, Eugenio Aguirre Benavides, and Roque González Garza, the more far-sighted members of his entourage, prevailed upon Villa to release him. Even then Obregón was not safe. For reasons that are now lost, Villa sent orders by telegraph to waylay and shoot him when his train reached Torreón, but fortunately for him, Aguirre Benavides and another general had heard the orders and personally guaranteed him a safe-conduct south. He had left Torreón only minutes before his pursuers arrived.

All was now ready for war between Villa and the First Chief. As ever, Villa wasted no time. He was already entraining his troops when, on 30 September, he and his chiefs in the north issued their manifesto of grievances and declaration of their reasons for taking up arms. Nevertheless, there were many people on both sides who were not willing to permit a division of this magnitude in the revolutionary ranks. Carranza had eased their path by offering his resignation to the Convention, which he still hoped to control. It was, after all, one of Villa's stated grievances that the chiefs who were being summoned were all Carrançista supporters. When Obregón reached Mexico City his influence –despite, or perhaps because of, all that had gone before–was thrown behind those seeking a peaceful settlement. No sooner therefore had he reported to Carranza, than he joined Lucio Blanco, the chief mover in the peace plan, in consulting with the other Constitutionalist leaders. They agreed he should go with the delegation to Zacatecas to meet with the Villista delegates and others representing the Centre, and from there the ultimatum was sent back to Carranza that if he wanted peace, he had to accede to the formation of a Convention, not a junta, and that it would meet, not in the capital, but on the neutral territory of Aguascalientes. The seventy-nine chiefs who responded to Carranza's call and met on 1 October, therefore, faced only the question of which of them would represent the Constitutionalists.

The lawyer Luis Cabrera had organized the junta for Carranza, but the soldiers were in the majority and restive at being invited to ratify rather than discuss. They nominated as president of the body the young general from Zacatecas who had been one of the first in arms against Huerta. Significantly Eulalio Gutiérrez was young: at thirty-four the youngest man to hold high political office in Mexico since Miguel Miramón over half a century before. An ex-miner, he had been a member of the proscribed Liberal Party under Díaz and entered the Revolution as an anti-re-electionist in 1909. Both his record and his pleasant personality made him acceptable to all factions. But beside him, Carranza, when mumbling from the rostrum dressed in a blue civilian suit and wearing a long white beard, looked a figure from another age. Loyally, they refused to accept his resignation until the Convention met at Aguascalientes, but there were few who were not prepared to drop him for the sake of peace.

Aguascalientes in 1914 was a town of 45,000 people situated at an altitude of 6,280 feet some 360 miles to the north-west of Mexico City. The capital of the state of the same name, it takes its title from the many hot springs to be found in the neighbourhood. Despite its altitude, the climate is very mild and the death-rate (in peacetime) very low. Like many Mexican towns, it was well built-up in the middle, but sprawled off towards the edge, where the dirt roads degenerated rapidly into mere tracks and the pavement came to an end. The city enjoyed a passable water-supply, and the system of tunnels underneath the centre was used in part for wells or cesspools. Otherwise it was commended to the Convention more for its situation than for its amenities, though these its members would not have found very worthy of note. It was here in the Morelos Theatre on 10 October 1914 that the Convention assembled.

By almost unanimous agreement among the Carrançista generals, they had left all their civilians behind, Obregón himself being one of the most outspoken in proclaiming their irrelevance. They were, however, a selected group, as compared with the Villistas, who came in virtue of the forces they commanded. But their independence of thought was very similar, and the first action of the Convention was to proclaim itself a sovereign body and to elect a new president for their deliberations, Antonio I. Villareal, a radical Carrançista. Every delegate then swore an oath of allegiance to the Convention and signed a large Mexican flag on the rostrum, which became the banner of the Revolutionary Convention of Aguascalientes.[2]

The First Chief, who ignored the Convention to the point of not being represented, proceeded as if it did not exist. Villa was disgruntled that the chiefs in Mexico City had not accepted Carranza's resignation. However, he did send Colonel Roque González Garza as his personal agent. The Zapatistas simply did not turn up. In the end the Convention designated Felipe Ángeles to go to Morelos and carry a personal invitation on their behalf. Then on 26 October an interim delegation of twenty-six from the Army of the South, having passed unmolested through Mexico City by rail, entered the Morelos Theatre as if it were a pass that might conceal a trap.

Once convinced that they were among friends, they proceeded to demonstrate the particular combination of qualities that had made them both the most enduring focus of the Revolution and the least successful at attaining a national hearing. Even their numbers were in doubt, the figure of 60,000 men in arms claimed on their behalf seeming absurdly high for a movement that had had so little impact outside its native territory. First Paulino Martínez spoke of the agrarian cause, demanding adherence to the Plan of Ayala, and was warmly cheered by the Villistas. Then Antonio Díaz Soto y Gama, one of Zapata's secretaries and a self-proclaimed anarchist, took the rostrum. He challenged the assembly to defy both Villa and Carranza. It was time to throw off personalist feelings, to speak as Mexicans. And the fact was that Mexico was not independent, and would not be independent until she had thrown off the lies of history. At this point, carried away by his own words, he picked up the flag on the rostrum, crumpled it disdainfully, and declared that he would never sign it, for it was 'the flag of the clerical reaction headed by Iturbide'. Immediately the theatre was in uproar, a hundred guns trained upon the speaker. When silence was achieved, he said that he did not mean to profane the national colours and would follow them as loyally as any, a sentiment that his southern colleagues emphasized heavily after him. What was much more significant, if less immediately moving, was the declaration of both González Garza and Felipe Ángeles that the principles of the Plan of Ayala were those of the Division of the North, a sentiment that was backed by every Villista delegate present.

Had the southerners not insisted on not becoming members of the Convention until the Plan was accepted, things might have turned out differently. But, as ever, they were unaccustomed to parliamentary ways. By the next day, Obregón had taken their measure. When Díaz Soto repeated the claim of their numbers, he intervened to ask why they had not taken Mexico City with 60,000 men, when he had done so with only 26,000! With the Carrançista majority still in control, the Convention voted to accept the Plan of Ayala 'in principle', but Obregón followed up his advantage by producing a letter from Carranza saying he was 'disposed to retire', but if he was to do so, Villa and Zapata must do so too. Having thus rent the Convention, he worked hard to unify it behind his followers' policy, which significantly emerged as the resignation of both Carranza and Villa and the designation of a new President. Finally on 2 November the factions agreed on a compromise candidate, and a message was duly sent to Carranza notifying him that his resignation had been accepted and that the Convention had nominated as Provisional President, Eulalio Gutiérrez, the miner from Zacatecas.

Carranza had not resigned. Even if he had, it is doubtful if certain of his followers could have afforded it. Both Pablo González and Francisco Coss, the military commander in Puebla, took the decision as a sign that the Convention was dominated by Villa, an impression that Villa did nothing to dispel by moving a large number of troops south into the State of Aguascalientes. On the other hand, Lucio Blanco, Carranza's commander in the capital, showed signs of defecting, even before the election. On 1 November, therefore, the First Chief took a train to San Juan Teotihuacán on a quiet Sunday visit to the celebrated Pyramids. Once on his way, he changed trains and fled to Tlaxcala, a small town 90 miles to the east, once an important Indian citadel. From there he moved to Puebla, where his Cabinet and the archives accompanied him.

Carranza, therefore, was in rebellion against the Convention, and in a very weak position. His only hope was that the Constitutionalist generals who had voted for his replacement–Obregón, Blanco, González, Villareal, and Hay–would have second thoughts about the fact that Villa had patently not retired, and realize that any government which had to depend on him to execute its wishes was bound to

1 Early Railways: steam-hauled goods train passing through
El Infiernillo Gorge, Mexican Railway

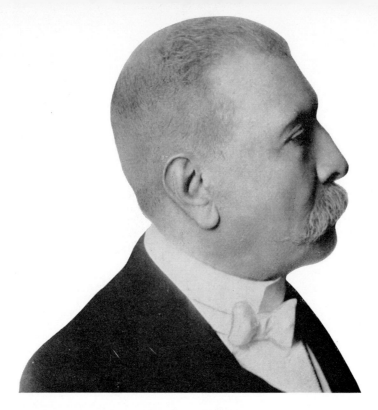

2 Porfirio Díaz (1830–1915)

3 Mexican oilfields, about 1910

4 Francisco I. Madero (*left*), arriving with his wife at the Palace
of Cortés at Cuernavaca (Morelos), receives a salute from the
bodyguard of General Emiliano Zapata

6 Federal troops in action, 1913–14

5 Victoriano Huerta (in civilian dress) and aides

7 An incident in the Delahuertista rebellion, 1923

8 Venustiano Carranza

9 Álvaro Obregón

10 Pancho Villa at his desk

11 Emiliano Zapata at a banquet

12 President Emilio Portes Gil arrives to open an educational centre, flanked by José Manuel Puig Casauranc, Secretary of Education (*left*), and Aquilino Villanueva, Secretary of Health (*right*)

13 Plutarco Elías Calles

14 President Lázaro Cárdenas (*right*) at a mass agrarian rally, 1938

15 President Miguel Alemán at home with his family

16 Two ambulance workers try to rescue a student from the
granaderos, 1968

19 Luis Echeverría Alvárez on campaign in the State of Tabasco

20 The Shrine of Guadalupe

23 Olympic Mexico

25 Colonial fountain of the Alameda, Mexico City, with the Latin American tower in the background

24 Giant Statue of Morelos, Lake Patzcuaro

26 The peak of Ixtaccihuatl

27 The Bay of Acapulco

become either his tool or a plaything. In fact, as the Convention drifted into war, more than half its delegates left to return to the First Chief. The most important of these was Obregón. But none of them had the forces that they had formerly commanded, and Obregón saw that the capital was almost isolated already. When Lucio Blanco was ordered to evacuate it, he defected to the Convention, a critical move which brought down the entire structure of Constitutionalist defences in the north and centre. As in the previous year, Mexico City lay open to Villa, and this time there was no one to hold him back.

In his extremity Carranza had only one possible escape. On 9–10 November 1914 he gave the United States the guarantees he had previously refused; the marines evacuated Vera Cruz and it was occupied by the troops of Candido Aguilar. The port now became the Constitutionalist capital, and Carranza's lifeline to the outside world.

Villa, despite his impatience, was careful not to occupy Mexico City first. Instead, the moment it was abandoned by Lucio Blanco, the Zapatistas began to appear in the streets from the direction of Xochimilco, and martial law was declared by their commander. Zapata himself paid a flying visit to the city; then retreated to Xochimilco where he invited Villa to meet him. He did not occupy the National Palace. That was taken over by Eulalio Gutiérrez on 3 December, but no one paid any attention either to him or to the government he set up. Villa escorted him into the city, but with only a small escort, and withdrew again at once before meeting Zapata at Xochimilco the following day.

At this meeting the two chiefs, so dissimilar in other respects, were united both by their own backgrounds in relative poverty, and by their hatred of Carranza. Having sealed their friendship with cognac and a mutual proscription of their enemies, they settled down to the serious business of planning the campaign. Zapata with the Army of the South was to strike towards Puebla. He would need guns and ammunition, which Villa would supply. Villa himself would strike at Vera Cruz. They left to Gutiérrez the problem of eliminating the Carrançistas in the Pacific states. Then, having reviewed their troops in the capital, they parted for good.

Their strategic appreciation was, as it later appeared, hopelessly over-optimistic. On paper the Villistas held most of the country, and the Carrançistas were reduced to a few small enclaves. But those enclaves were on the outside, around the ports including Vera Cruz and Tampico. The fact that they were there at all meant that Villa had to import all his arms overland from the United States, and the fact that even quite small enclaves were behind him, in the north, was a prospective danger to his supply-lines. Had he struck immediately at

Vera Cruz he might have finished the fight at one blow. But he hesitated, and in his hesitation, he lost his opportunity.

The Zapatistas, on the other hand, carried through their campaign at Puebla with great success. Yet having captured it, they were reluctant to go further. Meanwhile the Villistas ran riot in Mexico City, shooting anyone to whom they took a dislike. The diplomats, who had refused to follow Carranza to Vera Cruz, were not over-impressed with the standard of order maintained by the government of the Convention. United States enthusiasm for Villa, which had been high, fell off sharply. Part of the trouble was that Villa's staff was simply not sufficient to fill governmental posts and still leave him enough to give him good advice. He went back to the north to pursue a fruitless campaign to free his flank from the forces of the Constitutionalists in Jalisco, then at Christmas returned to the capital to keep an eye on Gutiérrez, whom he suspected correctly of wanting to act on his own and being in negotiation with the Constitutionalists in the north and north-west.

In fact, Gutiérrez was too painfully honest to keep his negotiations secret from anyone except Villa, who eventually read all about them in an American newspaper. The President was rapidly becoming disenchanted with the Convention. When it reassembled in Mexico City at the beginning of January, it had plunged into a long debate on the future form of government, and, led by the Zapatistas, who had gained considerably by the removal of the Carrancistas, was talking about reducing his powers to those of the figurehead of a parliamentary system. He responded to an invitation from Obregón to open a correspondence about the desirability of his leaving the capital. This Villa read of in the course of a flying visit to the border. On his way south, he received further news from Ángeles. On 5 January Ángeles had inflicted a stinging defeat on the Constitutionalist forces in the north-east at the battle of Ramos Arizpe. The Carrancista generals, Maclovio Herrera and Antonio Villareal, had fled, but by bad fortune Villareal's archives had fallen into Villista hands. In them were letters from the President.

The day of the vote in the Convention on the parliamentary system, Villa sent a telegram to General José I. Robles in the capital ordering him to kill Gutiérrez. Robles was no longer his subordinate, however, but Minister of War in Gutiérrez's Cabinet. He advised the President of the message. In the middle of the night Gutiérrez left the capital on horseback with his entourage, taking with him more than half the contents of the National Treasury. The noise of the hooves on the cobbles awoke Roque González Garza. He had no troops to pursue the fleeing President, and instead went to the Convention to assume control of the government in its name.

Gutiérrez, on the face of it, was unlucky. He failed to make contact with the largest body of troops prepared to support his government and for a month he retreated northward, harried by the forces both of Villa and the Convention. Finally he reached the independent territory controlled by Saturnino Cedillo in San Luis Potosí. After further vain attempts to appeal to the nation when he found Cedillo was not prepared to help, he resigned his claim to the Presidency. But he was more fortunate than most, for he was able to make his peace with Carranza and retired peacefully into civilian life.

Roque González Garza, on the other hand, looked for the moment to be one of the most powerful men in the nation. The personal representative of Villa, the Convention now deposited in him, as its president, the executive power. But it was a mirage–a power he was not permitted to exercise. The Zapatistas took advantage of the change to create a semi-parliamentary system with no separate executive–in fact, government by convention. This might have mattered more had it had anything to govern. In practice neither Zapata nor Villa paid any attention to it. The military situation was too critical.

On 4 January Puebla had been retaken by Obregón from the Zapatistas. Once they had captured it, they did not bother to maintain an adequate garrison there, and Obregón met with no resistance other than from the pro-Zapatista forces of Juan Andrew Almazán. Then the Almazanistas retreated in turn, while Obregón re-formed for the strike on the capital. Here again the Zapatistas bolted on hearing of the approach of the Constitutionalists, and the Convention itself left the capital on 26 January for Cuernavaca. Once there, González Garza was as much overshadowed by Zapata as Gutiérrez had been by Villa. The Convention continued to meet and to debate. As it moved back and forth to the capital, according to the shifts in military fortunes over the next eight months, it continued to debate the great problems of Mexico, and set about solving them on paper. But only on paper. The real fact was that militarily Obregón had cut off the south from communication with the north, and the outcome of the political battle would depend on the outcome of the great trial of strength between Obregón and Villa.

'Pancho' Villa

'Pancho' Villa was an elemental. Everything that he did was larger than life. Yet he was entirely human–animal in his passions and rages, but capable of great devotion and conscious of the need for higher values. Unlike Zapata, he could understand another point of view from his, though he shared all Zapata's hatred of the wealthy landowners of the old régime. It is paradoxical that it was he, rather than the southern chieftain, who became the personification of unthinking violence in Mexico; and yet the fact that he did so derived in some ways more from his good qualities than his bad.

Villa was born Doroteo Arango – the name under which he became famous was a self-adopted pseudonym. His parents, Agustín Arango and Micaela Quiñones Arámbula, were poor countryfolk, and he himself was brought up to work hard in the fields and to ride better than anyone else in the neighbourhood. Then, when he was entering his teens, he was orphaned. The young Doroteo was now head of the family. While working to support it, he fell foul of one of the *rurales* and, angered by his insolence, killed him. What that insolence was, no one now knows; legend has it that he tried to rape one of Doroteo's sisters, which is not improbable, but is not necessarily true. The famous temper which later made the entire Division of the North shake was already in evidence.

There was no hope for the young man but to take to the hills. The vengeance of the *Porfiriato* for his particular crime was certain. But the name Doroteo was too ladylike for a bandit, and a pseudonym had advantages in that it would protect his family. He called himself simply 'Pancho' Villa. But why he chose that particular name is a mystery. Villa's life abounds in them.

He was born in 1878 and is said to have been sixteen when he became an outlaw. From that time, about 1894, until 1909, a period of about fifteen years, there is nothing but picturesque legend and stories told much later to fill the gap. Villa was a bandit, so much is certain. He was a successful bandit, who was according to the best traditions generous to the poor, and particularly unpopular with the landowners of Chihuahua because he persisted in stealing their cattle. On the other hand, anyone who wants to make anything out of banditry is well advised to rob the rich, since they have more money. Cattle-rustling in southern Chihuahua and northern Durango (his usual territory) would have been particularly profitable, because the herds could be run over the United States frontier to the north. And Villa became a very important bandit indeed, with a substantial band of followers.

From time to time he emerged from legend into fact: as in the celebrated incident when he rode into Chihuahua and took ice-cream on the Plaza before shooting a deserter from his band and escaping in broad daylight. But he emerged permanently only in 1909 when he came to know Abraham González, the anti-re-electionist candidate for the governorship, and respected him for his bravery. So when in 1910 Madero issued his call for a general revolt, Villa responded to it. Tradition has it that he joined it on 17 November 1910, the day before the affray in Puebla; but after the initial failure of the general revolt, the first tangible sign of his appearance came only in February 1911 when he joined Madero in Puebla. His faithfulness to the Maderista cause never wavered, and after Madero's death was transformed into virtual reverence for both his memory and that of González.

His talents as a soldier and a leader of soldiers were apparent from the moment that he presented himself with a disciplined force at his command. Starting as a captain, he was rapidly promoted to colonel and took part in the junta at Ciudad Juárez on 1 May 1911 where the peace terms were discussed. He played an important role in storming the city when Orozco's forces mutinied. In recognition of his services he was given the honorary rank of colonel of *rurales* when peace came, and retired to Chihuahua to engage in legitimate stock-trading.

It was not in Villa's nature to endure peace for long, however. Nor, though he had by then been married for many years, and his wife was living in Chihuahua, did he settle down there. Instead, when news came of the revolt of Pascual Orozco, he entered the battle on behalf of the government, and at Torreón linked up with the military under the command of Victoriano Huerta. He fought at both Conejos and Rellano, being promoted to the rank of brigadier-general for his bravery. His defence of Parral was, as it ultimately turned out, one of the turning-points of the war, as it made the later stages of the campaign possible. But at Jiménez matters took a serious turn. Huerta had customarily used the *rurales* to carry the brunt of the attack, holding the regular forces in reserve. Now he summoned Villa from Parral and demanded to know why he had not obeyed an order which had been sent to him by telegraph. Villa claimed that he had never received it. Huerta refused to accept this explanation, and at a drum-head court martial Villa was found guilty of insubordination and sentenced to be shot.

He was saved only by the good fortune that Raúl Madero, brother of the President, was on Huerta's staff and telegraphed to Mexico City for him to be granted a reprieve. Madero did grant it, but instead Villa was sent to the Penitentiary in Mexico City in order to uphold Huerta's authority. This experience was very important for Villa's future career. He was a poor country boy who had never had any formal education, and he had never had time to learn. In prison he learned to read well enough to get through a newspaper, and to write. Even more important, he met Gildardo Magaña, a Zapatista, who told him about the Plan of Ayala and sowed the seed of the future alliance between North and South. After some months, Villa was transferred from the Penitentiary to the Carcel Militar. From there, at the end of 1912, he managed to escape, aided in his flight by one of his jailers, Carlos Jáuregui, possibly with the connivance of the government.

Once out of prison, it was too risky for him to stay in the country.

He avoided the terrain he knew and where he was known. Instead he made his way overland to Guadalajara and thence north up the Pacific coast through Colima, Manzanillo, Mazatlán, and Nogales. In Sonora, before crossing the frontier into the United States, he met Mayortena, then governor of the state, who gave him money and helped him on his way.

Villa did not linger long in the United States. He crossed to El Paso, Texas, and it was there that he read the news of the *Decena Trágica*. Having received fresh aid from Mayortena, he and eight other companions rode south through the river at 9 o'clock one evening late in February 1913, and in seven days were in San Andrés 439 miles away. Apart from the horses, which they had 'borrowed' from a local riding stable (Villa later repaid his debt twice over), they had only what they stood up in, and, according to John Reed, 'two pounds of sugar and coffee, and a pound of salt'.[3]

Within a month, Villa commanded a force of three thousand men. Others were in the field also, in particular Rosalio Hernández, based on Santa Rosalia, Maclovio Herrera and Manuel Chao of Parral, and Tomás Urbina of Jiménez. In September 1914 he was chosen as their chief by the others and became commander of the Division of the North. It was a fantastic achievement, and only one thing was needed to complete it – the capture of Torreón, chief railway junction for most of northern Mexico. As we have seen, Villa was unable to hold Torreón against Federal reinforcements on its first seizure (30 September 1913), but with renewed strength disconcerted his opponents, first by switching his forces to the extreme north to capture the port of entry at Ciudad Juárez (15 November), and then by striking south again through Ojinaga to take the city of Chihuahua on 8 December. Having entered the city he proclaimed himself Military Governor of Chihuahua and proceeded to improvise a government for the war-torn state.

Here as always Villa went to work like a whirlwind. Though he lacked formal education he had proved his administrative ability in the military field, and it is not too much to say that he had improved considerably on all principles of military organization known in Mexico up to that time. Once he had learnt to read, he appears to have devoured, if with painful slowness, a great deal of information about the history of his country; in his administration he substituted verbal discussion and immediate decision on specific points for the long-winded course of Mexican bureaucracy – and he got results.

Some of his results followed directly from his military methods. He printed paper money in large quantities, and shopkeepers accepted it because they had no safe alternative, even though it was backed by nothing except his signature. He succeeded in levying taxes, owing to the confidence the return of trade promoted, and dealt harshly with anyone suspected of speculation, with the result that profiteering in foodstuffs fell off sharply. Particular attention was given to Spaniards, to whom Villa was especially hostile; like many other Mexicans of a country background he knew them principally as middlemen and retailers, and believed that they were profiteering.

It was a cruel war, and the shooting of prisoners was common to both sides. Curiously enough, Villa's own excesses in this respect were at the time considered of little importance compared with the crimes, real and alleged, of Victoriano Huerta. Partly this was because they were committed *en caliente*, but partly it must have been because Villa was simply living up to his bandit image. Those who had the opportunity to see him at close quarters confirm that many of his actions were impulsive in this as in other respects. He was capable of great generosity, and could forgive a penitent who had erred. On the other hand, he was ruthless with the captured Orozquistas, whom he regarded as traitors to the Maderista cause. Worst of all, he was too forgiving with the crimes of his subordinates, in particular with those of Rodolfo Fierro, the 'Butcher of Ojinaga', whose sport it was to shoot prisoners with his own hands, sometimes upwards of a hundred in a single evening. In February 1914 Fierro shot an English expatriate named William Benton who had had the audacity to come to him and demand that he leave his property alone. Benton was a headstrong fool, but he was not in the wrong, and his death made the British government very doubtful about Woodrow Wilson's respect for Villa.

For the most extraordinary paradox about Villa was certainly the regard he inspired in the ex-President of Princeton, the President of the United States. Perhaps it was the attraction of opposites. Perhaps it was due to the good press that Villa, with his extravert and sociable nature, enjoyed in the United States. Or perhaps it was the honest way in which he dealt with the many unofficial agents whom Wilson sent to probe his intentions. He admitted freely that he was uneducated, that the administrative life did not appeal to him. When he eventually reached Mexico City, it was with great hesitation, and almost schoolboy daring, that he eventually tried the seat of the Presidential chair. His place was in the saddle, and he knew it.[4]

Violence

It is an illusion shared by a great many otherwise intelligent people that there is something purifying about human violence. From the safety of their armchairs, European and North American writers have for years bewailed the complex and tangled mat of social problems presented by Latin America. All too often they have—often very regretfully—come to the conclusion that the only cure for those problems is a violent revolution.

In the ten years from 1910 to 1920 just such a phenomenon occurred in Mexico. A nation threw all its energies into an internal war of such dimensions that there are few who question that it was one of the most destructive conflicts in human history. In those ten years Mexico sustained a net population decrease from 15,160,369 to 14,334,780 (1921). It is probable that the 1921 census is underestimated because of the legitimate fear people had by that time developed of anyone who was in any sense an official, and might be connected with conscription. It is also probably true that the fall in population was as much due to disease (in particular influenza), as to violence. But the fact remains that wartime is normally a time of population growth, and at the most conservative estimate something of the order of half a million people died during this time who might otherwise have lived.

Had these people all been ardent militarists or dedicated revolutionaries it might be possible to discern (according to one's own prejudices) something desirable about these facts. But of course they were not. Starvation and disease hit most cruelly at the weak, the feeble, and the old. The spectacular assassinations, the betrayals, the bestial massacres left the vast majority of the leaders untouched, and for those that fell, there were many more to step into their places. Mexico by 1920 was a land sick of war, but she was also a country in arms; militarized, restless, and eager for the excitements of the decade to come. Consequently the history of that decade is far from edifying. It does not look—however one regards it—as if violence was a selective method of producing a better political or social leadership. If such a leadership did in fact emerge, it was in face of the problems of the day, and its first task was to curb the vast hordes who were feeding on the substance of the state and had become accustomed to doing so. This problem has never been fully overcome. It is much to the credit of the Mexicans that they admit as much and do not try to take refuge in vague and optimistic generalities.

Secondly, on a rather cruder level, the population collapse was immensely damaging to the nation's immediate prospects of economic growth. Not only was each life lost valuable in itself, but it was also a precious economic resource for an underdeveloped country, and where the lives concerned were the youngest and most vigorous elements of society with the courage to fight for their convictions, they were especially hard to replace. The effects of the setback can be seen in the very slow rise of population in the inter-war years, from 14·3 million in 1921 to 16·5 million in 1930 and 19·6 million in 1940. Thereafter it spurted upwards to reach 25·8 million in 1950 and 34·9 million in 1960—the figure for 1970 being over 48 million.

It is of course often argued that the purpose of violence in a revolutionary situation is simply negative – it removes those individuals and groups who stand in the way of social progress. Again, the experience of the Mexicans is not very encouraging. It is hard to point to a single important member of the political élite of the *Porfiriato* who perished as a result of the Revolution. General Reyes is the only exception of any consequence. To a man the *cientificos* escaped with not only their lives but also their money. It seems that the violence of a revolution such as the Mexican was in fact so indiscriminate that those with power and influence had very little to fear. Some of the great *hacendados* of Morelos even managed to stay on their estates right up to the final consolidation of agrarian rule in the state, and to some extent at least to work them.

It can reasonably be argued that in the end the old hacienda system did give way, and this is to a considerable extent true. What the general statement disguises is the extent to which the change merely reflected a 'move out of land' by the wealthy, either to alternative investment or investment overseas. Their place was quickly taken by speculators. Many of these speculators came from among the new revolutionary élite, the generals and members of their families.

As far as the balance of material costs is concerned, however, the picture is much less clear. To take an important example, there is the impact of the period of violence on the railways. By 1915 almost half the boxcars and a great number of locomotives had been destroyed. The track, particularly near the major towns, had been repeatedly torn up and bridges dynamited. Roadbed, embankments, and tunnels, on the other hand, were substantially intact. Trains continued to run, though at a much reduced speed, and entirely at the will and for the purposes of the military authorities. In short, the basic investment in railways was still intact against the day on which it could again be used productively.

To suggest that violence in any way *improved* the railways (or any other economic structure), on the other hand, would be ridiculous. Mexican railways today are not absurdly bad by North American standards, but they are certainly so by the standards of Europe or Japan. Not only was a great deal of damage done to them, but more than ten years of use and reinvestment were irretrievably lost, never to contribute significantly to the development of the Mexican economy. Furthermore, the ending of hostilities did not and could not mean an immediate return to economic growth. Priorities had first to be settled, plans made, the equipment found, and all the while the doubt that attends any major disruption of the social order weighed against any fundamental change in the way of doing things.

Industry recovers from violence more easily than agriculture. The maldistribution of land before the Revolution was so acute that its sharing-out could result in a general improvement of living standards which would be noticeable and effective—and eventually was. First, however, was needed just that sort of recentralization that had already been achieved by the *hacendado*. This was to prove a difficult choice for later governments and still is to a considerable extent unresolved today. Mexico achieved a measure of social justice, and in the achievement, violence played a part. But its effects were neither as simple nor as beneficial as might be assumed from the events that followed. Nor did they suggest that a more equitable improvement of living standards might not have been achieved through a more orderly progress in which economic growth and the extension of opportunity went hand in hand.

It may lastly be argued that such a growth could not have been achieved under the pre-revolutionary system. The answer to this depends on the assumption that the *Porfiriato* could have outlived Díaz himself. It seems highly questionable. It was the very fragility of the system that made Madero's Revolution successful. The ability to plan for the present, by the fact of the dependence on the mortality of one man, had been achieved at the cost of being prevented from planning for the future. It is human to want to see dramatic changes in one's own lifetime, but it is a fault in revolutionaries as well as in rulers when it comes to dominate their thinking to the exclusion of the humane ends of society.

[1] The writ of *amparo* is a powerful and effective provision of Mexican law for redressing grievances both against the person and against property. See Miguel Lanz Duret, *Derecho constitucional mexicano*, 5th edn. revised (Mexico, Norgis Editores, 1959), 316 ff. ('Del juicio de Amparo').
[2] For a full account see Robert E. Quirk, *The Mexican Revolution, 1914–1915; The Convention of Aguascalientes* (Bloomington, Indiana University Press, 1960).
[3] Reed, op. cit., 118.
[4] He was also fortunate in the recording of his ideas by Martín Luis Guzmán, *Memoirs of Pancho Villa*, trs. V. H. Taylor (Austin, University of Texas Press, 1965).

The Revolution XIII: Villa versus Obregón

MEXICO CITY FELL TO OBREGÓN on 28 January 1915. The city, abandoned by the Zapatistas, was of no great strategic importance in the coming battle, but it did confer a certain prestige on the Constitutionalists and on Carranza. It was a prestige he was at pains to shun. The Constitutionalists continued to have their capital at Vera Cruz, and every action of Obregón was designed to reduce the supposedly proud and reactionary city to insignificance, and to punish it and its inhabitants. The retreating Zapatistas had destroyed the waterworks at Xochimilco, which proved impossible to repair. There was just sufficient water to drink, conveyed along the old aqueducts of the colonial period, but it was of poor quality, and without replenishment the drains rapidly became noisome. Worse still, food supplies, which had formerly been dominated by the trade from Jalisco, were cut off, and Obregón refused to make good the deficiency. The rich, the Spaniards, and, above all, the Church could afford to pay for supplies, he said.

Obregón's treatment of these three groups was such that when on 11 March his troops suddenly pulled out of the capital to meet the threat from the north, the Zapatistas were acclaimed as liberators. Meanwhile an important change had occurred. Cut off from the Convention, Villa had set up his own temporary government, and on 4 February had notified foreign governments that it would deal with business until the links with the south were restored. In foreign eyes, and in particular American ones, this made Villa President of Mexico in all but name. Both inside and outside Mexico, the great drive south was daily expected that would drive the Constitutionalists into the sea and restore some kind of order. In Mexico City, looted of everything movable, and just beginning to recover from the siege, a new verb had been coined: *carrançear*, meaning 'to steal'. It looked as if within weeks the Villistas would again be in the capital and together with the Army of the South would at last establish a viable government for the whole country.

Operating from Monterrey, Villa was in the process of consolidating his control over the essential coalfields of Coahuila, preparatory to launching an attack on Pablo González's forces defending the

171

oilfields of Tampico. He had clearly realized that in the military conflict the important thing was military resources. The capital had nothing to offer: despite what he said in public he had no confidence in the ability of the Zapatistas to defend it, and he could not afford to send a force so far south and risk it being cut off. For Obregón's army, though it had had to abandon the capital, still lay across the line of communication to the north. Still less, until his rear was secured, could Villa afford to move his whole force south.

It was therefore Obregón, drawing reinforcements, who moved first. By the end of March he had reached Querétaro. At the beginning of April he encamped in Celaya, a small town in the State of Guanajuato at which there was a junction between the National and the Mexican Central Railways, situated in a fertile and well-watered plain. In the meantime news of Obregón's advance had reached Villa, and stung him into action. The Division of the North was moved south to the nearest town, Irapuato, and there prepared for battle.

At Celaya, Villa was still close to his own territory, while Obregón's lines of communication from Veracruz were greatly extended. It was the ideal moment for the Zapatistas to strike from the Constitutionalist rear. But they did not move significantly, pleading a lack of ammunition which was in fact much less important than a lack of will. The Zapatistas were, in fact, much more concerned to stop the Convention leaving the capital for the north, and held it back long enough for it to be cut off. For from it they were wringing the first adequate supply of money their movement had ever enjoyed; with this money and by their own efforts they were turning Morelos anew into a garden. In the spring of 1915 it was one of the few places in Mexico, apart from the extreme south, that was so fortunate.

Villa, however, believed a false report that the Zapatistas had come to his aid. Full of confidence, he did not even trouble to leave Irapuato when his advance guard made first contact with the Constitutionalists outside Celaya on the morning of 6 April. Throughout the day, as the battle built up, he developed no strategic plan and maintained no reserve of fresh troops. Instead his men continued the same technique of frontal charge which had won all their previous victories. Obregón, on the other hand, had profited by the accounts of the Great War then raging in Europe. The soft soil around Celaya was criss-crossed with ditches which were easily extended into a system of trench fortifications. From the safety of these his riflemen and machine-gunners were able to inflict crippling losses on the charging Villistas at relatively small cost.

The first battle of Celaya lasted for the whole of that day and most of the following one. At last the Villista attack fell off, and at that moment Obregón sent in his reserve of cavalry in a charge from the flank that sent his opponents back in retreat to Irapuato. No attempt was made to follow them. Both sides needed time to recuperate. A week went by while Villa gathered in his forces, leaving in the north only a few troops under Felipe Ángeles to hold their ground there. His forces included some thirty guns with which he expected to blast a path for his attack. First thing in the morning of 13 April they laid down a barrage on the Constitutionalist lines and the second battle of Celaya was under way.

Once again the Villistas charged in the centre, but once again, in face of trenches and barbed wire, they suffered heavy losses. On this occasion they did not, as in the first battle, even succeed in making a momentary breakthrough. The Constitutionalist lines had been extended into a broad semicircle commanding every way of approach. After fighting throughout the night without success, the repetition of the cavalry charge that had decided the first battle threw them into complete confusion. This time, however, though they abandoned their weapons and artillery in their flight, they were not allowed to escape without pursuit. Harried by the Constitutionalist cavalry and followed by an infantry advance, the Villistas were forced to abandon their base and unable to regroup. They had lost at least six thousand men, whose dead bodies were strewn along the railway track on both sides for miles.

The second battle of Celaya destroyed the legend of Villa's invincibility, and was the decisive factor in the end of his ascendancy. For he was forced to recall his forces from Tampico, and in particular to conclude his efforts to control Jalisco, whose situation was essential to the link with the Army of the South and any pretension to national hegemony. All, however, might still be saved if, in a third battle with Obregón, Villa could secure a decisive victory, and it was apparent to everyone that it would not be long before that battle took place.

Álvaro Obregón

Up to the battle of Celaya, Obregón had been content to remain very much in the background as far as the press was concerned. He was a technician and an able one; though he was popular with his men and had a good sense of humour, he wanted to get on with winning battles and was content to leave the politics to the First Chief whom he served. Celaya catapulted him into the limelight, but once it was over, no one seemed to know much more about him than they did before. Villa's way was not his way, and given history's fondness for the spectacular, Obregón has attracted little attention, even from Mexican historians.

The facts about his early life are well enough known. He was born on 19 February 1880, at Siquisiva, a hacienda in the ranching State of Sonora, and was the youngest of eighteen children. He came of a good local family: his father had once been quite wealthy but had lost most of his money by supporting the Emperor Maximilian. The young boy had some desultory education from his older sisters and also for a time in Huatabampo and Alamos. Then he went to work. For a time he worked in a flour-mill, showing the technical bent which was later to be one of his most marked characteristics. But it was on the land that the future lay, and after building up capital as an expert with farming equipment while working for others, he was able in 1906 to buy his own small farm at Huatabampo from the Federal government. With typical humour he named it 'Quinta Chilla' (Penniless).

Having only just got his farm into production, it is not surprising that Obregón, whose wife died after bearing him two children, should have taken no part in the Madero Revolution. At the age of thirty-one he was, however, of modest wealth and a man of consequence in his locality. So at the end of 1911 he was elected as *presidente municipal* of the municipality of Huatabampo. At the outbreak of the Orozquista rebellion, he became one of those who responded to the call of Governor Mayortena for reinforcements, and, by bringing 300 men to Hermosillo to fight, received the rank of lieutenant-colonel in the state militia. The raw recruits were fortunate to have good instructors, and Obregón soon found himself in command of the cavalry in the Sonora column. The column set off across the mountains to Chihuahua and met the Orozquistas in full retreat from Huerta's forces. In the battle that followed, Obregón distinguished himself by capturing the enemy artillery, was promoted to full colonel, and commended by Huerta himself.

Obregón had found his vocation. It was not long before he had further opportunities to practise it. As for so many others, the occasion came with the *Decena Trágica*. In Sonora, unlike Coahuila, the governor did not even attempt to put up a fight. He resigned and was succeeded by his local rival, Ignacio L. Pesqueira. Pesqueira reactivated the state forces and in April 1913 the Sonorans acknowledged the authority of the First Chief. Subsequently their stand was ratified by the state legislature. But first they had to fight. Obregón's first task in March was to secure the frontier towns, giving the Sonorans from the beginning the priceless advantage of access to supplies from the United States. For some time the Federals were held up in Chihuahua, but it was not long before they entered the state. On 13 May, at Santa Rosa, 40 miles from Hermosillo, the Federals under General Luis Medina Barrón encountered the Sonoran forces, under the command of Colonel Obregón. Although the revolutionaries numbered more than the 1,500 Federals, the latter relied on their experience and made a frontal charge on the Sonorans. Obregón had planted his artillery with care, however, and the charge gave him the opportunity that he needed. The timely arrival of some five hundred reinforcements under Colonel Salvador Alvarado enabled the Sonorans to win a complete victory. From that time onwards Sonora was effectively outside Federal control.

However, outside Sonora the war was going very badly for the Constitutionalists, and soon the First Chief himself had taken refuge there. It was not until the capture of Chihuahua by Villa in November that the tide turned, and meanwhile the Sonorans had to fight on another front, far to the south of their state, in Sinaloa. Obregón, now a brigadier-general, besieged first Guaymas, and subsequently Mazatlán, but in both cases without result. At Mazatlán the Constitutionalists were severely handicapped by lack of naval support. Ultimately, after the appearance of the rift between Carranza and Villa, Obregón's army for the first time acquired a crucial significance. Largely isolated from the others, the Army of the North-West (as the First Chief had designated it) became the only one able to move.

However, there were difficulties to be overcome first. The siege of Guaymas had been left to Alvarado. Yet Carranza had, in pursuit of constitutionality, made the mistake of restoring Mayortena to the governorship without considering first where his sympathies might lie in the event of a split with Villa, who had, as we have seen, been his protégé. As Alvarado was a partisan of Mayortena, it was necessary to leave a substantial garrison in the north of the state. These forces, commanded by the former Maderista Commissioner of Police of Agua Prieta, Plutarco Elías Calles, were therefore not available to Obregón for the drive south. The situation, which considerably exacerbated relations between Villa and the First Chief, was only eased when in August 1914 Obregón occupied Guadalajara.

We have already seen how Obregón came to lead the forces that occupied Mexico City, and how he failed to take account of the Zapatistas. In his first negotiations with Villa on behalf of the First Chief there was from time to time more than a hint that he himself was striving for an agreement between generals which he was prepared to force on Carranza if necessary. If this was so, and it does seem very likely, then Villa himself must be held to have destroyed it by his impetuous threats and, above all, by his last attempt to have Obregón assassinated at Torreón. Throughout, Obregón showed great physical courage–a fact that strengthened his position considerably. The opportunity to sum up Villa at first hand, however, must have weighed heavily with him when laying his plans for the battle of Celaya, and his grasp of classical strategic principles showed there more clearly than ever.

After Celaya, Obregón had undoubtedly become the military man of the hour. If he had chosen to exert his authority, it is doubtful if the First Chief could have long withstood it. His policy of divide and rule had finally reached its limit.

However, Obregón pursued his campaign towards the city of León in Guanajuato. In a further battle there he could complete what Celaya had not. Though the Villistas had been forced to evacuate Monterrey, the loss of Tuxpam – the Gulf Coast port and oil port second only to Tampico – to them was a rude reminder that Villa was not yet beaten. The decisive battle at León was fought early in June, yet such was the state of chaos in communications by this time that it was over a week before the result of the battle became known to the outside world. Villa had been beaten. And in the course of the fighting a Villista grenade had exploded beside Obregón, shattering his right arm. In severe pain and bleeding profusely, the Constitutionalist general somehow managed to draw his service pistol with his left hand, put it to his head, and pulled the trigger.

Voices: The Convention

'I, gentlemen, will never sign this banner. We are making a great revolution today to destroy the lies of history, and we are going to expose the lie of history that is in this flag. That which we have been wont to call our independence was no independence for the native race, but for the creoles alone. And if the heirs of the conquerors, who have infamously continued to cheat the oppressed ones and the indigenous . . .'[1]

'Ownership of the lands and waters within the boundaries of the national territory is vested originally in the Nation, which has had, and has, the right to transmit title thereof to private persons, thereby constituting private property. Private property shall not be expropriated except for reasons of public use and subject to payment of indemnity. The Nation shall at all times have the right to impose on private property such limitations as the public interest may demand, and the right to regulate the utilisation of natural resources in order to conserve them and to ensure a more equitable distribution of public wealth.'[2]

'As an additional part of the plan that we proclaim, be it known: that the lands, woods, and water usurped by the *hacendados*, *científicos*, or *caciques*, under the cover of tyranny and venal justice, henceforth belong to the towns or citizens in possession of the deeds concerning these properties of which they were despoiled through the devious action of our oppressors. The possession of the said properties shall be kept at all costs, arms in hand.'[3]

'Col. Álvaro Obregón assumed the command of the forces of the

State. Immediately I presented my request to enlist in the Army of the Revolution. Francisco Peralta, who held the rank of lieutenant, replaced me in the Comandancia of Police and through this circumstance I was given, soon, the rank of lieutenant, 1 March 1913. It was the most decisive moment of my life, because my principles and convictions were entirely in accord with revolutionary ideas. The first thing was to destroy the enemies of legality.

'I have to confess that from the time I began a military career I had the intention of reaching the highest rank. This ambition, natural in any man, would give me the opportunity, if it were realized, to make the objects of the Revolution come true and to aid in the raising of the life of our people.'[4]

'One hears a great many stories of Villa violating women. I asked him if they were true. He pulled his mustache and stared at me for a minute with an inscrutable expression. "I never take the trouble to deny such stories", he said. "They say I am a bandit, too. Well, you know my history. But tell me; have you ever met a husband, father or brother of any woman that I have violated?" He paused: "Or even a witness?" '[5]

'All our anxious tensions express themselves in a phrase we use when anger, joy or enthusiasm cause us to exalt our condition as Mexicans: "*¡ Viva México, hijos de la chingada!*" This phrase is a true battle cry, charged with a peculiar electricity; it is a challenge and an affirmation, a shot fired against an imaginary enemy, and an explosion in the air. . . . When we shout this cry on the fifteenth of September, the anniversary of our independence, we affirm ourselves in front of, against, and in spite of the "others". Who are the "others"? They are the *hijos de la chingada*: strangers, bad Mexicans, our enemies, our rivals.

'. . . The person who suffers this action is passive, inert and open, in contrast to the active, aggressive and closed person who inflicts it. The *chingón* is the *macho*, the male; he rips open the *chingada*, the female, who is pure passivity, defenseless against the exterior world. The relationship between them is violent, and it is determined by the cynical power of the first and the impotence of the second. . . .'[6]

'Those were the days in which each one of us travelled in his special train with as much impudence as if they were only hackney-carriages. Because of this the majority of our political conversations, important or idle, often were coloured by the landscape of a railway journey and scented by coal smoke and hot steam. Trains of generals, trains of civilians came and went on the main lines, passing each other on sidings and at stations. The goods service had disappeared, or almost so; the passenger service hardly existed. All was war convoys or fleeting engines followed by a saloon car and a brakevan, where there travelled, with the speed of lightning, the armies and the animating ideas of the revolutionary hurricane. In their meeting places the locomotives saluted one another, their crews gossiped, and, if the trains carried politicians of rank, the travellers got down from the train and talked gravely.'[7]

[1] Antonio Díaz Soto y Gama, as quoted in Quirk, *The Mexican Revolution 1914–1915*, 108.

[2] *Constitution of the United States of Mexico*, 1917, Art. 27.

[3] *Plan de Ayala*, 1911.

[4] Abelardo L. Rodríguez, *Autobiografía* (Mexico, Novaro Editores, 1962), 61–2.

[5] Reed, op. cit., 124.

[6] Octavio Paz, *The Labyrinth of Solitude: life and thought in Mexico* (New York, Grove Press, 1962), 74–6.

[7] Martín Luis Guzmán, *El águila y la serpiente* (10th edn. Mexico, Cia. General de Ediciones, 1964), 364.

The Revolution XIV: Constitution

IT WAS, AS ONE HISTORIAN HAS PUT IT, 'an act of carelessness which profoundly affected the future of Mexico'. One of Obregón's captains had cleaned his general's pistol the day before the action at León, and he had forgotten to reload it. And as Obregón tried in vain to shoot himself, he was disarmed by an aide, Lt-Colonel Jesús M. Garza. While a doctor was fetched, he advised his staff that he was likely to die anyway, and said: 'Tell the First Chief that I have fallen fulfilling my duty and I die blessing the Revolution'.[1]

But he did not die. His arm was amputated, and, as he lay in bed convalescent, General Hill, the acting commander, was able to report the rout of the Villistas. On 5 June the Constitutionalists entered the city of León and the battle was over. Within days General Amaro and his colleagues had won a further victory at Silao. During the summer months Villista resistance crumbled rapidly.

Meanwhile, after the battles at Celaya the Constitutionalists had again cut off the food supplies of Mexico City, and in the face of starvation the discord between the Villistas and the Zapatistas had virtually brought the Convention to a standstill. In this brief period before the coming storm, however, it had had the distinction of becoming the first representative body seriously to come to terms with the problems of social reform in Mexico. The members could not remain aloof from the problems of the starving poor, when those poor broke in on to the floor of the hall and made their pleas in person. Their programme adopted guarantees for labour and for land rights; legislation was passed for the prohibition of religious education and for the establishment of divorce. But there was no money for food, and the solution dear to the hearts of the delegates – to take it from the rich – would not work, as after a winter of shifting currencies there were no more rich. Not in Mexico City, at least.

Finally the worsening situation forced the Convention to meet again, despite its differences. On 9 June it resolved to remove González Garza from the office of Chief Executive, and to exercise the executive power itself. For practical purposes, however, the executive was delegated to the most neutral figure available, Francisco Lagos Cházaro, a former governor of Veracruz. He was,

179

however, a President without authority, and soon to be without a base. Reports of disorders in the capital were causing concern in the United States, and Carranza, who wanted United States recognition, at last needed the city which he had finally come to realize was indeed the 'Capital of the Republic'. The task of recapturing it was entrusted to Pablo González.

So cautious was that general that the task took the entire month of June. The Zapatistas fought bravely with very little ammunition to hold the line of defence on the Grand Canal, but they were disorganized by a shift of front and lost control of the area on 9 July. Two days later González marched into a city that had already been abandoned by its defenders. Only five days later he withdrew suddenly. Obregón's capture of Aguascalientes in the second week of July had led Villa to try to relieve the pressure on his forces by striking at his communications. The capital, which had suffered so much from so many invaders, suffered most from being left without them. The Convention made no effort to reoccupy the city, and order broke down completely. Finally on 2 August the Constitutionalists drove out a Zapatista force under Amador Salazar and brought the capital permanently under their control, though it was many weeks before the Constitutionalist government cared to move there from Vera Cruz. Still the government of the United States, which always showed that unaccountable fondness for Villa, failed to move, until Villa's own increasing irritation began to tell against him. Early in September the Villistas lost Torreón to a Constitutionalist army under General Francisco Murguía. Soon afterwards the Convention, which had sought refuge in Toluca, was dispersed by the arrival of a Constitutionalist army. A rump of it continued to have some pretensions of authority and Lagos Cházaro continued to maintain a peripatetic government in the northern deserts into the first week of January 1916, but to all intents and purposes the only serious rivals to Carranza, either military or civil, had been reduced to insignificance. On 19 October 1915, very belatedly, the government in Washington faced facts and recognized the administration of the First Chief as the *de facto* government of Mexico.

By this time Felipe Ángeles, who had advised Villa in vain to adopt more modern tactics, had withdrawn from Mexican politics and gone as Villa's agent to Washington in a vain hope of securing American aid, or at least mediation. Once there he found it prudent to remain. Some of the other Villista commanders were able to go back to the Constitutionalist side. Villa himself remained in arms, but continuing losses of support and a ban on ammunition from the United States reduced him virtually to the state of an outlaw, though not yet of a bandit. He now controlled only Chihuahua and part of Sonora, Saltillo having fallen to the Constitutionalists. Mexico was, however, still very far from being at peace. In the south the Zapatistas had fallen back on Morelos, but were able to maintain themselves there, since the Constitutionalists made no serious attempt to dispossess them. Villa made a further attempt at a change of front when on 1 November 1915, having crossed the mountains into Sonora, he attacked the frontier town of Agua Prieta. The town was, with considerable care, protected at the instance of its commander, General Calles, with a ring of trenches on the Obregón pattern, and after three days Villa had to retire. In the bitterness of defeat he blamed his reversal, not on his own failings, but on the government of the United States, against which he plotted his revenge. And in some sense he was right, for President Wilson had allowed Calles to import the munitions he needed across United States territory, thus departing not for the first time from his self-proclaimed principles of neutrality. Even more significantly, perhaps, Villa, who had always favoured night attacks, had found the battle-field well lit up by brilliant searchlights, the power for which undoubtedly came from Arizona.

Thereafter Villa, whose forces met with a crushing defeat when they tried to strike at Hermosillo, returned to the life of the bandit he had previously been. A number of sporadic incidents, nevertheless, still occurred to remind Americans that he was still at large and that his anger was directed against them and their property. On 10 January 1916 Villistas murdered seventeen Americans in a train ambush at Santa Ysabel. It was an ideal opportunity for Wilson's enemies to accuse him of weakness. Then on the night of 8–9 March 1916 there occurred a dramatic incident that made Villa once again a national and, in fact, an international figure.[2]

In the early hours of the morning of 9 March the United States garrison at Columbus, New Mexico, was roused by the sound of shots. Villista forces were making a simultaneous attack on the camp and on the town, which was soon in flames. The American troops quickly rallied and drove off the invaders in under an hour from the initial surprise; they then cut the boundary wire and pursued them into Mexican territory. A small force of Carrançistas stood by without getting involved, and the retaliatory forces soon returned to their own base. They found from papers that had been abandoned in the rush that the attack had been planned two months before.

Although at the time there were a number of people in the United States who ascribed the whole incident to the machinations of sinister capitalist investors anxious to bring about a war between the United States and Mexico, there is no real doubt that Villa not only committed his forces to it, but led the attack in person, probably to remind the world of his existence and to prove his personal valour by attacking what he clearly conceived as the power that had been responsible for his ultimate downfall in his own country. Reaction in the United States was strong, and there was unequivocal feeling in favour of a punitive expedition. There was no confidence that the nominal government of Mexico could take any effective action, and indeed, though Carranza went through the motions of directing forces in pursuit, from the beginning it was the movements of troops north of the border that he was principally wary of. Within three days he had alerted the garrison at Vera Cruz against a possible landing and prepared his commander in the north to sever rail and telegraph links in the event of invasion.

As usual unaware of the extent of anti-American feeling in Mexico, the administration of President Wilson decided in favour of the punitive expedition, and asked Carranza to approve it. His reply, as eventually given, was that troops could only cross the border provided the right were reciprocal and subject to certain conditions. In turn the State Department treated this as an acceptance, which it was not, and the mobilization went ahead of a force suitable for the task. On 15 March it crossed the frontier into Sonora; its mission being to disperse the Villista band rather than, as was stated in the papers, to capture Villa himself 'dead or alive'.

Insofar as this was its stated task, it was fairly successful. The band of American soldiers struck south to the Mormon colony at Colonia Dublán; thereafter it continued to follow the Villista trail, closely watched by patrolling Carrançistas. As it got further south, hostility grew, and although Carranza permitted its provisioning by civilian means over Mexican railways, local friction led to a number of armed incidents, culminating in the destruction of an entire troop on patrol at Carrizal, Chihuahua, on 21 June. Carranza's government adopted a hostile attitude to American protests. It had shown its goodwill by sending no less a personage than its Secretary of War, General Obregón, to negotiate with the American General Scott. But it was not prepared to accept anything less than total withdrawal, being painfully aware of the possible political consequences of accepting anything less. After Carrizal, it again showed its goodwill by proposing mediation by other Latin American states. Again, however, its position was inflexible, and for six whole months the negotiations dragged on without conclusion. This time, being in the throes of the Presidential election, President Wilson was not able to yield either. Meanwhile the force remained in Mexico.

While the stalemate lasted Villa himself was not idle. In September 1916 he captured Chihuahua and gained both reinforcements and much-needed supplies of ammunition; in November he returned, and held the city for two weeks before being forced again to withdraw. Finally, on Christmas Eve, he occupied Torreón. Villa was once more a power in Mexico, or so it seemed, and he lost interest in the United States. Already preoccupied with the growing threat of involvement in the European War, President Wilson correctly decided to withdraw the expedition without further delay, and on 5 February 1917 the last troops crossed the border on their way north. They had not caught Villa, but then they had not really tried to, and they had gained a great deal of experience of armed combat which the United States was going to need in April. Yet ironically, by seemingly failing in its purpose, the punitive expedition certainly helped to confirm the impression in Germany that the United States as a military power could be safely disregarded, and that was a serious mistake.

It was not a mistake that had always been made. At the beginning of the war in Europe the United States had already been involved in a conflict in Mexico for internal reasons. The nature of that conflict had made it clear just how much Wilson and his pacific Secretary of State, William Jennings Bryan, were reluctant to go to war, but also how great was their concern with events in Mexico. The logical way for Germany to ensure that the United States continued to remain aloof from the European conflict was to guarantee that Mexico remained a serious problem for her.

Having arranged for Huerta to leave his native country on a German cruiser, the Imperial government had at its disposal a useful agent. In April 1915 they had enabled him to return to New York. After conferences with German agents there, on 25 June the ex-President of Mexico left by rail ostensibly for San Francisco and the Panama-Pacific Exposition, but in fact for the small settlement of Newman, New Mexico. There, as he left the train, he was arrested on the orders of an agent of the State Department, together with his colleague General Pascual Orozco, who had been waiting with a car to drive him over the frontier.[3]

When the two generals were taken to El Paso, Texas, they were, to the government's alarm, treated not as rebels but as heroes. After two days Orozco managed to escape, and Huerta was thereupon, quite illegally, lodged in the county jail. Even there he refused to make any terms for his release and was eventually transferred to the military prison at Fort Bliss. While he was there the news of German intrigues in the United States itself broke, aided in every possible way by the British government. The disclosures became a prime factor in determining Wilson to recognize Carranza, despite his doubts about his real qualities and intentions, because above all else the need of the United States was now for a strong, united, and friendly Mexico.

In prison, Huerta developed jaundice. When on the point of death he was released, so that the United States government would not be accused of murdering him. Nevertheless, Federal troops remained on guard at his bedside until he lapsed into a final coma. He died on 14 January 1916. By then Orozco was already dead, shot with four companions by a posse of Federal marshals, Texas rangers, and troops of the Thirteenth Cavalry who surprised the five men in a canyon in Culberson County, Texas, on 30 August 1915.[4] Neither incident reflected favourably on the conduct of United States justice towards Mexicans in the border areas.

The deaths of Orozco and Huerta removed two of the three Mexicans on whom the Germans had been counting to lead a successful revolt. The third, Félix Díaz, was supposed to lead a simultaneous rising in the south, where in Oaxaca his family connections still counted for a great deal. Ever optimistic, he went ahead despite the lack of northern support, and arrived in Mexico in February 1916. For some months his movement was the most serious opposition to Carranza in Mexico, its one major setback being its failure to make an alliance with Zapata, who remained coldly aloof. It is quite likely that German agents envisaged Villa as filling the role that Huerta and Orozco were no longer able to play, and there is certainly no doubt that Villa took the financial aid the Germans were so eager to extend. However, by the time that Díaz became effective, they had already, for a while, lost interest. The incapacity of the United States seemed so manifest that there was little need to embroil her further, and in any case it was becoming plain that Wilson was adamant in refusing to be baited.

Much more attractive was the possibility of establishing good relations with Carranza himself. For one thing, he was already in power, and it was easier to negotiate with him than to overthrow him. And secondly, Carranza himself was inclined to favour Germany, particularly given his constant fear of United States aggression. In the latter part of 1916 he was importing arms from Japan against the possibility of foreign attack. And Carranza, who controlled the Tampico-Tuxpam district, was in a position to let the Germans have what they needed more than anything else, a refuelling base on the far side of the Atlantic against the day of unrestricted submarine warfare which by November 1916 had been fully accepted in Berlin as the necessary next step. The only remaining question was when it would come into effect, and it did in fact come into effect on 31 January 1917, when the punitive expedition was still on its way back to the United States.

The fact was that Carranza had survived—if only just—any other combination of revolutionary chiefs that 1916 had been able to produce. Three factors were of crucial importance. The first was military: with Obregón as Secretary of War and Marine the Carrançista forces gave before attack, but never failed to hold together and to come back in force. The second was political: the fact that at Vera Cruz Carranza had come to accept, if very reluctantly, the emergence of two nascent political groups which were to be of the greatest importance for the future. The first of these, the agrarians, had received its recognition in the Decree of 12 December 1914 and the Law of 6 January 1915 which proclaimed the slogan 'Land for the People'. The other, the growing force of urban workers, had been acknowledged as vital by Obregón in Mexico City, who permitted the reopening of the anarcho-syndicalist Casa de Obrero Mundial on agreement that the workers would furnish him with reinforcements for his troops. These reinforcements–the six celebrated 'Red Battalions'–were of poor quality, and their separate existence was abruptly terminated by Obregón's precipitate withdrawal from the city, but his decree of 26 April 1915 was ratified by the First Chief and formed the first concrete advance secured by trade unions in Mexico. Significantly, in neither case had the advances registered been secured by parliamentary debates, though had the Convention survived, the legislation proposed there would have anticipated much that was only established two years later.

The third factor in Carranza's favour was economic. Not only did he control almost the entire territory of the republic, but he controlled almost all its wealth. At no earlier point could this have been said. And that wealth gained value daily under the forced draught of the Great War. Mexico was outwardly in ruins, her people starving, her communications disrupted, her fields untilled. Typhoid, typhus, malaria, and tuberculosis ravaged the towns; bandits and thugs terrorized the countryside. But the government was recovering a semblance of normality, and Mexico City itself was showing signs of restoration, of prosperity, much of it based on the flow of oil and mineral products to the Western Front.

This recovery was symbolically marked by the first steps towards the formal restoration of constitutional rule. In his new security Carranza could now become at long last President of his country. On the eve of the anniversary of the *Grito de Dolores*, on 14 September 1916, the First Chief issued a proclamation summoning a Constitutional Convention. The proclamation laid stress on the fact that its authority was derived from the Plan of Guadalupe, and emphasized that in so proceeding the government was following a procedure no more irregular than that of the Convention of 1857.

Elections were held on 22 October and the Convention met on the anniversary of the Revolution, 20 November, in the provincial splendours of the Academy of Fine Arts at Querétaro–a former chapel recently whitewashed inside. The delegates were only moderately representative. In some congressional districts no candidate had run; in the rest only unopposed returns were made. In any case, to ease their labours, a very long and detailed draft of the proposed constitution had been prepared by a committee led by the lawyer Luis Cabrera; and this the 151 delegates who met on 1 December were set to consider. It was hardly surprising that they made short work of it.[5]

Two-thirds of the Constitution of 1917 was taken over unchanged from the document of 1857. Where the new charter outlined the basic structure of government it did not depart greatly from its predecessors. Such modifications as there were were in the direction of executive supremacy and away from the Liberal notion of congressional responsibility. The Vice-Presidency was abolished altogether, leaving the President supreme as the chief executive and free from the rivalry of a potential successor. He was given what the Liberals of 1857 had denied him, a veto over legislation, in whole or in part, and the right to initiate legislation which must receive the immediate attention of Congress. To confirm what had during the previous three years been the regular practice of Carranza and of those to whom he delegated the power, the right of making laws by executive decree was also established. The new Mexican President was not going to have to strain the constitution in order to exercise the powers of a Juárez or a Díaz.

A useful provision that reflected the distaste of foreigners which had grown up during the Revolution was established in the notorious 'Article 33'. This enabled the President to deport at will any foreigner 'whose presence he judges inconvenient'. Huerta would have liked that.

But the new President was not going to be omnipotent. There was one very important check on his power–the reason why the whole Revolution had been initiated. The principle of no re-election was established. At the end of four years the President would have to yield his place to another who might hold him to account. In his short term, he could safely be trusted, therefore, with powers officially greater than any of his predecessors.

More controversial were the clauses dealing with those matters in which the Laws of the Reform had been transgressed. Article 3, laying the responsibility for elementary education on the Federal government, was particularly controversial. Carranza was very reluctant to see any extension in this area at all, while a vociferous, so-called 'Jacobin', minority called for a scheme of education which was overtly socialist. The result was a compromise which said nothing of the aims of state education, but did make it universal and compulsory, and if not socialistic, certainly anti-clerical. How much so would depend on those who had the task of carrying the provision into practice.

Article 3 has to be read in conjunction with Article 130. This established that it was for the Federal government to make laws concerning religion, and that inferior governments acted only on its behalf. Congress could not, however, make any law establishing or prohibiting any religion. On the other hand, the state did not recognize 'those religious bodies termed churches' as having a legal personality, and their ministers were only ordinary professional people. The legislatures of the states could determine how many were needed in their areas, and they must in any case be native-born Mexicans, not foreigners. Clerical journals or political parties were strictly prohibited. Finally, in accordance with Article 27 of the constitution, *all* property formerly held by Churches would become the property of the state, who would allocate it for their use as it thought fit.

Here the constituent delegates had gone much less far ahead of the draft, but had spelt out in much greater detail the restrictions on church activity which they wished to impose.

The most important respects in which the Constitution of 1917 departed from its predecessor, however, was in the field of social provision. The Constitutionalist movement had to pay its debts to the agrarians and to labour. Both groups ensured that they got as much as they could, and the result was a series of guarantees that went far ahead of anything then obtaining in any other country.

Article 27 dealt with the land question. It began by decisively stating: 'The property of lands and waters included in the limits of the national territory belongs originally to the nation, which has had and has the right to transmit the domain in them to individuals, thus constituting private property'. This was a close rendering of the position in colonial times, and a further paragraph in detail revoked the Mining Law of 1884. Alarm in mining circles was to some extent guarded against by the provision that expropriation could only be conducted for causes of public utility and on indemnification, but the right of the state to intervene to regulate the extraction of minerals, to break up estates, to create new towns, to develop agriculture, and to avoid damage from the elements was carefully expressed. All these things constituted public utility.

Property in lands, prohibited entirely for Churches, was subject to regulation for all public companies, who were confined to that necessary for their stated purpose. Above all, all lands were subject to the decree of restitution of 6 January 1915, and the rights of *pueblos* to hold lands in common were spelt out. At last, therefore, the government of Mexico had agreed that the farmers of Morelos–and elsewhere–were entitled to what they wanted. It remained to be seen how and when they would get it.

The farming interest in Mexico in 1916 was very considerable. The urban labour interest, by contrast, was very small. The workers who had formed the vanguard of labour organization, those who had taken part in the 1906 strike at Cananea, had been miners, influenced by the same doctrines as influenced their colleagues to the north of the frontier and propagated by the brothers Flores Magón in their paper *Regeneración*. Insofar as there were practically no other organized workers in Mexico, they were certainly representative of organized labour. But the majority of urbanized workers were actually to be found in the Core, in the cluster of new industries, such as textiles, paper, and public utilities, that had grown up under the patronage of the *Porfiriato* in the pursuit of a traditional policy of import-substitution. The confused conditions of the Huerta dictatorship had given the anarcho-syndicalist organizers a chance here to show what they could do, and they had been quick to respond to the offer of official support made by Obregón during his military occupation. At Querétaro they were to gain their reward. Mexico received, somewhat to the surprise of onlookers, the most advanced labour code that the world then had to offer. It was a fact of profound significance, perhaps only made possible by the relative weakness of labour, but in retrospect it offered the foundation on which a powerful political force could come into existence, and it permanently changed the face of Mexican political and social life.

Carranza himself asked only that the Convention in Article 73 of the draft constitution grant the power to legislate for labour matters to the Federal government. There were only two representatives of labour in the Convention, and neither of them sat on the committee that discussed the question. Yet out of it came so many different proposals for labour and social welfare that in the end they were, as Professor Cline puts it, 'packaged' in Article 123, entitled 'Concerning Labour and Social Welfare'. The principal concern of delegates was obviously that the provisions of the draft Article 5, seeking finally to outlaw debt-slavery in Mexico, were wholly negative. What they sought to do was to establish that the regulation of labour was a social duty, a public responsibility of high moral significance, and a field in which revolutionary Mexico could set an example to the world.

Article 123 began with a number of simple provisions establishing a maximum working day of eight hours, the abolition of child labour, the right to a minimum wage 'sufficient, taking into account the conditions of each region, to satisfy the normal necessities of life for the worker, his education and his modest pleasures, considering him as a head of a family'. His wages had to be paid in good money and he was entitled to a double rate for overtime, to clean living conditions, and safety at work. Alcoholic beverages were not to be sold nor games of chance played in factories. To guarantee his rights, he had the same rights as his employer 'to join together to defend his respective interests'. The right to strike was established, together with arbitration tribunals to adjust disputes, and a guarantee of wages if the employers arbitrarily refused to accept their decisions. Finally, the right of the government to establish social security funds was expressly stated.

Despite the lengthy debates on these and other important issues, the Convention, working day and night, ending in 'permanent session', did not take long to create its final draft of the constitution, which was duly promulgated by the First Chief on 5 February 1917 –important anniversary of the battle of 1863 and an occasion for a public holiday, particularly symbolic as the occasion on which the punitive expedition was making its retreat from Mexico. No time was lost in holding elections under the new constitution. They took place on 11 March. As a result, Carranza at last became President of Mexico, the inauguration ceremony taking place on 1 May. His irregular methods of avoiding the provision on no re-election had worked, but they were not forgotten. The first problem the Constitutionalists had to face, now that they were at last constitutional, was a general disrespect for constitutional restraints which had endured so long as to have become habitual.

Political Discourse

It may seem elementary to non-Spanish-speaking readers to point out at this stage the importance of realizing that Mexican political argument takes place in a different vocabulary. In the early revolutionary period, however, the vocabulary was already complex enough. It comprised, apart from the usual political bombast, a tradition of violent metaphor and extremely scurrilous personal attack, both public and private. Once habituated to this, it is difficult to shake off, and one of the problems of writing the history of Mexico is that whereas in some other countries one knows well that what is printed is only part of the truth, in Mexico it is not necessarily the same part.

After 1917 a considerable amount of Marxist terminology entered the Mexican political vocabulary. Since in those days the understanding of it was fragmentary, and in addition Marx had little or nothing to say about the peasantry that was polite, its relevance to

the conditions described is often only partial. It did, however, succeed in frightening quite a number of onlookers, as well as deceiving
the Russians into believing that Mexican experience was unimpor-
tant and could therefore be safely disregarded. The synthesis presented here is therefore based as far as possible on facts as they have
been recorded, but suggests an individual interpretation which
differs at times considerably from the values placed on these facts by
others.

[1] John W. F. Dulles, *Yesterday in Mexico: A Chronicle of the Revolution, 1919–1936*
(Austin, University of Texas Press, 1961), 12–13.
[2] Clarence C. Clenenden, *The United States and Pancho Villa* (Ithaca, N.Y.,
Cornell University Press, 1961).
[3] Barbara Tuchman, *The Zimmermann Telegram* (London, Constable, 1969), 66–
83.
[4] Meyer, op. cit., 130–4.
[5] 'Djed Borquez' (pseudonym of Juan de Dios Borjorquez), *Cronica del Consti-
tuyente* (Mexico, Ed. Botas, 1938).

The Revolution XV: Constitutionalism

As FIRST CHIEF, Carranza, it must be said, had been successful. As President he was not. Most of his problems stemmed from just those qualities of caution, conservatism, and suspicion that had enabled him to survive the political turbulence of the pre-constitutional years. To begin with, there was a honeymoon period as the interests who had received promises in the constitution waited for them to be delivered. They soon became impatient. When they did so, Carranza was not one to adjust his policy.

However, it should not be overlooked that during the period of the elections, the world had changed drastically. The Allies already appeared to be on the point of losing the Great War in Europe, and Carranza was being pressed more enthusiastically than ever to help Germany with material aid. Then in rapid succession came the secret decision of the Germans to begin unrestricted submarine warfare, the opening of the campaign, and the collapse of Russia. In anticipation of American hostility, the German Secretary of State, Zimmermann, had sent the famous telegram No. 158 dated 16 January 1917 to Ambassador Bernstorff in Washington for transmission to the German minister in Mexico. The minister was to invite Carranza's government to join in an offensive and defensive alliance with Germany against the United States. Mexico's reward was to be the return of her 'lost territories' of Texas, New Mexico, and Arizona.

The message was still undelivered when on 3 February the United States broke off diplomatic relations with Germany. President Wilson still intended to resist to the last any actual outbreak of hostilities, but Zimmermann decided to wait no longer. On 5 February a further telegram directed von Eckhardt, the German chargé d'affaires in Mexico, to deliver the message as a Note at once. It was a curious and important coincidence that on the same day the last troops of the punitive expedition left Mexican soil and that Carranza proclaimed the Constitution of 1917. His position vindicated, as he saw it, both internally and externally, Carranza felt secure and could afford not to be stampeded into such a doubtful venture.

On 1 March news of the Zimmermann telegram appeared in the

United States press. Intercepted on the Atlantic cable and decoded in London, then traced in its final version by the British chargé d'affaires in Mexico, the telegram had been communicated by London to Washington by way of Ambassador Page, and its message to the Americans was that while Germany had been talking peace, her leaders had been planning to make war. The uproar in the United States was felt in Mexico too. Despite strong German offers of monetary aid, Carranza refused to be drawn in, and, after the United States had declared war on Germany on 2 April, the First Chief (as he still was) officially informed the German minister that Mexico would remain neutral, after first announcing publicly at the reception of the new American ambassador (3 April) that no secret agreement existed between his government and that of Germany.

Mexico, racked by famine and disease, had had enough of war. During the same month of February, Pablo González had made a final attempt to win military glory by eradicating *Zapatismo*. Wholly defeated by flexible guerrilla warfare, on the 14th he announced a total withdrawal of all forces from Morelos. It was effectively the end of his career. Yet paradoxically he achieved something that none of his predecessors had been able to achieve. As a direct result of the withdrawal of his forces, the Zapatistas broke up within days into a bunch of warring factions. On 18 May Otilio Montaño, the author of the Plan of Ayala, was shot by his former *compañeros*.

The agrarian cause had triumphed. *Zapatismo*, as such, was finished. The movement lingered on through the disastrous harvest of 1918 and the disease and pestilence that followed, but the men who made up its base of support were having a hard time to stay alive. In the winter of 1918–19 the Spanish influenza swept southward from the capital. Zapata himself was still alive and a national political figure, publicly appealing for support from other revolutionaries who detested the post-war corruption and cynicism of the Carrançistas. Zapata's fatal mistake was to underestimate that corruption's and cynicism's capacity to harm him. Pablo González had been unable to defeat him in the field, but González was now a pre-Presidential hopeful for the elections of 1920 and was prepared to eradicate his humiliation any way he could. His agent was the dashing young Colonel Jesús Guajardo, commander of the 50th Regiment in Cuautla.

Guajardo had been imprisoned for dereliction of duty, and then released. Zapata's spies reported that he was inflamed with hatred against his general. Zapata wrote to him; the letter was intercepted and taken to González who used the treason expressed in it to force Guajardo to act as his stalking horse. Zapata, though suspicious, came to a proposed meeting at Chinameca–with a very large escort.

There on 10 April 1919, his forces outnumbered ten to one, he was shot down, as with his ten bodyguards he entered the place of the meeting, by the guard of honour drawn up on either side to receive him.

In May 1917, however, all this lay in the future. No one then predicted the collapse of the agrarian leadership, which enabled Carranza to make only token attempts at carrying out the land distribution policy foreshadowed by the constitution. The fact was, though, that it was not an easy thing to do. Land tenure was a highly complicated legal question, and, though it was logical to begin by attempting to restore the illegal seizures of the past decades, it was another matter after all those years of fighting to determine what was legal and what was not. Thus, though the Presidency of Carranza recorded few material gains for the agrarian cause, it was a very important period for the emergence (usually at state level) of new figures who were to carry out the land policy in the 1920s and '30s.

Their emergence was aided by the withdrawal from active politics of Álvaro Obregón. Irritated beyond endurance by the fact that his former chief, now the battles were over, preferred more pliable men, he withdrew to his estate in Sonora. There he devoted himself to the cultivation of chick-peas. He was very successful and made a great deal of money out of them.

A great many people in Mexico City were doing very well, mostly out of the war in Europe. But in the states it was still an age of turbulence. Throughout 1918 and 1919 the principal excitement in politics was the disposition of state governorships in preparation for the grand contest. In Tabasco, in the Gulf, the radicals were pushing for political power, and the provisional governor was accused of irregularities. The contest for power in the frontier State of Tamaulipas went even further when on 10 February 1918 an attempt to assassinate two of its leaders in the park of Chapultepec resulted in the death of one of their escort and the wounding of Federal Deputy Emilio Portes Gil. A month later General Caballero tried to seize the governorship by force. In August the governor of Guerrero revolted. To the south, moreover, Félix Díaz and other conservatives were still in revolt. Yet none of these incidents mattered very much in themselves, for the government was strong. In particular, it was strong financially. Its previous dubious record made the Allies even more anxious to help it. A new external loan was contracted, the death penalty for forgers decreed, and in 1918 a tax placed on the petroleum which was supplying the mechanized war on the Western Front.[1]

As 1918 gave way to 1919, however, the political contest became keener; so much so, in fact, that on 15 January Carranza felt constrained to issue a public warning against initiating campaigning too soon. With the ending of the war, the influence of the October Revolution in Russia began to be felt. One of the first places where it was noticeable was in Tabasco, where the radical General Greene became governor on 10 March. The sudden upswing in radicalism favoured Obregón, who had been careful to retain his identification with the workers' interests. As ever, Carranza responded conservatively and cautiously, but those close to the administration pressed for more action. Among them was General Calles, now Secretary of Industry, Commerce, and Labour. On the other hand, Carranza did take action against clerical attacks on the constitution by arresting various journalists. And he refused to intervene in Tabasco, where a miniature civil war was soon in full swing.

His inaction extended to the Presidential elections themselves. Anxious to conserve his power to the last, he viewed with great disapproval any attempt to force his hand, but it was known that he favoured neither Obregón nor González, and was looking for a more pliable candidate. It was therefore by Obregón that the situation was broken, when, on 1 July 1919, he declared his candidacy for the Presidency in a lengthy document attacking the prevalent corruption and quiescence of the government. Carranza used this attack as a pretext for formally declaring his opposition to Obregón, but to block the general something more was needed. The oldest maxim in politics is that one can't stop somebody with nobody. And though Carranza had not found nobody to serve his turn, he had found a candidate who was almost as negative. His name was Ignacio Bonillas, Mexican ambassador in Washington, an engineer and a technician, and like Carranza himself, a civilian, who as Carranza put it was 'a man of culture, of ample preparation, able to resolve the great diplomatic problems' which he foresaw in the post-war world.

Through the *Partido Liberal Democrático* a boom was created for Bonillas and in March 1920 he was recalled from Washington to take up his candidature. He was much handicapped by persistent delays to his campaign train caused by the Obregonista railway workers, but his campaign was well financed and government-backed. Obregón, on the other hand, got a disappointing reception, and was careful to back his peaceful efforts on tour by talking to all the military officers of the need to resist any attempt at 'imposition'. He and his supporters made fun of Bonillas as a political unknown, suggesting that he had been in the United States so long that he had forgotten how to speak Spanish.

The first crisis of the constitution had arrived. If Bonillas were to be elected, it would hardly be because of his own qualities, and the promises of the constitution would be forgotten. Obregón, on the other hand, stood for reform, but he could not be elected over government hostility, and a reversion to the habit of force would be a serious setback for the cause of constitutional development in which the Revolution had been nurtured.

Carranza resolved the dilemma. At the beginning of April 1920 Obregón was summoned to the capital as a witness in a treason trial. No one who recalled the recent deaths of Zapata in Morelos and Ángeles in Chihuahua (where he had returned to rejoin the revolutionary cause) could doubt that in going there he would be putting his life at the hazard of numerous enemies. Yet to flee would be to lose his candidature. As the trial progressed it seemed that the intention of it was to show that Obregón was implicated. The government was already moving troops into Obregón's home State of Sonora, a step that was vigorously contested by its governor, Adolfo de la Huerta. In a significant move, he had appointed General Calles, who had just resigned from the Cabinet to support Obregón, as director of military operations for the state's militia. As Obregón himself went to and from the trial he was closely shadowed by police, and it appeared only a matter of time before he would be arrested. There was no alternative to flight.

After supper on the night of 11 April, Obregón, driving through a park with three friends, changed hats with one of them and jumped out of the moving car. With the aid of his friends on the railways, carrying a lantern and with a large coat concealing his missing arm, he was smuggled aboard a train early the following morning, and hidden behind some baskets of chickens. From there he went, not north to Sonora as might have been expected, but south into the State of Guerrero. There he was found, sound asleep under a tree, the following day by General Fortunato Maycotte, who had received orders to arrest him. Maycotte put himself at the orders of his former commander, and with that act, the revolt against Carranza was under way.

Adolfo de la Huerta

The revolt of 1920 was a tragicomedy in the best tradition of grand opera. Appropriately, it was headed by a musician.

Adolfo de la Huerta, the governor of Sonora, it should first be said, was in no way related to Victoriano Huerta. He was born in Hermosillo, Sonora, on 26 May 1881, and had his primary education in Guaymas and his secondary education in the city of Mexico, where he studied accountancy and music. He did very well in both and became a teacher of music, but the death of both his parents in 1900 cut short his studies. From his youth he showed in addition a strong interest in politics, and he took part in the early stirrings of the

Revolution of 1910 when he was working in the National Bank in Sonora. He was one of the many inhabitants of the state moved to fury by the 'pacification' of the Yaqui, and when the time was ripe he left Guaymas on a railway handcart in order to establish contact with them. The friendships then made were to stand him in good stead later.

He had already met Calles when he was an assistant schoolmaster in Guaymas in 1894. After the success of the Madero Revolution he met Obregón for the first time. The soldier found the young politician somewhat incomprehensible. He said, and appeared to believe, that whether they were his friends or his enemies, the men with the support of the people should rule. It was Calles, however, who encouraged de la Huerta to run for the state legislature, which he did successfully. As a keen Maderista he did not hesitate to place himself at the service of the Constitutionalist government after the events of February 1913. After some difficulty, he made his way with a friend to Coahuila and found to his relief that Carranza had pronounced against the new government. Carranza was glad to see him. By a fortunate coincidence he was at that moment looking for a person with a knowledge of English to carry out a commission for him in Eagle Pass, Texas, and from that moment on, de la Huerta's star was in the ascendant.

By October 1913 he had become *Oficial Mayor* (Chief Clerk) of the Department of *Gobernación* of Carranza's peripatetic government. He served in this capacity until in 1915 he was entrusted with the portfolio itself in an interim capacity, and he was still in charge of the department in April 1916 when Carranza named him to be provisional governor of his native state. In that capacity he was the man responsible for restoring settled government in the state, reconstituting the courts and holding elections. But his term offered two important pointers to the future: the restoration of the communal lands taken from the Yaqui and the encouragement given to the development of workers' organizations among the state employees. At the end of June 1917 he handed over the governorship to Calles, who had been elected as his successor, and returned to the Department of *Gobernación*. It was not long, however, before he was given instead the honorific appointment of Consul-General in New York—Carranza was becoming nervous about the number of men from Sonora in high places and was taking precautions to reduce their influence as far as possible.

In the elections of 1918 he maintained his political position by being elected senator for Sonora, and shortly afterwards he succeeded Calles as elected governor of Sonora, after a turbulent campaign, mostly by car, during which there were two separate attempts made to assassinate him. According to his own memoirs, the campaign cost de la Huerta only 2,000 pesos, the balance being made up by the candidate's own energies. But this time he was to have little or no time to leave his mark on the state. Events in Mexico were moving too quickly, and by the time he was inaugurated in September 1919 Obregón had already announced his candidature for the Presidency in 1920.

The unpopularity of Sonora in governmental circles had already led to a claim–vigorously contested by the state government–that under the terms of the Constitution of 1917 the Sonora River was the property of the nation. Technically the Federal government was correct. However, the dependence of the Sonorans on its waters made the question something more than technical. Their concern grew when a number of agents of the Department of War began to arrive in the state, ostensibly to train schoolchildren in the use of arms, and when the Federal government expressed its opposition to the agreements with the Yaqui which de la Huerta had secured. News came north of the movement of troops intended for Sonora, leading to a public statement from the governor that the Federal government was intending to renew the punitive policy of Díaz. That this charge was substantially true appeared to be confirmed when, on 4 March 1920, Carranza named General Manuel M. Diéguez as Federal commander in Sonora. De la Huerta protested, but, more usefully, countered by naming General Calles as commander of the state forces.[2]

Once appointed, Calles pressed forward vigorously with preparations for revolt. It was these preparations for revolt that alarmed the government, but though they therefore endangered indirectly Obregón in Mexico City, they were in fact only the natural consequences of the plans that had already been made. It was Sonora that initiated the revolt, not Obregón. This fact was recorded by the manifesto of the revolt, the Plan of Agua Prieta, which was signed at the scene of Calles's victory over Villa and issued twelve days after the outbreak of hostilities. Subsequently de la Huerta himself signed it with enthusiasm, not altogether surprisingly, since it was he whom it proclaimed as the Supreme Chief of the so-called Liberal Constitutionalist Army. The purpose of the army was to reverse the trend of Carranza towards political factionalism by marching on Mexico City, installing a Provisional President to be named by Congress, and holding new elections in the spirit of revolutionary unity.

After the appearance of the Plan, virtually all the leading generals rapidly deserted the government cause. The only major exception was Pablo González. His army of 22,000 men was the largest in the country, and as the third officially declared candidate for the

Presidency, in opposition to both Bonillas and Obregón, it was not necessarily clear which faction he would support. In the event, after meeting the President, he simply withdrew to the country, effectively leaving the capital undefended.

Carranza resolved once again, as in 1915, to withdraw from the capital and set up his government at Vera Cruz. Times had changed. The Presidential convoy that left the capital on 7 May 1920, headed by the Presidential Train (the *Tren Dorado*), was nearly eight miles in length, and consisted of some 10,000 persons, their family possessions, and some 11 million pesos from the National Treasury. Before it had got very far, a surprise sortie from the rear had disabled about half of it. The rest, after two days of harrying, got as far as Alijibes, Puebla, before being forced to a halt. The track had been torn up, the trains were out of water and could get none, and worst of all, news had reached the President that the forces in Vera Cruz had joined the mutiny. Since in the meantime Pablo González had occupied the capital there was no orderly retreat.

After a ferocious battle on 14 May, Carranza and his closest followers left the column on horseback. There were only seventy of them in all, but the President rejected all notion of a safeguard for himself and resolved to fight to a finish. For the moment, however, it was difficult enough for the party to make its way across the broken countryside, enveloped in mist and cut through with rivers swollen by heavy rain. On the evening of 20 May they met up with the local commander, General Rodolfo Herrero, who conducted them personally to a safe refuge in the tumbledown hovels of the hamlet of San Antonio Tlaxcalantongo, otherwise entirely deserted.

Several of his followers–who counted among their number some of the most distinguished men in Mexico–scented a trap. Carranza, however, encouraged them to make the best of their situation, and lay down to sleep in a dilapidated hut, wrapped in a horseblanket. At 4 in the morning of 21 May the party were roused by the sound of shots. Concentrated fire was directed at Carranza's hut, and at the place where he was sleeping, and there, while at his injunction most of his followers fled to safety, he died.

When the column of General Herrero had finished hunting for the men they particularly wanted to shoot–especially Bonillas, who had had the good fortune to be sleeping on the extreme edge of the clearing, and so escaped–they ransacked the President's belongings. The President's secretary, the Secretary of *Gobernación*, and two generals who had stayed with him to the last, were then forced to sign a document saying that Carranza had shot himself, after which they were allowed to join their escaped companions in Villa Juárez. From there they accompanied the body to Mexico City, where, in return for their loyalty, they were placed in prison. Rodolfo Herrero, however, who was brought to the capital for an investigation, remained at liberty.

On 24 May, on the day that Carranza was buried in an ordinary grave in Mexico City, according to his own final wish, the Congress met to vote for a Provisional President. Obregón had made known his preference for de la Huerta, but Pablo González, who had renounced any attempt to secure the definitive Presidency, had hopes of securing the interim post. However, the voting went heavily in favour of de la Huerta, who was selected to serve by 224 votes to 29.

In fact, de la Huerta was still at the state capital of Sonora, Hermosillo, when the news came by telegraph of the events at Tlaxcalantongo. Immediately he arranged for a special train, and left for the capital on 22 May. It says a great deal for the abysmal state of transport in the country that the deputies should have shown concern whether or not he could cover the 900-mile journey in the nine days before he was due to take up office. But he did make it, and late in the afternoon of 1 June rode through the streets of the capital in an open carriage to the Chamber of Deputies, where in the presence of the leading figures of the Revolution, he took the oath of office.

The theme of de la Huerta's interim Presidency was harmony. The principal Carrançistas who were in jail were soon released, and the new President stated publicly that all exiles were welcome to return to the country whenever they wished. The only prominent figure to leave Mexico at once was Bonillas, who chose voluntarily to return to live in the United States, where he died a few years later. Despite the doubts of Calles and the hostility of Obregón, de la Huerta even successfully arranged for the formal surrender of none other than 'Pancho' Villa, who wished at long last to retire. He was given a pleasant hacienda in a remote part of Durango, far away from the main population centres or communications, and a sizeable pension for himself and each of his men. However, ironically, General Jesús M. Guajardo, who had arranged the trap that killed Zapata, and had subsequently led the successful operation that destroyed the rear part of Carranza's convoy, foolishly went into revolt against the new government and was shot. His revolt was part of a generally weak movement in favour of Pablo González, who, unlucky as ever, was captured, court-martialled, and sentenced to death. At the last, his luck changed and de la Huerta commuted the sentence. He chose, like Bonillas, to live in the United States.

Unrest continued on a lower level. Congress suspended the state government of strongly socialist Tabasco, and watched with disapproval rather than with alarm the political brawls and assassinations that were currently taking place in Yucatán. Presidential diplomacy, however, was successful in ending a threatened separatist movement in Lower California, and the new government was evidently stronger than its predecessor had ever been. A crucial factor here had been the recovery of most of the state assets which Carranza had attempted to remove. At Alijibes the bullion of the National Treasury had been carefully guarded at the instance of the young Adolfo Ruiz Cortines, and so had passed safely into the hands of the interim government. This done, Ruiz Cortines retired into the obscurity of the government Statistical Department, from which he did not emerge for fifteen years. But the government's credit was greatly enhanced.

One man, however, gained most conspicuously from the emergence of the new régime. This was General Calles, who was appointed as Secretary of War and Marine, principally because of his personal friendship with the President. It was he who was responsible for maintaining order in the country while the government carried out its principal purpose–that of holding elections. The elections themselves took place peacefully on 5 September, with Obregón, as the candidate of the newly reorganized *Partido Liberal Constitucionalista*, securing a large and in some places suspiciously unanimous majority over the only serious opposition candidate, Alfredo Robles Domínguez–himself a revolutionary of unimpeachable standing.

Two remaining achievements of the interim government can be credited personally to the President. One was the immediate acceleration of the land distribution which had begun only hesitantly under Carranza. The other was the establishment of friendly relations, for almost the first time in Mexican history, with the government of Guatemala, where the dictator Estrada Cabrera had just been overthrown. All these achievements, however, would have been meaningless had the government not duly fulfilled its main purpose: to hand over the power of the state intact, at midnight on 30 November, to General Álvaro Obregón. It is only fair to record that without the personal honesty, frankness, and good humour of the Provisional President, such a thing might well have been impossible, and in retrospect the policy of harmony appears a significant contribution to the bettering of Mexican social life.[3]

[1] There is no formal history of this period as yet. An annalistic account which is reliable is Alfonso Taracena, *Mi vida en el vértigo de la Revolución Mexicana* (Mexico, Ed. Botus, 1936).

[2] For the Sonoran side see Barry Carr, 'The Peculiarities of the Mexican North, 1880–1928', University of Glasgow, Institute of Latin American Studies, Occasional Papers No. 4, 1971.

[3] See *Memorias de Don Adolfo de la Huerta según su proprio dictado* transcribed by Lic. Roberto Guzmán Esparza (Mexico, Ediciones 'Guzmán', 1958).

The Revolution XVI: The Sonora Group

As a result of the efforts of de la Huerta, Obregón faced very few major internal problems on his accession to power. He was therefore free to devote his attention to the place of Mexico in the outside world.[1] In the aftermath of the Great War, it was not an attractive prospect. Relations were bad with all the Great Powers, on account of the losses that their nationals had sustained during the Revolution. They were now making use of the Mexican government's desire for international recognition to arrange financial settlements of various kinds.

The most pressing of these was the question of the United States. The government of President Wilson had already let the interim government know that it was prepared to accord recognition on three conditions. Mexico would have to reorganize her National Debt, agree to the establishment of a Mixed Claims Commission to deal with losses incurred by American citizens, and, above all, make it clear that the provisions of the 1917 Constitution would not have retroactive effect in depriving American oil companies of their existing rights to the subsoil. Negotiations on this basis were a matter that required great diplomacy. Early in 1921 this evident need was met by President Obregón recalling Alberto J. Pani from the embassy at Paris, and appointing him Secretary of External Relations. Pani, an engineer by training, had been an anti-re-electionist and had served as Subsecretary of Public Instruction in the Cabinet of President Madero for a brief time before becoming Chief of Public Works for the Federal District. He had then joined the Constitutionalist Revolution, and after early service as a confidential agent for Carranza, had served on various diplomatic missions in the United States, before in 1917 being recalled to serve as head of the Department of Industry and Commerce. A year later he was appointed to Paris. From there he had watched the Sonoran revolt with great coolness, and did not hurry to return to Mexico.[2]

Pani's appointment was regarded with some suspicion by his new colleagues, who were, moreover, afraid of the extent of the influence which his evident abilities had gained over Obregón. The most important of these was de la Huerta himself, who was Secretary of

Hacienda, and so responsible for financial negotiations. It was de la Huerta's turn to negotiate first, and to his disadvantage, for he had to negotiate against the background of a general depression, which seriously reduced Mexico's exports of metals, sisal, and cattle. To counteract the effects of this on the national revenue it became necessary in June 1921 to levy increased taxes on petroleum, but as the companies were reluctant to pay, and a United States warship appeared off the shore at Tampico, the government were forced to accept part of their payment in their own bonds.

The first round of negotiations took place between de la Huerta and Thomas W. Lamont, president of the International Committee of Bankers on Mexico, in Mexico in September 1921. It was concerned principally with the question of the foreign debt, but complicated by the question of the oil taxes, which the oil companies wished to have settled as part of a package deal on their future rights in Mexico. As a result, no agreement was reached.

In May 1922 de la Huerta went to New York for the second round of negotiations, and found himself not only up against formidable opposition there but also the hostility of Pani at home. Time and again de la Huerta advised Obregón to break off negotiations, but they continued, until it became apparent that the major obstacle to any agreement would be the ability of the Mexican government to pay. Nevertheless de la Huerta was able to extract from the bankers a promise, which he believed to be valid, of a further loan which would enable this difficulty to be overcome. Accordingly, on 16 June 1922, he put his signature to what became known as the de la Huerta-Lamont Agreement, recognizing a total indebtedness of over U.S. $500 million on bonds and notes, a further debt of U.S. $400 million for arrears of interest, and the obligation to pay current interest in full after 1928. In the meantime payment would be partly in scrip, the cash payment starting at $15 million in 1923 and rising by fixed amounts thereafter. The debt was secured on the entire proceeds of the oil tax and the entire earnings of the railways—if any, which was doubtful.

Despite Pani's opposition, the Cabinet eventually accepted the agreement in default of anything better, and in September it was ratified by Congress. It was now up to Pani to carry on the negotiations.

He started with one advantage. While in New York, de la Huerta had been invited to Washington by President Harding and had established friendly relations with him and other members of the administration. This was not necessarily an easy thing to do, since the Secretary of the Interior in that administration was Albert Fall, formerly senator from New Mexico and a long-term advocate of

American intervention in Mexico. The Treaty of Friendship and Commerce, therefore, which had originally been proposed by the State Department in May 1921 was much more commercial than friendly. Subsequently Obregón had made clear his desire for an agreement and had encouraged the Mexican Supreme Court to issue a ruling that the 1917 Constitution was not retroactive for companies or persons who had begun to extract oil, or to take steps to have it extracted, before the constitution came into effect. Despite this important move, negotiations with the State Department continued extremely slowly, with much haggling over small legal points.

Both Obregón and Harding became impatient with this process and agreed that the negotiations could be more quickly handled between representatives of the two Presidents. The representatives–two from each country–met at Avenida Bucareli 85, in the city of Mexico, in May 1923 and continued, with intermissions, until August. The discussions were informal and private, rather than secret, and were on the whole extremely friendly, despite considerable differences in the ideological position of the two sides. They resulted in two formal agreements, under which the two governments set up two commissions, one to handle claims since 1868, the other to handle those specifically arising out of the Revolution. On 31 August the United States recognized the government of Mexico in time for Obregón to announce the fact in his annual Message to Congress the following day. Her example was rapidly followed by other countries.

What created a major political upheaval in Congress and the Cabinet was that at the conclusion of the discussions, both pairs of commissioners signed the minutes of their proceedings as a record of what went on. Obviously there was much in these that was distasteful to one or another political faction, and within days there grew up the legend of a 'secret agreement' by which Mexico, it was said, had wholly conceded the right to enforce her own laws to her powerful northern neighbour. Insofar as there was a clear understanding on the part of the United States commissioners that the Mexicans had agreed not to expropriate the lands of foreigners except for village landholdings, and then only with compensation, and that this was a necessary precondition for any agreement, they were right. But the proceedings were not secret, only controversial, and in a sense the government, by accepting the principle of no retroactivity, had committed itself in such a sense from the beginning.

The nature of the upheaval, however, derived from the shifts in political forces which had occurred as a result of the events of the preceding two and a half years.

Despite their promising beginning, they had not been quiet. There was only one important revolt–that of General Francisco Murguía and associates in the north and west in mid-1922—which was ruthlessly put down by Obregón's Secretary of War, Francisco Serrano, with the deaths of its main leaders. Other potential rebels were bought off or, if recalcitrant, simply executed for 'intention to rebel'. Obregón was careful to pay Serrano's own gambling debts, which were notoriously high, and Mexico was full of wealthy generals driving around in large grey motor-cars or living it up at the casinos. But as quickly as possible many of them were transferred to the reserve and by 1923 the army had been reduced from over 100,000 to 60,000 and its budget from 61 per cent of the national budget to 36 per cent—a figure which left decidedly more funds for those still active.

At the same time Obregón built up the cavalry arm, which, as in the time of Díaz, was used for maintaining internal security in a country where unrest had generated endemic banditry. He was careful to keep soldiers out of the Cabinet and out of most of the provincial governorships. Though this led to considerable feuds in the states, it did have the desired effect of weakening militarism. Banditry, however, continued, its most spectacular victim being 'Pancho' Villa, who was assassinated in Parral, Coahuila, on 20 July 1923 as a result of a dispute over land.

The shift of emphasis away from the problems of the military did, at the same time, enhance the problems of the civilian. The effect was that the ruling coalition began to break up, and as it did so, it brought down the *Partido Liberal Constitucionalista*. In mid-1922 the Labour/Liberal coalition party that had brought Obregón to power—the successor of Carranza's vehicle—collapsed. It was displaced by the *Partido Cooperatista Nacional*, which, though it dated back to 1917, had hitherto played only a minor role in Congress. The basic reason for the collapse of the PLC was the failure of its members in the Congress to control the policy of the President. At first, the PCN made no such mistake, welcoming into the fold a large number of members of the defunct ruling party, much to their own advantage. But as 1922 gave way to 1923 it was clear that their position, though overwhelming on paper, was very insecure. The challenge came from the Left, where General Calles, who was known to be Obregón's choice for his successor, was establishing strong links with the rival *Partido Laborista*.

This last, though not strong in Congress, was powerful in terms of strength on the ground, and no one had forgotten the advantage that alliance with the workers in 1920 had given to Obregón himself against Carranza. When Jorge Prieto Laurens, President of the PCN, ran for the governorship of San Luis Potosí, Calles backed as his rival the agrarian Professor Aurelio Manrique. Obregón in the event refused to recognize either, and as a result many prominent members of the PCN, especially the young agrarian leader Emilio Portes Gil, who had pledged their support already to Calles, found themselves in a very difficult position.

The unrest in Congress paralleled demonstrations in the streets and strikes in the country at large. A crisis was at hand. The Bucareli conferences acted as a precipitant to the troubled situation. The immediate result was the resignation of de la Huerta from the Cabinet, specifically attacking Obregón's intervention in the State of San Luis Potosí as the reason for making it immediate. At once the PCN invited him to become their candidate in the Presidential elections, and, after a delay of nearly a month, during which the PCN lost considerable strength, he accepted.

Alberto J. Pani succeeded him at the Department of *Hacienda* and lost no time in denouncing his predecessor's alleged mismanagement of the public finances, which were, undeniably, in an appalling state. The new Secretary's solution in this situation was to order a general 10 per cent cut in government salaries, including all ranks of the army.

After this, matters proceeded rapidly towards a confrontation. In the middle of November the Agraristas (an agrarian splinter group) started the formal rush to Calles by adopting him as their Presidential candidate. Almost simultaneously the PCN convention nominated de la Huerta. PCN defections, however, had continued, and when Congress met at the end of November it was apparent that their support, including all allies, had already fallen below the critical number needed to control Congress. In the circumstances, it was therefore highly improbable that if their candidate were elected, the Congress would certify the returns. Those supporters of de la Huerta who were already negotiating with the army redoubled their efforts.

There had for long been a good many generals who regarded the ascent of the relatively junior General Calles with distaste. Given the general dissatisfaction of their colleagues at the government's financial stringency there were now others to listen to them. Amid rumours of *coups* and possible attempts on his life, on the evening of 4 December 1923, de la Huerta boarded a sleeping-car on the night train to Vera Cruz, and safely concealed in the lavatory, escaped from the capital.

José Vasconcelos

If there is one thing for which the Obregón government will always be remembered, and rightly so, it is not for its political manœuvrings, its financial instability, or its foreign policy, but for its new departures in education. These have given the Mexican Revolution its unique place in human history, and the credit for them is generally given to one man, José Vasconcelos.[3] Of course, they were much more than the achievement of one man, but there is an important truth concealed in the legend which deserves recognition.

José Vasconcelos was Secretary of Education in the Obregón government. It is often said that this department was the creation of Obregón. This is not so; it was the successor of the old Department of Public Instruction which was first created by none other than Victoriano Huerta and subsequently incorporated in the Constitutionalist system while at Vera Cruz. No provision was, however, made for it in the Constitution of 1917, and it became one of the first tasks of de la Huerta's administration to secure the constitutional amendment necessary for its restoration. It was the lobbying of Vasconcelos, who was then at the age of thirty-nine an old revolutionary and Rector of the National University, which secured the necessary legislation and in July 1921 he was, logically, appointed the first head of the new department.

Vasconcelos was an enthusiast and an individualist. Though born in Oaxaca, he had had a chequered education, eventually becoming a lawyer in 1907, and he had taken an active part in the Revolution of 1910, serving as a confidential agent of the Maderista movement in Washington, D.C., an experience which he was later to record in autobiographical form in his *Ulises Criollo* (A Creole Ulysses; 1936). As a confidential agent his mission was partly propagandist, partly lobbying, and partly seeking financial aid, a task in which he seems to have had no particular success. Nevertheless, he had an agreeable time in Washington, as he admitted quite frankly: too frankly, for some of his later readers. Subsequently he became Secretary of Public Instruction under Eulalio Gutiérrez, but much of his revolutionary experience was gained in the twilight world of revolutionary diplomacy, moving at the same time in the international world of culture and art in the United States and Europe.

His passion for education, his ability to work hard, and his tireless capacity for the intricacies of political negotiation (provided it was in a cause in which he wholly believed, and not otherwise) came together in his work at the education ministry to make him truly formidable. Unlike his colleagues, he was not at this stage interested in politics in any respect apart from that necessary to advance the interests of his own department. Unlike them, too, he had the knack of dramatizing its essentially humanitarian work, beginning by opening a demonstration school in the slums of the city where the children were clothed and fed before being given elementary instruction. In the aftermath of the Revolution he received extraordinary support from his colleagues, and soon education emerged as second only to defence as the biggest spending department in government.

With rare logic he concentrated these resources which, though considerable, were far from adequate, on an all-out attack on the problem of primary education. Primary schools were established throughout the country, backed by a government-inspired pro-gramme to print cheap textbooks and cheap reprints of the classics which could make education meaningful to adult readers. In a move which was later to be imitated in Cuba in 1961, he encouraged youth-ful students from the university and secondary schools to go out into the country and bring education to the masses. With the university authorities, however, he had considerable trouble. He had been suc-ceeded as rector by Antonio Caso, whose brother, Alfonso Caso, he dismissed from his post as professor for inciting students to rebel against his policy. The great Mexican philosopher resigned in sym-pathy with his brother, and the students rioted in the streets until they were dispersed with the traditional fire hoses.

What dramatized the programme of education, however, was the encouragement Vasconcelos gave to art. The buildings of the new Department of Education were used as one of the first great scenes for the work of the Mexican mural painters who were to fix the visual image of the Revolution for the succeeding generations. Realizing the potential of this visual medium, in both scale and depth of impact, Obregón and his colleagues permitted similar use to be made of other public buildings, while the work was crowned by Vasconcelos's pat-ronage of a vast new stadium for the capital which when inaugurated with an audience of 60,000 people became the largest meeting-place in Mexico.

Despite all his achievements, Vasconcelos became increasingly disillusioned with the government of which he was a member and in July 1924 resigned before the end of his term of office. Almost penni-less, he left the country in sadness and went abroad, but the work he had done so much to encourage went on. Eventually he too returned.

Pensadores *and Writers*

The figure of the *pensador* is a familiar stereotype of Latin American society. He is seen as a man who in the genteel tradition of letters is well read in philosophy, the novel, and poetry, who from his study contemplates the world and circulates his ideas to a few like-minded spirits either by intensive discussion or correspondence, occasionally by short books. His occupational disease is *proyectismo*–the tendency to daydream after fanciful ideas for setting the world to rights, which cannot and never could be carried out in the real world. It is a carica-ture, but it is an honourable one, for the *pensador* has been in the fore-front of the struggle for liberty.

The problem of the thinker in Latin America has generally been held to be the small size of the educated élite.[4] Mexico has had her share of *pensadores*; her literary tradition is strong; and she has pro-duced many good books, some world-famous. Today she is the great publishing centre of Latin America, even in some ways of the Spanish-speaking world. Yet it is still in some sense true that there is a division in the élite which keeps the educated part of it separate from that part which has done well and acquired wealth. Education is most valued by the lower-middle and the lower-upper classes; for the rest it is a matter for children rather than for adults, and during long years of the revolutionary period boorishness, uncouthness, and savagery were all too easily made the sign of a potent leader. The arrival of the 'American way of life' unfortunately has reinforced some of these ill-effects, since the respect for it is associated with Americans whose occupations or social goals in Mexico are not normally bound up with the pursuit of humane letters.

The Spanish literary tradition of the colonial period was one of devotional poetry and religious meditation. Neither is particularly conducive to direct involvement with the material world. The *conquistadores* left the records of their deeds, starting with Cortés himself, and reaching a rare level of literary attainment in Bernal Díaz del Castillo's *History of the Conquest of New Spain*. They spoke of martial glory and great deeds. The eighteenth century left elegant essays and the bitter criticisms of exiles of a reactionary Spain which were only partially true. The divergence of interests of which they spoke helped to bring on the powerful, overwhelming desire for independence. By the early nineteenth century it was not to Spain that Mexicans looked for inspiration but to France.

In the days of the Wars of Independence there was throughout Latin America a heady sense of making history, of forging a new world and a new future. Something of this informs the work of the great conservative historian of the early Independence period in Mexico, Lucas Alamán, who had served as Secretary of External Relations, and was to die in that post. His last and greatest work, the *Historia de Méjico desde los primeros movimientos que preparon su Independencia en el año 1808 hasta la época presente*, completed three years earlier, was, however, politically unpopular and even for him it was hard to reduce the broken story of Mexico's early independence into anything like a creditable story. Neither the wars of the mid-century nor the long rule of Díaz were to foster the spirit of critical inquiry, and the spread of positivism which accompanied both turned education away from letters in the direction of science and engineering, with important consequences for the decline of taste in the age of the *Porfiriato*.

The *pensador*, however, flourished in this climate. Projects for colonization, for development, for transport, agricultural improvement, and the encouragement of useful manufactures, sprouted freely. The novel languished – one could not compete with the metropolitan culture of Paris. It was the age of the literary critics, rather than the writers; an age of talk about books, rather than of the writing of books. It was the curiosity of the age of the Revolution that was to reverse this. It is the novel of the Mexican Revolution that has become its internationally famous product, not its intellectual rationality.

The process of revolt against science began before the Revolution, with the intellectual revolt against positivism associated with the *Ateneo de la Juventud* and the humanism of the philosopher Antonio Caso – the same who was to cross swords with Vasconcelos and to exert such a permanent influence on Lombardo Toledano. Caso's disciples stressed intuition as a guide to action. In the early years of the Revolution his work began to receive a wider circulation, beginning with the appearance of his *Problemas filosóficos* (1915) and given definitive form in his main work, his *La existencia como existencia y como caridad* (1916). He founded the modern Mexican philosophical tradition which was to be so powerfully reinforced by José Gaos and other Spanish exiles after 1939. More significant, perhaps, was the fact that the strength of this tradition operated against the easy acceptance of the rather simple-minded and mechanical form of Marxism which had begun to be prevalent in revolutionary circles. The thought of the Mexican Revolution was in its own stream of descent from that of the French Revolution of 1789 and owed little to other models.

The emphasis on living, on feeling, on intuition shows very strongly in other writings of the period, including especially those of Vasconcelos himself, whose memoirs subordinate accuracy to vitality and are virtually fictionalized. It comes as no surprise, therefore, to find that the novels of the Revolution are strongly historical in tone, presenting the stories of individuals as a theme in the greater concern of the Mexican experience as a whole. It was Mariano Azuela, the quiet, good-humoured country doctor with deep experience of human nature who initiated the genre in 1916 with the publication of his *Los de abajo* (The underdogs). He wrote in the heat of the moment, an eyewitness of the events he describes, and he wrote of ordinary people. They are not the 'lower class' of the sociologist, not the 'proletariat' – but what the Mexicans call *la gente humilde* (the humble people), *la clase trabajadora* (the working class), or *los pobres* (the poor). Some of them, too, were not of these classes, and he wrote of them with equal accuracy and sharpness: of the cowards, the traitors, the newly poor, the rich who had been suddenly cast down, the men on the make. He wrote of them all, as they were then. There is no sentimentality, only charity; the romantic dreams of hopes for the future do not warm the present, and the cold figures of post-war economic growth do not soften the years of asperity and horror.

Not all other writers could achieve the same standard, and not all

novels of the Mexican Revolution are good. The literary preciosities
of the late nineteenth century did not disappear all at once. They survived in memoir form well into the 1930s as minor politicians tum-
bled over one another to explain themselves; the minor ones, for the
major ones were slow to do so. The one exception of the early period,
Adolfo de la Huerta, did not compile his memoirs until the 1950s.
They consist of strong, straightforward narrative like the memoirs of
Emilio Portes Gil or the recollections of Abelardo Rodríguez.
Obregón left the only important military memoir of ten years of
fighting.[5] Of Carranza, Calles, and Cárdenas we have no major
literary remnant.

A serious loss in the early years of the Revolution was in the tradition of satire that had enlivened the intellectual life of the *Porfiriato*.
It was a tradition that went back in Mexico to the early years of
independence and *El periquillo sarniento* (The Itching Parrot) of José
Joaquín Fernández de Lizardi (1776–1827), published in 1816,
which has been regarded with justice as the first novel in Latin
America. However, satire does not flourish in times of revolution;
more precisely, perhaps, satirists do not flourish, though in the visual
medium cartoonists did. With this element temporarily in eclipse, the
efflorescence of the novel of the Revolution in the 1930s–with its
asperities already softened by the glow of time–came to an end in a
period of self-satisfaction. In the years immediately after the war, at
the time when the modern school of Mexican historiography was
being developed and beginning to tackle the great problems of the
Mexican past, literary life was once again fitful and frenetic, and,
above all, once again looking back over its shoulder at what was
going on in Europe.

Since 1960 this has changed dramatically. In the field of the novel
one of the best-known names is that of Carlos Fuentes. His *La muerte
de Artemio Cruz* (1962) retraced the paths of the Revolution in the
mind of a dying man, an ex-general and *nouveau riche*. The theme of
the complexity of human motivation, the difficulty of exact judgement, and the imprecision of assessment is an expansion of that of his
earlier *La Región más Transparente* (translated as *Where the Air is Clear*–
1958), which was a study of the pointlessness of life in post-war upper-
class society. But it is a much more uncomfortable book, not just for
the abundance of clinical detail which reminds the reader vividly and
incessantly of his own mortality, but for its lack of comfortable certainties. Other writers, such as Luis Spota, have attacked the tendency of certain strata of Mexican society to defer to foreign values,
particularly those of the United States. It is a recurrent theme.

Nowhere is it more striking than in the work of the philosopher
Leopoldo Zea, who has turned in recent years to making a series of

short and extremely generalized but precisely stated critiques of aspects of Mexican political thought. All deal with the conflict, stated in essay form by himself and two colleagues in *Magia y cibernética* (1959), between spiritual values and humanist ideals ('magic') and material advancement and the worship of technology ('cybernetics'). It is in the tendency to identify this last element precisely with the influence of the United States, though, that the thesis is questionable. The conflict is universal, rather than specific.

The work of delineating those features of the Mexican character which could be seen as specifically Mexican was undertaken by the poet Octavio Paz as early as 1950, and his *El laberinto de la soledad* (The labyrinth of solitude)[6] combines intense and perceptive introspection, from which he himself is not excluded, with a broad sense of human destiny which informs all his works. His subject is Mexicanism, the consciousness of being Mexican, of love for a country which has suffered so much. Despite all, it is intensely vital and optimistic.

In every generation the Mexican writer has tended towards the side of the progressive opposition. Even Justo Sierra, leading intellectual of the *Porfiriato*, had doubts about positivism, and transmitted them to his followers. While Antonio Caso was pursuing the path of philosophy, his brother Alfonso Caso became an anthropologist. In the present generation theory and practice have come together in a more realistic attempt to appraise Mexico's national inheritance and to conserve the best while improving the lot of all. If one has to single out one historian who has personally contributed the most to a greater understanding of that past and a great deal more by inspiration, it would undoubtedly be Daniel Cosío Villegas, author of 'big books' subjecting the life of Mexico between the Reform and the Revolution to the most detailed scrutiny of modern scholarship.[7] Not only has he, through the Colegio de México, trained able young historians to follow in his footsteps and explore the history of the Revolution as well, but together with other leading intellectuals such as the economist Víctor Urquidi he has played an important role in developing a school of higher studies relevant to every aspect of modern Mexican life.

It should be stressed, however, that there are historians of equal distinction elsewhere in Mexico, and that the University of Mexico, with its direct responsibility for the teaching of so many students, has not neglected its responsibilities in promoting their interests. The sociologist Pablo González Casanova, who is Rector of the University at the time of writing, has explored personally the subject of democracy in Mexico (*La democracia en México;* 1965) in the spirit of Spinoza. After his experiences of the incidents of 1968 he has continued to defend the spirit of free inquiry. When in 1971 a number of

Mexico's leading intellectuals, including Octavio Paz and Carlos Fuentes, actually set about the difficult and thankless task of creating a political bloc alternative to the PRI, it was to a generation and more of diligent inquiry that they owed their right to do so, and to their own participation in national life too.

In Mexico today, therefore, the *pensador* has stepped down from his ivory tower and entered the practical world of politics. There may be disputes about the forms of government and the deficiencies of the régime. There is general agreement on the need to serve Mexico, and the duty to do so. Today's writers are no less intelligent or well informed than their nineteenth-century forerunners; in fact it is in their generation that the age-old gap between 'Mexicanists' and 'internationalists' is ceasing to exist, as Mexicans play their important role on the greater stage of mankind.

[1] Not, however, in the sense implied by E. J. Dillon, *President Obregon, a World Reformer* (London, 1923).

[2] See also Alberto J. Pani, *Apuntes autobiográficos* (Mexico, Manuel Porrua, 1950).

[3] The principal autobiographical source is José Vasconcelos, *A Mexican Ulysses, an autobiography*, trs. & abridged W. Rex Crawford (Bloomington, Indiana University Press, 1963).

[4] See Fred P. Ellison, 'The Writer', in *Continuity and Change in Latin America*, ed. John J. Johnson (Stanford, Stanford University Press, 1964) for a good study.

[5] *Ocho mil kilómetros en campaña* (3rd edn. Mexico, Fondo de Cultura Económica, 1960).

[6] Trs. Lysander Kemp (1962). See also Samuel Ramos, *Profile of Man and Culture in Mexico*, trs. Peter G. Earle (Austin, University of Texas Press, 1962) and from a different angle Frederick C. Turner, *The Dynamics of Mexican Nationalism* (Chapel Hill, University of North Carolina Press, 1968).

[7] *American Extremes*, trs. Americo Paredes (Austin, University of Texas Press, 1964), introduction.

The Revolution XVII: Labour in Power

THE DE LA HUERTA REBELLION was the ultimate test of Obregón's policy of holding the army in line with heavy bribes. It opened as a re-run of the revolution of 1920. On 7 December, from a hotel in Vera Cruz, de la Huerta issued the so-called 'Plan of Vera Cruz', in which he denounced Obregón in the same terms and for the same crimes as he had denounced Carranza in 1920. Among his remedies for the situation were agricultural credits, better education, votes for women, and the abolition of the death penalty.

This last would not have been one moment too soon. General Francisco Múgica, on his way to Mexico City under the escort of an army colonel and accused of anticipating the revolt that was on the point of breaking, was shown by his escort a telegram from the President informing him that Múgica had been shot trying to escape. The colonel did not take the hint, and was cashiered, but he was in good company. Well over half the army was in revolt, or something of the order of 50,000 men, well armed and equipped by the Mexican government itself. The defections had begun on 30 November with General Rómulo Figueroa in Guerrero, and included over a hundred *divisionarios* alone, even General Fortunato Maycotte, who took the precaution of first approaching Obregón and drawing $100,000 for 'campaign expenses'. General Enrique Estrada, from Guadalajara, formally renounced his allegiance by telegraph on 7 December and was denounced by the President for being both a false friend and a disloyal soldier. The first became commander in the south, the second in the east, and command in the north went to General Guadalupe Sánchez.

Had these three been able to agree on a battle plan, all might have been well with their ambitions, but they did not do so, and they were not even wholly in agreement on who, if anyone, was supposed to be leading their revolution, or, more precisely, just whose revolution they were each following. Hence Puebla, which had fallen to the Veracruzano forces on 14 November, was recaptured by forces under General Almazán within a week.

In Jalisco the government forces, under General Lázaro Cárdenas, suffered an initial defeat from the numerically superior forces of

General Estrada. Cárdenas was wounded and captured. A sortie by rebel forces into Cárdenas's own State of Michoacán, however, was repulsed with heavy losses, and Estrada had to bring up his own troops to redress the balance and take the state capital, Morelia. The brothers Colonels Manuel and Maximino Ávila Camacho were captured there and threatened with death if they did not sign the Plan of Vera Cruz; when they refused to do so they were, however, released.

The government refused to be rattled. Taking advantage of their internal lines of communication, they devoted their major effort to the eastern front. At Estación Esperanza on 28 January government forces under General Martínez inflicted a crushing defeat on the forces of General Guadalupe Sánchez, who lost his campaign train and was lucky to escape on horseback. De la Huerta was forced to abandon the port for an alternative capital in Frontera, Tabasco.

By this time, the beginning of February, the President was already leading his forces in person against the rebels in the west from Irapuato in the State of Guerrero. On 10 February he secured an overwhelming victory at Ocotlán, forcing the followers of Estrada to abandon Guadalajara before Estrada himself could return there to save the day. Estrada's forces were located by government aircraft and harried; his men fled; and he himself eventually escaped to California after enlisting in the Federal army as a means of disguise! His principal companions were captured and shot.

With this débâcle, the fate of the revolt was sealed. The United States government under President Coolidge firmly backed the government they had so recently recognized, and facilitated the shipment of arms and ammunition to reinforce the Federal forces. But it was the United States control of sea communications that was to prove crucial after the rebel government had taken refuge beyond the Isthmus. Cut off from the outside world at Frontera, Tabasco, de la Huerta in the end had to cut his direct connection with the forces in Mexico in order to go personally to seek aid in the United States. With his departure General Cándido Aguilar, who became supreme chief in his absence, sought to recover the failing fortunes of the southern revolt by striking into Chiapas. Disease and desertions soon brought about the disintegration of his forces. General Salvador Alvarado, who had managed to escape from Ocotlán to join him in Chiapas, was killed by one of his own men, and the survivors fell into Federal hands or took refuge in Guatemala. Meanwhile every effort was devoted in Oaxaca to hunting down General Fortunato Maycotte, who was finally captured as a fugitive suffering from acute thirst in the sands of the Isthmus near Salina Cruz. There, after being tortured to make him give up the money he was believed to have been carrying, he was court-martialled by the military authorities and shot on 14 May.

The aftermath of the revolt was marked by a wave of executions. Few were spared who had taken an active role, the most celebrated being the lawyer Ramón Treviño, who when captured by the military authorities claimed that as a civilian he could not be shot. On the orders of the Secretary of War, his appointment as a general was published next to the warrant for his execution.

The military had done very well out of the revolt. They had been re-equipped at considerable expense, and the desertions had enabled Obregón to promote a great many new generals who might be hoped at least to stay loyal until the end of his term. The respite was used to make a start on creating a professional army in which promotion would be on merit and by examination; but in the few months remaining to him Obregón had no chance to make much more than a token effort in that direction.

What was much more significant was the extent to which the revolt had discredited the civilian political forces opposed to the rise of the labour interest. Suppression meant the installation of 'Calles men', and of these one of the more significant would be the newly-elected governor of Puebla, Vicente Lombardo Toledano, a socialist and a labour organizer. It also meant the recruitment of workers for the Federal cause, but this action was more symbolic than real. What gave it a greater meaning was a series of events stemming from the nature of the revolt itself. In its first days, various interests, including the large landowners, had been encouraged to rise in revolt against the socialist governor of Yucatán, Felipe Carrillo Puerto. The governor had fled by rail to Quintana Roo, where he had been captured by forces sympathetic to former Governor Salvador Alvarado; he was then brought back to Mérida, given an illegal court martial, and shot.

It was an act which probably stemmed purely from the personal hostility of the local military. But it was one which was used by Calles and Obregón to accuse the entire Delahuertista movement of being inspired by capitalist and reactionary elements. There were in Mexico City a great many people, however, who because of their hostility to the Bucareli treaties did not see it that way. Senator Francisco Field Jurado, senator from Campeche, was one of them; he firmly continued to direct the opposition to ratification. Then on 14 January, Luis N. Morones, a deputy, the founder of the *Partido Laborista*, and organizer of the trade union federation, the *Confederación Regional de Obreros Mexicanos* (CROM), denounced Field Jurado and his followers as supporters of the rebels and threatened 'a tooth for a tooth, a life for a life'. Boldly, Field Jurado announced that he would go to the Senate and vote against the convention nevertheless, but as he left the building a week later he was riddled with bullets from a car without licence plates. At the same time, other senators were kidnapped and though they were later released unharmed, the remainder of their colleagues prudently decided to pass only a token resolution expressing their desire for an investigation. No one was ever punished for the crime, and Morones was cleared on his assertion that he had nothing to do with it, which he may indeed not have done.

With the death of Field Jurado, PCN resistance to the treaties soon collapsed. The elections in July went off relatively quietly, and Calles, as candidate of the *Partido Laborista*, was elected by 1,340,634 votes over 250,050 for General Ángel Flores, the best compromise candidate the remainder of the PLC and PCN were able to agree on. The ascendancy of the PL, even backed as it was by the strongarm methods of the CROM, did not go unchallenged, and in a brawl on the floor of the Chamber of Deputies in November 1924 Morones was shot and wounded.

The four-year term of General Calles, which began with his formal inauguration on 1 December 1924 in the new National Stadium, was to confirm this ascendancy. There was a considerable degree of continuity between the new administration and the old, but, for example, though Pani continued at the Department of *Hacienda* and General Aarón Sáenz was retained as Secretary of External Relations, Morones himself was brought into the new Cabinet as Secretary of Industry, Commerce, and Labour and Dr José M. Puig Casauranc, a keen Callista, became the new Secretary of Education. So the new President from the beginning exercised a firm control over his administration. This control, however, tended increasingly towards support for the labour interest as a permanent base for backing the government.

It was the paradox of the Calles administration that at the same time it presided over the most rapid rate of expansion of the Mexican economy down to that time. The inauguration of Calles coincided with the return of prosperity, and in the gaudy years of the mid-twenties prosperity meant large cars, smart suits, and a lavish display of gold cigarette cases and diamond rings. The new Secretary of Labour was second to none in his fondness for the visible signs of economic success. Yet under Calles's rigid, autocratic, and frequently irritable direction, government activity broadened out into a real drive to promote the material basis of social welfare for a wider public.

Fundamental to this was the restoration of finances. In 1924 Calles became the first Mexican President to reap the benefits of an assured income for the state from the first regular income tax. By 1926 the banking system, which had been derelict since the days of Victoriano Huerta, was restored and the control of finance vested in a new single bank of issue, the Bank of Mexico. The introduction of a paper currency that actually commanded confidence finally did away with the host of currency expedients of the revolutionary years that had resulted in a permanent but acute shortage of exchange. At the same time, by the Pani-Lamont Agreement of October 1925 the government was able to modify in its favour the agreements made with its foreign creditors by de la Huerta in 1922.

This done, the government was able to turn its attention to the financing of development. The first problem was the lack of transport. The National Railways were placed under a separate government-controlled corporation and money spent on their restoration. In 1927 the old Southern Pacific railway link down the west coast was finally completed, as far as Guadalajara, where it linked up with the lines of the National Railways. Meanwhile the government had to deal with the even more pressing problem of the roads, which at the opening of the automobile age were still almost wholly the old colonial highways; that is, where they had not fallen into total disrepair. Outside the capital there were only two all-weather roads in the entire country. A commission was set up to carry out a major programme of trunk roads and funded out of the proceeds of a 3 per cent petrol tax.

Certain obstacles to change were also removed. It was Calles who 'closed the doors of the barracks'[1] by the firm alteration of the military establishment directed by his Secretary of War. General Amaro commanded universal respect as a dashing military figure who wore gold earrings in the old Indian tradition. Some generals were retired, others transferred, and the pressures for professionalization were stepped up. As a consequence of the election campaign of 1928, there was a brief military revolt, ended by a dramatic assassination of eleven of its leading protagonists on the Cuernavaca road. It was this incident that has given Calles a reputation for bloodthirstiness, but examples of personal ruthlessness on his part are few, though spectacular compared with those of his predecessor.

Calles continued the Obregón policy of fostering public education. As a one-time school inspector he might have been expected to do so; certainly Puig Casauranc received constant help and economic aid. It was but one aspect of a high moral tone that pervaded his public speeches. He saw three enemies of the people: the clergy, vice, and ignorance; and he fought all three.[2]

Above all, Calles advanced the programme of agrarian reform which the *coup* of 1920 had done so much to accelerate. The reasons for the acceleration were straightforward. There were two sorts of historical circumstances in which reform had to proceed. In some cases, land had been taken away from the common ownership of villages and given to big landowners or foreign companies, and the villages still survived and had evidence of title. Under Carranza a start had been made in enabling those villages to reclaim their lands. In 1920 the interim government of Adolfo de la Huerta had gone further in providing for the endowment of villages where they could no longer prove title. The amount of land distributed jumped accordingly, and under Obregón totalled more than a million hectares in all.

In other cases, however, and particularly in the Core and south, villages had been entirely swallowed up by the haciendas and their inhabitants reduced to the state of debt slavery. This presented a much greater problem, and it was not to be given a solution until the time of Lázaro Cárdenas. Calles, though, despite his political dependence on labour, or perhaps because of it, removed the remaining impediments to endowment and distributed three times as much land as his three predecessors. His policy was clear and articulated; it also explains many of the political pressures that were to affect his successors.

'I speak and fight for the compliance of the agrarian policy of the Revolution', he had said in one of his campaign speeches (20 September 1923),

> for in this lies the right of the people to live. To satisfy this necessity, the breaking up of the large estates which are yet intact and which, because of their size and the system under which they are worked, constitute a monopoly of the soil, must be brought about through evolutionary proceedings, amply planned and studied, backed by a firm system of agricultural credit and by the organisation of cooperative societies by the small farmers.[3]

Calles envisaged a large-scale reform leading to small peasant holdings. The experience of the past few years now convinced him that only by dividing the land up would the necessary incentive be found to work it efficiently. The Law of Ejidal Patrimony (1925) therefore provided for the parcelling-out of communal lands to individual owners. At the same time endowment and distribution were stepped up.[4] Nor was the need for supporting legislation forgotten. The Law of Ejidal Credit brought about the establishment in 1926 of the National Bank of Agricultural Credit, which was subsequently to play a major role in expanding productive capacity. In addition, work was begun on the extension of irrigation, the absence of which was the main obstacle to effective land use in the desert areas of Sonora and Sinaloa. After the time of Calles a great deal of this work languished until the 1950s again brought its urgency to the fore.

In the industrial field the new government's stronger adhesion to the labour interest brought results. By backing the expansion of the CROM at the expense of the Communist-dominated *Confederación General de Trabajadores* (CGT) it promoted the rapid growth of a large, if rather unhealthy, labour organization able to improve the conditions of its members at the expense of the employers rather than at the expense of the government. The number of strikes fell dramatically after Calles came to power. The expansion of the economy was evidenced by the general increase of production in all fields except oil, where bad labour relations with suspicious foreign companies combined with the exhaustion of wells overexploited in the war years to fuel the Great War effort. Even this was not seen as a great setback when so much else was going well. Then on 4 February 1926 the situation was abruptly changed by the outbreak of a conflict which Calles himself had invited, but which was to cast a shadow over the last two years of his personal rule.

Plutarco Elías Calles

Plutarco Elías Calles remains the most controversial figure in Mexican history this century. Only Luis L. León among his contemporaries has made a serious attempt to give credit where credit was due,[5] and the only easily accessible biography of him—not a long one at that—is frankly hostile.[6] Ironically, despite this artificial obscurity in his own native country, he is probably the only Mexican President to have found his way into an important work of English literature, D. H. Lawrence's *The Plumed Serpent*, thinly disguised as 'Socrates Tomás Montes'. Lawrence portrays him as 'sincere and passionate', all his ideas European and American, an atheist worshipped in Christian terms while surrounded by the ancient Aztec religion of blood and death; in this, as in so many other things, Lawrence is at once wholly wrong and at the same time not too wide of the mark.

Almost everything about Calles's early life is uncertain. He is stated to have been born at Guaymas, Sonora, on 27 January 1877, and was certainly baptized in the parish church there on 28 December 1878, when the statement about his birth-date was recorded. There seems no doubt therefore that we can reject at least one of the claims of his enemies, that he was not a Mexican by birth. He was the son of Plutarco Elías Lucero and María de Jesús Campuzano, who afterwards as a widow married a Juan Calles, who gave his surname to the young boy. Apart from some confusion about his mother's maiden name, this too seems to be reasonably well established.

Elías (Elijah in English) is certainly not a regular Spanish surname, but there was nothing obscure about the family in Sonora. Plutarco's great-grandfather, Rafael Elías González, was governor of Sonora in 1837; his step-grandfather, Juan José Calles, of Arizpe, Sonora, had held military and civil posts and had been mortally wounded in battle against the Imperialists in 1865; his father, a businessman, had served as a state deputy in 1875 and as Prefect of Guaymas in 1877–79. The Elías family were wealthy enough to be of the minor aristocracy, though they were generally held to be of Levantine, and were suspected of being of Jewish, ancestry. The nickname of 'El Turco' (The Turk) given to Plutarco as a boy reflects this belief. He was always touchy on the subject–a fact that only served to exacerbate the allegations of his enemies–and grew up morose and unsociable. When Adolfo de la Huerta met him in 1895, and, learning he was a fellow-citizen of Guaymas, asked him what family he came from, he replied with characteristic brusqueness 'My own'.[7] He finished his education in Hermosillo, the state capital, and in 1894 became a school-teacher.

In those days in Mexico school-teaching was a job of low social status, badly paid and regarded with contempt. It is quite likely that Calles's pupils did, as is alleged, give him a scurrilous nickname suggesting his addiction to drink, and that he used to thrash them soundly. However, in 1903 he was promoted to the post of Inspector of Schools, and this argues a certain degree of ability as well as some family influence and a great deal of political reliability. It is the next stage of Calles's career that has in fact created the most startling legends. He is said to have embarked on a quite startling career of petty crime, beginning by embezzling the funds of his schoolmasters' common room. Having had, it is said, to give up his teaching career in consequence, he is then supposed to have again absconded with the funds. His brother is then said to have put him in charge of the bar of the Hotel Mexico.[8] The hotel having burnt to the ground, supposedly with his help, the young Calles is then alleged to have acquired from the insurance sufficient money to set up in business at Fronteras, where he is variously supposed to have been in partnership with a North American in running a flour-mill, which failed, and ranching (with a bit of cattle-smuggling on the side). All this looks very like the sort of gossip that could in Mexico collect round a rather pushy young man determined to make money where he could. At the most, the factual basis is that he tried his hand at a number of business ventures but found none of them particularly congenial.

The reason why he had to do so is also clear—he was already involved in politics. He was active in the 'Club Verde' which emerged in opposition to the Porfirista state government and which subsequently joined Madero's following. The reason why he had to leave Guaymas was the publication of some short articles in opposition periodicals—something the *Porfiriato* did not expect from an Inspector of Schools. For this purpose his characteristic, aggressive style, crude but effective, was ideal. With the triumph of the Maderistas he obtained his reward, the post of commissioner of police in the crucially important frontier town of Agua Prieta, Sonora. Here was an opportunity not only to make a reputation, but also to make a lot of money from the American visitors who swarmed over the border in search of the night life. And this, it is said, he did by investing in his own bar. If so, the experience put him off alcohol for life.

Up to this point it appears that Calles had no actual military experience. It was forced upon him because in the absence of regular military forces he was responsible for the defence of the town, and he seems to have had his first experience of battle at the time of the Orozco rebellion. His formal military career, however, began in 1913 when he joined the Constitutionalists as a lieutenant-colonel, and was almost at once nominated by Obregón *Comandante Militar* of the state capital, Hermosillo. From then on his star rose rapidly. It was he who, though unable to gain the confidence of Carranza's nominee for governor, ex-Governor Mayortena, held on to the all-important border crossing-points for the Constitutionalists and so denied them to the Villistas. So impressed was Carranza with his loyalty, that when Obregón left the state with his men, it was Calles whom he left behind in charge of all the state's military forces, so securing his rear. It was with these forces that he carried out his celebrated defence of Agua Prieta against Villa's last thrust into Sonora in October and November 1915, when he used all the lessons he had gained from study of war in Europe against the formidable *Dorados* and won.

His military successes guaranteed him nomination for the governorship of Sonora on 4 August 1915. With Villa defeated, Sonora became one of the most orderly parts of Mexico, and he governed it sternly and efficiently. His reforms stretched into almost every area of the state administration. He amended the state constitution to control the judiciary; reformed the Civil Code, introducing, among other innovations, provision for divorce—later to become a major industry in the state; and reformed the collection and spending of taxes. He founded a Technical School for the training of the orphans of the Revolution, and greatly improved labour relations. But his two most controversial changes were the prohibition of the sale or distribution of alcoholic beverages and the expulsion of all Catholic priests from the state.

In 1916 he laid down the nominated governorship, but was elected again to complete the term until 1919, when he was brought into the Cabinet by President Carranza as Secretary of Industry, Commerce, and Labour. He held this post for less than a year before resigning it in February 1920 to aid the campaign of Obregón, and so made much less of a mark here than in the state, where he was soon to be called by Governor de la Huerta to act again as commander of the state forces in face of the threat from the Federal government.

The success of the Plan of Agua Prieta, which bore so much of Calles's hand, made Calles himself one of the three most powerful men in Mexico. De la Huerta, in whose Cabinet he served as Secretary of War and Marine, soon destroyed his own chances of further advancement by going into revolt, and for almost all the Obregón Presidency, Calles as Secretary of *Gobernación* was the President's right-hand man, fixer, trouble-shooter, and chief supporter. It was this man who now became President of Mexico and ultimately was to become almost synonymous with the Revolution itself.

But what was he really like? Lucien Romier described him for the *Revue des Deux-Mondes* in 1927 thus:

Tall in stature, massive shoulders, a face at once of violence and of reserve, with a sort of enlightenment in his gaze. There is not a single feature nor a single gesture in this man which betrays a drop of Latin, Anglo-Saxon, or, with greater reason, Celtic blood. He is not Oriental with the deceptive Oriental indifference. He is not the agile Indian. He is not semitic. He is a type apart. Imagine a quiet wild beast who will suddenly rend an attacker.[9]

As Carlos Pereyra, who hated Calles, said, Romier's portrait leaves a lot of wild beasts to choose from.[10]

Portraits of Calles confirm what all descriptions of him suggest, that there was something ominous about him. It is a heavy face but a strong one, entirely Mexican (whatever that may mean), the face of a bronze rather than of a stone statue. In life, however, and in conversation it was frequently crossed by a smile or a laugh; though in a sense puritanical, an impression strongly reinforced by his fondness for dark clothes, Calles had a pronounced if rather rough sense of humour. His greatest resemblance north of the frontier was not, as Pereyra suggested, to the figures of the so-called 'Wild West', but to those new heroes of his own time: the detective, or the boss of a great city.

And what drove this man on to the height of power that he did achieve? Not surely merely a personal ambition or a desire to avenge his own wrongs. His most striking characteristic, his intense and over-reaching anti-clericalism, may have been inherited, but it was inherited within the Mexican tradition, and not from his blood father's family at that, but from social tradition. Calles was neither a madman, as Catholics were wont to hint, nor a Protestant business-man, as his appearance was inclined to suggest to North American visitors, but a Mexican socialist, fired with the zeal to avenge cen-turies of wrongs. And his socialism, like his military strategy, was always Fabian.

Religion

The fundamental role of religion in Mexican life can hardly be gainsaid. To this day Mexico, though nominally atheistic, is over-whelmingly Catholic, and her Catholicism is not just the religion of the poor peasants or their relatives newly arrived in Mexico City, but that affected publicly by the *nouveaux riches* who in all other respects affect the manners and customs of the United States. The Catholic priests, monks, and nuns who braved incredible privations, physical danger, and ever-present death in order to convert the inhabitants of New Spain did their work well.

We have already seen how the Church attempted to protect the Indian against the Spaniard, and how a priest came to be the hero of Mexican independence. We have seen how many men of the nine-teenth, and not a few of the twentieth, century owed their first educa-tional opportunities to church schools and those who taught in them. And we have seen how Díaz came to a tacit agreement with the church hierarchy to protect them in return for their political support. What we have not seen is the extent to which the Church was itself divided, and the effect that this had on the climate of opinion in Mexico.

Socialism in Mexico was, after all, also an imported European product. The attitudes of the Church in Europe towards social re-form were transplanted to the New World, and not without some effect upon it. Though, therefore, in terms of formal structure one finds socialist organizations in existence in Mexico as early as the time of the Reform, it is straining more than one historical point to see them as the forerunners of the social movements of the twentieth century in any direct sense. These do derive directly from the founda-tion at St Louis, Missouri, in 1906 of the *Partido Liberal* of the Flores Magón brothers, and from the great strike at Cananea in the same year—the first example of mass industrial conflict in Mexico. But the impulse for both these events came primarily from the United States, not from the Mexican past.

Religion, however, did derive from the Mexican past, though it had been accommodated to Christian forms. The Reform, in Tannenbaum's words, began the process by which the Church was 'reduced to a hierarchical skeleton'. But as he recognized, it left the real faith of the people essentially untouched. And in the later years of the *Porfiriato*, when the church hierarchy made the terrible mistake of becoming closely associated with the maintenance of the dictatorial system, there were many within the Catholic fold who were stirred by the new ideas on satisfying material as well as spiritual needs for the Mexican people. Charity was no longer sufficient; in fact, in Mexico, it never had been sufficient.

The most dramatic exposition of these ideas came in the Encyclical *Rerum Novarum* of Leo XIII in 1891, though the Pope had from his accession in 1878 made the social question the central theme of his pontificate. Significantly the Encyclical, despite the great weight deliberately placed on the circumstances of its publication, was not discussed publicly in Mexico until 1895.[11] Yet it is hard to see how, in that repressive climate, it could have been. The circumstances of its invocation in 1895 were quite remarkable; the Church, beginning to revive, was emerging as an alternative base of political support to the régime, and hence as a potential opposition. In preparation for his re-election Díaz was gathering together every possible evidence of support, not excluding the foreign business community. The Church was uniquely in a position to give, not only support, but even legitimacy—but there was a price to be paid, and that was the awakening of interest in the social question among the laity.

In the early years of the twentieth century there was a dramatic flowering of Catholic organizations designed to provide a new and effective expression of lay involvement, beginning with a Catholic social conference in Puebla in 1903. Catholic workers' organizations began to appear, paralleling Catholic interest in agrarian problems, and at the Eucharistic Congress held in Guadalajara in 1908 the Church declared its support for a minimum wage and a wide range of individual social safeguards. From there it was a short step to the emergence at the fall of Díaz in 1911 of the National Catholic Party.

The Catholic Party had a short and unfortunate life. It pursued a strictly legal course within the constitution of the day, and its defeat in 1911 came as a surprise to few. However, its dedication to legalism in the wake of Huerta's seizure of power was to present it with an unacceptable dilemma. If it continued to take part in the electoral process—as it did—it was liable to become associated closely with the régime itself, and when the régime fell, this was to prove its undoing. What remained was two things: the revived bond between the clergy and the laity, which never thereafter wholly waned, and a new sense of the power and relevance of belonging to the international world of Christendom, from which the Church's power had come in the first instance. It was the interaction between these two aspects that was to make possible the resistance of the Church to secularization in the 1920s, and, ultimately, made it successful.

For Catholics in other parts of the world Mexico became an awful image of atheism. It was infinitely worse, because infinitely nearer home, than the anti-religious movement in the Soviet Union. It was in the first instance the Catholic community in the United States that developed this image for the English-speaking world, but their colourful denunciations were backed by cooler and better-written works.[12]

At home, in Mexico, the anti-religious fervour had some strange consequences. Priests were forbidden to appear in public in their habits. Churches were forced to accept during service the presence of large throngs exercising their citizen rights to make use of a public building for conversation. Photography by foreign visitors or journalists of scenes of 'religious fanaticism', such as the pilgrimage to the Shrine of Guadalupe (where the penitents advance across the courtyard on their knees), was strictly forbidden. Yet though anti-clericalism remained strong throughout the Cárdenas administration, it was his successor in 1940 who became the first post-revolutionary President to announce his own religious faith publicly, and it was evident that the declaration brought him as much support as he forfeited. The attempt to fight fanaticism with fanaticism was perhaps doomed to failure from the start; it remains to be seen how the new casual acceptance of religion as a social function of status or behaviour stands the test of time, but it can hardly be doubted that in this sense, success is a greater danger to the effective survival of religious belief in Mexico today than persecution and suppression ever were in the past.

[1] Luis L. León, 'El presidente Calles', *Historia mexicana*, 10: 320.
[2] Plutarco Elías Calles, *Mexico before the World; Public Documents and Addresses of Plutarco Elías Calles*, ed. and trans. Robert Hammond Murray (New York, The Academy Press, 1927).
[3] Calles, op. cit., 8.
[4] Portes Gil, *La crisis política de la Revolución y la próxima elección presidencial* (Mexico, Ed. Botas, 1957), 21.
[5] Luis L. León, op. cit.
[6] Fernando Medina Ruiz, *Calles, un destino melancólico* (Mexico, Editorial Jus, 1960); see also Daniel Moreno's brief account in his *Venustiano Carranza, Álvaro Obregón, Plutarco Elías Calles* (Mexico, Libro-Mex, 1960).
[7] de la Huerta, *Memorias*, 16.
[8] Anita Brenner, *The Wind that Swept Mexico: the History of the Mexican Revolution 1910–1942* (Austin & London, University of Texas Press, 1971), 126, calls him 'the rocky-jawed ex-bartender'.
[9] Medina Ruiz, op. cit., 14.
[10] The reference is to Carlos Pereyra's *México Falsificado*.

[11] Alicia Olivera Sedano, *Aspectos del conflicto religioso de 1926 a 1929* (Mexico, INAH, 1966), 31.

[12] Francis Clement Kelley, *Blood-drenched Altars* (Milwaukee, The Bruce Publishing Co., 1935); cf. Graham Greene, *The Lawless Roads* (London, 1950). Evelyn Waugh, *Robbery under Law: the Mexican object-lesson* (London, Chapman & Hall, 1939) said of Mexico: 'It is a waste land, part of a dead, or at any rate, a dying planet. Politics, everywhere destructive, have here dried up the place, frozen it, cracked it, and powdered it to dust'. But he was talking of oil, not religion.

The Revolution XVIII: Cristeros

THE CAUSES OF THE CRISTERO WAR reach far back into Mexican history. The dual nature of the Conquest, the tradition of war against the infidel, and the hierarchical structure of the Church and its association with the last years of the Díaz régime stood in opposition to the role of the clergy in the Wars of Independence, the Church as protector of the Indian, and the ambiguous uncertainties of the aftermath of the Reform. If it was never entirely forgotten that the Church was in some sense *foreign*, it was also never entirely forgotten that it stood for certain values of goodness, peace, and respect for the best of the past.

However, if generations had contributed to the dispute, it was Calles who precipitated it. In doing so, he acted in what he considered was the spirit of the Revolution, the new force that spoke for the people of Mexico. This was a strain that owed little to Madero; much to Villa, with his defence of the poor against the rich; but—curiously enough—most to the almost playful irreverence of Obregón. In Mexican society with its cult of virility (*machismo*), there was always lurking under the surface a contempt for the priest as not being a real man. It was the military experience, rather than ideology, that brought this to the surface. The tricks he played on the priests he captured in Mexico City, finally turning them loose in open country to walk home as best they could, were in this vein; as was the report of his medical adviser that they were all fit to walk, but that many of them were suffering from venereal diseases. It was this kind of calculated disrespect that was characteristic of Calles's approach to religion, and in the Mexico of the early 1920s this meant effectively that neither he nor Obregón sought to restrain the more overt anti-clericalism of others more ideologically committed.

The crucial issue was the question of lay education. The Constitution of 1917 had, it will be remembered, not merely reinstated the provisions of the 1857 Constitution limiting the powers of the clergy, but had added to them a provision prohibiting religious bodies from establishing schools and the clergy from teaching in them. The archbishop of Mexico, Monsignor José Mora y del Río, courageously reiterated his opposition to this and other provisions, but even he came under physical attack, and in the more remote parts of Mexico priests and even bishops were roughly treated. The new socialist governor of Tabasco, Tomás Garrido Canabal, was extreme in that he ruled that no priests could practise in his state unless they were married–which, of course, meant none–but others took advantage of their powers to license as few as they dared. At the same time Obregón looked with favour on efforts to establish 'socialist education' in the state schools, and this meant deliberate instruction in atheism.

Such moves did not lead to severance of diplomatic relations with the Vatican. The Apostolic Delegate of the day, José Ridolfi, titular archbishop of Apamea, is said to have intervened for the release of Madero in 1911. His successor fled from Mexico at the beginning of 1914, but only a few months later he was replaced by Luis Filippi, titular archbishop of Sárdica. Monsignor Filippi, who remained throughout the Constitutionalist period, determined on a counter-offensive against the Obregón government. At the top of the small mountain called the Cerro del Cubilete, in the State of Guanajuato, as near as possible to the geographical centre of Mexico, in January 1923 he laid the cornerstone of a vast monument to Christ the King (*Cristo Rey*) and so lent his official weight to a ceremony in which the bishop of San Luis Potosí solemnly proclaimed Christ the King of Mexico. He was forthwith expelled from the country on the grounds that he had broken the law of the land in taking part in a religious ceremony in the open air.

The expulsion did not check clerical enthusiasm. Although the new Apostolic Delegate soon had to retire for reasons of ill-health, preparations were pushed ahead for a vast Eucharistic Congress to be held in the capital itself in October 1924. The organizers were not over-careful to avoid transgressions of the admittedly very severe restrictions on their activities, and several of their planned activities had to be called off. But Obregón's actions in the matter were limited and it was clear that most of the opposition came from elsewhere.

With the inauguration of Calles a dramatic change occurred. To begin with, he was prepared strongly to back the anti-clerical programme of Garrido Canabal and his sympathizers. More importantly he gave covert encouragement to the appearance of a schismatic Church, the so-called Catholic Apostolic Church, which among other things allowed its priests to marry. This body took over, amid considerable public controversy, one of the capital's most central churches–like all others in Mexico officially the property of the government to dispose of as it would.

From then on the situation deteriorated rapidly. Calles had already planned, it seems, to introduce legislation giving effect to the anti-clerical provisions of the constitution. This was in line with his general policy with respect to other legislation. When press reports began to suggest that the archbishop of Mexico was opposing such moves, Calles gave immediate effect to some of them by ordering them to be followed by government employees forthwith, and the archbishop then exacerbated the situation by stating publicly that his position was indeed as it had already been reported. It was an unfortunate coincidence that the statement appeared on the anniversary of the constitution, 5 February 1926.

The government responded at once by expelling some 200 foreign priests and nuns, followed two months later by the newly arrived Apostolic Delegate himself. Several bishops, in particular the bishop of Huejutla, in the State of Hidalgo, advocated open resistance, and he, being the most inflammatory, was arrested and tried for sedition. The response of the archbishop to these two acts was to permit the establishment of the so-called *Liga Defensora de la Libertad Religiosa* which when the government's laws against the Church came into effect – on 31 July – immediately responded with full non co-operation and a boycott of the government. The laws themselves prescribed sentences for members of the clergy who opposed the government, and under these most of those who organized the resistance were soon arrested or detained. Backed by cheering crowds of workers, Calles made no attempt to avoid the conflict, which he blamed entirely on the church leaders. When 31 July came, church services stopped, for with the support and approval of Pope Pius XI the whole country had been placed under an interdict. Though presented with a petition bearing more than two million signatures, which it refused to accept, Congress backed the President in his stand.

It was not long before it became apparent that Calles had overlooked one thing. He could arrest the bishops, expel foreign priests, and place restrictions on Mexican ones. But he had underestimated the anger of the laity. Deprived of their regular duties of the care of souls, there were many priests who were prepared to lead them in guerrilla warfare against the government, and in the three States of Jalisco, Guanajuato, and Michoacán there soon appeared a full-scale army fighting under the battle-cry 'Viva Cristo Rey' ('Long live Christ the King'). From this cry they soon became known as the 'cristeros'. Not only were they numerous, they were also well armed, and their leader, General Rodolfo L. Gallegos, knew what he was doing. The fact that the hierarchy officially opposed the resort to violence made little difference. Nor, for that matter, did it stop Calles from expelling many of them from the country.

For two years the rural conflict raged. It was a savage conflict, marked by appalling atrocities on both sides.[1] Because of the sporadic way in which the conflict had broken out, the first stages went badly

for the rebels, who by resorting to attacks on trains and other surprise attacks did, however, manage to keep the conflict in being.
When the first leader of the movement, General Gallegos, was killed
in battle by Federal troops in May 1927 it appeared that the movement might be on the point of breaking up. The emergence of
General Gorostieta as commander of the forces in Jalisco, however,
provided a more dynamic leadership, and stalemate prevailed at the
outset of the Presidential campaign of 1928.

It was here that Calles had run into his most serious problem, and
the one that was eventually almost to defeat him – the succession.
There was no question but that Obregón wanted the job. But the
Revolution had above all been fought for the principle of no re-election, a principle which the Revolution of Agua Prieta had much
strengthened. On the other hand, it was a fact that there was no other
candidate who commanded general revolutionary support. Calles
himself favoured the labour leader Morones, but he was anathema to
the Obregonistas, and the question was really decided by the Obregonista majority in Congress. In 1926 they pushed through a constitutional amendment to allow a candidate who had already served a
non-consecutive term to stand again. It was a proposal which, after
all, touched their own interests closely. Shortly afterwards they
added to it a provision increasing the length of the Presidential term
to six years, with effect from the 1928 election.

Obregón delayed the formal announcement of his candidature
until he could make it in such a way that it would appear to have
been forced on him at the will of a grateful nation. He used the
effective argument that at this stage it was necessary to modify the
principle of No Re-election in order to secure that of Effective Suffrage – in other words to contest the political power of the incumbent
government. The two other military candidates in the field – Generals
Arnulfo R. Gómez and Francisco R. Serrano – he dismissed as un-
worthy of serious consideration. Neither had, perhaps, particularly
high hopes of attaining the Presidency by election, especially Serrano,
whose incurable craze for gambling had now left him on the wrong
side of bankruptcy. But Obregón's announcement made it abun-
dantly clear that their only hope was to take the traditional Mexican
alternative.

A major military parade on 2 October went off with an air of
tension as the Secretary of War, General Amaro, juggled with the
order of battle to avert the danger of the explosion taking place in the
capital. As they left, some of the troops declared for Gómez and
Serrano. Serrano was staying in the Moctezuma Hotel in Cuernavaca, awaiting news of the hoped-for uprising. Instead, on the orders
of President Calles, troops quickly arrested him and his principal

followers. On hearing of the crisis, Obregón had taken his place with the President at Chapultepec, and there, when news came of the arrests, the two men agreed that the fourteen prisoners should be shot forthwith. Accordingly without further delay they were bound and taken to a wood by the side of the Cuernavaca road and summarily shot. When the news was received elsewhere in the country any other support for the revolt rapidly fizzled out. Among those that were killed in other incidents were the governor of the State of Chiapas in the south and the brother of ex-President de la Huerta, in the State of Sonora. General Gómez, who had had more luck than his fellow-candidate, was defeated in a brief skirmish a week later, but managed to escape for almost a month before being betrayed and executed.

The stir caused by the revolt had hardly died down when it was quite forgotten in face of the development of the Cristero revolt. On 13 November 1927 while Obregón was driving through Chapultepec Park his car was blown up by bombs thrown from another moving vehicle. Somehow the ex-President survived virtually uninjured. The sensation came from the fact that the government obtained a captive, and he, while in hospital, disclosed that he knew a house where a Jesuit priest, Father Miguel Pro, and his brother, a Cristero organizer, were in hiding. There was no evidence linking the Pro brothers to the crime, but Calles hardly needed evidence, and they too were summarily executed, in the police station in the capital before numerous officials and photographers.

Obregón himself had, in fact, no connection on this occasion with the shootings. As he now had no opponents to contest, he took his time about resuming his campaign, and there was little enough that was interesting about it. One attempt was made on his life and several others on the lives of his followers, while a bomb did some damage to the Chamber of Deputies but not to the deputies themselves. Once elected, the President-elect made a triumphal progress down the west coast of Mexico, retracing the ground of his great military campaign of 1914. Everywhere he was welcomed. Finally, on 15 July, he arrived in the capital, where he was due to be welcomed the same evening at a victory banquet at a restaurant with the somewhat ominous name of La Bombilla ('Little Bomb'). There, surrounded by celebrities, listening to music from the orchestra while he ate and chatted, he was sketched by a small man in a brown suit who said he was a cartoonist. Midway through the meal the cartoonist took his sketches up to show to the President-elect, who smiled at him in a friendly way, and then looked across the table at a friend. As he did so the cartoonist shot him three times in the face with a pistol, and he fell forward dead over the table without another word.[2]

Intrigue

Mexico is unusual among the nations of the world in the pattern of her international relations. She is a strongly neutralist state close to a major world power; that is not unusual. She has become such a state as a result of a turbulent and often unhappy history, but that too does not mark her out. What *does* is the particular form of that history. No one doubts the importance of the War of Independence, the War of 1847, the War of the French Intervention; yet it is not these wars that shaped Mexican history so much as the phenomenon of which they were a result, that Mexico has ever since independence been a focus of intrigue.

It is a repetitive pattern. At first formless and undirected (except inasmuch as it involved the actions of Americans such as Poinsett), foreign intrigue has since 1847, if not since 1838, been directed at the dominant influence of the United States and the Anglo-Saxon hegemony of the Caribbean. In the 1860s the source of intrigue was the French. During the Great War it was the Germans. In between, the British were active, already conscious of the extension of American influence. But since 1918 a new dimension has been given to the question by the development of ideological conflict.

Ideological conflict was of course not new, in any sense. To the generally known facts about the role of Masonry in the civil strife in Mexico in the two decades after independence, Brandenburg has added a great deal of detail about subsequent developments which suggest that it enjoyed considerable importance again in the 1930s.[3] Portes Gil, Ortiz Rubio, Rodríguez, and Cárdenas were all Masons — the last the grand master between 1929 and 1931 of the Mexican Independent Symbolical Grand Lodge (founded 1927) which under his Presidency became an important bond between government officials and local leaders up and down the country. The importance of this is twofold. It confirms the active role of Masonry as a political force in Mexico throughout the nineteenth century and even down to our own time. But it also illuminates the struggles of interpretation of the direction of the Revolution; foreign influence remained strong in many lodges into the 1920s and its removal was one of the chief causes behind the formation of the Cárdenas Rite.

On the other hand, the ideological positivism of the Díaz régime was not associated with conscious penetration by any foreign power. Certainly the British did not arrive in Mexico bearing with them copies of Herbert Spencer's *Social Statics*. The French colony remained influential in Mexico throughout the same period, but it was not a centre of intrigue; Mexicans looked to Paris as a centre of culture, and, if wealthy enough, went there to be educated; but the government of the Third Republic was careful not to repeat the errors of the Empire.

It was left therefore to the Soviet Union in the early 1920s to make the running against American influence in Mexico. Recognition of the Soviet Union in 1923 brought a Soviet minister in Mexico, Stanislas Pestkovsky, who was recalled in 1926 and replaced by Aleksandra Kollontai, the first woman envoy accredited to a country in the Western Hemisphere. During her term of office relations between the two countries were friendly and there was no sign of any cooling of friendship on the part of the government of President Calles. However, in 1928 she was replaced as minister by Dr Aleksandr Makar who clearly had very different orders. The PCM were ordered to stop the peasants supporting the government, but the Communist peasant leader in Veracruz who attempted to do so was shot by the local military commander. A major diplomatic offensive was opened against Mexico as a tool of United States imperialism, with attacks in the Soviet press, public denunciations abroad, and agitation among members of the PCM in Mexico itself.[4]

The reasons for this extraordinarily ill-timed offensive are hard to understand. Russia badly needed friends abroad, and the Mexicans generally were by no means unsympathetic. But the Soviet government seems to have resented Mexican initiative in advising a peaceful settlement of differences with China, and to have misinterpreted it as a sign of a *volte-face* in foreign policy. Part of this misjudgement arose from the arrival in Mexico in 1927 of the new United States ambassador Dwight Morrow, and from his evident success at establishing a close personal relationship with Calles. Both men were very interested in scientific agriculture, and Calles, who was wont to take along on his tours of the country anyone whom he wished, found Morrow a congenial companion.[5]

Calles was always receptive to new ideas, and it would not have been surprising if Morrow had been able to influence him to some extent. Exerting influence, after all, is one of the expected duties of any ambassador. However, it is probably incorrect to ascribe the slowing-up in the land programme to Morrow's influence–as some have. Calles was already becoming concerned at the failure of land which had been distributed to be adequately worked, owing to the lack, in many places, of adequate water and transport for produce. In late 1926 the revolt of the Cristeros had spread to the point that suggested to the least sensitive of politicians that the ordinary agricultural worker was not very happy about existing policies. And Morrow's influence was certainly being directed on Calles to reach a settlement with the Church. This he steadfastly refused to do, despite its obvious attractions in removing the drain upon his budget; halting the land distribution was a saving which postponed the water crisis and alleviated hostility as well.

What Morrow did do was to establish good public relations for the United States, symbolized by the flight of his son-in-law, Colonel Lindbergh, from Washington to Mexico City at Christmas 1927 as well as by the careful respect he showed towards the Mexicans. This was a very different type of ambassador, and a very different view of the United States, from that to which Mexicans had become accustomed. Far from intriguing behind the President's back, Morrow was exceptionally cautious to make no move or no initiative without, as diplomats are supposed to do, first clearing it with the Head of State. It was on these foundations, laid at the time of President Coolidge, with whom Calles talked by telephone on the occasion of the opening of direct service between the two countries, that the Good Neighbor policy of Presidents Hoover and Roosevelt towards the rest of Latin America was to be developed.[6]

It may well be that the Russians were right to be suspicious, since a *rapprochement* alone would have been taken by them to be a sign of ideological impurity. But it would have been far wiser if they had not tried to bully the Mexican government. Ultimately, in a serious failure of Soviet security, a paper giving details of their plans to wreck the Mexican petroleum industry came into the hands of President Portes Gil, who in 1930 had no hesitation in ordering the Soviet minister to leave the country. Diplomatic relations were severed, and were not restored until 1942.

With the course of Soviet intrigue in post-war Mexico it is not necessary to deal here. It presents no very unusual features except its extent. The Soviet embassies in Mexico and Montevideo between them act as the twin centres of Soviet intelligence, diplomacy, trade, and espionage for the whole of Latin America. A particular importance devolved upon Mexico in that until very recently there was no focus of Soviet activity at all in Central America because there was no regular diplomatic mission. Since Central America is regarded by most parties as a particularly vulnerable point in the continental defence strategy of the United States its importance in the age of the Cold War is obvious, and even today it has by no means disappeared. For this continual importance, the emergence of Cuba as a centre of Communist authority within the Americas is largely responsible. It has become an article of faith for overseas observers that no diplomacy is possible in Mexico that is neither ineffective, nor deliberately aimed at the United States and her supposed hegemony.

This viewpoint seemed to receive added confirmation from the diplomatic initiative of General de Gaulle in 1957. In a move that recalled the palmy days of the Second Empire, he made his overseas tour of the Americas an occasion not only for exciting French nationalism in Quebec but also for eroding Anglo-Saxon influence in Mexico by deliberately recalling Mexico's debt to French culture. Excitement in the press of the English-speaking world was immense. Most of it, however, turned out to have been hasty. Such an initiative could have been important had one of two things been the case: that France was able to exercise actual power in the Caribbean region, or that United States influence in Mexico was a deliberate creation of state policy. In fact, cultural ties do not necessarily imply political power or control, and American influence in Mexico is largely the creation of the Mexicans themselves—where, indeed, it is anything more than the superficial evidence of technical and material modernization, in which Mexicans have contributed a very fair share to the world at large.

Voices: The Twenties

COLONEL CHARLES A LINDBERGH   MEXICO CITY
WASHINGTON D C

    IT HAVING REACHED MY KNOWLEDGE THAT YOU INTEND A FLIGHT FROM NEW YORK TO HAVANA IN THE ANTILLES I INVITE YOU TO DO SO VIA MEXICO WHERE YOU MAY REST ASSURED OF THE WARMEST WELCOME

        PLUTARCO ELIAS CALLES
        PRESIDENT OF THE REPUBLIC

PRESIDENT CALLES   WASHINGTON D C
MEXICO CITY

    AFTER THE WISHES OF COLONEL LINDBERGH I HAVE THE HONOR TO INFORM YOU WITH PLEASURE THAT TODAY AT 12:26 HE STARTED ON HIS DIRECT FLIGHT TO MEXICO

        MANUEL TELLEZ
        AMBASSADOR

        TALLULAH LA
TO U S NEWSPAPERS

    AN AIRPLANE BELIEVED TO BE COL LINDBERGHS WAS SIGHTED AS IT PASSED OVER TALLULAH BY FRANK HULE A TRAIN DISPATCHER AT 11:10 CENTRAL TIME TONIGHT

        ASSOCIATED PRESS

        HOUSTON TEXAS
TO U S NEWSPAPERS

    AN AIRPLANE BELIEVED TO BE THAT OF COL LINDBERGH PASSED OVER HOUSTON AT 2:20 OCLOCK THIS MORNING

        ASSOCIATED PRESS

                                    MEXICO CITY
TO MANY US NEWSPAPERS
    THOUSANDS OF MEXICANS WERE AT THE VALBUENA FLYING FIELD
AT DAWN THIS MORNING EAGER TO GREET COL LINDBERGH AT 8:40
PRESIDENT CALLES ARRIVED ACCOMPANIED BY HIS ENTIRE CABINET
WITH REPORTS AT 10:30 THAT COL LINDBERGH WAS HALF WAY
BETWEEN TAMPICO AND MEXICO CITY NINE MEXICAN ARMY AIRPLANES
HOPPED OFF TO MEET HIM RETURNING SCOUT PLANES LANDED AT
11:42 WITHOUT HAVING SIGHTED COL LINDBERGH SILENCE ALMOST
APPROACHING GLOOM PREVAILED OVER THE GREAT CROWD AS THE
25TH HOUR PASSED WITH LINDBERGHS WHEREABOUTS UNKNOWN THE
AUTHORITIES SET FIRE TO DRY GRASS WHICH COVERS THE FIELD TO
MAKE A SMOKE SIGNAL BOTH PRESIDENT CALLES AND AMBASSADOR
MORROW WERE UNABLE TO CONCEAL GRAVE EMOTIONS
                    THE ASSOCIATED PRESS

                                    MEXICO CITY
NEW YORK HERALD TRIBUNE
NEW YORK CITY
    THE INTREPID AMERICAN FLYER BROUGHT HIS SPIRIT OF SAINT
LOUIS DOWN ON VALBUENA FIELD AT 2:39 FROM THE CROWD
DELIRIOUS SHOUTS OF JOY
                    JACK STARR-HUNT

                                    MEXICO CITY
PRESIDENT CALVIN COOLIDGE
WASHINGTON D C
    IT PLEASES ME PROFOUNDLY TO SEND YOUR EXCELLENCY MY MOST
CORDIAL FELICITATIONS AT THIS TIME WHEN COLONEL LINDBERGH HAS
ARRIVED IN MEXICO CITY AFTER HIS NOTABLE FLIGHT
ACCOMPLISHED WITH GREAT SUCCESS
                    PLUTARCO ELIAS CALLES
                    PRESIDENT OF MEXICO

                                    WASHINGTON D C
COLONEL CHARLES A LINDBERGH
MEXICO CITY
    THE PEOPLE OF THE UNITED STATES ARE PROUD TO APPLAUD THE
SUCCESSFUL CULMINATION OF ANOTHER OF YOUR COURAGEOUS
VENTURES I WISH TO ADD MY HEARTIEST CONGRATULATIONS TO YOU
IN BEING THE FIRST TO FLY WITHOUT A STOP BETWEEN THE CAPITALS
OF THE TWO NEIGHBOR REPUBLICS
                    CALVIN COOLIDGE

NEW YORK TIMES
NEW YORK CITY

MEXICO CITY

PRESIDENT CALLES ISSUED A STATEMENT TONIGHT 'THE LATTER
PORTION OF COL LINDBERGH'S FLIGHT OVER TERRITORY ABSOLUTELY
UNKNOWN TO HIM OVER ZONES OF A PARTICULARLY DIFFICULT AND
DANGEROUS NATURE BECAUSE OF A LACK OF MEANS OF
COMMUNICATION AND THE DEVIATION FROM HIS ORIGINAL ROUTE PUT
TO THE PROOF HIS GREAT SKILL FOR NAVIGATING ALOFT HIS
MARVELLOUS RESOLUTION AND ENERGY ALONE PREVENTED HIM FROM
COMING DOWN MAINTAINED HIM IN HIS FIRM INTENTION TO REACH
MEXICO WITHOUT A STOP.'

NEW YORK TIMES
NEW YORK CITY

DETROIT

'THAT'S ALL THAT MATTERS,' SAID MRS LINDBERGH, TOLD OF HER
SON'S SAFE LANDING IN MEXICO CITY 'HE HAS ALWAYS TALKED OF
SEEING MEXICO.'[7]

'My class in Hispanic-American Sociology started with a good
number of students. Purposely I avoided any obligation to deal with
history, for that subject has never been to my liking, and at any rate,
sociology lends itself better to ramblings which end up in the study
of ideas and theories; facts do not interest me'.[8]

'Comrades: the moment has arrived to show the "gentlemen"
that we know how to administer; that we are the builders and not
them; it is necessary that we say to them that without the workers
this sumptuous cathedral would not exist; that without the workers
this palace would not exist; that without the workers there would not
be this park where all can come to take recreation and to breathe the
scent of flowers; lastly, without the workers railways, motor-cars,
buses would not exist; nothing that is useful to man would exist
without the workers'.[9]

'Señorita Natalia Calles, daughter of President Plutarco Elias
Calles, is a devout Roman Catholic. So is her dashing sister, Ernes-
tine. So is their mother. But President Calles has said: "No influence,
national or international, including the grunts of the Pope, will cause
the Government to vary its attitude [toward suppressing the Catholic
clergy]".

'Therefore, the Calles womenfolk were in a delicate position, last
week, on the eve of Señorita Natalia's wedding to Señor Carlos
Herrera, a minor government official. Would big, burly Papa Calles
insist that his daughter should have only a civil marriage, demand
that she live out of wedlock in the eyes of Roman Catholics?

'Papa-President Calles resisted tears, supplications. Señorita Natalia Calles was united in wedlock exclusively by the Mexican civil power. Then, on separate trains, the bride and bridegroom sped to San Antonio, Tex. At Mexico City the Papa-President clamped down his censorship, forbade Mexicans to print that at San Antonio a Mexican bride and groom achieved union through the Holy Roman Catholic Church.'[10]

'All this determines the magnitude of the problem: but the same circumstance which perhaps, for the first time in its history, confronts Mexico with a situation in which the dominant note is the lack of "caudillos", ought to allow us—is going to allow us—to orientate the policy of the country definitively towards paths to a truly institutional life, enabling it to pass, once and for all, from the historical condition of "a country of one man" to "a nation of institutions and laws".'[11]

---

[1] Sedano, op. cit., 255.

[2] Dulles, op. cit., 355–61.

[3] Frank R. Brandenburg, *The Making of Modern Mexico* (Englewood Cliffs, N.J., Prentice-Hall, 1964), 191–204.

[4] Stephen Clissold, introduction to *Soviet Relations with Latin America, 1918–1968: a documentary survey* (London, Oxford Univ. Press for RIIA, 1970), 3–8.

[5] Harold Nicolson, *Dwight Morrow* (London, Constable, 1935).

[6] Bryce Wood, *The Making of the Good Neighbor Policy* (New York, Columbia University Press, 1961).

[7] *Time*, 26 December 1927.

[8] José Vasconcelos, writing of his exile in Chicago in 1926, in *A Mexican Ulysses, an autobiography*, 217.

[9] Felipe Carrillo Puerto, Governor of Yucatán, 1 May 1922 at Mérida, in Robert Blanco Moheno, *El cardenismo* (Mexico, Libro-Mex, 1963), 161.

[10] *Time*, 28 February 1927.

[11] Calles, Message to Congress, 1 September 1928, quoted in Emilio Portes Gil, *Autobiografía de la Revolución Mexicana, un tratado de interpretación histórica* (Mexico, Instituto Mexicano de Cultura, 1964), 383.

The Revolution XIX: The End of Militarism

THE ASSASSINATION OF OBREGÓN came as a shock even to a country habituated to violence. The distraught Obregonistas visited some of their fury on the assassin himself, but though he was struck and bruised, he was safely removed to the Central Police Station, where at first he refused to make any statement. The Obregonistas then turned their suspicions towards Calles himself. The President had gone at once to the police station where the prisoner was; finding that he was silent, he had then gone to Obregón's house, where the body of the dead general had been taken. The Obregonistas made their distrust of him plain. In the end their demands crystallized round their doubts of Roberto Cruz, Calles's chief of police, and when they were able to agree on the name of a replacement, Calles appointed him on the spot without even going through the formality of asking for Cruz's resignation.

The new chief of police, General Antonio Ríos Zertuche, an Obregonista of unimpeachable loyalty, took full charge of the investigations. While the body of Obregón lay in state in the Palacio Nacional, the assassin was tortured, but he refused to confess. However, a Chinese laundry mark on his clothing enabled the police to trace his home and interview his wife and parents, who were as yet wholly unaware of the deed. Armed with this information, they threatened him with action against them if he did not talk. Eventually he agreed to do so, and conducted them to a house in Zaragoza Street where a religious group headed by a Madre Conchita lived. With the identification of the assassin as a religious fanatic, most doubts about the complicity of the President were resolved. Calles had, therefore, survived the initial shock.

It was another question for him to regain his authority. The majority of the Obregonistas continued to be angry and suspicious. Calles himself was deserted and the political life of the country revolved around the Chamber of Deputies, which, with a strongly Obregonista majority, would have to take the next steps to restore constitutional order. The one thing that was clear was that Calles could not hope to succeed himself, and there was great hostility to the labour interest as represented by Luis Morones, who had fled from the capital as soon as the news of the assassination had become known. Morones had opposed the re-election of Obregón. His resignation from the office of Secretary of Labour became the occasion for a cabinet reshuffle which enabled Calles to bring the moderate Obregon-istas into the government. These changes culminated at the beginning of August in the appointment of the young agrarian leader, Emilio Portes Gil, to the key post of Secretary of *Gobernación*.

Throughout August the turbulence continued. As ever in Mexico, no rumour was too wild or far-fetched not to be believed by some-one, and the agitation of Callista supporters revived in favour either of an extension of the Presidential term or in favour of the retroactive application of the constitutional amendment for a six-year term. It was noticeable, however, that representatives from Sonora itself were hostile to both proposals. What Calles himself had decided remained a mystery until 1 September, the day Congress reassembled and the President went before it to deliver his annual message.

As befitted the solemnity of the occasion the streets were lined with troops, which served the additional function of offering some protection against further assassination attempts. There was, however, no disturbance, though the President's reception, as he entered the Chamber of Deputies surrounded by his bodyguard, was tepid. His speech was forthright and to the point. It was time for Mexico, he said, to give up the habit of rule by 'strong men' and to create truly democratic institutions. Accordingly he had made the irrevocable decision, in spite of all the pressures exerted on him to continue, to leave the Presidency at the conclusion of his term on 30 November and never to seek it again. It was for Congress to nominate a Provisional President to succeed him, and to select an election date for the choice of a successor, ensuring that the domination of one group in the selection of candidates be ended and political intolerance reduced. A reminder of political realities was his repeated call to the army to guarantee the maintenance of order and the security of the institutional structure arrived at.

There was very little question but that there would soon be another military revolt. The only question was when, and whether the government could be prepared for it. Much would depend on the name of the Provisional President. To avoid unnecessary conflict, Calles summoned leading generals to the Palacio Nacional on 5 September and advised them to keep 'perfect unity' and to stay out of the struggle for the Provisional Presidency altogether. Among those approving of the President's advice, the most notable was General Escobar. General Almazán accepted the decision with reluctance, saying pointedly 'I deem any divisional general more able to occupy the Presidency than any civilian', a view with which his colleagues were perfectly in agreement.[1] Since a large number of deputies and senators were willing to agree on the name of Emilio Portes Gil for the office, the thirty-seven-year-old lawyer from the frontier State of Tamaulipas was ultimately nominated on 25 September without a dissenting vote, and with only two abstentions.

Revolutionary opinion had closed ranks. But at the same time, with the nomination of 20 November 1929 for the elections for the definitive Presidency, it was clear that electioneering would begin almost at once. Portes Gil was a prominent agrarian; in the politics of Tamaulipas he had backed one of the first labour laws under Article 123, and he had shown the political gifts of conciliation and organization. But he was still going to find it difficult to be anything more than a cypher in office, given the shortness of time in which he had to work. Within days the irreconcilable Díaz Soto y Gama was speaking openly in the Chamber of Deputies of the tendency to see Calles still as the indispensable leader – the *jefe máximo* – of the Revolution. It was a clear pointer to the dangers to come.

Calles's actions in the last days of his Presidency reflect his ambiguous position. He made no objection to Portes Gil's demand for the inclusion in the Federal budget of a vastly increased estimate for land redistribution. He agreed with Portes Gil that new blood was needed in an administration that had changed very little in eight years. To further this, one very important move was made: the recall from the post of ambassador to Brazil of the engineer Pascual Ortiz Rubio, who was to take over the portfolio of *Gobernación* in the new administration. Lastly Calles asked all prominent members of the government to remain at their posts until after 21 November, thus making them ineligible for the next year's elections. The only one unaffected was Aarón Sáenz, who was already on leave from his governorship, and could therefore be considered as the most likely candidate the following year.

On 30 November, however, at his inauguration, Portes Gil demonstrated his independence by outlining the programme of his government, which he was careful to stress would not just be holding the next elections. Consolidation of the Revolution and fighting corruption were the twin goals. Continuity with the past was stressed by the retention of three members of the Calles Cabinet: General Joaquín Amaro, at War and Marine, Luis Montes de Oca, at *Hacienda*, and Genaro Estrada as Subsecretary *encargado* at External Relations. But it fell to Portes Gil to appoint the large number of new Federal judges needed by the purging of the judiciary which had been a major plank in Obregón's programme, and other appointments reflected the shifting balance of power.

What Calles envisaged as his new role was only evident the following day with the appearance of a manifesto signed by him and other colleagues, calling for the creation, as the first step in establishing new political institutions, of a new political party, independent of old groupings and interests. It was to be called the *Partido Nacional Revolucionario*–the National Revolutionary Party (PNR). As such it was the first, and still the most successful, of Latin American 'revolutionary' parties. This, however, was not by any means apparent at the time. In fact the first impression was that it was a fiasco, since several prominent men refused to serve under Calles, and an attempt by Morones to challenge Portes Gil was so firmly put down that Calles inevitably suffered. Considering discretion the best policy, Calles withdrew from the PNR, reaffirming his loyalty to the new government. Shortly afterwards, he left for France.

Aarón Sáenz had been Calles's candidate. The withdrawal of Calles was a great setback to his chances of becoming the nominee of the new PNR, but a more serious objection was his own personality. However, neither of the two declared candidates, General Antonio I. Villareal and José Vasconcelos, were acceptable alternatives, even had they enjoyed official favour. Vasconcelos was identified with the cause of socialist education and reformism, and as a civilian was unacceptable to the military, while Villareal had left Obregón to join the de la Huerta rebellion and so was unacceptable to the Obregonistas. Their campaigns were quite independent, and they ran into much hostility, particularly Vasconcelos, who was campaigning with a band of youthful but vigorous followers for an end to authoritarianism and a return to the principles of Madero.

When the convention of the PNR met in Querétaro on 1 March 1929, Sáenz was still the front-runner, but he had further lost ground. Stung by the Vasconcelistas, the committee of the PNR had taken up so radical a position that they were hard to outflank, and measured by this standard, Sáenz began to look moderate. A new contender who looked on paper much more plausible was the new Secretary of *Gobernación*, Pascual Ortiz Rubio, who was much more acceptable to the agrarians, of whom the President was one. And above all things the President wanted agrarian support, for the expected revolt was now imminent, and he needed agrarian help in order to defeat it. Sáenz, seeing which way the wind was blowing, withdrew. On 4 March the PNR formally came into existence, and as its first official act nominated Ortiz Rubio for the Presidency. The revolt had begun just a day earlier.

It began subtly when the commander of the forces in Veracruz, General Jesús M. Aguirre, telegraphed that the governor was in revolt. The telegram was to excuse him from sending troops to Mexico

City which he, in fact, was planning to use to seize the capital. The object of the intended *coup* had been to place General Escobar in the Presidency, and its pretext was to have been the nomination of Sáenz; the disclosure of the plan by accident forced the hands of the conspirators. Escobar assumed the part written for him, and a prepared 'Plan' denounced imposition and Calles, 'the Judas of the Mexican Revolution'.

At the moment of crisis a serious accident altered the course of Mexican history. The Minister of War, General Amaro, who had for so long worked under Calles on the reduction of the military forces, and who in conjunction with Portes Gil had anticipated and planned for operations in the event of just the sort of revolt they were witnessing, was incapacitated. He had been struck in the eye by a polo ball, which had destroyed the sight of one eye. Only one man was available to step into his shoes who commanded the necessary attention and that was Calles himself, and so, despite his intentions, he returned to the government. The campaign itself was brief. Only nine states were affected, and these were widely separated, so that although altogether over a quarter of the army was in revolt, nowhere were the rebels numerically very strong. Escobar himself, after the usual misleading telegram, seized Monterrey, but was unable to hold it and after two days it was recaptured by loyal troops under General Almazán. The revolt in Vera Cruz fell apart and its leaders were captured and shot after court-martial. Calles in person took part in the operations in the north in which aircraft played a major role in hunting down rebels. Torreón was taken with the aid of agrarian forces under General Saturnino Cedillo; Durango fell to the forces of General Cárdenas and Almazán smashed the main body of Escobaristas at Jiménez. Then the government troops advanced into Sonora: the troops of Cárdenas advancing through Sinaloa along the railway with the aid of Federal gunboats, and those of Almazán from Torreón northwards, making use of both armoured cars and aircraft. By the end of April the revolt had ended. It had cost the lives of 2,000 persons, of whom, as Portes Gil pointed out, only three were generals, the rest of the rebel leaders having taken refuge in the United States.

The forces having been reorganized, Calles resigned his emergency office on 22 May and retired once again into private life.

Emilio Portes Gil

Emilio Portes Gil was the only statesman of the Revolution to write its autobiography,[2] and he was one of the few people who could have done so, for reasons that will become apparent when one considers the course of his life. He was born in Ciudad Victoria in the frontier State of Tamaulipas on 3 October 1891 and received his preparatory education there, but in 1906 entered law school in the capital and first came into contact with the Maderistas there in 1909. He continued to enjoy the advantage of student status until he graduated as a *licenciado* in 1915, and then went straight into the Department of War and Marine. From then until his retirement in 1961 – more than forty-five years later – he was to hold a unique series of offices which brought him into contact with nearly every aspect of Mexican government.

His first piece of good fortune was in making an early acquaintance with Sonora, for he was sent there as a judge of first instance and rapidly rose through the profession. In 1917 he was elected a deputy to the XXVII Congress, the first under the new constitution – he was to serve in that capacity twice more between 1920 and 1924. He rapidly consolidated his hold on the politics of his native state, of which between 1924 and 1928 he was to be first *ad interim* and subsequently constitutional governor, and in 1920 took the decisive step of support-ing the revolt in Sonora. Given the strategic position of the frontier State of Tamaulipas, with its close proximity to the oil-wells and port of Tampico, his choice was certain of a favourable reception.

Throughout the politics of the mid-1920s the burly and jovial figure of Portes Gil weaved a sure course. The impression of joviality and good humour was far from being a misleading one, but the tight mouth of the politician indicated resolution and the mind behind it was acute. Though strongly identified with the agrarian interest in Tamaulipas, he had devised for the *Partido Socialista Fronterizo* (PSF), which was the vehicle for political control in that state, a system of functional representation which worked unusually effectively, and in his left-wing stance he was careful to avoid the excesses of the leading personalities of Yucatán or Tabasco. But it was in the capital that the future lay, and in the difficult days after the assassination of Obregón it was there that he was to be seen. His choice as Secretary of *Gober-nación* after Obregón's death resulted from his consistent but moderate pro-Obregón stance and his importance as an agrarian leader, and his choice as Provisional President followed naturally.

The first way in which his selection as President was important was that a civilian was chosen at all. It is true, as has been said, that in some ways Portes Gil came one year too early to have his full impact on Mexican politics. In the late twenties the military and business were both riding high, and an agrarian radical who spoke the language of socialism – however engagingly – was preaching to the deaf. By 1930 many more people were in a mood to listen – but Ortiz Rubio was President, and Calles, by interfering in his government, deprived it of what little initiative it had. The point is that the appointment of Portes Gil, as he has since claimed, did restore the principle of civilian government. Of those who came after him, none was a military *caudillo* in the old sense, and even Ávila Camacho was essentially a soldier of the wartime emergency.

Secondly, the position of Portes Gil enabled him to play a vital role in the creation of the PNR, as has already been shown. In return, it was to provide him with a vital outlet for his energies when as a youthful ex-President of only thirty-nine years of age he had to look around for ways to keep himself occupied. As Secretary of *Gobernación* in the Cabinet of his successor, an almost unique situation, he was too near the top to be safe; as president of the PNR for the first time he drew up its statutes and secured its foundations, yet ironically found that he had only succeeded in making it safe for Calles. In his second term as president of the PNR in 1935–36 he was to give it a very different direction; though ultimately to his own disadvantage, this is the form which it has retained since in all its various reincarnations.

In between he had not only served Mexico as her ambassador to France—then still the most prized of diplomatic posts—but also as her first representative to the League of Nations, to which Mexico acceded in 1931. He had returned to Mexico to serve in the top legal post of the government of President Rodríguez. Somehow he also found time to write: his first book to attract general attention being his monograph polemic on *La lucha entre el Poder Civil y el Clero* (1934), which aroused considerable criticism abroad as an attempt to bridge the policies of Calles with the more tolerant spirit which Portes Gil himself had done so much to encourage.

It was to writing that he was to turn again after 1936, when he returned to the practice of the law, and his *Quince Años de Política Mexicana* (1940) is at one and the same time an account and a justification of his political actions. It was appropriate therefore that twenty years afterwards, after several further books, many articles, a spell as Mexico's first ambassador to India, and a term at the head of the National Securities Commission, Portes Gil should have been asked, on the occasion of the fiftieth anniversary of the Revolution of 1910, to contribute an essay on the spirit and doctrine of the Revolution to the memorial publication. Out of this was to grow the monumental *Autobiografía.*

Portes Gil has for most people been overshadowed for the latter part of his career by the figure of Lázaro Cárdenas. Yet much more precisely than Cárdenas he represents the conscience of the Revolution (if revolutions can be said to have consciences), and if one man can be credited with the impetus that led to the continuation of the agrarian reform under López Mateos, that man is Portes Gil; it was he who set the tone for the choice of the official party candidate, at a time when Cardenistas and Alemanistas were too much embattled with one another within the context of the Cold War for either to be able to win a decisive advantage. Unlike Cárdenas himself, he always appreciated that the effectiveness of the concept of the official party lay in its continued unity of operation rather than (though not to the exclusion of) its ideological purity.

Peasants

The word 'peasant' in English has an unfortunate connotation; its literal use in the Mexican context is almost always misleading and sometimes quite wrong. The Spanish word *campesino* is rather less rustic; it means something much more approximating to farmer or farm-worker depending on context.

A complication is that many writers now tend to define the term 'peasant', not in its own environment, the countryside, but in relationship to the demands and pressures of the outside world. Thus Oscar Lewis describes Tepoztlán as

> a peasant society in the sense that it has an old and stable population, the villagers have a great attachment to the land, agriculture is the major source of livelihood, the technology is relatively primitive (hoe and plow), and production is primarily for subsistence, with barter persisting, although the people also participate in a money economy. Moreover, the village is integrated into larger political units such as the state and the nation and is subject to their laws.

But he goes on to add that in consequence of the incursions of the outside world the community 'has developed that peculiar combination of dependence on and hostility towards government which is so characteristic of peasants and colonial peoples', and this is an equation that has to be approached with great caution.[3]

Peasants by the fixed nature of agricultural production are intensely vulnerable to the tyranny and depredation of local bosses. Naturally they make use of what superior power they can reach in order to control them. The appeal to the 'justice' of a superior against the depredations of an inferior is one of the oldest motifs in human history; its significance in the Mexican context lies in the constant change of overlords since the Conquest which has driven the peasant communities back on their own resources, where, as in the case of Tepoztlán, their communities lie close to such centres of power and cannot remain unaffected by their instability.

Tepoztlán is a village and *municipio* in the north of the State of Morelos, directly adjoining the boundary of the Federal District in a steep and hilly area of great natural beauty. It was first studied by the American anthropologist Robert Redfield in 1926–27 and subsequently restudied by Oscar Lewis in 1943 and again in 1956–57. In addition to the anthropological studies that have been published on life in the village, there is also the opportunity to observe life in the remarkably similar community of 'Azteca' as seen by an old Zapatista, his wife, and his son, in Oscar Lewis's *Pedro Martínez*. In many ways the life of the village is representative, showing the catastrophic drop in population that accompanied the Conquest, the growth of religious power under the colonial period, the forced labour in the mines at Taxco and Cuautla, and the decline of the pre-Conquest economy towards subsistence level. Independence passed almost unnoticed in a period of relative prosperity that lasted for a further thirty years.

Then with the Laws of the Reform came the break-up of the church lands and the emergence of local *caciques* who took over political control, forcing many to work as day labourers on the big estates they were developing. Tepoztlán was luckier than many villages in that the communal lands of the village, where the poorest could opt to make a living by hoe cultivation of maize on the steep slopes, were not themselves seized by the *caciques*, though the villagers were forbidden to work them so as to force them to labour on the estates instead. It also benefited from the building of the railway in 1897 which brought alternative work to the village, as well as lighting, piped water, and steel ploughs. At the first sign of revolt in 1911 the villagers overthrew the *caciques*, but proceeded to quarrel violently among themselves as to what should be done next, with fatal results. Worse was to come. Invading and marauding armies during the first years of the Revolution laid the village waste with most of the rest of the state; many lived in the hills for months at a time, and of the houses that had been there before the Revolution, some lucky people who returned in 1919–20 found only the roof tiles that they had providently hidden in ditches. When Oscar Lewis first went to the village in 1943 the shortage of livestock, butchered during the Revolution and hitherto not adequately replaced, was still serious. The attempts to recoup losses quickly by burning the surrounding forests for charcoal not only destroyed a precious natural resource, but gave rise to constant recriminations and ended in bankruptcy.

The decisive change for the village came in 1929 when the community were granted ejidal lands from a nearby hacienda; with this in the period down to 1940 came the building of flour-mills to relieve the women of the burden of graining corn by hand; the construction of an all-weather road which enabled the villagers to go into Cuernavaca and gave them, and in particular the women and the young men, a considerable measure of additional personal freedom; and the building and expansion of the school. With this came the most dramatic cultural change. In 1920 the villagers had still been primarily Náhuatl-speaking–speaking among themselves the old language of the Aztec

Empire. By 1944 only half the villagers were bilingual and only five spoke Náhuatl alone; the younger people, feeling that their elders used it only for 'quarrelling and scolding', were hostile towards it. With this came contact with the outside world. In 1943 only a few had battery radios; in 1956 there were more than eighty, and the fortunate ones cultivated bus-drivers to swop their radio batteries with that of the bus and so recharge them – with what effect on the bus can only be imagined! But in 1949 movies had come to the village, and newspaper reading increased; in the post-war period newspaper reading showed a noticeable decline, and in 1956 the village got its first telephone exchange. Contact with the outside world shows many variations, but the trend away from the traditional isolation accelerates.

As it does so, the traditional suspicion, the avoidance of demonstrativeness or friendships outside the extended family give way to a more competitive spirit and the pursuit of material benefits. Many of these are in themselves desirable. Women in particular have benefited from the disappearance of the traditional pattern of hard and unremitting labour; paradoxically today it is the men who are isolated in the fields during the day and who resort to alcohol to ease the discomfort of social contact in the evenings. There is more alcohol and it is more varied, though the traditional *pulque* is still in great demand. In the 1940s the old pattern of religious festival observance, with its accompanying hierarchies of officials giving status within the village community, still survived intact, embodying forms from pre-colonial days. By 1956 it had collapsed. In fact the villagers have become more Catholic in their religious observances rather than less, though the traditional prayers over the growing crops and incantations designed to bring good luck in the unpredictable, difficult life of the farmer are not neglected.

Three important developments stand out in the post-war years. First stands the arrival of a resident doctor about 1950. In the worst years of the Revolution there were no doctors at all, even in the nearby towns, and thousands of children died who might have lived, as in the case of the family of Pedro Martínez, of 'the stomach' or of natural hazards such as the bite of a scorpion. Even in the 1920s doctors were still scarce, and the traditional healers (*curanderos*) in great demand. Now there is a regular free Federal clinic and the possibility of hospital treatment for serious cases; the villagers do not seem to understand much about what the clinic does, but they do appreciate it.

Secondly there is the pressure of would-be residents from Mexico City and tourists in search of local colour. In 1943 land was simply not for sale. Since then prices have risen drastically, and a community of outsiders has grown up in the midst of the village, many of them upper-middle-class Mexicans.

Lastly, there has been the opportunity for enterprising young men from the village to earn money as *braceros* (migratory contract labourers in the United States), bringing into the village at a time the equivalent of two or more years' pay from a few months' work. The problem of much of Mexican farming–apart from the flat lands of the north and north-west–is that this sort of injection of capital can do little to improve its yield because of the steep slopes and poor plots which the villagers of Tepoztlán take for granted. But it does benefit their lives in many ways, though often at the cost of severing their contact with some of their most able sons. Many go to Mexico City, and all too many there end up in the struggling slum communities that the Federal government is now working so hard to remove.

Tepoztlán, as will be seen, began to develop striking differences from the traditional pattern of peasant life almost from the end of the violent phase of the Revolution. The question is, how typical is it in the recent period? Certainly in its proximity to Mexico City it is not, and this is important. If we turn to the south of Mexico and the village of Zinacantan, studied by Evon S. Vogt and his associates, we find ourselves in a very different, yet still recognizably related, situation. The people of Zinacantan in the highlands of Chiapas speak Tzotzil, a Mayan language, and their social organization and way of life show strong links with each period of their culture's past; but that past is much less accidented than that of the State of Morelos. Time has moved much more slowly here. The workers of the Harvard Chiapas Project have been able to attain an amazing level of documentation –one that puts it on a par with the local history of a European country or of the United States–and they show that realities vary exceedingly from one part of the country to another. The villagers of Zinacantan found great resistance to their petitions for ejidal land even in the reforming 1930s, and have, on the other hand, been very dramatically affected, almost for the first time in their long history, by the building of the Pan-American Highway to San Cristóbal in 1950.

Evon Vogt found great consistency too in the pattern of the villagers' beliefs, a process which the anthropologist calls replication. Replication refers to the way in which the Tzotzil way of life is built around basic concepts; concepts which are applied to all sorts of phenomena and used by all levels of society to derive appropriate rules of conduct towards them. 'In sum', writes Vogt, 'in the socialization process within the family, in the ritual life of the baptismal, wedding and curing ceremonies, and in the supernatural world inside the mountain "fathers" and "mothers" are "embracing" their children'.[4] Furthermore, by the related process which the anthropologist calls encapsulation–'the conceptual and structural incorporation of new elements into existing patterns of social and ritual behaviour'[5]–the

Zinacantecos can keep these basic concepts essentially unchanged. By appropriate rituals they have accepted the new school in Paste, the Pan-American Highway in NaChih, and, of course, the Harvard Field House, whose visiting anthropologists themselves have separately been incorporated into such complex rituals of the society they have been studying as those relating to *compadrazgo*, the bond of brotherhood through godparents, and the borrowing of money. After all, they were equally able in the past to accept the Catholic faith and a continuous stream of new civil magistracies.

While no anthropologist expects that any specific patterns of behaviour and beliefs could have remained unchanged for a period as long as 1,300 years, it does appear that the changes in Tzotzil culture patterns have been sufficiently regular for a modern understanding of that culture to improve our understanding of Maya life in the Classic period, though it should be remembered that present-day communities exhibit marked differences one from another.

Most resistant to change is the economic system. As Vogt says:

If one could remove certain elements from the economic system (machetes, axes, flashlights, chickens–which probably replaced turkeys–sheep, horses, mules, pigs, fruit trees, and some items of clothing) the system resembles what we can reconstruct for the Ancient Maya.[6]

Housing is essentially changeless, while clothing maintains the same conventions, with substitution of materials that became available in colonial times or more recently. (It could be added, however, that the economic elements named, all of which derive directly or indirectly from the Spanish invasions, are in themselves of great, sometimes overwhelming, importance.)

With this in mind, it is perhaps less surprising that one can infer that the social order of society in ancient times was not so very different either. The house groups of the ancients were probably patrilocal extended families living around courtyards. These in turn were grouped in patrilineages, in clusters approximately the same size as present-day villages, and these were settled around important sources of water. In turn, numbers of these settlements can be expected to have maintained a ceremonial centre of some size. It is suggested that each pyramid in such a centre, as visitors to Yucatán can see to this day, was perhaps associated with a specific tribal ancestor or ancestors, their modern descendants having a similar relationship to a shrine in a nearby mountain, to which at set times of year pilgrimages are made. The priestly offices were probably then as now held in rotation by those members of the clan who had accumulated a sufficient surplus of wealth to be able to undertake office. The rotation of office imposed on the Mayas by their obsession with the passage of time and the calendar automatically circulated power among the kin groups, creating a stabilized pattern of relationships well adapted to the settlement and resettlement of their shifting plots of cultivation.

Professor Vogt stresses the Zinacantecos' adherence to their concepts of time and space by pointing out that continuity can run in both directions. The Zinacanteco devotion to the values of hard work, punctuality, and thrift not only flies in the face of the absurd stereotypes of peasantry in general and Mexican peasants in particular, but gives firm evidence for the existence of a 'protestant ethic' without Protestantism. If, as he suggests, these values can enable the Zinacantecos ultimately to be incorporated within the structure of 'modern' Mexico without going through those stages of migration, proletarianization, and urbanization which formerly seemed to be a necessary evil, then they will have served them well, far beyond the hopes of their ancestors.

This in turn raises the interesting question of how far the culture of modern Mexico is indigenous. Often criticism of the 'traditional structures' of Latin American societies seems to be based on the assumption that the structures in question were imposed by the Spanish Conquest. Thus it is constantly being said that Spanish colonial society lacked a 'middle class', or that the political troubles in Mexico in the nineteenth century stemmed from the fact that there were only two classes – the rich and the poor. These statements are not true as Wolf has shown in his study of the region around Querétaro,[7] where in the eighteenth century there was a very large middle class which formed the foundation for Mexican independence movements. In modern Querétaro two things stand out in the analysis of class structures.[8] One is the ambiguous role of the upper class: they have not been annihilated by the Revolution; but neither have they been supplanted by the *nouveaux-riches*. The other is the unequivocal role of the agricultural labourer, the *peón*. He is by general agreement at the bottom of the social pyramid in terms of status, income, and opportunity alike. And the social structure of this large Mexican town is an essentially modern affair, the creation of the Mexicans themselves, for Querétaro had no pre-Conquest existence as such.

In Mexico as elsewhere status is a product both of money and of acceptance. Acceptance is not easily accorded in the absence of money, and lineage in itself counts for only as much as the subject can make it. The characteristic of the peasant society is not poverty, for in any terms modern Mexican peasants may be comparatively well off, measured by the standards of Mexican urban society. It is the lack of acceptance of status, bred of the tendency of peasant societies to keep their measurement of status within the community and to conceal evidence of prosperity until it can no longer be concealed, which enables other groups to maintain their own relatively high self-esteem. The problem for the modern Mexican peasant is maintaining his own importance, particularly in relation to the middle-class groups which dominate the political process of the republic. But it must not be forgotten that it was men from that middle class, who recalled their own youth and their own struggles in a different environment, who kept their promises to the peasants of Mexico and gave them what they now have.

[1] Dulles, op. cit., 390.

[2] Emilio Portes Gil, *Autobiografía de la Revolución Mexicana*.

[3] Oscar Lewis, *Tepoztlán: Village in Mexico* (New York, Holt Rinehart, 1960), 1.

[4] Evon Z. Vogt, *Zinacantan. A Maya Community in the Highlands of Chiapas* (Cambridge, Mass., The Belknap Press, 1969), 578.

[5] ibid., 582.

[6] ibid., 589.

[7] Eric R. Wolf, 'The Mexican Bajío in the Eighteenth Century', in Robert Wauchope, ed., *Synoptic Studies of Mexican Culture* (Middle American Research Institute, Tulane University), XVII, 177.

[8] Andrew H. Whiteford, *Two Cities of Latin America, a Comparative Description of Social Classes* (New York, Doubleday Anchor, 1964).

The Revolution XX: The Party

GIVEN HIS POSITION, Portes Gil's interest in establishing and strengthening the powers of the PNR was bound to be great. In fact, the strength of suppressed agrarianism was to make Portes Gil the major influence in the shaping of the new party over a period of nearly eight years. Its structure and its very statutes were modelled on those of the political machine with which he controlled his native state, the *Partido Socialista Fronterizo* (PSF) of Tamaulipas.[1]

As President Portes Gil gave the new party unmistakably official status, as well as financial support, by levying a precept on all government salaries for its upkeep.[2] This was to be the turning-point in the emergence of a new and ultimately powerful sector of revolutionary opinion—that of the new official class, whose wellbeing was now bound closely to the success of the government. Official status alone would not have made the new party the strong centralizing force that it proved to be. Far more important was the fact that the structure of functional representation characteristic of the PSF proved at national level to be highly effective in cutting across regional loyalties to traditional *caudillos*. Time was needed to give the party's influence time to work in this direction. It was secured by the spectacular rise in land distribution that enabled Portes Gil to ride out the Escobar rebellion; his government's military strength being in striking contrast to the relative inefficiency of the Calles administration in facing the Cristeros when peasant support was denied it.

In June 1929 Portes Gil took a further important step in opposition to the Calles policies, and towards national unification, by reaching an agreement with the Church. After a long series of mysterious conferences and hurried journeys, with the influence of the American ambassador, Dwight Morrow, being exerted in favour of a peaceful settlement, the President and the archbishop of Mexico, Leopoldo Ruiz y Flores, were able to announce on 22 June 1929 that an accord had been reached under which services could be resumed while the principal laws governing religion were still enforced. Most of the confiscated churches were made available once again to the clergy and some 14,000 Cristero soldiers surrendered to the government.

It would be wrong, however, to conclude that the interests of labour were neglected. Under Portes Gil work was completed on the Federal Labour Code which finally made the provisions of the 1917 Constitution effective, though the code itself was not promulgated until 1931.

Other important moves were the establishment of the autonomy of the National University (June 1929), as a means of ending the struggles of the past decade between students and representatives of the government; the establishment of 'circuit schools' to combat rural illiteracy in remote areas; and the campaign against gambling machines in the northern states. Coming as he did from a frontier state, Portes Gil shared much of the puritan hostility of Calles himself to the gambling and drinking which he associated with the influence of Prohibition-age America. In his time at Chapultepec, no alcoholic beverages were served at official banquets.

Portes Gil therefore departed to a remarkable extent from the traditional form of interim government and succeeded in carrying out a positive programme. As he afterwards admitted, though, he had already made one mistake. This was to ask Calles, while still President, to recall Pascual Ortiz Rubio from the Rio embassy so that he could be appointed Secretary of *Gobernación* in the new administration. Ortiz Rubio, an engineer by training, had a good revolutionary record and, as governor of Michoacán, had played a bold part in opposing Carranza's plans for the succession. He was generally regarded as upright and progressive. But he had served abroad as an ambassador for some ten years, and his personality and views had been modified accordingly.

As Ortiz Rubio was personally uncommitted his candidature for the Presidency grew spontaneously. Calles accepted it as an unexpected windfall when on his return to Mexico Ortiz came to pay his respects to him before taking up his post. At the same time he was initially most careful to follow a course that would facilitate his candidature as far as humanly possible. He was, of course, duly nominated, and in the aftermath of the Escobar revolt there was never any real chance that he would not be elected.

It is a fact, however, that many people believe that there was. The reason for this is that his only serious opponent in the election was José Vasconcelos, whose generous estimate of his own abilities as a candidate was accepted by a small group of intellectuals at its face value. Vasconcelos had undergone a dramatic ideological shift to the Right, which took him away from the militant socialism of the Obregón era and back towards the traditional liberal posture of the anti-reelectionists; his campaign was a protest against the evolution of politics into the machine age, behind which he saw the figure of Ambassador Dwight Morrow as the evil genius of Anglo-Saxon influence. Several scattered incidents occurred: clashes between anti-re-electionists and PNR supporters, resulting in the death of three Vasconcelistas, and Vasconcelos and his followers complained continuously about harassments from state bosses and others.

Amid much tension the country went to the polls on 17 November 1929. Vasconcelos had already gone north to Guaymas to await the results, and had drawn up a Plan of Guaymas on the assumption that the vote would go against him. And so it did. Ortiz Rubio was declared elected by 1,948,848 votes to 110,979 for Vasconcelos, with 23,279 going to a minority candidate. Declaring that he did not wish to share the fate of Ángel Flores (who had died shortly after the 1924 election – according to the Vasconcelistas, from poison), Vasconcelos withdrew to the United States, where he claimed the results had been published before the polls closed.[3]

Ortiz Rubio, like Calles before him, spent the months between election and inauguration in composing his Cabinet and in paying an official visit to the United States, before making a triumphal progress back to his own country. On 5 February 1930 he was inaugurated in the National Stadium in the presence of large crowds. About an hour later, on leaving the National Palace after swearing in the members of his Cabinet, he was shot in the jaw by a young man at almost point-blank range. His wife was hit on the side of the head and various other members of his entourage wounded.

The new President was able to walk into the hospital, and even to take the oath of office of the governor of the Federal District, Dr Puig Casauranc, before lying down on the operating table. He was hospitalized for only a short period. But the experience seems to have had a disastrous effect on him. Even after he was fully recovered, he behaved like a recluse, appearing seldom in public and travelling only in a specially made bullet-proof limousine. He was derided for his lack of courage and lost public respect.

His colleagues suspected both Portes Gil on the one hand (who was Secretary of *Gobernación* in the new administration), and Calles on the other. Most of the Cabinet were strong Callistas, and had been chosen with every evidence that the President intended to follow the Calles line as that of the PNR. However, Portes Gil was the chief in the government of the majority (or so-called 'red') faction of Congress and served initially as the new president of the PNR. The 'white' or Ortizrubista faction of the PNR was therefore relatively weak in the country. Since, despite severe tortures, it proved impossible to connect the would-be assassin with anyone of political moment – though he was believed to be a Vasconcelista – the incident did no more politically than to strain further very strained relations. In other ways its consequences were grave. Among other reprisals taken against real or suspected Vasconcelistas, the massacre of more than sixty at Topilejo, between Mexico City and Cuernavaca, by the military commander of the Valley of Mexico, stands out for both brutality and the total lack of legal redress afforded to relatives.

The country was now beginning to feel the full effects of the Great Depression. The first consequence was the withdrawal of foreign capital, which had a direct effect on the government's ability to carry out its programmes. When the President held his first cabinet meeting on 20 March 1930, Calles, though not a member of the administration, was present, and argued strongly in favour of halting the land distribution programme. This, it seems, was not just for general economic reasons. Calles had always been concerned about the modernization of agriculture, even before Dwight Morrow encouraged his interest and made use of his rural tours to talk to him informally and confidentially. He undoubtedly saw in the distribution of land to small landowners the danger of adding to the economic crisis by reducing production.

The result was not a foregone conclusion and in the event it was indecisive. The land distribution programme was abruptly halted.[4] But the 'red' majority in Congress were still able to secure agrarian legislation, in particular the long-awaited Act to forbid the use of the legal process of *amparo* to landlords obstructing distribution. However, in the executive branch power was now to pass rapidly back into the hands of Calles, who had become the centre of government during the Presidential disability, and whom men soon began to call the *Jefe Máximo* (Supreme Chief) of the Revolution.

Ortiz Rubio became increasingly deferential to Calles himself. Callers stopped at Calles's house in Chapultepec before coming to see the President. A wag chalked on the gates of the Castle the couplet:

> Aquí vive el presidente
> El que manda vive enfrente.[5]

But Ortiz Rubio's subordination to Calles did not mean that Calles could do what he liked. The PNR received strength from the very closeness of the struggle, and the need to maintain a coalition of interests remained. Portes Gil himself found his position untenable; in October 1930 he resigned his posts in party and government, and left for Europe. When he returned in 1932 he found he could not even become governor of his native state again against Calles's opposition. But there were other factors and personalities at work. Calles replaced Portes Gil as president of the PNR with the young General Cárdenas. Cárdenas built the PNR into a machine loyal to the incumbent President, a move which, though in the short term identified with the interests of Calles as *Jefe Máximo*, held obvious long-term implications for the future of the system of divided control. He was therefore driven to resign in September 1931 when a prominent Ortizrubista was wounded in a shooting incident and the opportunity taken to reshuffle the Cabinet. Moving into the Cabinet as Secretary of the key department of *Gobernación*, his place as president of the PNR went to a prominent Callista, General Pérez Treviño.

What happened next demonstrated just how military status and backing made Cárdenas stronger politically than Portes Gil had been in a similar position. He held the office of Secretary for some two weeks. Then all four of the leading generals resigned from the Ortiz Rubio Cabinet together. With this sort of guarantee, Cárdenas was able to retire to Michoacán as governor, and to outflank Calles on the Left with a radical programme directed at labour.

Meanwhile, in a condition of stalemate, the Calles domination of the government continued. As the international economic crisis deepened, the government began to look more and more helpless. All sorts of dramatic events were going on in the outside world, recognized by Mexico in the classic statement of the right of other countries to choose their own governments (the Estrada doctrine), but at home the President was almost invisible and inactive. In the end it was Calles who realized that the only way to get himself out of a weak position was to force Ortiz Rubio's resignation. The resignation was loyally submitted to Calles, addressed as 'Supreme Chief of the Revolution', and on 2 September 1932 Ortiz Rubio laid down the Presidency with visible relief. The burden had begun to tax his health severely.

His last year of office had been marked by almost continuous discord at the Secretaryship of *Hacienda* and frequent cabinet changes. From January 1932 onwards the President had been deprived of almost all the members of the Cabinet who were personally loyal to him. Luis Montes de Oca had been replaced by Alberto Pani at *Hacienda*, while a new member of the Cabinet was a former Undersecretary to Calles at the post of War and Marine, to which he had now returned as a result of the changes of October 1931. This was General Abelardo L. Rodríguez, a relatively non-political general from Sonora who had once been a professional baseball player, had served as a soldier throughout the Constitutionalist period, and had been governor of and responsible for the financial development of neighbouring Lower California, during which he had amassed a considerable fortune.[6]

It was Rodríguez whom Calles now nominated as Provisional President of the Republic to complete the six years for which Obregón had originally been elected in 1928; for, under the 1917 Constitution, where there was less than half the Presidential term to go, no general election was needed and a substitute President would be appointed by Congress. Rodríguez was not Calles's first choice: a list of three names had been presented to the PNR bloc in Congress by the president of the party, in the order Alberto J. Pani, General Joaquín Amaro, and Abelardo L. Rodríguez. It was Rodríguez's own popularity that gave the nomination to him rather than to the others. A sign of the times was the lack of change in his Cabinet. Calles now retired once more, and Lázaro Cárdenas became Minister of War and Marine, while Portes Gil was brought back into the Cabinet as Procurator-General of the Republic. Neither could be seen as in a commanding position, but the suggestion was one of national conciliation with a slight inclination towards labour.

The policies of the new administration followed the same pattern. Its principal task appeared to be to implement the Federal Labour Code of 1931, which was a task of some complexity, and government speeches heavily stressed social policy. But the agrarian interest was cared for too, and, rather hesitantly, the distribution of land was resumed. It soon accelerated, and by the end of his term, Rodríguez in twenty-six months of office had distributed nearly twice as much land as his predecessor had in twenty. His work in this field was crowned by the appearance of the Agrarian Code of 1934, which provided for the first time for the 'fractionating' (i.e., division and redistribution) as well as the restitution of lands and endowment of villages. Needless to say, as a lawyer and as an agrarian, Portes Gil was active in the drafting of the code. Significantly, the operation of 'fractionating', in other words the division of the great estates into co-operative farms (*ejidos*) under collective ownership, was specifically provided for in the code. It was also written into the great Six-Year Plan (*Plan Sexenal*) which was to run from 1933 to 1939 and so would guide the hand of the new President whoever he might be, for five out of the six years of his term.

Rodríguez himself was a President of national reconciliation, and in any case his time was short. He did not choose to exercise the Presidential power as vigorously as he might have done. But he was undoubtedly a strong President. He called few Cabinets and the importance of individual members of the Cabinet began to recede once more before the imperatives of Presidential office. The new United States ambassador to Mexico, Josephus Daniels, commented:

> It was expected that Calles would be the power behind the throne and Rodríguez would do his bidding. In the first period of his administration they saw eye to eye, and when I reached Mexico the opinion prevailed that Rodríguez took orders from Calles. By 1934 it became apparent that Rodríguez was, in fact as well as in name, President of Mexico.[7]

He had good reason to know. Twice he had seen the President assert his authority—once when he held a full official dinner for Calles, who was only a private citizen, and once when he incautiously referred to the ex-President as the 'strong man of Mexico'. On both occasions the President sustained his point. His resistance to the attempt of his Secretary of *Gobernación*, Narciso Bassols, to revive the anti-clerical issue, resulted in the removal of Bassols from the Cabinet and the retention of the policy of reconciliation begun by Portes Gil. Pani, another prominent Callista, was sacked for criticizing the President in public.

The idea of the Six-Year Plan originated with Calles. Its antecedents were obvious enough. What was important was that Rodríguez adopted the idea as his own and put his full official weight behind it; in July 1933 he ordered all heads of departments to co-operate in its formulation. It was basically seen as a fundamental necessity to make land redistribution really effective and enable it to take place on a sufficient scale and in sufficiently large units to make it work. Calles, who had seen the consequences of over-small agricultural units during his tour in France, had, as we have seen, developed considerable caution about them. From the beginning the expansion of public education was seen as equally important, along with the rights of labour and the development of interior communications; the President himself subsequently added the need to create national mineral reserves to protect them from private exploitation.

The Plan, as it was actually presented to the Second National Convention of the PNR in December 1933, followed these guidelines closely.[8] It was an ambitious document, couched in broad terms, stating intentions rather than concrete goals; but a vast extension of the land reform on a co-ordinated basis was certainly intended by it. The only thing that remained to be decided was who was to carry it out. The principle of no re-election had been restored by Rodríguez to the constitution and though Cárdenas now appeared a very probable choice as candidate, he still had two rivals who were even more Callista than he was. In the event one, Pérez Treviño, withdrew and the other, Carlos Riva Palacio, Calles's closest friend, became president of the PNR before the convention began. Cárdenas was nominated.

There were three other candidates in the field, but against the energy of Cárdenas and the strength of the PNR machine there was little they could do. Even given the appalling transport conditions of the day, the candidate himself covered more than 18,000 miles in the course of his campaign, reaching towns and villages that had never before seen a potential President of the Republic. At the same time he did not shun the latest means of electioneering; on election eve the radio carried his final campaign speech across the nation from a studio in Durango. The result was an overwhelming and certainly largely genuine vote of support; and so it was confirmed that Cárdenas would have the task of implementing the country's first (and, as it turned out, last) Six-Year Plan.

Statistical

Table 1 : Presidential Elections since 1917

1917	Venustiano Carranza	797,305	98·1
	Pablo González	11,615	1·4
	Álvaro Obregón	4,008	0·5
1920	Álvaro Obregón (PLC)	1,131,751	95·8
	Alfredo Robles Domínguez (PNRep)	47,442	4·0
1924	Plutarco Elías Calles (PLM)	1,340,634	84·1
	Ángel Flores	250,599	15·9
1928	Álvaro Obregón (PLM)	unopposed*	100·0
1929	Pascual Ortiz Rubio (PNR)	1,948,848	93·6
	José Vasconcelos (PA)	110,979	5·3
	Pedro V. Rodríguez Triana	23,279	1·0
1934	Lázaro Cárdenas (PNR)	2,225,000	98·2
	Antonio I. Villareal (CRPI)	24,395	1·1
	Adalberto Tejada (Soc)	16,037	0·7
	Hernán Laborde (Comm)	539	neg
1940	Manuel Ávila Camacho (PRM)	2,176,641	93·9
	Juan Andreu Almazán (PRUN)	151,101	5·7
	Rafael Sánchez Tapía	9,840	0·4
1946	Miguel Alemán Váldes (PRI)	1,786,901	77·9
	Ezequiel Padilla (PDM)	443,357	19·3
	J. Agustín Castro	28,537	1·3
	Carlos I. Calderón	1,181	neg
1952	Adolfo Ruiz Cortines (PRI)	2,713,419	74·3
	Miguel Henríquez Guzmán (FdePPM)	579,745	15·9
	Efrán González Luna (PAN)	285,555	7·8
	Vicente Lombardo Toledano (PP)	72,482	2·0
1958	Adolfo López Mateos (PRI)	6,769,754	90·4
	Luis H. Álvarez (PAN)	705,303	9·4
1964	Gustavo Díaz Ordaz (PRI)	8,368,446	88·8
	José González Torres (PAN)	1,034,337	11·0
1970	Luis Echeverría Álvarez (PRI)	11,948,412	84·7
	Efraín González Morfin (PAN)	1,945,204†	13·8

* votes cast 1,670,453.   † total votes cast 14,092,867.

Table 2: Population of Mexico

Census	Year	Total population
1st	1895	12,632,427
2nd	1900	13,607,272
3rd	1910	15,160,369
4th	1921	14,334,780
5th	1930	16,552,722
6th	1940	19,653,552
7th	1950	25,791,017
8th	1960	34,923,129
9th	1970	48,313,438

Table 3: Presidents of Mexico by states and regions of birth, 1824–1970

State	1824-54	1854-84	1884-1910	1910-40	1940-70	Total
NORTH						
Coahuila	1	0	0	4	0	5
Durango	2	0	0	0	0	2
Nuevo León	1	0	0	0	0	1
Sonora	0	1	0	4	0	5
Tamaulipas	0	1	0	1	0	2
WEST						
Jalisco	2	0	0	1	0	3
Zacatecas	1	0	0	0	0	1
CORE						
Aguascalientes	1	0	0	0	0	1
Guanajuato	0	1	0	0	0	1
Hidalgo	1	0	0	0	0	1
México	0	0	0	0	1	1
Michoacán	1	2	0	2	0	5
Puebla	0	2	0	0	2	4
Querétaro	1	0	0	1	0	2
SLP	2	0	0	0	0	2
Veracruz	3	3*	0	1	2	8
SOUTH						
Campeche	0	0	0	1	0	1
Guerrero	2	1	0	0	0	3
Oaxaca	0	2	1*	1*	0	2
FEDERAL DISTRICT	4	4	0	1	0	9

* indicates one included under previous period.
Note: data for 1854–84 include two Regents for Empire.
Source: Manuel García Purón, *Los gobernantes de México*.

Table 4: Redistribution of land by Presidencies 1915–64

President	Dates	Months	Hectares	Ha.p.m.
Carranza	1915*–1920	66·5	132,640	1,995
De la Huerta	1920	6	33,696	5,616
Obregón	1920–24	48	971,627	20,242
Calles	1924–28	48	3,088,072	64,335
Portes Gil	1928–30	14·1	1,173,199	83,200
Ortiz Rubio	1930–32	30·8	1,468,745	47,687
Rodríguez	1932–34	27	798,982	29,592
Cárdenas	1934–40	72	17,889,792	248,469
Ávila Camacho	1940–46	72	5,518,970	76,652
Alemán	1946–52	72	3,844,745	53,399
Ruiz Cortines	1952–58	72	3,198,781	44,278
López Mateos	1958–64	72	16,004,169	222,280

* Includes preconstitutional period, 1915–17.
Source: Wilkie, *The Mexican Revolution; Federal Expenditure and Social Change since 1910*, 188.

Table 5: Gross National Product, 1940–64, in pesos of 1950

Year	GNP (millions)
1940	22·6
1941	24·8
1942	26·3
1943	27·5
1944	29·7
1945	30·5
1946	32·3
1947	33·5
1948	35·0
1949	37·1
1950	40·6
1951	43·6
1952	45·4
1953	45·6
1954	50·4
1955	54·8
1956	58·2
1957	62·7

1958	66·2
1959	68·1
1960	73·5
1961	76·0
1962	79·7
1963	84·7
1964	93·2

Source: *La economía mexicana en cifras* (Nacional Finciera, S.A., 1965).

Table 6: Government expenditure on the army 1924–60

Year	Govt. exp.	Army	Per cent
1924	261,519	114,510	43·8
1925	302,164	82,853	27·4
1926	314,322	86,155	27·4
1927	310,081	86,379	27·8
1928	287,244	85,452	29·7
1929	275,541	90,021	32·7
1930	279,121	73,490	26·3
1931	226,478	58,875	26·0
1932	211,624	55,030	26·0
1933	245,950	54,381	22·1
1934	264,740	54,210	20·5
1935	300,822	62,740	20·8
1936	406,098	70,412	17·3
1937	478,756	83,052	17·3
1938	503,764	84,303	16·7
1939	582,227	91,868	15·8
1940	631,544	120,488	19·1
1941	681,869	130,247	19·1
1942	836,848	154,331	18·4
1943	1,075,539	194,358	18·1
1944	1,453,334	213,088	14·7
1945	1,572,804	234,316	14·9
1946	1,770,543	252,892	14·3
1947	2,142,961	277,299	12·9
1948	2,773,364	306,314	11·0
1949	3,740,587	330,003	8·8
1950	3,463,290	346,331	10·0
1951	4,670,088	380,353	8·1
1952	6,464,230	467,739	7·2
1953	5,490,401	509,233	9·3
1954	7,916,807	640,867	8·1

Table 6—continued

Year	Govt. exp.	Army	Per cent
1955	8,883,120	709,046	8·0
1956	10,270,112	774,742	7·5
1957	11,303,248	903,697	8·0
1958	13,287,707	968,668	7·3
1959	14,163,433	942,125	6·7
1960	20,150,330	1,086,067	5·4

Source: González Casanova: *La democracia en México*, Table XIV.

Table 7: Strikes and strikers, 1920–60

Year	Strikes	Strikers
1920	173	88,536
1921	310	100,380
1922	197	71,382
1923	146	61,403
1924	136	23,988
1925	51	9,861
1926	23	2,977
1927	16	1,005
1928	7	498
1929	14	3,743
1930	15	3,718
1931	11	227
1932	56	3,574
1933	13	1,084
1934	202	14,685
1935	642	145,212
1936	674	113,885
1937	576	61,732
1938	319	13,435
1939	303	14,486
1940	357	19,784
1941	142	2,748
1942	98	13,643
1943	766	81,557
1944	887	165,744
1945	220	48,055
1946	207	10,202
1947	130	10,678
1948	88	26,424

1949	90	15,380
1950	82	13,166
1951	144	13,553
1952	113	18,298
1953	167	38,552
1954	93	25,759
1955	135	10,710
1956	159	7,573
1957	193	7,137
1958	740	60,611
1959	379	62,770
1960	377	63,567

Source: Wilkie, *The Mexican Revolution*, 184.

Table 8: Population by religious creed

Year	Population	Catholic	% Catholic
1930	16,552,722	16,179,667	97·74
1940	19,653,552	18,977,585	96·56
1950	25,791,017	25,329,498	98·21
1960	34,923,129	33,692,503	96·47

Source: González Casanova, *La democracia en México*, Table XV.

[1] Emilio Portes Gil, *Quince años de política mexicana* (Mexico, Ediciones Botas, 1941), 223.

[2] Alberto J. Pani, op. cit., II, 109; Jorge Vera Estañol, *La Revolución Mexicana, orígenes y resultados* (Mexico, Editorial Porrua, 1957), 629.

[3] If true, this incident does not necessarily prove Vasconcelos's implication that the elections were 'made in the U.S.A.'. Readers will recall that the *Chicago Tribune* anticipated the results of the American Presidential election of 1948, though in that instance they were wrong.

[4] Pani, op. cit., 113; Portes Gil, *Quince años*, 395–444; Nathaniel and Sylvia Weyl, *The Reconquest of Mexico: The years of Lázaro Cárdenas* (New York and London, Oxford University Press, 1939), 95–105.

[5] 'This is where the President lives; the boss lives across the way'. Pani, op. cit., 119.

[6] Abelardo L. Rodríguez, op. cit., is uninformative, but see 46, 93, 123 ff.

[7] Josephus Daniels, *Shirt-Sleeve Diplomat* (Chapel Hill, University of North Carolina Press, 1947), 47. Rodríguez himself (op. cit., p. 155) says: 'Calles jamás fue ni trató de ser el jefe de mi Gobierno'.

[8] Gilberto Bosques, *The National Revolutionary Party of Mexico and the Six Year Plan* (Mexico, Bureau of Foreign Information of the National Revolutionary Party, 1937) gives text; see also Ramón Beteta, *The Mexican Revolution, a Defense* (Mexico, DAPP, 1937).

The Revolution XXI: Cárdenas

LÁZARO CÁRDENAS BEGAN HIS PRESIDENCY with one piece of good fortune which his predecessors had not had. His term began with a peaceful election and in conditions of returning prosperity. He had, as we have seen, made one preliminary move of which they had not thought: he had toured the country thoroughly as candidate, making it his business to appear in person even in the most remote communities. Yet on the eve of his election he had still been very much the cautious party man, talking in the generalities of the party line. What showed that he intended to bring a new purpose to these was the speech he made on the occasion of his inauguration, in which he was much more positive, and his dramatic proposal that as President he would set aside an hour every day to receive telephone calls or visits from all citizens. It was a promise that he more than kept.

It is not to detract from the magnitude of Cárdenas's achievement to suggest that the most fundamental change he initiated was not that he carried out the plan before him—for others might have done the same—but that he did it in such a way as to end the domination of the 'Sonora dynasty' and to harness the PNR itself to the institution of the Presidency. It was his first major task to achieve personal power. He began with the advantages of military status and the personal goodwill of Calles. The most dangerous element of Calles's following, as long as it remained closely his, was bound to be the labour interest. Cárdenas had to woo this, while at the same time retaining the sympathy of the agrarians with whom he personally had more in common.

Cárdenas himself is a figure by no means easy to assess.[1] He was born on 21 March 1895 in Jiquilpan, in the State of Michoacán, the son of Dámaso Cárdenas and Felicitas del Río. His parents were comfortably off, though not rich, but the early death of his father deprived Cárdenas of the opportunity of secondary education. Having worked as a printer's apprentice, he obtained a job in the local rent office of the municipality; in 1913 when he was eighteen he heard the news of the Constitutionalist revolt; he freed the prisoners in the local jail and went off to fight. In a year's time he was a captain; the following year, a colonel. Though initially attached to a Villista unit he

266

made his way over to the Constitutionalist side in the crucial year of 1915. He was to display similar dexterity in 1920 when he supported the Plan of Agua Prieta and became a brigadier-general.

By this time, however, he has become almost invisible as an individual, having been a soldier for his entire adult life, and throughout the 1920s and early 1930s he is chiefly remarkable as a soldier only for one thing, though a very important one indeed: he was consistently humane. There are no atrocity stories about Cárdenas. To some extent his future identification with the labour interest might be said to have been prefigured, if it had not been so general and widespread at the time. And his contemporaries after 1924 consistently identified him as a 'Calles man', which implied a strong anti-religious stance; but at the same time his lack of personal enemies receives important confirmation from the fact that when captured during the Delahuertista rebellion he was treated with courtesy and subsequently freed.

During the early 1920s he first encountered the power of the international oil companies in the Isthmus. Legend has it that some clumsy local manager tried to bribe him, as so many other generals were bribed, and that he refused, insulted.

The circumstances surrounding his choice as governor of Michoacán in 1928 are entirely obscure. Michoacán, though generally regarded as part of the Mexican west or Core, partakes of much of the character of the north, and in an age of northern dominance he was a divisional general (promoted 1 April 1928) who was strongly sympathetic to the Calles policies. But he seems to have built up considerable regional support, a political base which he was to retain until the last years of his life. It was something more than a lucky chance for him that Ortiz Rubio, an ex-governor of Michoacán, should so soon afterwards have emerged as the Presidential candidate of the PNR for 1930. For it meant that it was he who was chosen to manage the campaign, who became president of the PNR and Secretary of *Gobernación*, if only for two weeks, and who meanwhile was able to retain his governorship for four years, until his term expired in 1932.

During this term as governor, when he was already emerging as a national figure and trying out his strength on the national stage, he developed the basis for the radical programme that he was later to pursue as President. Nor did he share in the collapse of fortune that afflicted those identified more closely with Ortiz Rubio, whom he thus decisively replaced as the *cacique* of his home state. And it was during this period that he became for the first time closely identified with the agrarian cause, which from then on he served with the zeal of a convert, without losing his original identification with labour. This balance, perhaps only possible to someone who came from Michoacán, explains how, as President, Cárdenas came at one and the same time to be the last of the northern Presidents (1920–40) and the first of the long sequence from the Core (since 1934).

Cárdenas was still at this crucial period a soldier, a factor probably decisive in his nomination as President. The view that he was always, despite, or perhaps because of, his military career, a civilian at heart is, however, scarcely disputable. As President he was conspicuously unmilitary, maddeningly disorganized, the antithesis of good staff-work or personnel management. He eschewed military uniform completely for baggy and rumpled civilian suits. However, he was still only happy at home in the saddle, travelling over some of the most difficult country in Mexico, always listening to complaints, difficulties, problems from the people of Mexico. He was never a desk-bound civilian, any more than he had been a desk-bound officer. His own instinct to shun ostentation was symbolized for many by his refusal to make use of Chapultepec Castle, splendid but remote, as his actual official residence. Instead he moved into a small residence in Chapultepec Park called Los Pinos, which was secluded but accessible, and this since 1934 has remained the official home of Mexico's Presidents.

In many ways this personal style of government had advantages, and it has certainly made Cárdenas a legend in the stories of the people of his country. But it did have one great failing. By choice Cárdenas immersed himself in minor problems and shrugged off a general overview of administration; by inclination he was unwilling to believe ill of others around him. While government became more rather than less presidential, the evil of corruption spread. Though the 1930s were not to exhibit the sheer greed and vulgarity of the 1920s or the late 1940s, they were a period in which important decisions were not taken which could decisively have influenced later developments.

With Portes Gil as his first Secretary of External Relations, it came as no surprise that from the beginning top priority was placed on the distribution of land, where possible in the form of *ejidos* or co-operative farms. The President himself was constantly interrupting other state business to rush off and deal with the problems of some small Indian community who had appealed to him for aid. The wry jokes that were made about this did not suggest that his heart was not in it. It was.

However, in one area Cárdenas did not intervene: in labour disputes, and the result was a wave of strikes which grew in 'geometric' proportions. As a result of these, labour began to win direct from employers what it would have otherwise cost the state too much to give. At the same time the strikes dealt the final death-blow to the old and now complacent CROM, whose leader, Luis Morones, had long been notorious for his personal vanity and ostentation. Unobtrusively, Cárdenas directed official favour towards the rival left-wing element of the labour movement and towards its leader, Vicente Lombardo

Toledano. Calles watched the erosion of his political base with alarm. But the clash was to come not over labour, but over land.

Even with the abolition of the restraint of *amparo*–the legal writ used in Mexico for redressing almost all grievances–the land reform programme still sustained considerable delay. The delay now arose rather from the inactivity of the judges than the fact of legal pretexts. Interference with the judiciary, however, had been such a scandal of the Díaz period that Portes Gil–after first carefully culling the bench–had established the principle of the permanence of judges on the Anglo-Saxon model. This principle Cárdenas now swept aside, much to the applause of the left wing and the more vociferous 'revolution-aries'.

Calles, who had been in poor health, had withdrawn to the north for treatment after the inauguration, while his long-time colleague had handed over the presidency of the PNR to General Matías Ramos. The arrival in the capital of the new Secretary of Agriculture, Tomás Garrido Canabal, for thirteen years ruler of Tabasco, which he had turned into a remarkable demonstration of secularism, atheism, and prohibitionism, illustrated that at least some of the values he stood for were strongly favoured by the new government. Garrido Canabal's fascistic 'Gold Shirts' were not as obtrusive in the capital as they were on their native stamping-ground, but they were there nevertheless. And the strikes were worrying. From some thirteen worthy of note in 1933 in 1934, under the influence of the new Federal Labour Code, the number had risen to 202; in 1935 it rose to 642. Now irritated beyond belief by the removal of legal restraints, Calles decided to speak out, denouncing the strikes as 'provoking, and playing with, the economic life of the nation'[2] (11 June 1935).

In the course of his speech Calles included references to the political struggles under Ortiz Rubio which were generally held to refer to that President's enforced resignation. Cárdenas could not afford to ignore the implication. Strengthening his position by calling for the resigna-tion of the entire Cabinet, he placed an aeroplane at the disposal of the ex-President and Calles flew into virtual exile at the remote seaport of Mazatlán. Portes Gil became president of the PNR, and Tomás Garrido Canabal was removed from the Department of Agriculture and replaced by an early supporter of Cárdenas, the long-time revolutionary *caudillo* of Nuevo León, General Saturnino Cedillo. There was no doubt now who was President.

With the departure of Garrido Canabal the anti-religious campaign was unobtrusively checked, with a return to a more conventional pattern of socialist education in the schools. Then Cárdenas, with Portes Gil at his elbow to organize candidates, set about systematic intervention in the states, eliminating governors who were potentially hostile. When this was done, Portes Gil himself was replaced; with his agrarian background he was potential competition that could not be ignored. Before this happened, the last round of the contest between Cárdenas and Calles had been played. In December 1935 Calles arrived unexpectedly in the capital by air direct from Los Angeles, accompanied by Luis Morones. Those prominent members of the party who flocked again to meet him immediately found themselves the victims of more or less direct pressure to desist, one of the most prominent of those demoted or transferred to less sensitive jobs being General Joaquín Amaro. Calles himself was subjected to a wave of demonstrations and even investigations of his past, which failed to reveal anything discreditable. However, although the ageing *caudillo* exercised considerable restraint, his supporters – those who had boosted him as 'Supreme Chief of the Revolution' in the first place – were less cautious. Then on 7 April 1936 the express train from Mexico City to Vera Cruz was blown up, with the loss of thirteen lives. It was taken as a signal of conspiracy against the government, and the enemies of Calles lost no time in indicating their feelings to the President. Two days later Calles was arrested in the early hours of the morning, taken to Balbuena airfield, and deported, this time to the United States.

The following month there returned to Mexico, with the approval of the President, Adolfo de la Huerta, who had spent the long years of his exile in the United States giving singing lessons. He was only the first of many other returning exiles. Cárdenas had solved the problem of Calles in the old way, but it was he who found out, for the first time in Mexican history, just what else could be done with ex-Presidents. He put them to work. De la Huerta himself became Visitor of Consulates and in 1946 Director-General of Pensions; Ortiz Rubio became (1935) head of the state petroleum corporation 'Petro-Mex'; Rodríguez subsequently (1943) became governor of Sonora. They were to show the way for all their successors, including Cárdenas himself.

The middle two years of Cárdenas's Presidency were those in which he determined the impact he would make on Mexican history. In the first twelve months of his term he had distributed as much land as Rodríguez had in his entire term. After the first exile of Calles the rate of redistribution grew even more spectacularly. At the same time, the departure of Calles emphasized the ascendancy of Vicente Lombardo Toledano. At the outbreak of the Spanish Civil War Mexico was the only Latin nation, and one of the few in the whole world, to continue to support the Republican government, which Cárdenas was prepared to support physically to the best of his power. In 1939 Mexico was to receive in turn an influx of some of Spain's most able sons, and to offer a refuge to General Miaja himself on the fall of Madrid. It was the heyday of the Left in Mexico, and in the late 1930s this meant more than a degree of sympathy with a Moscow where the notorious treason trials were only just getting under way. With Hitler as the apparent alternative, Moscow was treated with great forbearance for a considerable time.

Despite the disturbing situation abroad and signs of both Communist and Fascist agitation at home, 1937 was a year of considerable prosperity for Mexico, and the progress of the Six-Year Plan was a notable personal triumph for the President. He was now strong enough to dispense with the services of Saturnino Cedillo, who returned to his native state to nurse his ambitions for the Presidency. Cárdenas had, however, his own remedy for *caudillismo*–the reconstruction of the official party on the functionalist lines foreshadowed for it from the beginning. To symbolize the establishment of the new era, nothing less was required than its complete transformation. In December 1937 the PNR convention was persuaded to vote for its own dissolution. In its place there emerged the new *Partido de la Revolución Mexicana*, known as the PRM.

The new party was divided vertically into four sector organizations. Labour was represented by the *Confederación de Trabajadores Mexicanos* (CTM), headed by Lombardo Toledano; it was offset by the Peasant Sector *Confederación Nacional Campesina* (CNC), founded in 1935 to keep the agricultural workers out of the hands of the labour interest. Both were large organizations resting on a mass membership already running into millions. The third sector was only 60,000 strong, but it was in a way the key to the success of the whole arrangement. This was the Military Sector, in which the armed forces gained a regular voice in the processes of government, and so, it was hoped, would no longer feel the need to revert to violence when their ambitions were thwarted. The fourth sector, the so-called Popular Sector, was designed to provide a home for the middle class which, with the growth of bureaucracy along with the growth of government, might otherwise all too easily be a prey to right-wing demagogues or traditional conservatism. It had no special organization. Incidentally, at the same time, the passage of a Civil Service Law helped to consolidate the support of the bureaucracy for the régime, and the abolition of the compulsory dues which had formed the financial basis of the PNR made the new political arrangement considerably more attractive to them than the old.

The new régime was to confront its greatest test almost immediately. It came, however, not from inside Mexico, but from outside; and not so much from foreign governments, as in the past, but from the great international corporations engaged in the oil business. It will be recalled that at the time of Bucareli the Mexican government, then in a weak position financially, had had to give in effect a pledge against the application of the provisions of the Constitution of 1917 on sub-soil resources. It turned out that this pledge coincided with the failure of many of the early oil-wells that had been drilled in the first rush and had been heavily produced during the Great War. Before this happened, one of the largest, the El Águila Company, originally founded by the English entrepreneur Lord Cowdray, had been sold by him in 1917 to Royal Dutch Shell, of whose vast worldwide empire it now formed part. In 1936 and 1937 the Águila company had been a major scene of labour unrest as the CTM backed attempts by its workers to increase their pay and allowances.

As part of its programme of reform the government had secured, on 23 November 1936, the passage of a general expropriation law author-izing it to nationalize private property where it was deemed necessary for 'public or social welfare'. The first use of this law came in June 1937 when labour disputes on the National Railways were checked by expropriating the railways themselves and handing them over to the railway-workers to run. While foreign governments were still up in arms at this move, the government proceeded to enact a declaratory Act resuming the subsoil rights formerly acquired by the oil companies, which, however, they were allowed to continue to exercise on the government's terms. The principal of these was that the wages of the workers should be at once raised by one-third.[3]

The companies took the question to the courts and they, at the beginning of March 1938, ruled in favour of the government. It was clearly advisable for the companies to submit, and the government of the United States, in pursuance of its 'Good Neighbor' policy, advised its companies to do so. But the British government, sticking to a rather old-fashioned idea of international propriety, expressed strong disap-proval. It could hardly have done so at a worse moment; on 12 March Hitler's forces marched into Austria, and Britain had her hands full. Within a week, on 18 March, Cárdenas proclaimed the nationaliza-tion of all the properties of the foreign-owned oil companies, British and American, and almost without exception every Mexican backed him publicly and privately in the maintenance of Mexico's national sovereignty.

In the upshot, it is hard to say who came off best. The United States government maintained its moderate attitude and secured neither compensation nor arbitration, though late in 1938 it did secure an agreement on land claims which it had sought vainly for years. The British government sent three notes of increasing stiffness. Public collections were held throughout Mexico, and in May Cárdenas had the pleasure of sending a cheque for the indemnity to the British government and immediately severing diplomatic relations. But the British investors did get their money.

While Cárdenas was still at the height of his power, in May 1938, word came to him that Cedillo was preparing to revolt. He was one of the few men in the country who spoke out against the oil expropriation. But he was unlucky, and he was foolish.[4] He allowed himself to be edged into premature revolt by the army, and he had forgotten that the desert plains of San Luis Potosí now lay open to the eyes of men in aircraft. This, the latest military revolt to be attempted in Mexico, was a complete failure, and Cedillo himself was shot by his over-zealous captors, against the wishes of Cárdenas himself.

After this the rest of Cárdenas's government was in a sense anti-climax. The agrarian reform did not slacken, and by the end of the six years the total of more than 20 million hectares had been redistributed into *ejidos*. The power of the regional *caudillos* had been broken. The new government agencies displaced them as the source of benefits, and the peasants found that they could indeed free themselves from their former limitations with their aid. The labour movement remained powerful, though under their new ownership and management the railways did not work very well, and subsequently President Ávila Camacho was to transfer them from workers' control to the care of a state corporation. But from the spring of 1939 the principal domestic preoccupation became the choice of a new President; and it was clear that the main preoccupations of the man who was chosen would be finance and the war in Europe.

The main contenders for the nomination were all generals. The strongest was General Múgica, then Secretary of Communications and Public Works, who was favoured by the Left. Against him, however, there was the charismatic figure of General Almazán, whose right-wing following included those fascistic groups which by this time had become known collectively as the Sinarquistas. For all its Mussolini-like solidity on the surface, the ruling party was a coalition that had not yet had time to settle down. The choice of either of these candidates might split it beyond repair.

One cabinet member appeared possible as a compromise candidate. A large and affable man who was politically colourless, Manuel Ávila Camacho, the Secretary of War, not only held a post the importance of which was growing daily, but he had the added political advantage of a brother who like him had an excellent revolutionary record, and into the bargain was currently governor of the State of Puebla. If Cárdenas did back him, he did so with extreme finesse; despite the accusations of his enemies, there was no evidence of assistance, and he was to fulfil his promise of holding elections as fairly as possible. At its convention in November 1939 Ávila Camacho was the overwhelming choice of the party regulars, and General Almazán retired to run as an independent opposition candidate.

It was a stiff contest. In retrospect it was apparent that the Mexican economy had been running into difficulties since mid-1937 when there was a recession in the United States. In 1938 only the exports of silver–the traditional prop of the colonial economy–enabled the government to maintain a positive balance of trade. By 1939 the government's headlong plunge into nationalization was beginning to call for a heavy financial commitment, and in the autumn Cárdenas had to appear before Congress and call for an unpopular programme of self-restraint. The candidate of the PRM had a good record to point to, but not such a rosy future. Yet he remained calm, and Almazán did not. The streets were filled with his hysterical partisans and as the elections approached there were repeated clashes between youths in the street and even an abortive revolt in Monterrey. Then four days before the election Almazán made a serious tactical error by threatening revolt if the election was not fair. After that it hardly could be.

In those days the Mexican electoral law provided that the first faction to reach any polling booth had the right to organize it. On election day, 7 July 1940, both sides strove to take advantage of this. In Mexico City, where Almazanista support was particularly strong, gangs fought with clubs and sticks to secure possession of the booths, then denied access to the polls to all but their own followers. Outside the capital, however, it is likely that genuine popularity kept the majority in line. The result officially declared was suspiciously unanimous, but the huge crowds that had flocked into the Zócalo in praise of Almazán did not march.[5] They had confidence in Cárdenas, and he had promised them a fair count. Ávila Camacho was to be the next President of Mexico.

It was the end of one era and the beginning of another: the era of the Institutionalized Revolution. But for the moment the task was war and a general was again President.

Oil

Oil was known to the Aztecs, who called the black sticky substance *chapopote* and used it for religious purposes. They found it floating on lakes and rivers in the low-lying regions of the isthmus of Tehuantepec. No one took much account of this in Mexico until the beginning of the present century; it remained just an interesting curiosity.

The modern use of oil began with the discovery of the first oil-well in Pennsylvania in 1859 by a farmer who was drilling for water. It was the beginning of a vast industry which provided, at considerable profit to middlemen such as John D. Rockefeller and his business associates, mineral oil for lighting and improved lubricants for railways and stationary steam engines. No great refining processes were needed for either of these purposes and the light fractions were regarded as a dangerous nuisance, for it was their presence that made so many early oil-wells catch fire and burn out completely without ever becoming productive. Mexico's first oil-well was drilled in 1894, but its product then had no value and it was a commercial failure.[6]

In 1901 the English entrepreneur Sir Weetman Pearson was passing through Spindletop, Texas, on his way back to England from Mexico when he heard that oil had been found there. He inspected the spot, and recalled having seen, in the course of building the Tehuantepec National Railway, the deposits of *chapopote* which suggested the presence of an oil-field. It was not long before he had obtained concessions from the Díaz government to search for oil and in 1906 obtained further concessions to search for oil on government lands. He had several rivals in the field, the most important being Edward L. Doheny, the Californian oil magnate, who was prospecting for oil on private land which he had purchased and struck oil in small quantities in 1901. As it happened, however, it was Pearson (by this time Lord Cowdray) who brought in the first 'gusher' in Mexico to become fully productive in December 1910, a month after the start of the Madero Revolution.[7]

Cowdray's company, as was appropriate to its function of exploring government-owned lands, was a semi-official corporation in which the Mexican government held a considerable share. Its full name was the *Compañía Mexicana de Petróleo 'El Águila', S.A.*, but it was usually known as the Águila Company. Because it was official, and because it was deliberately encouraged to oppose United States interests, which had previously monopolized the sale of fuel and illuminating oil in Mexico, it incurred considerable hostility in the early years of the Revolution. Unremitting press attacks sponsored by the American companies sought to identify the British interests wholly with the old régime, and for many revolutionaries must have strongly helped reinforce their natural dislike of foreign interests generally, born of generations of bitter experiences.

In fact the Águila Company was given Madero's approval and encouraged to continue. Government investigation found nothing discreditable. However, when Huerta seized power, the company found itself in considerable difficulties. Huerta's urgent need for money caused pressure upon businesses to contribute to a government loan, and it was hard to refuse and continue in business. When the United States government came into conflict with Huerta, it was natural, though erroneous, for it to assume that Huerta was being upheld by European finance, and the oil interests were the most obvious candidates for blame. Meanwhile, United States interests extended and consolidated their holdings, and after the alarms over the capture of the Tuxpam-Tampico area were able to expand production considerably.

Cowdray himself never went back to Mexico after 1912 and by some happy instinct decided in 1917 to sell all his oil interests in Mexico to Royal Dutch Shell. Doheny sold his to Standard Oil of Indiana in 1925. It was the new owners, therefore, who had to cope with the problems raised by the Mexican Constitution of 1917 and the sudden and drastic drop in oil production that occurred in 1921, at the very moment that Mexico had become the world's second largest oil-producing country, with the exhaustion of the oil-wells at the end of the war. Not surprisingly, oil companies generally played safe and decided to invest as little as reasonable in such an unstable area. Oil production remained low throughout the 1920s. However, the Águila Company was the one exception and was rewarded by successfully bringing in the fabulously rich Poza Rica field in 1930 (fully productive by 1933), while the Americans were not willing to invest, given the unsettled state of the country and the doubts felt by their own government; both in the United States itself and in Venezuela there were much better opportunities for making money.

It was the age of the motor-car and the pattern of demand for oil had changed completely. Illuminating oil was being replaced for lighting purposes, in Mexico as elsewhere, by electricity; the diesel engine was replacing the steam engine; and there was a limitless market for petrol and aviation spirit. By 1938 the Mexicans calculated the private companies had made ten times their investment in profit. In retrospect one may well feel that the Mexicans were very fortunate not to lose more of their oil reserves before they were in a position to exploit them themselves. For by the time that the pressures were building up again in advance of the Second World War, Cárdenas was in power and the question of the state's right to the mineral reserves of the nation was no longer an issue. In 1937 Bolivia became the first Latin American nation to take over its local oil companies. Faced with the intransigence of the oil companies in 1938 Cárdenas knew that it could be done, and was well aware that the Mexicans had the competence and the skills to run their own oil industry.

In the post-war period Mexico has had a limitless capacity for all the oil her fields can produce. The state oil corporation has discharged its task of locating and extracting oil with great efficiency. It has, however, encountered the problems common to large nationalized enterprises of being regarded at one and the same time as a guaranteed job for its employees and as a corporation whose job it is to subsidize social welfare in remote regions by keeping prices down.[8] Only in the early 1960s did it become possible to break out of this dilemma by deliberate capital investment in refinery capacity designed to diversify its product and create a modern petro-chemical industry. Since the future use of oil is unlikely to be the present wasteful combustion of a useful and often essential chemical raw material, there can be no doubt that Mexico's future in this respect is bright.

Vicente Lombardo Toledano

Until his death in 1970, Lázaro Cárdenas was the one Mexican politician whose name was widely known outside Mexico. The Mexicans whose names were most widely known were, of course, sports personalities, and perhaps this is as it should be. Writers, artists, and professional men, too, were known to their publics–sometimes much further afield. Why then were politicians not so favoured? Three reasons suggest themselves. Most of them were not very interesting people. Those who were found themselves overshadowed by the institution of the Presidency which it was politically inexpedient to abandon. And the few not overshadowed found themselves ideologically constricted in expressing their personalities by the exigencies of Marxist antipathy to anything that smacked of a 'personality cult'.

Vicente Lombardo Toledano suffered from all three problems–yet no discussion of recent Mexican life can afford to ignore him. His early life was of no great interest even to his biographers, usually a persistently curious tribe when it comes to such details. A descendant of an Italian immigrant, he was born in the village of Teziutlán in the State of Puebla on 16 July 1894,[9] and was brought up in a comfortable middle-class household. He was educated at the Escuela Nacional Preparatoria and the University of Mexico where he was strongly influenced by the anti-scientism of the Ateneo de la Juventud and in particular by the humanism of Antonio Caso. His law thesis was strongly individualist and he did not turn towards Marxism until he was already strongly involved with the workers' movement. In one sense he never abandoned individualism, and he always wore his Marxism with a slight degree of embarrassment.

In 1917–two years before he took his degrees in law and philosophy–he joined the Universidad Popular as secretary, and organizer of the courses that it and its humanist founders set out to provide in adult education. As such he became, more or less inadvertently, a founding member of the CROM in 1918, and after five years of service in worker's education he was elected to the Central Committee in 1923. While he continued to teach and, perhaps more importantly, to hold teaching positions, he now found that the power of political patronage behind him gave him a dramatic political opportunity. The governor of Puebla had supported the revolt of Adolfo de la Huerta, and was removed; Lombardo was chosen to serve as interim governor to fill out his term. At its conclusion he returned to the capital to serve in the government of the city, later being elected a deputy to Congress for two terms, from 1924 to 1928.

Marxist jargon was much in the air in Mexico at this time, as we have seen, but it was not much understood, and Lombardo was in no way untypical in his socialist position. By 1927 he was speaking of himself as a Marxist, but his writings show he was pretty hazy about what Marxism meant, apart from the idea that the proletariat was the class of the future and that imperialism was a phenomenon of capitalism. More might have been expected from someone who was now secretary-general of the National Federation of Teachers. In fact, Lombardo's slow conversion to Marxism, culminating in his use of it to explain his resignation from the CROM in 1932, followed rather closely the general trend of opinion in Mexico, first under the influence of Calles and socialistic education, and subsequently under the impact of the Great Depression.

In October 1933 Lombardo emerged at the head of a possible alternative labour organization, the *Confederación General de Obreros y Campesinos de México* (CGOCM). It was much more militant than the CROM and soon succeeded in obtaining the affiliation of the bulk of Mexico's organized trade unions, by a combination of ideological self-justification and pursuit of better economic conditions through strikes. It was the CGOCM that was behind the strikes in 1934-35 which enabled Cárdenas to outflank *Callismo*. It had its rival, however, to the Left in the form of the Mexican Communist Party (PCM), and the political climate of the mid 1930s favoured the strategy of the Popular Front. Although not himself a Communist, Lombardo followed the Front pattern by organizing with government support the *Confederación de Trabajadores Mexicanos* (CTM) in February 1936 with Communist participation. He was soon to be confronted by a strong challenge from the Communists to direct the policy of the entire organization, and in averting this had necessarily to sacrifice something of the strength of the confederation as a whole. The price, as we have seen, was having to accept a permanent division of functions between the workers' organization and that of the agrarians.

The climax of labour strength and influence under Cárdenas came with the challenge to the oil companies in 1938. It was Lombardo who backed the strikes that brought about government intervention; it was he who called for the massive demonstrations in favour of the President; and it was he who subsequently registered the strength of the labour movement in Mexico by forming the nucleus of the Latin American Workers' Confederation (CTAL) and becoming its first president. However, this strength was not to last long.

It was eroded by the approach of war and the extraordinary evolutions forced upon non-Communist Marxists who had to cope with the sudden reversals of friendship of the Soviet Union herself and the Comintern, her creature. Although from the time that he proclaimed his Marxism Lombardo had been open to the suggestion that he was in fact a Communist, much sharper doubts were cast on his independence by his strong opposition to Trotsky's presence in Mexico. The suspicion that he was a fellow-traveller was reinforced by his sudden advocacy of neutralism in 1939 and his equally sudden turn towards belligerency against the Axis in 1941. At the same time he had, by creating a 'workers' militia' in 1938, incurred the hostility of the army, whose influence grew rapidly as war approached. Though he did serve out his five-year term as secretary-general of the CTM, he was not re-elected in February 1941, and the trend of the CTM under his successor was away from militancy and towards gaining the maximum advantage for the workers out of the wartime situation.

It was only after the opening of the Cold War, when Alemán (for whom he had spoken in 1945–46) was President, that Lombardo began to find himself isolated. He was now advocating the creation of a workers' party in opposition to the government, to be called the *Partido Popular* (PP). The price was his own expulsion from the CTM, which shortly afterwards was to withdraw from the increasingly Communist-dominated CTAL. In the same year, 1948, Lombardo successfully organized a rival labour grouping, which was subsequently to take the title of the *Unión General de Obreros y Campesinos de México* (UGOCM). It proved not only to be weak, but also the forerunner of a number of equally unstable splinter groups of the CTM. With experience the government gained in subtlety of treatment, and the splinter groups were to some extent fostered in order to provide a vehicle for Left sentiment within the revolutionary party. Meanwhile Lombardo had been forced to make overtures himself to the party to end his exile, and although from that time on he remained notionally independent of the PRI, by backing the official party candidates his party enjoyed a kind of semi-official status which marked it off sharply from the PAN or other real opposition groups.

The decisive moment came just before the beginning of the López Mateos administration, when the PP had already come out in favour of his candidature, and before the election, when the UGOCM led an attempt to take over lands belonging to foreign owners and forced the government to expropriate them. It was in turn outflanked by López Mateos himself. Meanwhile, however, with strong left-wing support, the workers who had been suffering from inflation in the early 1950s began to become restive. The new administration was greeted by a wave of strikes, culminating in the great railway strike, and it struck back at them sharply. The unrest continued for more than two years, in the course of which a number of prominent Left supporters had been arrested under the provisions of the wartime law on 'social dissolution'. Lombardo was not one of them, despite the fact that with the Cuban example before them the *Partido Popular* had added the epithet 'Socialista' to its title for the first time, and proclaimed itself openly a Marxist-Leninist party. With the reform of the electoral system in 1962 the PPS was at last able to win seats in Congress, where its fatal abstentionism had previously deprived it of what small representation it had won, and Lombardo in 1964 at last became a Federal Deputy as an opposition candidate.

One thread runs through the whole story of the Left in Mexico: a persistent failure to recognize the strength of Mexican nationalism. However, it is only fair to point out that it is a force that has been underestimated by others too, and always to their cost.

Voices: The Thirties

'Insofar as there exist contingents of human beings dispossessed of the lands of their forefathers, of their rights as men and as citizens and they continue to be treated as animals and as machines, it cannot be considered that equality and justice reign in the Americas'.[10]

'The prosperity of a country then [1900] was measured by the extension of its railroads or by the amount of its exports and any district whose production was valued at many millions of pesos was considered very wealthy although the majority of its inhabitants lived under conditions of such poverty that they hardly merited being classed as human'.[11]

'Experience in America has shown that the policy of uncontrolled working, and that on small areas, is a national blunder. Moreover, this method of working has produced wild speculation, and has resulted in the most deplorable waste'.[12]

'The current joke was that one morning while dispatching business in the capital his secretary laid a list of urgent matters, and a telegram, before him. The list said: *Bank reserves dangerously low.* "Tell the Treasurer", said Cárdenas. *Agricultural production failing.* "Tell the Minister of Agriculture". *Railways bankrupt.* "Tell the Minister of Communications". *Serious message from Washington.* "Tell Foreign Affairs". Then he opened the telegram, which read: "My corn dried, my burro died, my sow was stolen, my baby is sick. Signed, Pedro Juan, village of Huitzlipituzco".

' "Order the presidential train at once", said Cárdenas. "I am leaving for Huitzlipituzco" '.[13]

'By a rare beneficence of Providence it so happens that the nations who are at the moment accredited with the most war-like disposition, are deficient in oil. But it also happens that the sources of oil are, with the exception of those of Russia and the United States, located in small countries who could not hope to maintain their independence by force unaided, and the strong, peaceful powers control the supply, by arrangements more or less analogous to the one lately repudiated by Mexico'.[14]

'I began by asking him why he, the most famous Mexican writer of his day, was still practising medicine instead of devoting himself to literature. "After all", I said, "there must be hundreds of able and willing young physicians to look after your patients, but there is only one Mariano Azuela to write the classics of the Revolution. Surely. . ."

' "My friend", he interrupted, peering at me quizzically, a glance half-pitying, half-deprecating, "my friend, do you know how many copies of my books are sold here in Mexico? Naturally, you don't. Well, if the sale of any one of them should reach a thousand it would be a sensation. No. We Mexicans don't support our writers. Some day, possibly, but not now. Just take a look at the book stalls and what do you find. A lot of bad translations of second-rate French novels and the like. So I practise medicine and write when I can find the time" '.[15]

'Mexico has not had to alter even the slightest concept in its doctrine in order to find itself on the side of the nations who are currently struggling for the civilization of the world and the wellbeing of Humanity. Our authentic road has not changed. Our historic sense of honour continues to be the same that was expressed with arms, in the past, to defend our territory and to uphold our institutions. If to align ourselves with your country in the present emergency had implied for us an unforeseen change of course, our co-operation would not enjoy the unanimous support which Mexican opinion confers'.[16]

[1] There are two biographies of Cárdenas in English: William Cameron Townsend, *Lázaro Cárdenas, Mexican Democrat* (Ann Arbor, Mich., George Wahr, 1952) and Nathaniel and Sylvia Weyl, op. cit. For an opposition view see Carlos Alvear Acevedo, *Lázaro Cárdenas, el hombre y el mito* (Mexico, Editorial Jus, 1961). Roberto Blanco Moheno, *El cardenismo*, is more comprehensive than its title suggests.

[2] Dulles, op. cit., 629–31.

[3] For the Mexican view of the dispute at this period see *Oil Industry in Mexico*, 'Commentaries' Series No. 2 (Mexico, DAPP, 1938).

[4] Sir Owen O'Malley, *The Phantom Caravan* (London, John Murray, 1954), 174.

[5] Betty Kirk, *Covering the Mexican Front* (Norman, University of Oklahoma Press, 1942), 238–52.

[6] Furber, op. cit., 91.

[7] Desmond Young, *Member for Mexico* (London, Cassell, 1966), 133–4.

[8] Brandenburg, op. cit., 271–5. The best general study of the Mexican oil industry is that of Ernesto Lobato López, in *México: cincuenta años de Revolución I: La economía* (Mexico, Fondo de Cultura Económica, 1960), 315 ff.

[9] All factual details on Lombardo's life are taken from Robert Paul Millon, *Mexican Marxist: Vicente Lombardo Toledano* (Chapel Hill, University of North Carolina Press, 1966).

[10] Lázaro Cárdenas, address to the First Interamerican Indigenist Congress, 5 April 1940, quoted William Cameron Townsend, *Lázaro Cárdenas, Demócrata mexicano*, trs. Avelino Ramírez A. (Mexico, Biografías Gandesa, 1959), 128.

[11] *Oil Industry in Mexico*, 3.

[12] Statement attributed to Lord Cowdray, 1918, by John Kenneth Turner, *Hands Off Mexico* (New York, Rand School of Social Science, 1920), 25.

[13] Anita Brenner, op. cit., 91.

[14] Evelyn Waugh, op. cit., 88.

[15] Lesley Byrd Simpson, introduction to Mariano Azuela, *Two Novels of Mexico: The Flies, The Bosses* (Berkeley & Los Angeles, University of California Press, 1964), xi–xii.

[16] President Ávila Camacho's welcome to President Roosevelt at Monterrey, 1943, in Ávila Camacho, *La ruta de México* (Mexico, Secretaría de Educación Pública, 1946), 105–6.

The Revolution XXII: War or Peace?

ÁVILA CAMACHO WAS A CONSIDERABLE CONTRAST to his predecessor. Where Cárdenas had been a convinced, if not fanatical, atheist, he proclaimed himself in the course of his campaign 'a believer', and proceeded with his brother to attend Mass in public. Where his predecessor was diminutive and mobile, he was unusually tall and reticent though friendly. Where Cárdenas had gone about unaccompanied, except by a chosen colleague to whom he wished to talk, Ávila Camacho was once again shadowed by the hard-eyed gunmen who had guarded his predecessors. For the times were turbulent. Almazán did not attempt to lead a revolt, and it was not Mexicans whom they were wary of.[1] In a time of war Mexico was a centre of international intrigue and the fifth column and the Comintern strove for every advantage in a nation officially neutral and uncommitted, but so inconveniently near to a Great Power.

The Left, however, was on the defensive. In an act of characteristic generosity, Cárdenas in 1937 had become the only world leader prepared to give hospitality to the fallen Trotsky. He was not only allowed to live in Mexico, but also to write and receive visitors. Intentionally or unintentionally, his presence in Mexico caused great embarrassment for the Stalinist Communists among the CTM as well as for fellow-travellers such as Toledano himself. Cárdenas could have thought of no better way of keeping the Left in turmoil. Then in 1939 came the collapse of Republican hopes in the Spanish Civil War. Recriminations were multiplied as old battles were fought anew in recollection.

On 20 August 1940 Trotsky was murdered in his house by an assassin armed with an icepick. The assassin, who included among his names that of Jacques Mornard by which he was known at his trial, was generally recognized to be an agent of Stalin himself, and the breach of Mexican neutrality which the assassination implied cooled relations with the Left still further, while doing nothing to narrow the cleavages among it. Mornard was tried and sentenced to prison for twenty years; on his release in 1960 he chose to go to Cuba.[2] Though in his lifetime he had only a small following, Trotsky's period in Mexico has been an inspiration to younger Mexicans, especially students, in

recent years, and Trotskyite organizations were among those prominent in the disturbances of 1968.

In 1940, though, all this still lay in the future and the visible threat
came from the Right. The Sinarquistas were only the tip of the ice-
berg; a more important development in 1938 had been the appearance
of a right-wing political party, the *Partido de Acción Nacional* (PAN),
which was not clerical and which enjoyed a considerable measure of
business and professional support. It was Ávila Camacho's task to seek
to bring this support back to the revolutionary fold while at the same
time stimulating economic recovery and promoting the modernization of his country. Peasants now needed more than land, more even
than irrigation works and credit facilities; they needed transport, they
needed electricity, and they needed consumer durables. Oscar Lewis
found in Tepoztlán that the most desirable article for any Mexican
family was a sewing machine to make clothes and give the housewife
a measure of economic independence. With the world once again at
war the economy was enjoying the benefits of increased demand for
raw materials; the oil companies could no longer maintain their
hostility, and the state no longer had to depend on embarrassing
barter deals with the Axis Powers in order to offload their production
abroad.

The upshot was that the Revolution 'got down off its horse', as one
observer put it. It was even suggested that it had come to an end–a
suggestion which later writers have often rather uncritically accepted
at face value, though it depends for its weight on the idea that something called 'Revolution' was actually going on up to that time. On
the agrarian front, the speed of land distribution did fall off, though
there was relatively little arable land left for redistribution anyway.
On the labour front, the militant leadership of the CTM under
Lombardo Toledano was displaced by the moderate group, government-backed, led by Fidel Velázquez. 'National Unity' was the theme
of the day, and both Calles and Garrido Canabal returned to Mexico.

By December 1941, with the war going strongly in favour of the
Axis, Mexico as a neutral country was an oasis of stability and a
place of refuge. To the exiles of Republican Spain were now being
added a new wave of exiles from occupied France, as well as representatives of other European states, of whom the most spectacular was
to be King Carol of Romania, accompanied by Madame Lupescu.
Then came Pearl Harbor and the sudden and involuntary entry of the
United States into the ranks of the Allies. Mexico was now even more
isolated. The small countries of Central America and of the Caribbean had followed the United States into war with Japan with startling
rapidity in a matter of days, leaving Mexico alone in the North
American continent. Military expenditure rose and defensive posi-

tions were manned, ex-President Lázaro Cárdenas taking command of the Eastern Zone in case of attack from Japan. But it did not come.

On 13 May 1942 the Mexican tanker *Potrero del Llano* was torpedoed off Miami and sank with a loss of thirteen crew members. Mexico was already committed to co-operation with other powers of the Western Hemisphere in the event of outside attack, and relations with Germany strained as a result of Axis agitation. In April 1941 the President had affirmed his opposition to the Axis system in a public speech. At the time he met with considerable opposition from the Left, and Lombardo Toledano had accused the government of being involved in secret negotiations with the United States–a bitter charge in Mexican politics. However, the German attack on Russia in June brought a dramatic transformation. By the end of the year the Left were clamouring for more action against Germany, the government had (August 1941) closed German consulates as likely centres for espionage–as they had been during the First World War–and in September passed a stiff Espionage Act. Yet, as we have seen, the Mexican government did not join the general rush to declare war on Japan, and it seems it was restrained principally by the feeling that it was undignified and probably dangerous to be doing so at the instance of the United States. An actual attack on a Mexican vessel was just the kind of pretext that was needed to bring public opinion behind the government in the event of war, and the ultimatum that was sent to Germany virtually committed the country to war in the event of a repetition. Strong speeches from the Secretary of External Relations, Ezequiel Padilla, showed that the ultimatum had to be taken seriously, but events moved too quickly for diplomacy.

In less than a week he and the government had their answer. On 22 May another tanker, the *Faja de Oro*, was torpedoed with the loss of seven lives. Three days later President Ávila Camacho convened an emergency session of Congress, and on 28 May appeared before the deputies to ask for a declaration of war. After two days' debate it was passed. At the same time Congress gave the President unprecedented powers to suspend constitutional guarantees at will for the duration of the emergency.[3]

Observers universally confirm that for most Mexicans the great shock was not finding themselves at war, but finding themselves fighting with, and not against, the *gringos*. Even in the capital, public opinion as late as 20 May had been against entry into the war;[4] in the country districts the news was received with incredulity. It was, after all, the first formal declaration of war by a Mexican government since 1847. However, this war was very different from any that Mexico had known before. Initially Mexican military action was confined to strengthening and equipping the forces against the possibility of an attack by Japanese forces on Panama–an eventuality which in mid-1942 still seemed very probable. No immediate attempt was made to send Mexican forces overseas.[5]

Instead, in August 1942, a convention was signed with the government of the United States providing for the dramatic increase in the number of migrant contract labourers (*braceros*) crossing the northern frontier and so relieving the work force of the United States. Many Mexicans resident in the United States were drafted under a mutual agreement in the United States forces. By the end of the war over 14,000 had served under the American flag and many had done so with distinction. To their considerable surprise a number of Americans resident in Mexico had similarly found themselves serving in the Mexican army. That army, with Lend-Lease aid, was rapidly becoming not only one of the most professional, but one of the best equipped, in the Americas. Above all, Mexico became an important source for strategic war materials not available elsewhere, and with wartime powers, the government was able to effect a considerable measure of compulsory diversification in mineral extraction. Copper, lead, zinc, cadmium, antimony, and graphite were among those encouraged, and the henequén (sisal) industry of Yucatán enjoyed a brief Indian summer of prosperity as demand soared for ropes and matting.

On 16 September 1942, on the anniversary of the *Grito de Dolores*, Mexicans had a dramatic symbolization performed of the ideal of national unity. The ceremony took place at noon, and when the President appeared on the balcony of the National Palace where the bell of Dolores hangs, he appeared in the company of six living ex-Presidents of Mexico: de la Huerta, Calles, Portes Gil, Ortiz Rubio, Rodríguez, and Cárdenas. As they stood on the balcony, in a sight unparalleled in Mexican history down to that time, they linked arms to reinforce the message of their presence, that the unity of what Brandenburg called 'the Revolutionary Family' was indissoluble, even by war.[6]

It was an ideal rather than an actuality, of course, but it was none the less important, not because the ex-Presidents played their part in the war effort, as they did, but because the main problem of an active but non-participant role in the war for Mexico was that lesser men did not necessarily put the war effort first, or even before their own interests. War meant jobs for the bureaucracy and money for the middle class; the workers were determined not to be left out. In some fields, particularly on the railways, the determination of the workers to secure their own interests made effective working almost impossible. The government made use of force on several occasions, and in 1944 formed for this purpose a special paramilitary reserve known colloquially as the *granaderos*.

Despite the considerable interest of the United States in Mexican co-operation and assistance, unusual sensitivity was shown by the United States government in its handling of relations with Mexico, and great care was taken to demonstrate that under the Good Neighbor policy of President Roosevelt, relations were conducted with mutual respect and regard. In April 1943 Roosevelt, travelling through the southern United States on an inspection tour of munitions plants, unobtrusively crossed the frontier to pay a formal visit to President Ávila Camacho at Monterrey. Once the meeting had taken place, it was, of course, given full publicity as befitted only the second such meeting in the relations of the two countries. The fact that Roosevelt had gone to Mexico, and not Ávila Camacho to the United States, was received with great approval south of the Río Bravo.

In the last two years of the war, Mexican-American co-operation grew out of all recognition. It was to be symbolized in February 1945 by the despatch to the Pacific Front of a Mexican squadron of aircraft – Squadron 201 – which took part in the final attacks on the Philippines and Formosa. By the sending of this squadron, Mexico joined the ranks of members of the United Nations who actually took part in the war directly, the only other Latin American state to do so being Brazil. The squadron lost eight lives. Even before this, Mexico had gained international recognition for her part both before the war in the pursuit of peace, and during it in its restoration, and it was appropriate that in February 1945 she became the scene of the crucially important Inter-American Conference on Problems of War and Peace, which was to play such a major role in shaping the post-war diplomatic structure of the Western Hemisphere and setting the scene for the big debates of the next twenty years.

The Chapultepec Conference – as it became universally known – originated in the desire of the United States government to strengthen its hand for the formation of the United Nations Organization. American aims were the reaffirmation of existing wartime alliances and the maintenance of low tariffs in the post-war period. The Latin American delegates hoped for a united programme of post-war development in the economic and social fields, with the United States contributing the capital, as she had done for the war effort in Europe and the Pacific. They were to be disappointed and, worse, they were to be offended, by the evident belief of the United States delegation that their proper function in the world was to continue to act as primary producers for the industrial manufactures of the United States. This view of developing countries in those days was almost universal outside Latin America, and the Latin Americans were the first to challenge it.

And the challenge on this occasion was led by the host country – Mexico. The Secretary of External Relations, Ezequiel Padilla, had already achieved a personal diplomatic triumph in securing through secret negotiation the presence of Argentina at the conference, for Argentina for most of the war had been pro-Axis and an object of extreme suspicion to the United States. The participation of Argentina at Chapultepec was to lead to her, with the other Latin American nations, formally entering the war and so becoming charter members of the United Nations Organization. In his opening speech Padilla set the theme of the conference by proclaiming the need for a cycle of abundance in the Americas.

The Chapultepec Conference gave Padilla international stature and made him a strong candidate to succeed Ávila Camacho in 1946. (His chief rival was another civilian, the Secretary of *Gobernación*, Miguel Alemán.) This in itself was the most important contribution of the war to Mexico; the strengthening of the concept of civilian government. By accepting the ideas of the Atlantic Charter and the Four Freedoms, Mexicans had implicitly accepted that the era of military domination was over. Revolutions to the south in 1944, in Guatemala and El Salvador, had toppled military régimes and replaced them with reforming civil administrations with which Mexico had sought to establish friendly relations. The Mexican forces now included many who had studied at West Point or been trained by American instructors; their numbers were swelled by young recruits who had never taken part in the old revolutionary fighting and who now saw a new post-war world in which armies would be superfluous. Perhaps most important of all, there was no possible *caudillo* in the antique mould: Almazán was a spent force, tainted, though unfairly, by his pro-Axis supporters, and on 17 February 1945 the President's brother, General Maximino Ávila Camacho, who appeared the natural standard-bearer of the Right, and who aspired to that role, died suddenly at Atlixco, Puebla. This event had a dramatic counterpoint on the Left, and that was decisive.

After the entry of Russia into the war in 1941, Soviet diplomacy had displayed unexpected and sudden enthusiasm for the re-establishment of diplomatic relations with Mexico. This initiative was aided by Roosevelt, who enabled the Mexican minister in Washington to establish contact with Molotov. Diplomatic relations were formally re-established in December 1942. When they were raised to ambassadorial level in 1943, the Soviet Union emphasized her interest in the post by sending as her first ambassador to Mexico a former Undersecretary for Foreign Relations, Constantin Oumanski. Oumanski's embassy was so large and its contacts with the Mexican labour movement and other bodies so extensive that it was suspected of not being solely concerned with the maintenance of friendly relations with its host country. By 1945 it was widely believed that the Soviet Union was sponsoring a move for a *coup* from the Left, but this belief was never put to the test. Oumanski was killed in an air crash in Mexico City on 25 January 1945, and if there was any truth in the rumours (some as colourful as any to have circulated in a rumour-prone country), only one thing is certain: the fear of some such conspiracy powerfully strengthened the position of the man who was responsible, under the President, for the internal security of Mexico, namely Miguel Alemán.

At the end of May 1945, he was chosen at a secret meeting by the leaders of the sector organizations as the party's candidate for the Presidency in 1946 ('the Pact of the Centrals'). It was the end of the old PRM's short life. As a part of its adjustment to the post-war world the PRM, at its second conference in January 1946, was to dissolve itself and to be replaced by the *Partido Revolucionario Institucional* (PRI)–the Party of the Institutionalized Revolution. The most important difference from the older party, apart from the significant title, was the final disappearance of the Military Sector introduced by Cárdenas; the military were in future to be represented within the Popular Sector. The Popular Sector itself had been formally organized by Ávila Camacho in 1943 as the *Confederación Nacional de Organizaciones Populares* (CNOP).

Before turning to the problems of Mexico in the post-war world and the man who was to have to tackle them, it will be convenient to mention here some of the other developments of the wartime period. In Mexico, as in other countries, the fact that national energies were primarily concentrated on the war did not mean that other aspects of progress were neglected.

By far the most important was the new attitude to education. The concept of 'socialist education' favoured by Cárdenas was phased out. It had always been much more a euphemism for militant atheism than a designation of ideological commitment, and as such it generated unnecessary hostility. In 1945 Article 3 of the Constitution of 1917 was amended to remove the directives on the content of education. Meanwhile, however, the administration had devoted far more of its budget than any of its predecessors to actually building schools and training teachers, and under the direction of the Secretary of Education, Jaime Torres Bodet, the long-hoped-for massive campaign against illiteracy was inaugurated, on the principle that it was the duty of those who could read to teach those who could not. By 1950 Mexico was to be over 80 per cent literate–still a long way from the ideal, but a vast achievement for the seven years of the campaign.

For those who lacked even these opportunities, the introduction of

Social Security in January 1943 meant much more to them than the promises of the Constitution of 1917. A contributory scheme, it covered all registered workers for sickness, unemployment, or old age. For the moment its importance was overshadowed by the frenetic pace of wartime life and the visible extravagance of the *nouveaux-riches* bred by the war economy. Despite inflation Mexico was prosperous; even more obviously, she was becoming Americanized. The new urbanized Mexicans ate *sándwiches,* drank *cocacola* or *sevenup,* or at *cocktail parties* downed *jaiboles* on their way from their *clubes* to a *cabaret.* Advertisements were everywhere; the products of Hollywood swamped even the strong local film industry; and the new Institute of Social Security was a massive block of architecture on the American model.[7] It was post war in the New World.

Miguel Alemán Valdés

Miguel Alemán symbolizes with great exactness the post-war era in Mexico. His name is associated with some of the most dramatic advances imaginable in the living standards of the Mexican people. Yet in retirement he has been a controversial figure and his place in the official history of the past fifty years is by no means settled. Wealthy, politically influential, a friend of President Lyndon B. Johnson of the United States, he has been generally regarded as the leading representative of the Right within the Revolutionary Family. As such he has been the target of public abuse amounting to severe attacks on his reputation, and if not his person, at least his effigy.

Alemán was the first second-generation revolutionary to attain the Mexican Presidency after 1910. His father, Miguel Alemán (1884–1929), had an impeccable record in the Revolution: a Maderista, a Constitutionalist in June 1913, and a supporter of Obregón who rose to the rank of *divisionario,* by 1921 he was one of the leading men in Mexico. He nearly fell from grace in that year by supporting the plot against Obregón, but fortunately for him it failed before he had declared himself and his allegiance was not questioned. With the re-election of Obregón, however, his allegiance, like that of many others, finally failed. So in 1929 he made the fatal mistake of supporting the revolt in Vera Cruz of General Jesús M. Aguirre, and was killed in battle against the Federal forces.

His son, Miguel Alemán Valdés, was born at Sayula, Veracruz, on 29 September 1900, and graduated in law from the National University in the year of his father's death. After practising for a few years, he found that his own agreeable personality, coupled with the reputation of his father, made him a formidable candidate for election and one welcomed by the local organizers of the still unformed PNR. One thing stood in the way of larger ambitions: the continued influence of Calles. With this removed, Alemán's rise to influence was meteoric. In 1935 Cárdenas appointed him to the Supreme Court of the Federal District. Evidently he liked what he saw of him, for in 1936 Alemán was chosen to run for senator from his native state. In June of that year, however, Manlio Fabio Altamirano, who had just been elected governor of the state, was assassinated in Mexico City, and the young Alemán was chosen to replace him.

As governor he gave the state strong rule, exhibiting the traditional Veracruzano concern for the advancement of education and spending on it an exceptional amount, even by the competitive standards of the day. Then in 1939 he was chosen by Ávila Camacho to organize his election campaign, with the results that by now are familiar, and was given in return the post of Secretary of *Gobernación*. Writing in 1940 John Gunther could already describe him as 'the Ed Flynn of contemporary Mexican politics, the party fixer, the boss of the government machine'.[8] It may or may not be revealing that he also said that one of Alemán's favourite books then was *Contr'un*, by Étienne de La Boétie, a reply to Machiavelli's *Prince*.[9]

Alemán attained his position because he controlled important patronage in a key state, demonstrated consistent support for Cárdenas, particularly at the time of the oil expropriation, and was the prime mover in the drive for the candidature of Ávila Camacho. Circumstances were, however, to continue to favour him exceptionally. The Secretary of *Gobernación*, as the head of the department responsible for internal and police affairs, and elections, had always commanded important political forces. Moreover, Alemán had the good fortune to hold the office in wartime, when the maintenance of internal security was a prime consideration of external policy also, and he had therefore unusual responsibility and unusual powers. It seems clear that in the course of exercising them, he came to develop a close working relationship with the increasingly professional military forces. In the general reaction to civilism of 1945 he was a natural choice as a Presidential candidate who was a civilian, yet who was acceptable to the military and hence would not cause them to doubt the virtue of the unwritten agreement by which they had withdrawn from an active role in politics to the anonymity of the Popular Sector.

A few days before Alemán's choice by the sector organization in May 1945, Ávila Camacho had set the pace by indicating that the new President could be a civilian. When the end of the war came, he laid down his own emergency powers unobtrusively, and significantly emphasized reconstruction in his Speech to Congress on 1 September. It soon became clear that there was to be no new Six-Year Plan. Instead Alemán toured the country discussing with local leaders what needed to be done, and the ideas gathered were incorporated by a Roosevelt-style team of bright and able assistants into the so-called *Plan Alemán*.

There was also to be no repetition of the election-day chaos of 1940, for Mexico acquired a new and up-to-date electoral law in 1945 and polling day was entirely orderly. Alemán was elected with over 77 per cent of the vote. His only serious rival was his former colleague, Ezequiel Padilla, who got nearly 20 per cent; more significant was the fact that for the first time since the foundation of the official party the opposition succeeded in winning some seats in the Chamber of Deputies. They were to lose all of them again at the mid-term elections of 1949, but the lesson was not forgotten that official opposition was one of the generally recognized hallmarks of the democratic tradition as Mexico had inherited it.

The Alemán administration opened with promises to cut down corruption and improve efficiency. It was to close amid ugly charges of graft and nepotism, and its successor was to show up dramatically some of its shortcomings. Most of them stemmed from two features that became a permanent feature of Mexican life during the Alemán period: economic expansion and the desire of Presidents to complete and open major works within their own term of office. All this, however, was still in the future when on 3 March 1947 President Harry S Truman of the United States arrived by air in Mexico City for the first state visit by an American President in office to the Mexican capital. Truman, the first Southern-born President of the United States since Woodrow Wilson, was genuinely anxious to repair the wrongs of the past, and two things he did during his term of office were to mark a permanent change in United States-Mexican relations. The first was the quite spontaneous gesture, during his visit to Mexico, of placing a wreath on the memorial to the *Niños Heroes*. The second came three years later when, following an initiative from Americans living in Mexico, the United States returned to Mexico all battle trophies captured during the War of 1847 – an action which was subsequently reciprocated.

In April 1947 Alemán became the first Mexican President to visit Washington, an action endorsed by a vast public welcome on his return and a ceremonial visit of support to him by the ex-Presidents, still six in number, for Calles had died in 1945, in the United States.

Though expenditure on social welfare continued to rise during the Alemán Presidency, it was outstripped in emphasis by expenditure designed to strengthen and expand the economic infrastructure. The modernization of the railways was begun and the systems of Lower California and the south-east linked to the rest. The all-weather road network expanded until for the first time since the colonial period it was possible to travel overland to all parts of the republic except Lower California. The northern part of that territory, benefiting from the economic development around San Diego on the northern side of the frontier, was raised to statehood in 1951, though the desert southern territory still remained essentially an island most easily reached by boat from the mainland.

In the south, again borrowing ideas from the United States, the government initiated the vast Papaloapan Valley project, on the model of the Tennessee Valley Authority: a series of dams designed to control an almost ungovernable river, to provide irrigation, and to generate electrical power; it was to have a powerful influence on the development of neighbouring Oaxaca. On the other hand, critics of the régime noted that the rate of distribution of land slowed still further, and disapproved of the important new measures designed to protect the small property-owner by making his smallholdings inalienable.

The theory of industrial development that motivated Alemán and his followers was the one suggesting that the benefits would 'trickle down' to the masses. The benefits of increased electricity production were felt directly, and heavy government investment in the Altos Hornos steel-mills, the fertilizer corporation Guanos y Fertilizantes, and the petroleum industry (Pemex) had its ultimate effect in every part of the national economy. So too did the development of port facilities at Vera Cruz and Acapulco, necessary if overseas trade were to be expanded. Even the provision of a new water supply for the Federal District had implications outside the area it served. The agent of the government in this process was the powerful state development bank, Nacional Financiera, and its attentions were not limited to primary industry; through it the government, while encouraging unprecedented private investment in Mexico, actually expanded the area of state control. Among other industries to develop rapidly during this period, perhaps the one best known to visitors to Mexico was that of brewing.

But Alemán's main achievement—and the one which brought him most international prestige—was the construction of the new University City (*Ciudad Universitaria*) for the National Autonomous University of Mexico (UNAM), work on which was drastically accelerated to meet the deadline of the transfer of power. In consequence the great library building was almost empty of books, the striving for monumentalism having virtually exhausted the funds available. Less spectacular, but no less significant in the conscious creation of the new, highly-educated entrepreneurial class envisaged by the Alemanistas—who were of it themselves—was the foundation of the Instituto Politécnico in Mexico City and the encouragement of other centres of higher education. It is for these foundations, rather than for its brashness and its shortcomings, that future generations are most likely to remember the administration of Miguel Alemán.

UNAM

You will see it written that the National University of Mexico is the oldest university in the New World, antedating Harvard College in Massachusetts by over seventy years. This, though untrue, bears sufficient relation to the facts to be tolerable, but the discrepancy is nonetheless significant.

The first university in Mexico was created by *Real Cédula* of Charles I of Spain dated 21 September 1551. It was some eighteen months before the Royal and Pontifical University of Mexico opened its doors to students, but thereafter for over 250 years it performed its function well: providing the best that Spain could provide in the way of higher education to the inhabitants of New Spain. Though modelled on the pattern of the medieval university as established in Spain, it was as progressive as any institution of the day, and towards the end of the colonial period entered upon a new era of expansion with the opening in 1778 of the Royal School of Surgery and in 1792 of the Royal College of Mining.

With the coming of independence, however, like other universities in Latin America, the University of Mexico found itself in a difficult position. Dependent as it had been for so long on the support of the royal government, its leaders had difficulty in adjusting to the rapid turns of politics and the consequent uncertainties. What the royal charter granting it autonomy now meant was difficult to tell. For on the one hand, Conservatives were distrustful of any unregulated influence within the state; on the other, Liberals feared and distrusted the universities, with their clerical teachers, as bastions of conservatism. Besides the University of Mexico there were by now three others: in order of foundation, the University of Guadalajara (1791), founded by royal decree as part of the development of education in the last years of the viceroyalty; and the Universities of Mérida (1824) and Chiapas (1826). In the year that the University of Chiapas was founded, that of Guadalajara was closed – as it proved, only temporarily. But it was a sign of what was to come.

In 1833 the Centralist administration of Vice-President Gómez Farías not only closed down the University of Mexico, but decreed its dissolution into its constituent Faculties. Under the Centralists it languished. But worse was to follow. By the end of the Reform and the War of Intervention the University of Mexico had been suppressed three times. What was left, shorn of its ancient *fueros*, was little more than a series of government schools. Intellectual life in the country was generally at a low ebb, and the Universities of Mérida and Chiapas disappeared altogether, transformed into harmless Literary Societies.

The void in higher education was filled to some extent by the Church. In colonial times, the Jesuit colleges of Guadalajara and Mérida had enjoyed university status, including the power to grant degrees. These were, in a sense, the predecessors of the universities founded after them, but with the rise of the civil power they had ceased to be effective. Now in the second term of President Díaz the diocesan seminary at Mérida was translated with papal approval into the Catholic University of Mérida (1885); in 1896 the Pontifical University of Mexico was launched with great ceremony in the cathedral of the city of Mexico itself; and in 1907 a third Catholic university appeared in the city of Puebla, not to be confused with the State College which had antecedents in the Colegia del Espíritu Santo founded there by the Jesuits in 1578.

It was Justo Sierra who secured from Díaz the decree which founded the present National University on 26 May 1910, and its inauguration formed part of the great Centenary celebration. Firmly under the control of the Ministry of Public Instruction, of which Sierra was then head, it was his crowning of his life's work, and in 1948, on the centenary of his birth, the university recognized as much by publicly proclaiming him 'Maestro de América', a supremely significant honorific which is virtually untranslatable.

Throughout the 1920s the university, housed in numerous small and crowded buildings near the Zócalo in the heart of the capital, was a centre of turbulence and revolutionary ferment. The granting of autonomy to the university in 1929 by President Portes Gil did not end this. It did, however, mark the second important step towards the re-emergence of the university as a major educational institution, today once again one of the most important in Latin America. All that remained was for it to be rehoused in a more fitting manner. This task was one of the many assumed by President Alemán: to him the university owes its spacious University City on the outskirts of Mexico City.

Fourteen miles out of the centre, the university is served through its own terminal by numerous buses, on which the rates for students have been held down to a nominal level. With a total student enrolment in excess of 60,000, the campus has been planned on a huge scale. The arts building alone is more than a quarter of a mile long; the stadium is of Olympic scale and was in fact planned as a venue for the Games themselves. Dominating the centre of the main area is the windowless tower of the University Library, its external surfaces covered by complex murals depicting the advance of knowledge in

Mexico. Other buildings too are distinguished appropriately by murals which, though of uneven quality, are, as a collection, a fascinating record of the aspirations of Mexicans for their future and of no mean standing as art. Below the University Library, there used to be a large statue of Alemán himself. Since he came to be identified with the 'Right' of the Mexican Revolutionary Family, it was smashed up and daubed with slogans and swastikas in student disturbances in 1965.

The transition to the new site has never been complete: students still work in the old library built in the Díaz era a few blocks from the Zócalo, and student life in Mexico is not identified with the university alone, or even with the other modern universities that have come into being since 1910. Apart from two other universities in the capital itself, and the University of Guadalajara, these now include the Universities of Michoacán (1917), Yucatán (1922), San Luis Potosí (1923), Nuevo León (1932), Puebla (1937), the Universidad Autónoma de Occidente in Guadalajara (1935), Sinaloa (1937), Sonora (1942), and Guanajuato (1945). But far more important has been the emergence of the rival campus of the Politécnico; for it is natural that what students conceive of as a challenge to the entire system of society should come from that sector of society that has to compete for status.

---

[1] Ávila Camacho himself was, however, the subject of an assassination attempt on 10 April 1944 when he was shot and wounded by an artillery lieutenant named de la Lama.

[2] Brandenburg, op. cit., 124.

[3] See Ignacio Burgoa, *La legislación de Emergencia y el Juicio de Amparo* (Mexico, Editorial Hispano-Mexicana, 1945).

[4] Cline, op. cit., 269.

[5] For wartime speeches of the President, see Manuel Ávila Camacho, *México coopera con las Naciones Aliadas: nuestra bandera ondea en los campos de la lucha* (Mexico, Secretaría de Gobernación, 1944) and *La ruta de México*.

[6] Cline, op. cit., 271; Frank R. Brandenburg, op. cit., 3-7. Two living ex-Presidents were *not* present, Pedro Lascuráin, President for 56 minutes in 1913 before handing over to Huerta, and Roque González Garza, President of the Revolutionary Convention of Aguascalientes in 1915. They died in 1952 and 1962 respectively.

[7] Salvador Novo, *La vida en México en el periodo presidencial de Manuel Ávila Camacho* (Mexico, Empresas Editoriales, 1965).

[8] John Gunther, *Inside Latin America* (New York & London, Harper, 1940), 91.

[9] Étienne de la Boétie, *Discours sur la servitude volontaire, ou, Contr'un*; published in English as *Anti-dictator*, trs. Harry Kurz (New York, Columbia University Press, 1942).

The Revolution XXIII: The Age of the *Licenciados*

IN THE STRICT SENSE, in Mexico the title *Licenciado*[1] means one licensed to practise law. In a broader sense it is used loosely to refer to university-educated intellectuals. President Alemán himself was a *licenciado*, as were many of the young men who formed his team. Collectively they came to be referred to as 'the *licenciados*', and it is with Alemán that the age of the *licenciados* in Mexico–which is still going on–begins.

Alemán himself exercised unparalleled power for a civilian President during his term of office, and quite naturally expected to be able to nominate his successor to continue his policies. He had not reckoned with the wasting disease of *futurismo*–the Mexican version of the American 'lame-duck'–which struck his administration with the approach of its close in 1951. Many of the *nouveaux-riches* were observed in an unseemly scramble to get richer while they still could. Opposition was growing in traditional labour and agrarian circles to the denial of revolutionary values this implied, and the economy was badly overheated, while at the same time coming under some strain from the change in trade patterns accompanying the outbreak of the Korean War, towards which sympathies were divided. The devaluation of the peso in 1948 had failed to arrest the trend towards an unfavourable trade balance. Above all, inflation was becoming endemic, and the natural tendency was to blame the government, for it had always been ready to assume credit.

It was Cárdenas himself who became the decisive factor in the choice of the new President. Together with Ávila Camacho he led the opposition of the Left to Alemán's proposed nominee, and was able to block him. What neither he nor anyone else was able to do was to propound a satisfactory left-wing alternative–in the age of the Cold War traditional Mexican neutralism tended to reassert itself, and the President still controlled the political machinery of the nation. Speculation continued for an unwontedly long time, and the figure of the candidate was a subject of intense debate. (Six years later, in 1958, he became personified for most Mexicans by the cartoon figure of *El tapado* ('the hidden one'). A sign of the times was the enterprising cigarette company which brashly proclaimed that *El tapado* smoked their brand, though in fact he did not.)[2]

In 1952, however, the chosen candidate was hidden only by his prominence, for he turned out to be none other than Adolfo Ruiz Cortines, Alemán's Secretary of *Gobernación*, and hence a man who enjoyed the President's special trust. Ruiz Cortines had come a long way since his days in the Government Statistical Department. In 1935 he had moved into the government of the Federal District. Two years later he had been brought into politics as a Federal deputy from Veracruz, and his knowledge of finance had made him a natural choice for the job of treasurer of Ávila Camacho's campaign in 1940, under Alemán. He spent the war years with Alemán as chief clerk of the Department of *Gobernación*, but had returned to his native state to serve for four years as governor (1944–48) before being brought back into the government as Secretary when the sudden and unexpected death in Vera Cruz of Hector Pérez Martínez left the post vacant.

Ruiz Cortines was generally agreed to be a good choice, an able administrator of proven worth who had experience of many different aspects of Mexican government and who was himself of unimpeachable honesty. But he did not have an easy campaign. For the first time for years there was a serious candidate of an organized right-wing party in the field, for the PAN had capitalized on the disintegration of *sinarquismo* during Alemán's term and had decided to run a candidate in their own right. But a much more serious contender was the disillusioned General Miguel Henríquez Guzmán, who deserted the official party and formed a temporary rival to challenge the official nominee. He combined both pro-military elements and important groups among the *ejidatarios*, who felt they had been neglected, and miners, who felt they had been getting fewer rewards than others for their efforts. To add to the confusion, the former head of the CTM, Vicente Lombardo Toledano, led his splinter party of the Left, the *Partido Popular* (PP), into the fray, behind his own candidature, in an effort to regain his former position.

The result was unexpected. The combined total of the opposition votes amounted, as in 1946, to almost a quarter of the whole. But the bulk of them went to Henríquez. The PAN candidate ran a poor third, and the vote for Lombardo Toledano, which included the votes of the extreme Left and the Communists, was surprisingly small–less than 2 per cent. Within two years Lombardo Toledano was trying to lead his group back into the Revolutionary Family to jockey for position in 1958, and, having failed to do so, the PP were forced to endorse the official candidate in 1958 and try to pick up seats in Congress and the states as a basis for future efforts.

The new President soon showed that he was not going to remain long under the shadow of any of his predecessors. If his austere figure commanded confidence, the moderate but balanced composition of his Cabinet upheld it, and once in power his training as an accountant asserted itself. One of Alemán's close associates who claimed to have built a very long but non-existent road for which he had been paid, went to prison. Other prominent figures found themselves making embarrassing explanations – none, however, actually within the government. The monumental projects favoured by the previous administration were unobtrusively finished.

The theme of the administration was fiscal stability and the 'march to the sea'. In the realm of finance the government began, as we have seen, with serious difficulties, and in 1953 it was forced to devalue the peso to 12.50 to the United States dollar. From then on, however, the revival of trade began to work in its favour, and that parity was held, though inflation continued for some time to have serious implications for the lower-paid workers. Particular attention was, however, taken to see that new industry was developed in regional centres that had previously been neglected, and increased attention given to the support of the agricultural sector, both public and private.

The 'march to the sea' dramatized a number of things. In one sense it was a new version of an earlier policy of the Ávila Camacho administration to open up the *tierra caliente*. It meant roads – not monumental ones like the Mexico City-Cuernavaca Turnpike of the Alemán period, though this did, as it was intended, help open up access to Cuernavaca, Taxco, Chilpancingo, and the port of Acapulco, now becoming a booming tourist resort of international standing – but plain, ordinary roads as a means of getting from place to place. It meant important new oil pipelines and the extension of the electricity grid. And it meant state encouragement for the fishing industry, the expansion of fish and fish-meal production, and a further step on the road to making Mexico self-sufficient in food, though this was a hope which was continually frustrated by the boom in population. It was particularly ironic that the 'march to the sea' came to an end with a major earthquake in the south-west in 1957 and a series of hurricanes at the beginning of 1958 which destroyed much property in coastal areas and forced work to begin again.

In foreign policy the term of Ruiz Cortines was a quiet one, since it coincided with the 'thaw' in the Cold War and ended before the Cuban Revolution of 1959. But the traditional posture of the government was not substantially altered by its new prosperity. It demonstrated considerable opposition to the choice of Caracas as the site of the Inter-American Conference of 1954 and resisted strongly the move of the United States to express its disapproval of the left-wing government of Guatemala under Jacobo Arbenz, only to be caught short, as most other countries were, by the sudden collapse of the Guatemalan government in face of an exile expedition aided by the United States. Significantly President Arbenz went into exile in Mexico, where he died in 1971.

With the approaching end of the Presidential term Mexico was once again plunged into a fever of speculation. This time the decisive influence came from the Left and came early. It was ex-President Portes Gil who, in a broadside, initiated the whole process by calling for a revival of revolutionary fervour and, in particular, of the land reform.[3] It was clear from its reception elsewhere in the party that his call had to be heeded. Since his re-entry into politics in 1951, Cárdenas had been airing the views of the Left on the labour side and had constituted himself virtually as their spokesman; it was plain that he looked to a candidate who would give the workers the priority in governmental thinking that they had not enjoyed since 1940. Within the government the obvious candidate was the brilliant young Secretary of Labour, Adolfo López Mateos. He was disclosed as the official candidate by the PRI at the end of 1957.

Once he had ascertained that his name was acceptable to all factions within the party, Ruiz Cortines gave him every support. He had already suppressed the splinter party of the Henriquistas for their potentially dangerous Trotskyite tendencies; deprived of this nucleus, the factional Left of the official party came into line and received the endorsement of the PP. In a straight fight against Luis H. Álvarez, the candidate of the PAN, López Mateos won over 90 per cent of the votes cast. The incidental result was the strengthening of the PAN, which had successfully shed much of its *sinarquista* and fringe support, and assumed a position of constructive opposition to the government which did more to put it on its mettle than any of its previous challengers.

One of the first fruits was seen in the attention given by the new administration to the long-neglected north, and in particular to the region of the frontier, where the penetration of United States capital was again becoming very marked. It was coincidental, though not wholly accidental, that the redistribution of land, in which López Mateos was to surpass all his predecessors except Cárdenas, involved the settlement and opening-up of other near-frontier lands, particularly in the territory of Quintana Roo. For with the accession of Fidel Castro to power in Cuba only a month after his own inauguration, the main preoccupation of López Mateos throughout his Presidency, and the preoccupation which shaped all other government policies, was that of national security. In an age of guerrilla warfare, it was inadvisable to leave any remote area too long unattended.

The hallmark of the López Mateos administration was nationalism, the one sentiment that united all factions. But it was nationalism fairly and humanely interpreted. Mexico in foreign policy maintained a consistent stance in favour of allowing the Cubans to pursue their own revolutionary course unhindered, and did so despite the pressure of the United States (which transferred a considerable proportion of the former Cuban sugar quota to Mexico), and the often irritating quarrelsomeness of the Cubans themselves. Though at the time of the Cuban missile crisis in 1962 most Mexicans displayed some justifiable alarm at the prospect of coming within range of Soviet nuclear attack as a result of Cuban adventurism, Mexico remained the only country in the hemisphere to have diplomatic relations with Cuba and to maintain physical links with the island in the shape of a regular air service. The Mexican government refused to join in the condemnation of Cuba or to support her expulsion from the OAS. It received very little thanks.

This was partly because of the tough line pursued by the government in internal policy, where moves against possible infiltration verged at times on the dictatorial. The government had recalled as early as 1948 that it had in its hands since 1942 an Act passed by the Congress establishing a crime called 'social dissolution' and prescribing severe penalties for it. From then on its use against the militant Left became increasingly frequent. In 1959 the Communist leader of the railway-workers' union was arrested and imprisoned, and among others who followed, the most famous was the celebrated painter and muralist David Siqueiros, who found belatedly that political positions appropriate in the thirties were no longer acceptable. An embarrassing factor was the outspoken support of Cárdenas himself for the Cuban régime, though not for Soviet policy towards it. Another was rising student turbulence, agitated by the multiplicity of ideological cross-currents. Riots in 1960, as in 1921, were dispersed with fire hoses; in 1965, at the time of the American intervention in the Dominican Republic, they were to recur on a much larger scale, and the Mexican government began to become embarrassed at the enthusiasm of its own citizens of the future.

It was hard, however, to pin down the exact ideological complexion of the administration itself. In some respects it was far enough to the Left to silence its opponents on that flank. Not only was its land distribution massive in itself, but by the end of its six years a total of 27 per cent of the continental land surface of Mexico had been redistributed – a vastly larger proportion of the amount that could be considered in any way fertile – and over one-third of all people engaged in agricultural production had land of their own. Moreover, the government nationalized by purchase the electrical power industry, built its own oil refineries without more than a token representation of private capital, and forced foreign automobile interests to assemble their cars in Mexico or forfeit their market. It also took over control of two Mexican airlines.

On the other hand, the resources for this expenditure, though they were handled by an increasingly centralized developmental finance system, were still drawn overwhelmingly from overseas investors, most of them in the United States, where the government floated the first post-revolutionary dollar loan in 1963. Government relations with the United States continued to be very friendly. President Eisenhower had met Ruiz Cortines for the opening of the Falcon Dam on the Río Bravo in October 1953 and had welcomed him in turn to the United States in March 1956 to discuss common problems with the Prime Minister of Canada. He now lost no time in paying a post-inauguration visit to López Mateos at Acapulco in February 1959, a meeting which was reciprocated in Washington later in the same year, with a further return visit to Mexico. At these meetings were laid the foundations for a comprehensive settlement of outstanding disputes between the two countries. Two in particular stood out: the proper disposition of the Chamizal, a strip of territory isolated from Mexico on the northern bank by shifts in the course of the Río Bravo; and the problems of the Mexican farmers dependent on the waters of the Colorado River for irrigation in the State of Baja California del Norte, who were suffering from excess salination from over-use of the water in the United States.

Both disputes were, in fact, to take some time yet to settle. The Chamizal agreement was signed in July 1963 during the short Presidency of John F. Kennedy, who paid a state visit to the Mexican capital in June 1962. By it Mexico gained a small amount of territory, but, more importantly, agreement was reached on how to avoid similar disputes arising in the future. The problem of the waters of the Colorado, the two Presidents agreed, was also urgent, but it was not so easily solved.

It will be seen that if friendly relations were maintained, they were not, at governmental level, maintained at any cost to the integrity of the Mexican position. Facts, however, were to many Mexicans less important than impressions, and the impressions that many of them did have were of a return to the days of Díaz. Foreigners were once again welcome, business booming, the government all-powerful, opposition scant, and monuments everywhere. It was a very superficial view, and one which took no account of the deep and profound changes in Mexican society in the generation that had elapsed since 1934. Thus, when the name of the government candidate for the Presidency was announced in late 1963 there was a distinct shock. The name of Gustavo Díaz Ordaz, the Secretary of *Gobernación*, was not one to evoke universal acclamation, but he was a reasonable choice and he was duly elected.

Díaz Ordaz was above all an administrator, a man who had made his career in party and government. He lacked the charisma of his predecessor, but he did not depart substantially from his policies. Particular emphasis was placed on labour policies throughout the campaign, which was again a quiet one, and the new President came to power with less disturbance than any of his predecessors. The first signs of change came with the student disturbances of 1965. Though directed in the first instance against the United States, as has been seen, they were to confirm for the government the increasing radicalism of youth and to give it the unenviable task of repressing it. In the following year the government arrested more than forty people accused of the crime of 'social dissolution' – plotting to overthrow the government. Within a year or two, stirred by the example of Che Guevara and remembering Emiliano Zapata only as a heroic figure of the past, a small group of intellectuals were to take to the hills in Guerrero in the cause of Cuban-style revolution. Conflicting crosscurrents were generated by endemic civil war in Guatemala to the south, and the presence on Mexican soil at all times of large numbers of students from the United States bringing with them 'hippy' culture and an embarrassing interest in the rapid growth of marijuana under Mexico's cloudless and uncrowded skies.

The celebration of the fiftieth anniversary of the Revolution in 1960 had been a largely official occasion, rather overshadowed by events in Cuba. The government had since moved through a phase of trying to demonstrate the superiority of its own revolution by words to a desire to proclaim it by deeds. An old ambition of revolutionary governments was at last on the point of coming to fruition, for Mexico had been selected, after hard lobbying, as the scene of the 1968 Olympic Games. It was to be the climactic festival of the Mexican Revolution – and it succeeded in surprising almost everybody.

Art and Architecture

When the American John L. Stephens travelled to Chiapas and Yucatán in 1839–40 he took as his companion an English artist, Frederick Catherwood, with more than ten years experience in the study of the antiquities of the Old World. The incredible problems of getting to the ruins and of obtaining access to them first successfully overcome, Catherwood started to sketch some columns while Stephens scoured the surrounding jungle and found some fifty further objects worthy of note, before returning to tell Catherwood how much more there lay in store for him.

'I found him not so well pleased as I expected with my report' wrote Stephens afterwards.

> He was standing with his feet in the mud, and was drawing with his gloves on, to protect his hands from the moschetoes. As we feared, the designs were so intricate and complicated, the subjects so entirely new and unintelligible, that he had great difficulty in drawing. He had made several attempts, both with the camera lucida and without, but failed to satisfy himself or even me, who, was less severe in criticism.[4]

Catherwood's drawings, which despite his initial difficulties were of startling accuracy and beauty, were the first introduction to the world at large of the complex tradition of Maya art, and were no less foreign then to most Mexicans. At the beginning of the nineteenth century the tradition of art in Mexico was wholly Spanish, with the provincial crudities and occasional variations which distinguish it, often attractively, from the metropolitan original. The Spanish had already absorbed the alien tradition of Moorish architecture, creating a style which was neither European nor Moorish but a blend of the two. Given the native tradition of stone-working and the vitality of its artistic traditions, it is not surprising that the churches and public buildings surviving from the first century after the Conquest show an amazing variety and excitement within a basic sense of restraint. In the eighteenth century it developed into Baroque, with an exuberant use of fantastic ornament which ended in the delightful excess of Churrigueresque.

By the end of the colonial period, however, the neo-classical movement had already begun to impose a formalism on Mexican taste which was to lead to a rapid decline in inventiveness. Independence in itself probably made little difference. When Catherwood was making his drawings, there were few new public buildings being created and the repetitive uniformity from the outside of Spanish domestic architecture gave little hint of life within. With the Reform and the confiscation of church property many good buildings of the colonial period began to fall into decay, if, indeed, they were not physically destroyed. In the latter half of the nineteenth century the *nouveaux-riches* might move into the old houses of the aristocracy (as they have done again since the Revolution, where the houses survive, with the original coats of arms and symbolic decorations still intact), but it was much more likely that they would build new *châteaux* in the Second Empire style. All that was worst in French municipal taste went into the public buildings of Mexico during the age of the *Porfiriato*.

With the Revolution came two distinct developments. The excesses of the Empire style, its lumpishness and its absurdities, were reswept away. Led by José Villagrán García, who first demonstrated the new style with his 'Granja Sanitaria' at Tacuba in the Federal District, there grew up a school of modernism, in a plain unadorned style that stressed practicality and comfort. This style had the practical purpose of creating buildings of substantial size that were resistant to earthquake shock, and sometimes, as in the case of the National Lottery building in the capital, by José A. Cuevas, the results are disappointing. But its dominance is unquestionable, though international influences have encouraged younger architects to use a larger and apparently increasing proportion of glass to wall, which in the climate of Mexico is not an unmixed blessing. The Latin American Tower by Leonardo Zeevaert in the centre of the capital, the highest building in Mexico, gives a magnificent view of possible alternatives to this rather standard form: the slab-sided workers' housing on *pilotis*, evidently strongly influenced by Le Corbusier, the divided tower of the María Isabel Hotel; and the triangles of the National Railways and the Edificio Símbolo, by Mario Pani, centre of a workers' housing project. Nor should one forget the daring shell-vaulted roofs of Félix Candela, who came to Mexico originally as a refugee from Republican Spain.

The functional school has, however, a rival with which it has come to terms in the brilliantly coloured murals which adorn so many of Mexico's public buildings. Mexico inherited little of the Spanish school of painting except its concentration on religious scenes, and the tradition of painting that has directly affected the moderns is one of folk simplicity, blended with elements of diversity and repetition drawn from pre-Columban sources. The mural is the most striking evidence of its vitality, combining art and architecture in one unified whole.

The three names who would occur most widely in any discussion of Mexican mural painting in this century would probably be Diego Rivera, José Clemente Orozco, and David Siqueiros, the three who in the time of Obregón first had the opportunity to proclaim their view of the Revolution on the walls of Mexico's public buildings. Their murals were the visual equivalent of their manifesto that it was the duty of writers and artists to support the Revolution with their respective talents, and that their talents were no less important to it than those of the soldiers. The rather absurd gesture of the artist painting with a gun strapped to his waist served a functional purpose in protecting him from those who disapproved strongly of what he was doing.

The frescoes of Diego Rivera in the Palacio Nacional showing Aztec Tenochtitlan are delightful. Others do not have the subtlety of the best of Orozco's work, but they are much more representative, both of the strongly political message which they seek to convey, and of the chauvinistic way in which it is put over. The flaring colours are used to put over a black-and-white message: the revolt of the poor against the oppressors. The effigy of Zapata on a white horse in the Government Palace in Cuernavaca is contrasted with the figure of Cortés as a syphilitic gnome. Both Rivera and Siqueiros continued to maintain a strong Marxism long after it had ceased to be fashionable, and Siqueiros was imprisoned in 1959 for the crime of 'social dissolution'. Orozco stayed within the revolutionary tradition, but avoided the stereotyping imposed by the cult of socialist realism, though his best-known work still is probably the early murals in the Escuela Nacional Preparatoria.

In the University City the murals combine with the functional architecture to create a unique effect. The style is of a series of inter-connected pavilions, strongly reminiscent of the 1951 Festival of Britain. Pride of place, however, goes to two massive constructions which are quite different: the library and the stadium. The library is covered by a vast, intricate, and symbolic tapestry of natural stone by Juan O'Gorman, telling the story of the development of art and science in Mexico. It is stupendous in its effect, with a subtlety of effect deriving from the changing patterns of light around it. It contrasts strongly with the more raucous and conventional works on other buildings around it. The stadium is a superb dish by Augusto Pérez Palacios; the importance of its design lies not just in itself, but in the subtle way in which it is joined to the rest of the campus by underground walkways without distorting the balance of the whole. For this, and for such sensible and eminently practical details as the comfortable steps and useful covered walkways for protection against rain and sun, credit must go to the architects of the overall plan, Mario Pani and Enrique del Moral.

The size and omnipresence of mural art in Mexico, however, does not mean that the smaller scale of canvas and paint is neglected. Mexican scenery calls out to be painted, and few have been able to resist the spell. One of the most delightful artists simply to celebrate the glories of his native country, Miguel Covarrubias, is fortunate that through his book illustrations his work has enjoyed worldwide circulation. In his *Mexico South* he has combined his talent with his deep knowledge of his country's antiquities to produce something that is both profound and expressive.[5] Otherwise it would be invidious to single out individuals in a school which, despite the confusing and competitive pressures upon it, comprises as fascinating a cross-section of talent as anything the world has to offer today. The Mexicans have thoughtfully chosen to site their glass-sided Museum of Modern Art in Chapultepec where it is easily accessible and can be seen in tantalizing glimpses by passers-by, a decision that is fully characteristic.

Old and new come together in Chapultepec. Not far from the Museum of Modern Art there is one of the most remarkable complexes of human activity ever planned: the National Museum of Archaeology and Anthropology, designed by Pedro Ramírez Vásquez and Rafael Mijares. Its keynote is drama. The moment the visitor climbs up the steps and enters the vast concourse he is made aware of the fact that he is in the presence of power, symbolized by the vast upturned umbrella of concrete covering the courtyard through which water cascades in careless profusion as if to symbolize the presence of the vast Tlaloc, the Rain God of the ancients, the source of life and fertility for the whole of Mexico. The exhibits themselves are presented with equal drama, illustrated by murals and contrasted by bright colours everywhere.

Finally one must mention the Museum of Modern History, nestling to one side of the old Castle of Chapultepec. It curls in a triple spiral, the visitor entering at the top and leaving at the bottom of the slope, but unlike (say) the Guggenheim Museum in New York where a similar pattern is followed, the spiral is open, the scale is human, and the building itself fits easily and naturally into natural surroundings. It is the exhibits that matter, and they are very well done.

These museums are for all Mexico. The message is modern Mexican art and architecture, and, if it is not always followed, it still sets a standard which few countries in the world need not envy.

Adolfo López Mateos

Adolfo López Mateos was born in the year of the Revolution, 1910, on 26 May, in the township of Atizapán de Zaragoza, in the State of Mexico. As it was to be of considerable significance in his future political life, it is interesting to note that his place of birth was quite accidental. Being accustomed to spend a holiday in the village during the month of May, his parents had gone there as usual that year, and considered it was wiser not to attempt the return journey to the city of Mexico when it became apparent that the birth of their fifth, and as it turned out youngest, son was imminent.

Adolfo's father, Mariano Gerardo López y Sánchez Román, was a dental surgeon; his mother, Elena Mateos y Vega, was a native of the State of Guerrero who was descended from a hero of the War of the French Intervention, José Perfecto Mateos, and the Liberal spokesman of the Reform, Francisco Zarco Mateos. As such he was also a collateral relative of Don Ignacio Ramírez ('The Magician') – one of the most formidable intellectual influences on the Reform and hence on the entire life of mid-nineteenth-century Mexico. His father's ancestry was slightly less distinguished, but no less impeccably Liberal. It was, however, his mother's family who were to have the greater influence on the boy's future, for in the terrible year of 1915 his father died, and the five boys were brought up in very difficult circumstances.

The young Adolfo received his primary education as a scholarship boy in the capital at the Colegio Francés. The choice of Toluca as the place of his secondary education stemmed from the fact that some of his mother's relatives lived there. It was, however, a good choice. In order to keep himself the boy was able to gain employment in the library of the Instituto Científico y Literario, and when he qualified he was able to get a position as a teacher of history there, as well as holding the chair of Ibero-American Literature at the State Normal School.

The young López Mateos was good at sport as well as at academic work. In his youth, like many other Mexican boys, he played football. But he was always looking for fresh fields to conquer. It is on record that when he was sixteen he hiked with a group of friends to Morelia, the state capital of Michoacán, which in 1926 was a long and difficult way. However, he did not rest on his laurels. Armando de María y Campos records that later the same year he and his friends conceived the even more ambitious plan of hiking to Guatemala entirely on foot. They set out on the anniversary of the Revolution – 20 November 1926 – and took 56 days to get there. It is hardly surprising that on his return, López Mateos earned the nickname of 'El Guatemala' from the fact that he could not stop talking about it.[6]

Though little is known about his early political views, it seems clear that they must have been well to the Left of the revolutionary tradition, for in the 1929 campaign López Mateos emerged into politics as a fervent supporter of José Vasconcelos against what were then seen as the repressive forces of the Calles machine. In the aftermath of that stormy campaign, López Mateos left Mexico briefly, possibly for safety, possibly just out of a sense of disgust. He went to Guatemala for a short time, then worked for a spell in Tapachula before returning to the capital.

His introduction to public life, however, predated his involvement in the 1929 campaign. In 1928 he had served for a short time as private secretary to the governor of the State of Mexico, Colonel Filiberto Gómez, and subsequently as a local government official, before resigning to enter the political battle. Now it was to the State of Mexico that he returned, in March 1931 when he was appointed Professor of History in the Institute at Toluca. At Toluca his ability in public speaking came to the attention of Colonel Carlos Riva Palacio, who from the closeness of his friendship with ex-President Calles was already a leading figure in the PNR and was soon to become its president. When he became governor of the State of Mexico, he recruited the young López Mateos once more as his private secretary. Though Riva Palacio failed, as some had hoped, to get the nomination for President in 1934, his influence as president of the PNR was of great help to a young man who was just completing his law studies at the National University, from which he graduated in 1934. His thesis was entitled 'Crimes against political economy'.

Between 1934 and 1937 López Mateos worked in the National Workers' Development Bank and so gained important first-hand experience in industry, particularly the important sugar industry with its international ramifications. He attended international conferences in Washington and Geneva—experience which was to stand him in good stead in later life. Shortly before the outbreak of the Second World War the course of preferment brought him into a very different sphere, when as assistant chief of the National Institute of Fine Arts he was responsible for the encouragement of the theatre. In 1940, at the age of thirty, he married the niece of former Governor Filiberto Gómez, Eva Sámano. He had now moved on from hiking to mountain climbing, and they went climbing together.

In 1943, Isidro Fabela, the diplomatic historian, who was then governor of the State of Mexico, asked López Mateos to intervene in a dispute in his old college at Toluca. He did so with success, and as an unexpected consequence was named as its Rector, a post which he held for three years and discharged very effectively. At this period his heart was in teaching rather than in politics—when Fabela offered him a seat as a Federal deputy he turned it down, much to the older man's surprise. Though he did play a part in working for the nomination of Miguel Alemán, whom he had met during his days in the Bank, he was not seeking a place in the political arena for himself when he received it by a happy accident.

Fabela, unable to succeed himself as governor, had been nominated for the Federal Senate for the six years from 1946 to 1952. At the last moment, however, he was nominated to a seat on the International Court of Justice and withdrew from the election. López Mateos was nominated in his place by the state legislature at Toluca. He was now a senator. During his six years he continued to travel abroad, finally serving as head of the Mexican delegation to UNESCO. From there he was recalled by Ruiz Cortines after his nomination to organize his election campaign, a choice which carried with it the appointment of Secretary-General of the PRI and the ultimate reward of a seat in the Cabinet as Secretary of Labour and Social Security.

López Mateos was, of course, no stranger to Ruiz Cortines. As senator from his native state he had been called upon by the then Secretary of *Gobernación* to arrange for the nomination of candidates in

1948 for the Federal elections. The Secretary had been favourably impressed by the young senator, and they had become friends. In nominating him to the portfolio of Labour he was giving him a great opportunity, but he was also giving him a formidable task. Recent holders of the office had been weak and in the aftermath of the war and the Alemanista boom, the economy was badly overheated and industrial disputes flourished on all sides, as workers attempted to catch up with the falling value of the peso. With his natural gift for conciliation, based on his honesty and goodwill, López Mateos was able to make the Department of Labour an effective force in labour relations, and as it moved from a negative to a positive attitude in the conciliation of disputes, so the number of disputes it had to tackle fell spectacularly. At the same time the real wages of the workers rose noticeably. With this record, and the general feeling among Mexicans that it was time for a reinvigoration of the social policies of the 1930s, it was not surprising that López Mateos should have been widely supported as future candidate for the Presidency of the Republic even before, on 4 November 1957, he was announced as the choice for the nomination by the Peasant Sector organization of the party, the CNC. For the new nominee stood, in his own words, 'on the extreme Left within the Constitution'.[7] Sadly, hardly had this able and gifted man completed his term of office when he was struck down by illness and lay in a coma for six years before dying peacefully in 1970.

Recent Politics

Mexican government in recent times has been well described in detail by other authors.[8] Relating what they have said in the context of recent history we get something like this.

The Mexican government looks in some respects very like that of the United States, but the similarities are mostly superficial. The Constitution of 1917, which was based on that of the Reform, is very different in tone and phrasing, and is in great part original. Its roots go back to the Spanish Constitution of 1812, as we have seen, and its Bill of Rights (the first 29 articles) is modelled on the French. Above all, it supposes the traditional customs of pre-Columban and Spanish Mexico, and the judicial forms and customs of Roman Law.[8]

In practice, any appreciation of Mexican government must begin and end with the President. He is elected for a six-year term, is ineligible for re-election, and must fulfil the stringent requirement of being a Mexican citizen by birth and the son of Mexican citizens. He appoints Secretaries to head the various ministries; he is chief executive and solely responsible for the conduct of government; appoints the governor of the Federal District; and may suspend the government of the nominally independent states. As the government is extensively involved in the economy through state-owned enterprises, he is the manager of the railways, electricity, airlines, ports and harbour works, and many other establishments, as well as a wide range of Federal Agencies modelled on those of the United States.

The President's powers in everyday use extend to the regulation of Congress. To begin with, the Secretary of *Gobernación* (or Interior) controls the national police and is responsible for the conduct of elections. He and his fellow-Secretaries have a recognized duty to initiate legislation and they can appear before Congress and speak there, or, on the other hand, be summoned to give an account of themselves, though they are solely responsible to the President. The President does not just sign bills, but has the positive duty of promulgating them, and the generally accepted practice of skeleton legislation, not unknown in Britain and the United States, is used in Mexico also. Beyond this point, the President is recognized by custom as having the right to legislate by decree if he chooses.

The legislature, however, is not by any means powerless, though the overwhelming majority of the ruling party weighs against it, offering serious competition to the Presidency. The 120 members of the Senate all belong to the PRI, serving terms of six years, with half retiring every three. They too are ineligible for re-election, as is every other government official in an elective post. The Senate has the right of confirming Presidential appointments but does not now exercise a veto in practice, since expression of opposition is confined to the Chamber of Deputies. By a law of 1963 all parties getting more than $2\frac{1}{2}$ per cent of the national vote are entitled to proportionate representation in the Chamber, even though they may have won no seats on the single-member constituency system otherwise in use. Hence in the 1967–70 legislature, of the 210 deputies only 175 belonged to the PRI, and the PAN, the principal opposition party of rightish nationalist complexion, which only won three seats in the constituencies, had 20 seats. Two other parties, the leftist PPS and old-guard revolutionary dissident PARM, were given 10 and 5 respectively, 'to conform with the spirit of the law', though neither party had received the legal minimum. It was, of course, not inconvenient for the PRI thus to see that the PAN did not emerge as a clearly defined rival, and the PAN deputies protested strongly at the decision.

The judiciary has been much improved in the last twenty years. Its political functions, however, are not comparable with those of its counterpart in the United States, as in the Roman Law tradition jurisprudence is subordinated to professional opinion, and precedent is not automatically embodied in the adaptation of political forms to changing circumstances. Furthermore, in common with most other Latin American countries, Mexico traditionally drew her political civilians from an 'intellectual proletariat', that is to say, the products of the law school who used their training as an avenue of entry into politics. Only with the Law of the Judicial Branch of 1951 was the foundation laid for a fully professional service, and steps taken to remove the colossal backlog of cases from the Supreme Court.

In summary, the Federal government in Mexico is an efficient organization for decision-making, but it does not of itself make very obvious provision for the efficient processing of public demands or needs. This is even more true of state and local government. The power of the President to suspend state governments is only the ultimate power in a series which makes all state and local government the decentralized expression of the central power. Tradition favours this, of course, but it is significant that the reacquisition of these powers after the Revolution was much accelerated by Cárdenas's need to acquire a broad basis of popular support for his struggle against Calles, through his tours of remote parts of the country never previously visited by a Mexican President.

The President seldom has to suspend a state governor today because through the official party his power of nomination is in the first place almost complete. The state governor holds a position therefore corresponding in practice very closely to that of the French prefect, with a single-chamber state legislature as the only rival to power. There is no separate state judiciary in Mexico. Though the states enjoy concurrent taxing powers over a wide range of activities, in practice they are to a great extent dependent upon the Federal government for the economic benefits of transport, river valley development schemes, rural electrification, and the like, to an extent, indeed, which is hard to compare with that of regions of any country which has been economically developed for a longer time. As Scott says, the states are a 'poor third' to the nation and the municipalities.[9]

The municipalities hold their position because of their nearness to those who live in them. In a mountainous country in which population collects naturally in the valleys, the locality is the true fatherland, the *patria chica* of the authors and poets, and, for that matter, of the politicians. As late as 1950 there were only nine cities in Mexico (other than the capital) with populations over 100,000; that is, larger than that of Cambridge among British cities. The average municipality, among the 2,349 comprising units of local government, contained only about 11,000 people. 11,000 is approximately the population of Newmarket, and is not really large enough to support efficient municipal services other than lighting, drainage, and roadworks. But the Mexican municipality is not necessarily a town, for there are only some 200 towns in Mexico with a population of over 10,000. The other municipalities are rural areas and hence largely ineffective.

To monitor the effect of government decisions alone over so large an area so sparsely inhabited requires a highly developed organization. The PRI, which performs this function, has by now been the dominant force in Mexican political life for over a generation, and in this time the boundary line between party and state has got somewhat blurred. It is therefore hard to say whether it is modelled on the organization of the nation or vice versa. Technically it is one party divided into three sectors, but each of the three sectors has its own independent organization, and the hierarchies of each interlock with that of the party all the way down from the presidency to the municipality.

The three sectors of today are those of the Workers (the CTM) and of the Peasants (the CNC) and that curious amalgam known as the Popular Sector, the CNOP, which includes the bureaucrats, white-collar workers, the military, intellectual, and teachers' associations, and even individual members.

The membership of each of these sectors is officially something over two million, though since workers are automatically counted as members of trades unions and peasants as workers on collective farms, there must be a good deal of inactive membership and some overlapping. Members of committees are elected at each governmental level for each of the three sectors and these are crosslinked to the party in the following manner. At the top, there is a National Assembly in which representatives of all the sectors participate in the declaration of party policy every three years. A special convention in years in which Presidential elections take place nominates the candidate. Otherwise the ultimate voice in policy-making lies with the *Gran Comisión* of thirty members nominated by the Central Executive Committee. This committee is the directing body of the party, and if the Assembly corresponds to Congress, it corresponds to the President and his Cabinet. Its own president is actually nominated by the President of the Republic, as is its Secretary-general. Of the other members, three represent the sectors, and two the two houses of Congress. Separate Offices of Feminine and Youth Activities and the Institute for Political, Economic, and Social Studies are made responsible to the President.

Next there are thirty-two Regional Executive Committees, whose composition differs in having only one representative of the unicameral state legislatures, and the appropriate number of Municipal Committees with five members and no representative. It follows that at each level the three sectors contend with one another as virtual factions within the ruling party, but in such close proximity that divergences can be eliminated at the next higher level without undue disturbance. It follows, too, that intrafactional alignments have considerable importance in the light of the fact that any two sectors can outvote the third, subject to this overriding central control, and the persistent attraction of the benefits of central approval. As might be expected, the Workers' Sector, subject to the attention of the Left Popular Party, has developed an institutional faction system, the majority constituting the so-called BUO (*Bloque de Unidad Obrera*) and the Left faction within the party organized as the so-called CROC (*Confederación Revolucionaria de Obreros y Campesinos*). The very formation of the minority group, however, is a testimony to the success of the tripartite party and the failure of the political opposition to capitalize on its potential disunities.

The official party incorporates both the mechanism by which interests are brought into the political system and that by which they are arbitrated and a common programme formed from them. There is, however, no particular historical evidence that Mexican interests were ever in pre-revolutionary times particularly reticent in expressing themselves, provided that they were allowed to do so, nor that traditional deference to authority and habits of obedience did not enable the task of arbitration to be effectively performed under the reign of Díaz. The failure of Díaz lay in the failure of his régime to perform the no less important or necessary functions of recruiting new individuals into roles in the political system and providing for the instruction of the people in the maintenance of social behaviour patterns without the periodic use of violence.

Now the level of violence employed even today in Mexico in social control is considerably greater than that to which we think we are accustomed.[10] There seems good reason to suppose, however, that this apparent distinction is one of class and income rather than of national origins. From the works of Oscar Lewis we can have a better idea of life below the poverty line in Mexico than most of us who have the chance to take an interest in this subject have of the same culture in our own country; and yet Professor Lewis himself suggests that the striking feature of his disclosures is the existence of a common 'culture of poverty' between countries of very different social and ethnic backgrounds. There are more poor people in Mexico than there are in Britain, and they are poorer, but that is all we can say; in both countries social violence is commonplace within a particular social context. There is some reason to suppose that the price of declining political violence may be an actual increase in social violence, but the correlation is far from clear.

The degree of stability of the present system is best shown by the emergence since 1940 of a new type of Mexican President. To begin with, where Presidents between 1858 and 1910 came from the crowded south, and the Presidents of the revolutionary years from the desert north; each in their own particular time enjoying the advantages of their particular type of regional terrain for military manœuvres, the new-type President is an administrator and comes from the Core, the centre of industrial and agricultural activity. He must have a favourable appearance and personal reputation, but by no means the reputation of the traditional *caudillo*. In the new Mexico the need is for moderation in all but ability to organize and direct, and, unlike the *caudillo* again, the new President has actually proved his worth in administration or political work and served as governor of his state before being picked out for membership of the Cabinet and so inducted into the pattern of behaviour of the central authority. Ultimately he can be presented to the party as a candidate only by his immediate predecessor.

The incumbent President had, down to 1970, to take account of the opinions of the living ex-Presidents, who had been sardonically termed the Grand Electors. The candidate had to be acceptable to General Cárdenas on the Left, as well as to Señor Alemán on the Right, while the President himself had to take into account the reaction from his own policies and the need of the country for a distinct change. So effective has the compromise been since 1940 that distinctive Presidential programmes are part of the current coin of political discussion, while a noticeable long-term alternation has occurred between those generally termed Left and those generally termed Right. Of these perhaps the most striking contrast was between President Díaz Ordaz and his immediate predecessor.

Gustavo Díaz Ordaz was a citizen of the State of Puebla, a lawyer by training, and formerly a Professor of Administrative Law at the Catholic University of Puebla. He served as a deputy and a senator for Puebla before in 1952 being appointed to the post of director of legal affairs in the Department of *Gobernación* by President Ruiz Cortines. Under López Mateos he became Secretary of *Gobernación*, responsible for the all-important functions of police and internal security. Here was the essence of the Mexican situation, for while President López Mateos came to the Presidency as a very popular Secretary of Labour and proceeded to distribute more land to the peasants than any previous Mexican President, his chosen successor was regarded as a conservative, and gained his reputation as a cabinet member by imposing effective barriers to the spread of Cuban-inspired propaganda calling for more of much the same sort of achievement. Yet both men, incidentally almost the same age and from adjacent states, were unquestionably heirs of the Revolution, and both commanded the full spectrum of support within the PRI.

Voices: Recent Mexico

'. . . Fiscal inspectors do take what in Mexico is called a *mordida*, that is a bribe or a tip, in order to do or not to do a certain thing. This has several degrees. There is the *mordida* paid to have something done rapidly which one has a right to have done–that is really a tip. Then there is the *mordida* paid in order to have something done slowly which one does not want done quickly–this is going much further. The third step is to have something done to which one does not have a right, for example to smuggle merchandise into Mexico. This, unfortunately, does exist, but Mexico is not the only country where it does, and it does not happen at the ministerial level. That is to say, there has not been any president or minister of, let us say, the last five or six terms who has ever gained a significant advantage for himself through really illegal means'.[11]

'A loyal review of what is occurring in our country as in other parts of the world, leads us to see with different eyes the theme of development at any price and cost what it may. Let us forget for the moment the crimes and stupidities which have been committed in the name of development, from Communist Russia to socialist India and from peronist Argentina to nasserist Egypt, and let us see what has happened in the United States and Western Europe: the destruction of the ecological balance, the contamination of minds and lungs, the congestion and the miasmas in the infernal suburbs, the psychic ruin in adolescence, the neglect of the old, the erosion of sensibility, the corruption of imagination, the debasement of Eros, the accumulation of refuse, the explosion of hate. . . . Before this vision, why not go back and seek *another* model of development?'[12]

'Those who made the Revolution, those who now serve it and who will continue it in the future, let us give more bread, more room, a more worthy life to the people; let us ensure that the sources of work are multiplied; that our fields and our seas produce greater riches; let us bring roadways, electricity, health and instruction to the most remote places; let us exploit our natural resources for the common good; let us honour our heroes. In short, let us make Mexico greater'.[13]

'. . . Certainly, Mexico is not a capitalist country like the United States, France, federal Germany, or even Spain. But it is a capitalist country on the road to attaining sufficiently high levels of development. For example, the very fact that this country has been chosen as the theatre for the Olympic Games signifies that it has reached a high degree of development and equipment. One can see other signs in the intensity of foreign investment and the level of productivity we have attained here'.[14]

'The ex-Presidents of the Republic of Mexico on being interviewed said:

LIC. MIGUEL ALEMÁN: "I have great hope because it is a new stage in the country's progress. Licenciado Gustavo Díaz Ordaz arrives with the endorsement of the people of Mexico and with his great experience he will take Mexico to new goals of achievement".

'For his part Licenciado EMILIO PORTES GIL declared: "The ceremony of the transmission of powers is the most extraordinary event of the Mexican Revolution. Mexico enjoys peace and tranquillity and we have all recognized the enthusiastic and fruitful task of President Adolfo López Mateos. Licenciado Gustavo Díaz Ordaz was elected by the immense majority of the people of Mexico. We have confidence in him".

'General Lázaro Cárdenas was very laconic and said: "We have great confidence in the future of Mexico".

'General ABELARDO L. RODRÍGUEZ and RUIZ CORTINES gave their opinion together: "I am going to consult Señor Adolfo Ruiz Cortines, let it be him who gives his opinion". A.R.C. said: "What better guarantee for Mexico than the words of President Gustavo Díaz Ordaz!" '[15]

'In Mexico, all movements, the most democratic and the most just, have suffered too much from corruption. At the moment when the leaders of the movement were going to triumph, they have sold out to the government. And it is precisely that that we want to avoid with this movement. We have decided not to go to any "intimate" meeting, as we say among ourselves. All must be public. . . .'[16]

As a title customarily abbreviated 'Lic'.

[2] Robert E. Scott, *Mexican Government in Transition* (Urbana, University of Illinois Press, 1964), 204.

[3] Emilio Portes Gil, *La crisis política*.

[4] John L. Stephens, *Incidents of Travels in Central America, Chiapas and Yucatan* (New York, Dover Publications, 1969), 120.

[5] *Mexico South: The Isthmus of Tehuantepec* (New York, Knopf, 1945).

[6] Armando de María y Campos, *Un Ciudadano – Boceto para una biografía – Como es y como piensa Adolfo López Mateos* (Mexico, Libro-Mex Editores, 1958), 9.

[7] See Adolfo López Mateos, *Pensamiento en acción* (Mexico, Oficina de prensa de la Presidencia, 1963, 2 vols.); and *Presencia internacional de Adolfo López Mateos* (Mexico, 1963).

[8] See *inter alia* William P. Tucker, *The Mexican Government Today* (Minneapolis, Minn., University of Minnesota Press, 1957); Robert E. Scott, op. cit.; Brandenburg, op. cit.; L. Vincent Padgett, *The Mexican Political System* (Boston, Houghton Mifflin, 1966).

[9] Scott, op. cit., 46.

[10] For an interesting discussion of the reasons why this should not be attributed, as do Ramos and Paz, to the cult of *machismo*, see Evelyn P. Stevens, 'Mexican machismo: politics and value orientations', *Western Political Quarterly*, XVIII (December 1965), 848.

[11] Ramón Beteta, Oral History Interviews with James and Edna Wilkie, 17 December 1964, Mexico City, cited in James W. Wilkie, *The Mexican Revolution: Federal Expenditure and Social Change since 1910* (Berkeley & Los Angeles, University of California Press, 1967), 8.

[12] Octavio Paz, *México: la última década*, 1969 Hackett Memorial Lecture, Institute of Latin American Studies, The University of Texas at Austin.

[13] Gustavo Díaz Ordaz, Secretary of *Gobernación*, speaking on 20 November 1960, on the occasion of the fiftieth anniversary of the Revolution, quoted Florencio Zamarripa M., *Díaz Ordaz, ideología y perfil de un revolucionario* (Mexico, Editorial Futuro, 1963), 41.

[14] Mexican student, 1968, quoted in Claude Kiejman & Jean-François Held, *Mexico, le Pain et les Jeux* (Paris, Editions du Seuil, 1969), 43.

[15] Gustavo Díaz Ordaz, *Doctrina y programa de acción del nuevo gobierno* (Mexico, Ediciones del Centro de Estudios Nacionales, 1964), 18, comments on the occasion of the inauguration, 1964.

[16] Mexican student, 1968, in Kiejman & Held, op. cit., 35.

The Revolution XXIV: Tlatelolco

IN THE SUMMER OF 1968 representatives of the nations of the world began to assemble in Mexico for the Olympic Games. In modern times the Games have become traditionally an occasion for international ill-will on a colossal scale, and these were no exception. Hostility had been manifest from the beginning to the idea of Mexico as the venue for the games at all; the altitude was regarded as a serious drawback by the nations living at or near sea-level, and their feelings that their own representatives might be at a disadvantage tended to be more or less disguised as concern for the state of their health.

With the representatives came the reporters and newsmen. Mexican society, economy, and political life were under scrutiny as never before, and as the months passed every snippet of information helped build up tension in preparation for the great day of the opening. Workmen were still diligently finishing the major installations on round-the-clock shifts, and in ways faintly reminiscent of the Centenary celebrations of 1910 the capital was being tidied up for the occasion. Most Mexicans seemed to be looking forward to showing what their nation could do, and what the Revolution had achieved. And so they did–but not exactly as they had intended to.

The discordant note on this occasion came from the students. They were, to begin with, exasperated by the heavy demand on their inadequate educational facilities–inadequate because of their own sheer numbers rather than through any inherent defect. They were affected by the rise in the cost of living that accompanied the prevailing economic boom, and hence conscious of the disparities in economic wealth that were still a feature of the city. The slums on the approaches were being swept away, but the vast workers' housing projects were tending to create a new 'aristocracy of labour'. Their government, the government of the PRI, seemed to them to have lost any contact that it had once had with the people, to have become conservative and uncaring. It was a year of 'demonstration democracy' in Europe and in the United States, and affected by the prevailing mood, excited by the knowledge that at last they were under observation, they spilled out into the streets.

The incident that provoked the initial outburst that led to tragedy was a battle between two schools, one private and one technical, on 22 July. Over-anxious perhaps, the chief of police made what was to prove a crucial mistake; in breaking up the combatants he made use of the paramilitary riot police, the so-called *granaderos*. It was four days before the anniversary of the Cuban Revolution. The usual demonstrations on this occasion became the immediate cause of denunciations of police repression, and a large crowd tried to invade the Zócalo. Once again they were met by the *granaderos*, and the conflict rapidly escalated into a full-scale street riot with barricades being thrown up to enclose the student quarter around the Politécnico. For three days the *granaderos* fought to contain the students, who had hijacked a number of buses, and used petrol bombs and other improvised weapons to resist attempts to disperse them. On the 30th they were finally dispersed by the army using fixed bayonets; no one was killed, but several were wounded and the door of the Church of San Ildefonso was blown in by a bazooka.

The President offered publicly to forget the incident and to extend the hand of friendship to those who were loyal to the government. The students of the Politécnico, however, responded with a large demonstration in which the government were denounced as false revolutionaries and the agents of the American Central Intelligence Agency (CIA), somewhat improbably credited with organizing repression. A strike committee was formed. Throughout August the excitement grew, as large rallies were held quite peacefully in the Zócalo itself. Then on 28 August fighting broke out between the students and members of the crowds which were watching. The army was called in to disperse the crowd and in the process one student was killed. From then on the crowds grew in numbers, reaching more than 300,000 on 13 September in the Paseo de la Reforma.

At first the government negotiated with the students. Then it seems the government grew impatient. On 18 September troops were sent in to occupy the university. Several arrests were made. At the Politécnico a mass meeting determined to continue the struggle. Those present did not have long to wait; when their turn came on 24 September they turned out to have prepared for it. In the fighting several more students were killed. But the occupation of the buildings of the university and Politécnico was not only not enough to stop the demonstrations, it was very embarrassing to the government, who were upset by newsmen taking photographs of tanks on the pavements by the library. So on 1 October the troops were withdrawn from the university. To celebrate, the students organized a vast meeting for the following day in the Plaza de las Tres Culturas in the district of Tlatelolco.

The meeting began at five in the evening. Its aim was to secure the liberation of the Politécnico, a few hundred yards away. A large crowd listened to a series of speeches from the balcony of one of the large buildings surrounding the square. All was peaceful. Then, at twenty minutes past six a Very light was seen over the buildings. The speaker tried to halt a sudden panic reaction by appealing for calm, but was himself seized and choked by one of his neighbours. All around the platform, according to eyewitnesses, plain-clothes men who had been waiting for the moment now attacked the platform party, while behind the crowd the military forces that had surrounded the square throughout the meeting began to advance in formation, guns at the ready. What happened next is in dispute. Mexican papers claimed that the troops were fired on first from the rooftops; others have stated that they fired without provocation and without warning. What is certain is that they poured their fire, from pistols and automatic weapons, into the dense crowd at short range, and that the crowd, trapped as they were between the buildings and unable to escape, sustained dozens of casualties.

Mexicans, who habitually carry firearms as part of their everyday dress, would probably not find it surprising that the students used them. At any rate, the army detachment were soon engaged in a full-scale battle by the light of flares and a burning department store. After an hour and a half the firing was halted and prisoners shepherded away. According to the official statistics forty-three had been killed and over two hundred wounded, including members of the police and army.[1]

The effect of the Tlatelolco incident was to shock Mexico and the world into attention. Torrents of denunciations were loosed on the government, in particular the chief of police and the Secretary of Defence, General Marcelino García Barragán. It was the latter, in fact, who assumed full responsibility for the incident, which President Díaz Ordaz was later (in 1969) to take upon his own shoulders. But the incident inflicted such serious injuries on the student movement that despite threats to disrupt the Games, it ceased to be of any effective significance from then on. Not only had the deaths a sobering effect on the mass, but more than a hundred identified as ringleaders were arrested, tried, and sentenced to heavy terms in jail.

First of all, however, there were the Games themselves. From the point of view of organization they were an unqualified success, and the country at large benefited not only from the boost to the tourist trade, but from the construction of housing and sports facilities. Many of the more jaundiced predictions of the commentators were not fulfilled. No one collapsed and died, and, if the distance events suffered as a result of the altitude, the sprint events gained: the new Olympic and world long-jump record exceeded all expectations.

Then in the aftermath came the recriminations. In his Message to Congress in September, President Díaz Ordaz had already admitted that Mexican political institutions were in need of change. They had, as he said, been evolved in the context of a less developed country. No one, on the other hand, felt the same urgency as the students did to get on with specific changes; in particular, workers' leaders backed the government. An important exception was Carlos Madrazo, the former president of the PRI, and when he was killed in an air crash at Monterrey in June 1969, it was a serious setback to the cause of radical reform from within the party. The students called off their strike the month after the Games, but continued to organize demonstrations, which in turn influenced the traditional process of *ausculta-ción*. For in 1969 the party was once again looking for a new Presidential candidate, and it was confidently hoped that the choice would mark a return to the Left.

In November further discussion was pre-empted by the announcement of the official selection, this time by representatives of the Agrarian Sector (CNC). The name of the candidate was hardly a surprise – the Secretary of *Gobernación*, the forty-seven-year-old lawyer Luis Echeverría Alvárez. Like his predecessor before his election, his career had been almost entirely within the party until he became deputy to Díaz Ordaz at *Gobernación* in 1958. But since he had been the minister responsible for the police at the time of the Tlatelolco incident he was hardly to be seen as a conciliatory choice by the students, and the initial slogans of his campaign strongly emphasized the theme of the restoration of public order as the path to general happiness. Significantly, at about the same time, the Workers' Sector received a new Labour Code, revising that of 1931 considerably in their interests.

Despite the fact that his election was certain, the new candidate embarked on an exceptionally vigorous campaign, in the course of which he visited 900 municipalities and was believed to have come face to face with no less than fifteen million people. It was a remarkable achievement in its own right, and it was effective. At the elections in July 1970 he was chosen as President by 11,948,412 votes to 1,945,204 for his sole opponent, Efraín González Morfin, of the PAN. Before he took up office three important developments took place. The last sixty-eight students accused of crimes in connection with the disturbances at the Olympic Games were sentenced to prison terms of from three to twenty-five years, despite a plea for clemency from Dr Pablo González Casanova, the Rector of the National University. The new labour code was formally put into effect, establishing among other things: equal rights for women, the obligation of management to provide housing for employees, and the right of trade unions to maintain surveillance of the employers' tax returns in order to ensure that they were not being cheated. And the much disliked law against 'social dissolution' was formally repealed, though its provisions were in fact continued under legislation governing other crimes. It was, therefore, very much up to the new President to determine whether or not he would make a fresh start.

In one respect at least he had little need to. Relations with Cuba had deteriorated as a result of that country's opportunistic encouragement for the Mexican students. But the new Republican administration in the United States had begun badly in its relations with its southern neighbour, by mounting a large-scale campaign against drug-smuggling which had a serious effect on Mexican trade generally. As a result the campaign was brought to an end after only three weeks, though this in itself did not improve relations much. A more encouraging step was the resolution of the long-standing dispute over the ownership of the Presidio region and numerous islands in the Río Bravo, in favour of Mexico in 1969, and the agreement between the Presidents of the two countries at their meeting at Puerto Vallarta in August to establish permanent machinery for regulating disputes which might arise in the future from the continued tendency of the Río Bravo to change its course without consulting the wishes of human beings or their governments.

Though the inauguration did not bring an immediate change of policy, it was not long before its effects were felt. Ten of those imprisoned for taking part in the 1968 disturbances were released at Christmas 1970, eighteen more in January, and twenty-three in May 1971. In a series of messages to Congress, where increased but rather unsuccessful efforts had been made to boost opposition participation, the President welcomed the idea of social reform and expressed his own commitment to it. Then came a setback: on 10 June a large demonstration of some 8,000 students who were meeting peacefully to demand the release of those of their fellows and sympathizers still in jail. Suddenly a fleet of municipal buses drove up. A well-organized force of men, armed with machine-guns, pistols, and sticks, jumped out of them and attacked the demonstrators while the police stood by. At least four students were killed and thirty-five disappeared, a sinister development which caused the most serious alarm about their safety. The group responsible for this attack was identified as a right-wing organization known as *Los Halcones* ('the falcons'). It was apparent from the manner of their attack that they enjoyed some official connivance, probably from municipal officials. The President, however, denounced the organizers of the group as 'irresponsible' and stated that it enjoyed no official support from his government. When the Secretary of Justice presented his resignation for reasons of health in August, it was immediately accepted. Finally, the whole long and sorry story of the 1968 crisis came to an end on 28 December 1971 when the last twenty-eight prisoners were released.

It had left a deep scar on the complacency of the older members of the Revolutionary Family who had become used to a peace and prosperity such as Mexico had never known before, and who could not understand the restlessness of those who were, after all, many of them, their own children. It is only right to say that by world standards the Mexican authorities reacted throughout with remarkable tolerance, confidence, and even sophistication. If in the years before 1968 they had shown themselves perhaps a little too jumpy about the possibilities of infiltration and subversion, and if at the time of the Olympic Games they had allowed impatience to dictate a tragic policy at a critical moment, they recovered from both errors with flexibility. Yet it remained to be seen whether the government's offer to admit more opponents to a policy-making role would be taken up and made effective, or whether through default Mexico would once again become a battleground for urban terrorists and rural guerrillas; though if this last were really a possibility, it was not likely to be one from which many other countries were immune.

Revolution

Social scientists make a fundamental assumption about the nature of the relationship between theory and fact. For them, theories are seen, not as guides to individual behaviour in the light of general models, but as tools for the clinical investigation of social processes. The end of this search is a better theory.

This, however, should not be a point of pride unless the construction of new theories can be related to the processes and actions going on in the real world. And here the most formidable obstacle is the sheer mass of information at the disposal of the modern investigator. Analogy from the natural sciences suggests that there is nothing more constricting to the development of ideas than an elegant theory that happens to be wrong. An elegant theory has most chance of acceptance if it seems to order a very large number of hitherto unrelated facts.

So it is with the fashionable concept of social revolution. There is no general agreement on what a social revolution is,[2] but most concur that Mexico has had one and the majority of American states have not. This assumption is popularly used to 'explain' various social, economic, and political differences between Mexico and the others. The reason for this is simple. The precursors of 1910 said they wanted a social revolution in Mexico. People in ruling circles in Mexico today assume that they got what they wanted, and most observers, if they are doubtful about this claim, must at least concur that the domination of the men of the revolutionary era over the political process was so complete that there was little excuse for them not achieving their ends, nor probability that they would not do so.

What was it that the precursors wanted? Some, such as Madero (1908), wanted political power.[3] Some believed that the redistribution of political power would follow a redistribution of wealth, and others were concerned only with lifting the effect of political power from their own sector of interest, be it agrarian tenure or industrial organization. To achieve any of these ends it was first necessary to terminate the authority of the régime of Porfirio Díaz. It was not, it should be noted, necessary in all cases to replace it with another comparable authority, yet that is in fact what has happened in the long term. The termination of power, the transition to the first revolutionary government, was a political act. It was in fact accomplished.

This form of political action is the basic meaning of the word 'revolution', as violent political change is the factor common to the three major established usages: that of intermittent alteration of government, that of cyclical change of régime, and that of linear historical progression through foreordained stages of development.[4] Though these three concepts coexisted in the early years of the century, it is a historical fact that it was the third of them that held special place, probably for the reason that in that period, uniquely, monarchies of a sort were regularly being replaced by some kind of republic. In the pseudo-excitement that has subsequently been generated over the Russian Revolution of 1917 it is often forgotten just how widespread these changes were: Turkey, Persia, Portugal, and to a lesser extent Morocco and Russia herself had all been affected before 1910, and China followed suit after Díaz had fallen but before Madero had come to power. Meanwhile in the Western Hemisphere the Liberal revolution in Paraguay, the reign of the *civilistas* in Peru, and the revolt against military coercion from Nicaragua in Central America all in their way offered proof that the elements historians discern in the Mexican Revolution were not in themselves unique.

The decision to perform a political act, however, cannot take place in a vacuum. The individuals who take on the role of revolutionaries require ideological justification for their actions. In fact, it may be said that they require more justification than those who accept the *status quo* actively or passively. In the Mexican case, there was much objectively wrong with the Díaz régime, as even such a consistent apologist as Francisco Bulnes recognized.[5] In consequence, from the beginning there was propounded among the revolutionaries a variety of solutions, and the variety of solutions was reduced by the establishment of coalition of agreed proposals rather than by the ascendancy of one doctrine. This in itself was not surprising. Unlike the monarchies of the Ottomans or the Kajars, the *Porfiriato* was a strongly ideological régime, not just committed to a minimum programme of survival, but to a maximum programme of economic growth and self-improvement according to the 'scientific' laws of one of the founders of sociology. A coalition of opposition opinion was not therefore attained under it, in the way that it could be under a régime more obviously out of touch with the times.

The role of ideology on the broad phenomenon of revolution is twofold. To begin with, it is an essential ingredient in the process of dissent and 'transfer of allegiance' that makes the political event of governmental overthrow (transition) possible. Later, it is used to justify this act (but more particularly distasteful acts ancillary to that act) and hence legitimize the successor régime. To the extent that the myth of the revolution is accepted, that régime will find it easier to enforce whatever programme of social or economic change it may wish to pursue.

Ideology, then, is inseparable from revolution. It cannot be assessed quantitatively, only relatively. The Mexican Revolution is no more and no less ideological than any other revolution, or series of revolutionary events. However, since ideological justifications of these events, and the ancillary phenomena of terror and coercion, have been so various, we do encounter an exceptionally broad range of conflicting interpretations. In approaching these, it is important to recognize that they are not contemporary with one another: that they do, in fact, originate from different historical periods, and that they reflect variously the ideological attitudes to the Díaz régime, the degree of participation in the events described, the sympathy or otherwise with the programme of the successor government, and the degree of allegiance to the overall myth of the Revolution as it has developed since 1910.

Sources on the period of the Mexican Revolution may, therefore, be considered broadly under four categories: as to whether they are orientated in the first instance primarily towards consideration of the process of disaffection, the events of political change, the programme of social renovation, or the myth of revolutionary coherence.[6] Two warnings are, however, necessary. First, no one source considers the Revolution wholly under any one of these analytical categories, and in certain cases the criteria for consideration are somewhat specialized. Secondly, the concept of the Revolution (and, indeed, of revolution in general) is in yet another sense purely a literary device for describing the ordinary, everyday politics of a nation of an unusual type. It may well be, therefore, that ideologically orientated writers have in some instances attached 'revolutionary' significance to events which had they appeared in (say) the Victorian period in England would have received a rather different sort of publicity.

Within these categories, the sources may be graded according to their degree of proximity to the sequence of events. There is more than one continuum along which proximity can be measured. Geographical proximity ranges from the participant to the remote foreign observer, but within participants there are varying degrees of what we may call social proximity to the consequences of the event. No less important is temporal proximity, the measure of the ability to perceive the consequences of events. Largely in consequence of these factors, observers derive value judgements on the events they describe, but allowance must be made for distortion by other, closer experiences. These measures of proximity, it should be noted, are common to the perception of all social events, and not specific to the phenomenon of revolution.

As in the case of other historical periods, the general perception of the Mexican Revolution probably owes most to the synthesizing historian, anxious to present a coherent picture of a large number of partially related events. Such general histories are those of Miguel Alessio Robles (1938)[7] and more recently the documented account in compact form by Roberto Blanco Moheno (1957).[8] It would be quite wrong to suppose, nevertheless, that the historians in any sense 'created' the Mexican Revolution, in the sense that they have created, say, the Nineteenth Century or the Golden Age of Spain. Given the particular claim of revolution, they have opted to accept the myth (or ideological justification) of the precursors and of the men who made the Revolution of 1910–11. That is to say, they accept that it was a revolution that they made, and that it was they who made it. But beyond that, they accept the retroactive additions and amendments to that myth, made by the men of the 1920s and later.

Such acceptance (or commitment) is also that of the sociologist. One of the most significant recent attempts to apply sociological models to the revolutionary process in Mexico is that of Eliseo Rangel Gaspar. His *Hacia una teoría de la Revolución Mexicana*[9] owes something to both the economic determinism of Marx and the sense of individual alienation of Brinton and Pettee; but in general it falls squarely within the continental European tradition, of regarding revolutions as processes of social liberation and adjustment of all kinds of inequalities.

This intellectual tradition is, of course, continuous with that of the nineteenth century, and in particular with the revolt against positivism of the precursors of the Revolution. Some of them, such as Andres Molina Enríquez, in their own persons both contributed to the intellectual disillusion with the *Porfiriato* and subsequently recorded their observations of its consequences, in his case in *La revolución agraria en México* (1937).[10] At shorter range the positive accomplishments of the time might have been less impressive. Ramón Prida's *From Despotism to Anarchy*[11] is a valuable reminder that the process of revolution does not seem beneficent to many, or at least not before it has come to a conclusion and some semblance of 'normality' has again been attained.

On a larger canvas, the social process of the Revolution could be received more easily, either as an episode in the longer panorama of Mexican history, or as a regional variant of problems common to Latin America as a whole.

Wilfrid Hardy Calcott (1931) saw the Revolution, even before Cárdenas, as the current act in the longer growth of liberalism in Mexico.[12] As in other countries, the 1930s saw the widespread acceptance that the highest form of liberalism involved the denial of liberty to some in the name of social equality, an equation which a later age is inclined to accept only a little more critically. The consciousness of the Revolution as a step in Mexican evolution had, indeed, been propagated from the beginning by such indefatigable publicists as the North American John Reed (1914).[13] For him, agrarian reform was not a matter of statistical planning and preparation, irrigation, drainage, and transport, but dust-stained heroes galloping straight across the hot desert by the light of dawn.

Seen from the 1950s, scholarly inquiry cast more light on the muddle of revolutionary preparations and the betrayals of frightened semi-sympathizers. Cumberland (1952) and Ross (1955) do to some extent employ their knowledge of the future to compensate for contemporary disillusion with the Maderistas.[14] The disillusion was for less persistent investigators forgotten, in view of the crown of martyrdom conferred upon Madero himself through his violent end. For the Constitutionalists the dead President became *Madero el inmaculado*.[15] Those who were happy about subsequent events founded the modern school of Mexican historiography.

But many, too, were not happy. Madero's own colleague, Francisco Vázquez Gómez, in his *Memorias políticas (1909–1913)*,[16] considered that he had compromised the cause of the Revolution by his insistence on the paths of legality and constitutional action. Later, others were to claim that those methods were being persistently violated. Most vocal, perhaps, were the Vasconcelistas, supporters of the revolutionary educator and defeated Presidential candidate at the elections of 1929. His own writings, notably *Ulises criollo*[17] and its two continuation volumes, set the theme: it was to be carried to its ultimate conclusion by the annals of Alfonso Taracena's *La verdadera Revolución Mexicana*[18] (1960). In thirty-two serial parts, Taracena delineated the course of the revolutionary movement down to what he took to be its conclusion, in 1930, with the Age of Vasconcelos.

Certainly, the rule of Lázaro Cárdenas, though great in agrarian achievement, gave labour less than Calles and was not publicly less anti-clerical. It was not on that account, however, that it turned out to be disappointing in terms of cultural relics. Had Cárdenas appealed consciously to the intellectuals to support the Revolution with their pens, as the Cubans have attempted to do, the Mexican Revolution could have been supplied more effectively with a visible orthodoxy of ideology. Rigidity of thought, though, could easily have destroyed the political gains actually achieved. It is doubtful if the Mexicans could have done better with it, though it would certainly have enabled them to lay down dogmatic patterns of development for other Latin American countries.

Mexico is recognized in Cuba as in some sense an example for her own social upheaval.[19] It is in this sense that Mexico is treated by a critic of the Cuban scene, Boris Goldenberg, in his *The Cuban Revolution and Latin America*.[20] Thus, the process of social dissatisfaction in Mexico is linked to a similar process in a very different country and age, yet in a way that proves stimulating to consideration of the nature of social change, for the Cuban remedies for their ills have been very different. Goldenberg considers that the Mexican Revolution, as a programme of reform, failed. He does not consider that the Cuban Revolution has been a success.

In contrast to Goldenberg's view is that of which Tannenbaum, and latterly Ross, called the view of the Mexican Revolution as the 'preferred' revolution.[21] This is the publicist's summation of Latin American revolutions as being the product of common social forces: the assumption of John Gerassi and even, to some extent, of Tad Szulc in his *Prophets of the Revolution*. It is preferable, therefore–so runs the argument–for the revolutions of other countries to take the Mexican, rather than, say, the Cuban form. Not only may something be achieved, but relations with other countries (notably the United States) need not suffer in consequence. Such hopes are bound to be dashed. Internation hostility is in great part a product of its times, and United States-Mexican hostility at the height of the Mexican Revolution was as great as any.

The reverse of this view is the orthodox Marxist one, hinted at in the East German historian Friedrich Katz's *Deutschland, Diaz und die mexikanische Revolution* (1964).[22] Perception of its causes as lying in part in the reaction of the Díaz régime to competition between capitalist states for overseas influence suggests that the failure of the Mexican Revolution as a medium of social change resulted from its lack of understanding of the forces involved. Since it began seven years before the Russian Revolution it could not, so runs a more didactic argument, have achieved success before 1917. That is the view developed by the Soviet authors of *La Revolución Mexicana: cuatro estudios sovieticos*, edited by Moisei S. Al'perovich (1960).[23]

Another possible interpretation of the historical process of 1910 is now defunct, though it is represented by Bulnes in the work already cited and even in *El verdadero Díaz* (1920).[24] There is much that is logically pleasing about it. According to this view, Mexico before 1910 was a particularly efficient example of a form of polity particularly adapted to Latin American needs: namely, a dictatorship. The Revolution that followed was the product of decay and hence a pathological condition. Bulnes wrote at the time when the post-1910 era of warring factions had not yet given way to a new period of authoritarian rule. Had he written in the 1930s, he might well have found much in common between Díaz's Indian wars and the Calles solution, both military and civil, to the problem of *las patrias chicas*.

Though the Revolution as a process of disaffection and transfer of allegiance may be viewed on a local, national, or hemispheric scale, and on the other hand as a temporary or a secular phenomenon, all such treatments have in common a certain tendency to play down the fact that at the least such a process must be viewed as the product of numerous 'sub-routines' having an additive or multiplicative effect. Recent historical investigation, with its concentration on imparting objective precision to the record of events, lends new emphasis to the presence within the period of discrete phenomena which have either achieved no resolution or have acted to produce inconvenient incompatibilities in a modern state characteristically the product of coalition and compromise.

To the contemporary annalist and diarist such a perspective was inevitable. In terms of vigour and literary skill the period is distinguished, both by Mexicans and by foreigners. Few can have approached the early years of the Revolution without soon making the acquaintance of Guzmán's *El águila y la serpiente* (1917).[25] Its photographic clarity makes it no less valuable as an historical record than as a literary masterpiece. The uneasy alliance between military heroes and promoters of ideas for reform that it portrays is presented from a different perspective by Reed. Less well known is the view of this phase by the *pacíficos*, whose acceptance was the key to political stabilization in the 1920s. For them the memoir of Mrs King, *Tempest over Mexico* (1936),[26] speaks graphically of the futility of war and the waste of valuable lives it entails.

This period of violence (1913–17) would, however, be difficult to comprehend were it not for the detail available from contemporary sources of the miasmic atmosphere in political circles at its beginning. Two North American observers, Edward I. Bell and Mrs O'Shaughnessy, portray it from a liberal and from a moderate conservative standpoint respectively.[27] Both contribute to our understanding of the key political event, the assassination of ex-President Madero in

February 1913, the circumstances of which were so graphically recorded by the then Cuban minister, Manuel Márquez Sterling.[28]
Though none of these observers could foresee what the consequences of
the destruction of legitimacy might be for central authority in Mexico,
at least none was grotesquely wrong in supposing that the product
might be a continuation of the old *Porfiriato*. Carlos Toro's *La caida de
Madero por la revolución felicista* (1913), published only weeks after the
event, demonstrates the limitations of the conservative perspective.[29]
Its author presents as an accomplished fact that the restoration has in
fact occurred.

Yet such a mistake was certainly possible in the confusion of events,
and the deterioration of communications in Mexico at the close of 1913
meant an end to the possibility of checking the voices of rumour. The
impossibility of securing reliable evidence on the course of events even
without this handicap was demonstrated by the Smith Committee of
the United States Senate (1913)[30] and was to be demonstrated again
and again by its successors. These investigations, nonetheless, and
others like them, offer a unique body of information and misinforma-
tion to the student of the period and of the political pressures involved.
The complexity of these was recorded for the same period by a
moderate conservative historian, Ricardo García Granados, down to
the point at which his own first-hand experience ceased to be available
to him to act as guide. Though overburdened with the detail of military campaigns in the style of Caesar's *Commentaries*, his story is still of
great value in bringing order into the confusion of the times.[31]

For the 1920s and 1930s a similar task has been performed more
recently by Dulles in his monumental *Yesterday in Mexico*.[32] It is moderate but heavily anecdotal, and an essential quarry for students of the
period. For the era 1937–52 they can now also have the benefit of the
social observations of the writer and journalist Salvador Novo.[33]

The diplomatic historian, who is concerned in the first instance
with delineating the appearance of events at a particular fixed point of
view, offers a form of selection independent (to some extent) of
personal preferences, which resolves complexities. To him, those events
that have not materially contributed to the external impact of the
subject-country are of little relevance save as background or colour.
Thus an early resolution of Mexican history into a coherent pattern is
that offered by Hackett in his study of the revolutionaries' relations
with the United States (1926).[34] This is of particular interest, as it also
served to formalize the 'Wilsonian' view of the Mexican Revolution
as a social movement deserving the aid of the American government.
The Mexican historian and revolutionary Isidro Fabela subsequently
offered a definitive study of the diplomatic appearance of the Revolution from official and unofficial Mexican sources (1958).[35]

The use of outside diplomatic sources, apart from published memoirs, to amplify the internal pattern of Mexican public life in the 1910–29 period could technically have been possible at any time after the capture of German diplomatic papers of the period in 1945. The volume of material, however, was small and the concentration on European aspects of German diplomatic behaviour still paramount. Investigation therefore waited until the opening of the State Department files, made general in 1958. The pioneer work of Cumberland and Ross, already referred to, was therefore amplified by the study of the anarcho-syndicalist revolt in Baja California by Blaisdell (1962)[36] and of the Convention of Aguascalientes by Quirk (1963).[37] British diplomatic papers were also employed to determine the course of internal events in my own *The Mexican Revolution 1910–1914: the Diplomacy of Anglo-American Conflict* (1968).[38] The effect of the recent temporary opening of French archives remains to be felt and assessed.

Other forms of imposed viewpoint are theoretically possible. The biography is such a form. It would not be entirely fair to say that the Mexican Revolution lacks good biographies, and it would not be far from the truth. The contrasts between different periods are too extreme for any but the most dedicated biographer not to conclude that his chosen hero has feet of clay. In the light of subsequent events the life of Cárdenas by Nathaniel and Sylvia Weyl appears notably more 'accurate' than the more recent one by Townsend,[39] but this perception of 'accuracy' tells us little about the individual subject, in the sort of way that, say, the revisionist critique of Huerta by Sherman and Greenleaf (1960) does.[40] Accuracy not only involves an accurate perception of surrounding events, but also a logically satisfying relationship between those changing events and the evolving personality of one man.

Few Mexican biographies have yet achieved anything resembling this. Most remain content to outline the 'official' events in a man's life, such as, for example, the useful but limited survey of three great figures of the period by Daniel Moreno.[41] For the most part, revolutionary biography is autobiography. This is disappointing in view of the readiness of Mexican historians to approach their history in general in a critical and broadminded way. The English-speaking reader familiar with the history of the Cristero uprising only from McCullagh (1928) and Kelley (1935) welcomes the depth of Antonio Rius Facius's *Méjico cristero* (1960) by contrast.[42]

The view of the participant-observer, be he individual or, as diplomatist, representative of his country's role in the international arena, is therefore a view of the Revolution primarily as a sequence of events. If for greater coherence he has imposed an 'approach' (analytical framework) upon them, he has distorted and perhaps even destroyed the primary virtue of his work as a medium for the storage and reproduction of useful information. The autobiographer, by the fact of writing, performs an act which distinguishes him from the mass of participants in the events he is describing. He creates a retrospective justification for his own life and career. Of course this is valuable in itself. What is misleading is not that this operation is performed; it is that this particular sequence of events is described as forming the backdrop to a coherent programme, when in reality the theoretical element of the historical process was applied at discrete intervals in individual acts of interpretation and guidance by a large number of actors acting either singly or collectively. Where this rationalization might be tolerable over a longer time-span, it is much less so given the short duration of revolutionary events.

It is very difficult for human beings to accept that their own efforts to carry out social betterment may have been futile or, worse, harmful. Those participants who have been excluded from participation in the political process (or that part of it which seems to them to be of most importance) in the course of normal political manoeuvring, tend to lay the blame for this on personal prejudice, etc. This, however, recognizes an element of superiority in one's opponents which may well be difficult to accept. In consequence, the particular circumstances of a revolutionary sequence may be expected to provide a historical justification for defeat which will be used as such. It is much grander to be overcome by impersonal forces than by individual enmity or personal incapacity.

It would be wrong, however, to regard these variations as distortions of a 'pure' history of the revolutionary sequence. At each stage in the development of Mexican history over the past half-century there have been views as orthodox and as well established as those of José Mancisidor's *Historia de la Revolución Mexicana* or the multi-volume compilation *México, cincuenta años de Revolución*.[43] Such today are official statements by the Head of State like Adolfo López Mateos's *Pensamiento en acción*[44] or *Ideas políticas del Presidente Gustavo Díaz Ordaz*.[45] Yet the orthodoxy of the era of the Institutionalized Revolution is patently not that of the age of violence that preceded it. The reader of Florencio Zamarripa M.'s campaign biography of Díaz Ordaz[46] reads of a revolutionary career as an efficient member of the bureaucracy, and will certainly find no justification of the act of revolting against it such as he will in, say, the *Memorias de Don Adolfo de la Huerta*.[47] Yet if the period of Mexican history since 1910 were not called 'the Mexican Revolution' this fact would not in itself occasion surprise, still less become the basis for groundless supposition that the Revolution, having been a historical process in the first place, has now in some way come to an end![48] The coherence of the concept with the present is due not to process or events, but to the programme that has arisen out of them.

There are, in fact, four different aspects of the programme of 'revolution' subsumed under the collective title.

The dominant one is a programme of political reform: the creation of a political and social order by the development of a unified bureaucratic state. In view of the programme as originating in ideological terms as a revulsion against nineteenth-century concepts of progress through free competition, such a reversion to the tradition of Madrid and Seville is not entirely unexpected. It is the political concomitant of returning the title to sub-soil and riparian rights to the state. The mistake critics made was to focus on the aspect of European liberal constitutional doctrine that was concerned with the two-party system and cabinet government, and to ignore the no less important facts of career civil service structures, colonial administration of underdeveloped possessions, and the state's responsibility for the welfare of its citizens demonstrated when they became involved in trouble abroad.

The first outspoken statement of the Revolution not as a process of liberation but of ordering, of establishing stability, came from Calles, in his address of September 1928. It was embodied in his *La democracia institucional* (1930)[49] at the time when his ally and colleague Emilio Portes Gil was laying the foundation for the institutional system of today. As related in Portes Gil's *Quince Años de Política Mexicana* and, most recently, in his *Autobiografía de la Revolución Mexicana*,[50] it is seen as a planned extension to the national sphere of the kind of tight organization he had found necessary in his own state to carry out the kind of programme for which he stood. There is no reason to doubt this motivation.

What must not be forgotten, however, is that at all stages during the Constitutionalist period bureaucratic style and traditionalist approaches to government were very much in evidence. It was Carranza who began the extension of cabinet responsibility only mooted under the Madero period and the formidable volume of paper generated by the Constitutionalist government remains a monument to the methodology of its aspirations. As evidenced, for example, by Ing. Luis G. Franco's series of *Glosas del periodo de gobierno del C. General e Ingeniero Pascual Ortiz Rubio 1930–1932*,[51] the process was well advanced by 1932. Indeed, without such a high level of bureaucratization it is improbable that the economy of Mexico could have survived the vagaries of Cárdenas. Portes Gil sees the process of the Revolution as continuing down to the present. It is not necessary to go so far to see the political system as the principal link between the era of violence and the entrepreneurial expansion associated with *alemanismo*, and to observers like Cline the chief justification of the Revolution as a whole.[52]

Portes Gil, however, has when he speaks of the Revolution a second programme in mind to which the first is only subsidiary. This is what Tannenbaum recognized as early as 1929 as *The Mexican Agrarian Revolution*,[53] which for a country like Mexico falls into three parts: the redistribution of land title; the provision of essential water supplies through irrigation; and the possibility of rural credits to equalize losses and provide capital for stock and seed. The vigour with which Cárdenas implemented the first of these goals was to create hopes such as those expressed by Eyler N. Simpson that successful agrarianism might prove to be *the* feature of the Mexican Revolution.[54]

The hope has to a large extent proved to be justified, in sharp contrast to the contemporary position in the Soviet Union–for example–where a strong tradition of peasant radicalism was thoroughly extirpated. In a telling critique in 1957, however, Portes Gil was to charge that the earlier radicalism had been allowed to lapse by default.[55] The large-scale distribution of land by López Mateos has yet to give rise to any very assured assessment of its importance. It is conceded to indicate that the ideal of land reform remains, though the achievement of it is unlikely ever to be fully completed, while attacks on the efficiency of the co-operative system of the *ejidos* continue unabated.

The theme of the Revolution as a programme of labour reform has produced a mass of polemic but little of enduring value. The most striking feature, but hardly the most important, has been the development of study of early labour movements, beginning with *La huelga de Cananea*.[56] Since Marjorie Ruth Clark's study of labour in 1944, a biography of Vicente Lombardo Toledano and Ashby's considerable study of the labour movement under Cárdenas are the only works that have attempted to apply critical methods to the evaluation of what has actually been achieved.[57] On the other hand, Tannenbaum's *Peace by Revolution* was among the earliest of many studies showing the importance of this element as being equal to that of the agrarian reform, a theme well handled in such diverse modern works as Cline's *The United States and Mexico* and Lesley Byrd Simpson's *Many Mexicos*.[58]

The Mexican Revolution as an historical tendency can certainly also be considered as a programme of social betterment, not necessarily confined to the 'official', agrarian, or labour sectors, of the present-day PRI. It is in this broader sense that it has been treated by Wilkie. In his *The Mexican Revolution: Federal Expenditure and Social Change since 1910*,[59] he has made the first serious attempt to isolate the social component of actual government expenditure and to examine its variance against the background of successive government proposals and propaganda. Potentially highly controversial in the summary treatment of a vast bulk of very useful material; this work will no doubt find successors.

Wilkie assumes, of course, that something of value has actually been achieved. This assumption is criticized from the standpoint of an old revolutionary, by Jorge Vera Estañol.[60] Basically his conclusion is that the revolutionary process was such that the Revolution must have failed to achieve its objectives. Others have indicated specific points at which the Revolution seems to have ceased, but none basically sympathetic have put the case with such force. As a modern, educated in the tradition of recent French sociology, Pablo González Casanova approaches the same question from a different standpoint.[61] He is specific in defining the groups whom the social and welfare programmes have not benefited, and the reasons he sees for this. In this fashion he gives the force of numerical estimation to the social changes represented in the lives of his characters by the social anthropologist Oscar Lewis and his followers.[62]

None of these writers goes so far as to suggest that the only thing that is revolutionary about a social and welfare programme, however grandiose in concept, is the mystique by which it is 'sold' to interest groups. Yet surely some such caution is necessary? Revolution is not the only metaphor for social change, though it does happen to be the one currently fashionable. The celebrated cross-national survey of cultural and political attitudes by Almond and Verba[63] should remind us of how much Mexico has in common with, say, Italy, a country in which programmes of social reform no less comprehensive or effective have been justified largely on religious grounds. The expectations aroused by such programmes do not substantially differ, so why should the national element of ideology not be isolated and regarded separately?

For it is the element of nationalism that distinguishes the Mexican experience as being specifically Mexican. That element of the revolutionary programme that dealt with the elimination of foreign influence has seldom been isolated as the principal result of the Revolution, though given the assumption, it is certainly not the least considerable. Mention should be made here, however, of the pioneering work of Alfred Vagts in Germany.[64] From many points of view it is regrettable that there has been little or no comparable work on modern Mexico in France, one of the few exceptions being the work of Pierre Lyautey (1938).[65] It seems that French scholars have been fatally attracted away from recent times by the glamour of the French intervention, but, it must be said, the reluctance of successive French governments to grant access to official papers has made it difficult for them to do otherwise.

Those who see the Revolution primarily as myth are, at first sight, an incongruous group. Some there are like Carlos Pereyra who have the ability to express themselves and the mental toughness to resist each stage of the revolutionary programme.[66] They are regarded by every faction of the 'Revolution' as lying outside it. Others have stood before the Revolution and seen the policy of government recoil from them. The influential have made their peace with the Institutionalized Revolution; their excluded rivals' tribulations were recently given efficient description by Schmitt.[67] Brandenburg is a foreign observer who has made such a searching analysis of sordid motives in government that he avoids enthusiasm for the régime.[68] All three attitudes take the ideology of Revolution essentially for camouflage for the real powers and forces within. What they do not say or see is that the elements in the régime that are antipathetic to them are those inseparable from the operation of any political system of any size.

Apart from that, what these writers have in common is an exceptional remoteness from events. Characteristically, this is not a physical nor a temporal remoteness, but a social one; a conscious effort at alienation from the mainstream of Mexican life, the more intense for having experienced it at first hand.

There remain the modern poets, such as Octavio Paz, and novelists, such as Carlos Fuentes.[69] In the last analysis, in all societies, both Eastern and Western, the artist is a deviant element and Mexican artists are no exception. Being expressed in words the modern writers' perception is more subtle than that of their predecessors the painters, whose perception of alienation was direct and too visibly hostile to the régime of their day. It is still from this quarter that some of the most telling protests at the shortcomings of the institutionalized society have come, or are likely to come.

Significantly, not one of the writers, however alienated, dismisses the Revolution completely. This is natural, because even as a myth, it must be real to those whose craft is words. All, therefore, have had to grapple, to come to terms with the semantic content to a word, a phrase that is the essence of the Mexico of their immediate past and the making of their present.

This then is the problem raised by the works that we set ourselves for investigation. If the Mexican Revolution is a myth, it is a fact. If it is a fact, it is because it is made up of events. Those events occurred because men advanced theories as to what should be done to rectify the imbalance of the society in which they lived, and so brought them into being in their actual form. Having accepted them, they applied through them further theories in their own individual spheres of influence, material or insubstantial. Since these events and these theories, taken as a whole, lack agreed definitions, boundaries, content, or effect, the Mexican Revolution remains, even for the social scientist, incalculable. But if we can analyse it in this way and break down its individual structures for comparison with similar ones in other places and times, need we continue to regard the Revolution as unique and indivisible? For if not, it is hardly necessary to accept it, or to reject it, or any other Revolution, as a whole.

[1] Kiejman and Held, op. cit., 79–83.

[2] Lawrence Stone, 'Theories of Revolution', *World Politics*, XVIII, 2 (January 1966), 159. Mexico is discussed as a case study in the light of these theories in Carl Leiden and Karl M. Schmitt, *The Politics of Violence: Revolution in the Modern World* (Englewood Cliffs, N.J., Prentice-Hall, 1968).

[3] Francisco Indalecio Madero, *La sucesión presidencial en 1910* (3rd edn. Mexico, Imprenta de la Viuda de Ch. Bouret, 1911).

[4] Peter Calvert, *Revolution* (Key Concepts in Political Science) London, Pall Mall & Macmillan, 1970).

[5] Francisco Bulnes, *Toda la verdad acerca de la Revolución Mexicana. La responsibilidad criminal del presidente en el desastre mexicano* (Mexico, Editorial Los Insurgentes, 1960, first publ. 1916).

[6] Peter Calvert and John Simpson, 'Attributes of Revolution', unpublished paper presented to International Sociological Association, Working Group on Armed Forces and Society, at its conference on 'Militarism and the Professional Military Man', London, 14–16 September 1967.

[7] Miguel Alessio Robles, *Historia política de la Revolución* (Mexico, Editorial Botas, 1938).

[8] Roberto Blanco Moheno, *Crónica de la Revolución Mexicana* (Mexico, Libro-Mex Editores, 1957–, 3 vols.).

[9] Mexico, Talleres Gráficos de la Nación, 1964.

[10] Andrés Molina Enríquez, *Esbozo de la historia de los primeros diez años de la revolución agraria en México (de 1910 a 1920), hecho a grandes rasgos* (Mexico, Talleres gráficos del Museo Nacional de arqueología, historia y etnografía, 1932–).

[11] El Paso, Texas, El Paso Printing Company, 1914; published also in Spanish as *¡De la dictadura a la anarquía! Apuntes para la historia política de México durante los últimos cuarenta y tres años* (2 vols.).

[12] Wilfrid Hardy Calcott, *Liberalism in Mexico, 1857–1929* (Stanford, Stanford University Press, 1931).

[13] *Insurgent Mexico* (New York, Clarion, 1969).

[14] Charles Curtis Cumberland, *Mexican Revolution: Genesis under Madero* (Austin, University of Texas Press, 1952); Stanley Robert Ross, *Francisco I. Madero, Apostle of Mexican Democracy* (New York, Columbia University Press, 1955).

[15] Title of Adrian Aguirre Benavides, *Madero el inmaculado; historia de la revolución de 1910* (3rd edn. Mexico, Editorial Diana, 1964, first publ. 1962).

[16] Francisco Vázquez Gómez, *Memorias políticas (1909–1913)* (Mexico, Imprenta Mundial, 1933).

[17] Current edition Mexico, Editorial Jus, 1958 (expurgada); the complete work available in English translation by W. Rex Crawford as *A Mexican Ulysses, an autobiography* (Bloomington, Indiana University Press, 1963).

[18] Alfonso Taracena, *La verdadera Revolución Mexicana* (Mexico, Editorial Jus, 1960), 32 vols.

[19] Cuba, Government, National General Assembly, *Declaration of Havana* (Peking, Foreign Languages Press, 1962), p. 7, speaks of Latin Americans as 'the heirs of Zapata and Sandino'.

[20] London, Allen & Unwin, 1965; first published in German as *Lateinamerika und die kubanische Rsvolution* (Cologne, Kiepenhauer, 1963).

[21] Stanley Robert Ross, 'Mexico: The Preferred Revolution', in Joseph Maier and Richard W. Weatherhead, eds., *Politics of Change in Latin America* (New York, Praeger, 1964), 140.

[22] Friedrich Katz, *Deutschland, Diaz und die mexikanische Revolution: die deutsche Politik in Mexico 1870–1920* (Berlin, Veb Deutscher Verlag der Wissenschaften, 1964).

[23] Al'perovich, Moisei S., *La Revolución Mexicana: cuatro estudios sovieticos* (Mexico,

Fondo de Cultura Popular, 1960). See also J. Gregory Oswald, 'La revolución Mexicana en la historiografía sovietica', *Historia Mexicana*, XII, No. 3 (January–March 1963), 340.

[24] Francisco Bulnes, *El verdadero Díaz y la revolución* (Mexico, Editorial Nacional, 1960, first publ. 1920), 1: 'Una revolución es la reacción violenta saludable de un organismo, contra la infección que lo ha invadido'.

[25] Martín Luis Guzmán, *El águila y la serpiente: memorias de la Revolución Mexicana* (10th edn. Mexico, Cia. General de Ediciones, 1964, first publ. 1928).

[26] Rosa E. King, *Tempest over Mexico, a Personal Chronicle* (London, Methuen, 1936).

[27] Edward I. Bell, *The Political Shame of Mexico* (New York, McBride Nast & Company, 1914); Edith Louise Coues O'Shaughnessy, *A Diplomat's Wife in Mexico* (New York & London, Harper & Brothers, 1916).

[28] Manuel Márquez Sterling, *Los últimos días del presidente Madero* (*Mi gestión diplomática en México*) (Havana, Imprenta 'El Siglo XX', 1917).

[29] Mexico, F. García y Alva, 1913.

[30] United States, Congress, Senate, Committee on Foreign Relations, *Revolutions in Mexico*, etc. (Washington, United States Government Printing Office, 1913).

[31] Ricardo García Granados, *Historia de México desde la Restauración de la República en 1867 hasta la Caída de Huerta* (Mexico, Editorial Jus, 1956).

[32] John W. F. Dulles, *Yesterday in Mexico: A Chronicle of the Revolution, 1919–1936* (Austin, University of Texas Press, 1961).

[33] Salvador Novo, *La vida en México en el periodo presidencial de Lázaro Cárdenas* (Mexico, Empresas Editoriales, 1964); *Manuel Ávila Camacho* (do., 1965); *Miguel Alemán* (do., 1967).

[34] Charles Wilson Hackett, *The Mexican Revolution and the United States 1910–1926* (Boston, World Peace Foundation Pamphlets, 1926), IX, No. 5.

[35] Isidro Fabela, *Historia Diplomática de la Revolución Mexicana* (Mexico, Fondo de Cultura Económica, 1958).

[36] Lowell L. Blaisdell, *The Desert Revolution, Baja California, 1911* (Madison, Wis., University of Wisconsin Press, 1962).

[37] Robert E. Quirk, *The Mexican Revolution, 1914–1915; The Convention of Aguascalientes* (Bloomington, Indiana University Press, 1960).

[38] Cambridge, Cambridge University Press, 1968.

[39] Nathaniel and Sylvia Weyl, *The Reconquest of Mexico; The Years of Lázaro Cárdenas* (New York and London, Oxford University Press, 1939); William Cameron Townsend, *Lázaro Cárdenas, Mexican Democrat* (Ann Arbor, Mich., George Wahr Publishing Co., 1952).

[40] William L. Sherman and Richard E. Greenleaf, *Victoriano Huerta, a Reappraisal* (Mexico, Centro de Estudios Mexicanos, 1960).

[41] Daniel Moreno, *Venustiano Carranza, Álvaro Obregón, Plutarco Elías Calles* (Mexico, Libro-Mex, 1960).

[42] Francis McCullagh, *Red Mexico: a reign of terror in America* (New York, Louis Carrier, 1928); Francis Clement Kelley, *Blood-drenched Altars* (Milwaukee, The Bruce Publishing Co., 1935); Antonio Rius Facius, *Méjico cristero* (Mexico, Editorial Patria, 1960).

[43] José Mancisidor, *Historia de la Revolución Mexicana* (Mexico, Ediciones El Gusano de Luz, 1958); Mario de la Cueva, *et al.*, *México, cincuenta años de Revolución*, III. *La política* (Mexico, Fondo de Cultura Económica, 1960).

[44] Adolfo López Mateos, *Pensamiento en acción* (Mexico, Ediciones de la Oficina de la Presidencia de la República, 1963. 2 vols.).

[45] Gustavo Díaz Ordaz, *Ideas políticas del Presidente Gustavo Díaz Ordaz*, ed. Roberto Amoros (Mexico, Editorial Ruta, 1966).

[46] Florencio Zamarripa M., *Díaz Ordaz, ideología y perfil de un revolucionario* (Mexico, Editorial Futuro, 1963).

[47] *Memorias de Don Adolfo de la Huerta según su proprio dictado*, trsc. Lic. Roberto Guzmán Esparza (Mexico, Ediciones 'Guzmán', 1958), 244 ff.

[48] Cf. Stanley Robert Ross, ed., *Is the Mexican Revolution dead?* (New York, Alfred A. Knopf, 1966).

[49] Mexico, Talleres Tipográficos de *El Nacional Revolucionario*, 1930.

[50] Mexico, Ediciones Botas, 1941; Instituto Mexicana de Cultura, 1964.

[51] Luis G. Franco, *Glosas del periodo de gobierno del C. General e Ingeniero Pascual Ortiz Rubio, 1930–1932* (Mexico, 1944, 11 vols., various titles).

[52] Howard F. Cline, *The United States and Mexico* (Cambridge, Mass., Harvard University Press, 1963; revised edn. 1967), 370.

[53] Frank Tannenbaum, *The Mexican Agrarian Revolution* (New York, Macmillan, 1929). cf. the same author's *Mexico: the struggle for peace and bread* (London, Jonathan Cape, 1965, first publ. 1951).

[54] Eyler N. Simpson, *The Ejido, Mexico's Way Out* (Chapel Hill, University of North Carolina Press, 1937).

[55] Emilio Portes Gil, *La Crisis política de la Revolución y la próxima elección presidencial* (Mexico, Ediciones Botas, 1957).

[56] Manuel González Ramírez, ed., *La huelga de Cananea* (Mexico, Fondo de Cultura Económica, 1956), Fuentes para la Historia de la Revolución Mexicana, 3.

[57] Marjorie Ruth Clark, *Organized Labor in Mexico* (Chapel Hill, University of North Carolina Press, 1944); Robert Paul Millon, *Mexican Marxist: Vicente Lombardo Toledano* (Chapel Hill, University of North Carolina Press, 1966); Joe C. Ashby, *Organized Labor and the Mexican Revolution under Lázaro Cárdenas* (Chapel Hill, University of North Carolina Press, 1967).

[58] Frank Tannenbaum, *Peace by Revolution: An Interpretation of Mexico* (New York, Columbia University Press, 1933), reissued 1966 as *Peace by Revolution: Mexico after 1910*; Cline, op. cit.; Lesley Byrd Simpson, *Many Mexicos* (Berkeley & Los Angeles, University of California Press, 1966).

[59] Berkeley & Los Angeles, University of California Press, 1967.

[60] Jorge Vera Estañol, *La Revolución Mexicana, orígenes y resultados* (Mexico, Editorial Porrua, 1957).

[61] Pablo González Casanova, *La democracia en México* (2nd edn. Mexico, Ediciones Era, 1967).

[62] Oscar Lewis, *The Children of Sánchez; Autobiography of a Mexican Family* (London, Secker & Warburg, 1962).

[63] Gabriel A. Almond and Sidney Verba, *The Civic Culture, political attitudes and democracy in five nations* (Princeton, N.J., Princeton University Press, 1963).

[64] Alfred Vagts, *Mexico, Europa und Amerika unter besonderer Berücksichtigung der Petroleumpolitik – eine wirtschafts-diplomatische Untersuchung* (Berlin/Grunewald, Dr Walter Rothschild, 1928).

[65] Pierre Lyautey, *La révolte du Mexique* (Paris, Plon, 1938).

[66] Carlos Pereyra, *Mexico Falsificado* (Mexico, Editorial Polis, 1949).

[67] Karl M. Schmitt, *Mexican Communism: A Study in Political Frustration* (Austin, University of Texas Press, 1965).

[68] Frank R. Brandenburg, *The Making of Modern Mexico* (Englewood Cliffs, N.J., Prentice-Hall, 1964).

[69] Octavio Paz, *El laberinto de la soledad* (Mexico, Fondo de Cultura Económica, 1959), publ. in English as *The Labyrinth of Solitude*, trs. Lysander Kemp (New York, Grove Press, 1962); Carlos Fuentes, *El región más transparente* (Mexico, Fondo de Cultura Económica, 1958).

1 The extent of Mexico in 1822, with territory later lost in the north to the United States and in the south to Guatemala, etc., including territory in dispute

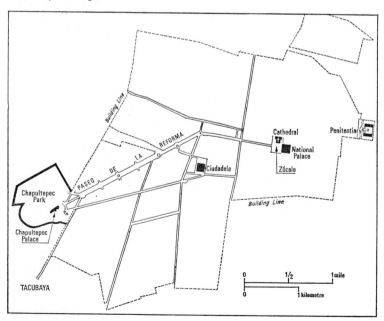

2 Mexico City in 1916

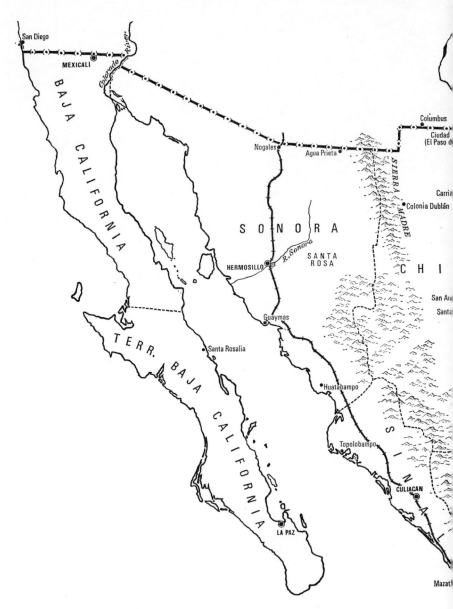

3 Mexico: general map

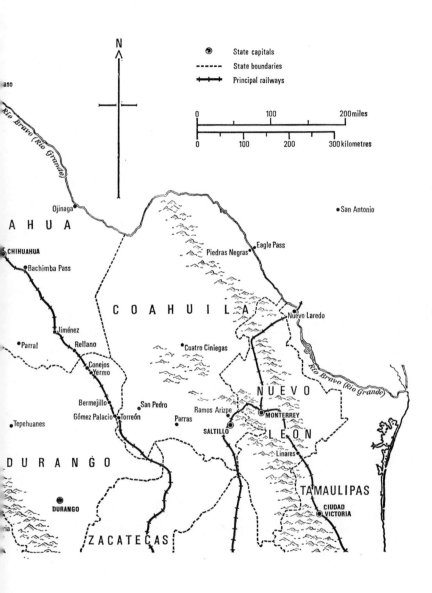

Legend

- ⊚ State capitals
- ----- State boundaries
- +-+-+ Principal railways

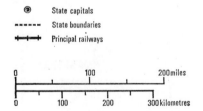

```
0                    100                    200 miles
|----|----|----|----|----|----|----|----|----|
0        100        200        300 kilometres
```

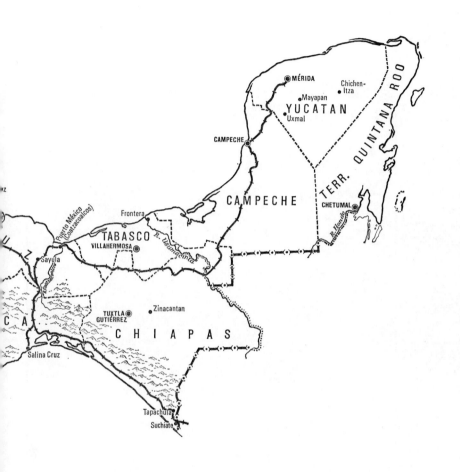

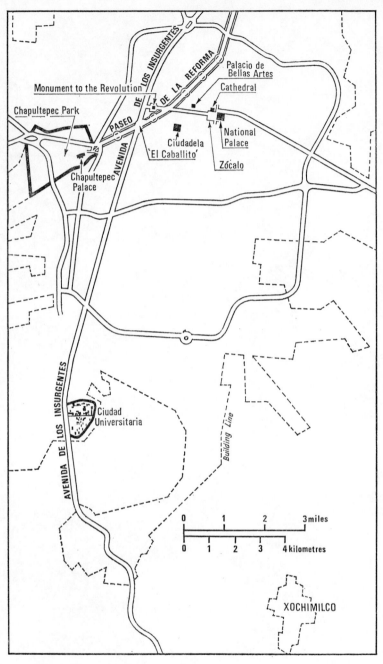

4 Mexico City today

Index

347

Printed in Great Britain
by W & J Mackay Limited, Chatham

DATE DUE

9 1989

F1231.5 .C273 1973
Calvert, Peter. cn
Mexico / by Peter Calvert.

c.1
100105 000

3 9310 00043097 3
GOSHEN COLLEGE-GOOD LIBRARY